Roget's

Pocket

Thesaurus

Roget's
Pocket
Thesaurus

A Dictionary of Synonyms

JOHN O. E. CLARK

BARNES
&NOBLE
BOOKS
NEW YORK

This edition published by Marboro Books Corp,
a division of Barnes & Noble Inc.
by arrangement with the Harrap Publishing Group.

1992 Barnes & Noble Books

ISBN 0-88029-778-6

Printed and bound in the United States of America

M 9 8 7 6 5 4 3 2

Preface

Roget's Pocket Thesaurus is a book for both users and students of English. It is a constant reference source for the many occasions when finding the right word is essential, or when variety and interest need to be brought to writing.

The book contains an alphabetical listing of key English words. The part of speech of each word is identified, and the synonyms listed in up to three categories. First are synonyms of the literal meaning (denoted by the abbreviation *lit.*), second the figurative synonyms (*fig.*), and third, if appropriate, specialist synonyms (*spec.*). This last category includes words from the arts, sciences, and technology. Where an entry represents more than one part of speech, the following order of presentation is strictly observed.

n	noun
vb	verb
adj	adjective
adj (pa.pt)	adjective (in form a part participle of a verb)
adj (pr.pt)	adjective (in form a present participle of a verb)
adv	adverb
prn	pronoun
prp	preposition
cnj	conjunction
art	(definite or indefinite) article

This consistent order of presentation is for ease and speed of access. In many cases it does not necessarily correspond with the important or frequency of usage within the language of the parts of speech represented by the entry. The different meanings of a headword are represented by groups of synonyms separated by semicolons.

A

abandon n *lit:* dash, elan, recklessness, unconcern, uninhibitedness, unrestraint, verve, wildness. **vb** *lit:* desert, evacuate, forsake, jilt, leave, leave behind, maroon, quit, relinquish, retire from, withdraw from; *fig:* abort, cede, desist, discontinue, give up, leave off, renounce, resign, stop, waive.

abbreviation n *lit:* abridgment, condensation, contraction, curtailment, reduction, shortening, truncation.

abduct **vb** *lit:* carry off, elope with, kidnap, run away with, seize, snatch.

abet **vb** *lit:* aid, assist, back, be an accomplice, encourage, help, incite, prompt, second support, sustain.

abhorrent **adj** *lit:* contrary (to), detestable, disgusting, distasteful, hateful, horrible, horrid, loathsome, offensive (to), repellent, repulsive.

abiding **adj (pr.pt)** *lit:* constant, continuing, enduring, firm, immutable, lasting, permanent, persevering, persistent, steadfast, tenacious, unchanging.

ability n *lit:* adeptness, aptitude, capability, capacity, competence, dexterity, expertise, facility, faculty, flair, gift, knack, power, proficiency, skill, talent.

abject **adj** *lit:* contemptible, cringing, debased, despairing, despicable, fawning, forlorn, groveling, hopeless, humiliating, ignominious, low, mean, servile, slavish, sordid, worthless, wretched.

able **adj** *lit:* accomplished, adept, capable, competent, dexterous, efficient, expert, fitted, gifted, practiced, proficient, qualified, skilled, skillful, talented.

abnormal **adj** *lit:* anomalous, atypical, deviant, exceptional, extraordinary, irregular, mutant, odd, peculiar, queer, singular, strange, uncommon, unnatural, unusual.

abolish **vb** *lit:* abrogate, annul, cancel, do away with, eliminate, erase, expunge, get rid of, invalidate, nullify, put an end to, quash, repeal, rescind, revoke, stop, terminate, void, wipe out.

abortion n *lit:* miscarriage, stillbirth; termination; *fig:* abandonment, calling off, cancellation, freak, monster, monstrosity, postponement, travesty.

about adv *lit:* active, almost, around, close by, here and there, moving, near by, nearly, roughly, stirring, virtually. **prp** *lit:* adjacent, beside, close by, concerning, concerned with, dealing with, referring to, regarding, respecting, treating.

above n *lit:* aforementioned, aforesaid, foregoing. **adj** *lit:* aforementioned, aforesaid, earlier, foregoing, on high, overhead, preceding, previous, prior. **adv** *lit:* farther up, heavenward, higher, in/to heaven, on high, on the next level upward, overhead, upward. **prp** *lit:* farther up than, higher than, over; *fig:* after, beyond, more than, past, superior to.

abrasive n *lit:* grinder, scourer. **adj** *lit:* fricative, grating, scratchy, scuffing, wearing; *fig:* chafing, grating, rasping, rough, sharp.

abridge vb *lit:* abbreviate, condense, contract, cut, reduce, shorten.

abroad adv *lit:* at large, away, being spread, circulating, current, far and wide, in circulation, out of the country, outside, overseas, publicly, widely.

abrupt adj *lit:* blunt, brusque, curt, gruff, hasty, hurried, precipitate, precipitous, sharp, sheer, short, steep, sudden, terse, unexpected, unforeseen; *fig:* broken, disconnected, discontinuous, jerky, uneven.

absence n *lit:* being away, defection, deficiency, desertion, lack, nonattendance, nonexistence, omission, want; *fig:* abstraction, inattention, preoccupation, reverie.

absent adj *lit:* away, deficient, elsewhere, gone, lacking, missing, nonexistent, not present, out, wanting; *fig:* abstracted, distracted, faraway, inattentive, oblivious, preoccupied, vacant.

absolute n *lit:* entirety, independent entity, totality, whole. **adj** *lit:* autocratic, autonomous, categorical, certain, complete, conclusive, consummate, decisive, definite, downright, entire, out-and-out, positive, pure, sheer, sovereign, supreme, sure, total, unadulterated, unambiguous, unequivocal, unlimited, unmitigated, utter, whole; *spec:* constant, fixed, invariable (in physics); modifying, qualifying (in grammar).

absolve **vb** *lit:* acquit, clear, discharge (from), exculpate, excuse, exempt, exonerate, free, pardon (from), release, remit, shrive, vindicate.

absorbing **adj (pr.pt)** *lit:* arresting, captivating, engaging, engrossing, fascinating, gripping, intriguing, riveting, spellbinding.

abstain **vb** *lit:* cease, desist, forbear (from), keep (from), refrain (from), refuse, reject, stop.

abstract **n** *lit:* condensation, digest, imaginative/nonrepresentational work, outline, paraphrase, précis, résumé, summary, synopsis. **vb** *lit:* appropriate, condense, detach, isolate, outline, paraphrase, précis, remove, separate, steal, summarize, take. **adj** *lit:* conceptual, conjectural, fantastic, hypothetical, imagined, imaginative, nonrepresentational, notional, theoretical, visionary.

absurd **adj** *lit:* crazy, daft, driveling, farcical, foolish, frivolous, idiotic, inane, irrational, jejune, laughable, ludicrous, lunatic, mad, moronic, nonsensical, puerile, ridiculous, senseless, silly, stupid.

abundant **adj** *lit:* ample, copious, luxuriant, overflowing, plenteous, plentiful, profuse, rich, teeming.

abuse **n** *lit:* derision, despoliation, disparagement, exploitation, ill-treatment, imposition, insults, invective, maltreatment, misapplication, misuse, oppression, opprobrium, vilification, vituperation, wrong. **vb** *lit:* betray, deride, despoil, disparage, exploit, ill-treat, impose on/upon, insult, inveigh against, malign, maltreat, manhandle, misapply, misuse, oppress, swear at, take advantage of, vilify, vituperate against, wrong.

abusive **adj** *lit:* cruel, defamatory, derisive, disparaging, exploitative, insulting, libelous, offensive, oppressive, rude, scathing, slanderous, vilifying, vituperative.

academic **n** *lit:* don, fellow, lecturer, man or woman of letters, master, polymath, professor, scholar, student, tutor. **adj** *lit:* bookish, erudite, hypothetical, intellectual, learned, literary, scholarly, studious, theoretical.

accelerate **vb** *lit:* expedite, further, go faster, hasten, hurry, increase speed, speed up; *spec:* change velocity (in physics).

accept vb *lit:* assume, bow to, defer to, receive, take; *fig:* accede to, admit, agree to, consent to, pass, recognize, stipulate, take on, undertake.

acceptable adj *lit:* admissible, agreeable, all right, bearable, fair, gratifying, passable, pleasing, satisfactory, tolerable, welcome.

access n *lit:* admittance, entrance, entry, means of approach, passage, path (to), road (to), way (to).

accessible adj *lit:* achievable, approachable, at hand, attainable, available, convenient, friendly, manageable, nearby, on hand, open (to), possible, reachable, to hand.

accident n *lit:* blow, calamity, chance, collision, contretemps, crash, disaster, fluke, happening, luck, misadventure, mischance, misfortune, mishap, mistake.

accommodate vb *lit:* adapt, adjust, board, cater for, conform, entertain, have room for, help, house, lodge, modify, oblige, provide, put up, quarter, reconcile, serve, settle, supply.

accommodation n *lit:* adaptation, adjustment, berth, board, housing, lodgings, modification, place, provision, quarters, reconciliation, reservation, room, seat, service, settlement, space, supply.

accompany vb *lit:* attend, be with, come with, escort, go with, happen with, join with, occur with, supplement; *spec:* play for, provide backing for (in music).

accomplish vb *lit:* achieve, attain, bring about, bring off, carry out, complete, do, effect, finish, fulfill, manage, perform, realize.

accord n *lit:* agreement, concurrence, correspondence, entente, harmony, rapport, sympathy, unanimity, understanding; *fig:* motivation, volition, wish. vb *lit:* afford, agree (with), be unanimous (with), confer, concur (with), correspond (with), give, grant, harmonize (with), render.

accordingly adv *lit:* appropriately, consequently, correspondingly, for this reason, hence, so, suitably, therefore.

account n *lit:* balance, bill, charge, consideration, description, explanation, history, inventory, invoice, ledger, narration, note, profit, recital, reckoning, record, register, report, score, statement, story, tale, tally, worth. vb *lit:* assess (to be), believe (to be), consider (to be), deem (to be), give an explanation (for), give a reason (for), hold (to be), reckon (to be), think (to be).

accountable   **adj** *lit:* answerable, comprehensible, explicable, liable, responsible, understandable.

accumulation   **n** *lit:* accretion, aggregation, amassing, buildup, collection, conglomeration, gathering, growth, heap, hoard, increase, load, pile, piling up, stack, stock, stockpile.

accurate   **adj** *lit:* correct, exact, precise, meticulous, right, scrupulous, strict, true, unerring.

accusation   **n** *lit:* allegation, arraignment, charge, impeachment, imputation, indictment.

accuse   **vb** *lit:* allege, arraign, blame, bring a charge against, charge, denounce, impeach, impute, indict.

accustom   **vb** *lit:* acclimatize, familiarize, get used (to), habituate, inure, train.

ache   **n** *lit:* anguish, longing, pain, pang, pining, soreness, suffering, throbbing, yearning. **vb** *lit:* be in pain, suffer; hurt, pain, put in pain, throb; feel (for); have sympathy (for); hunger (for), long (for), pine (for), yearn (for).

acid   **n** *lit:* corrosive; *fig:* hallucinogenic drug; LSD. **adj** *lit:* corrosive; acerbic, acrid, biting, pungent, sharp, sour, tart, vinegary; *fig:* acerbic, caustic, cutting, keen, mordant, stinging, trenchant, vitriolic; ill-natured, ill-tempered.

acknowledge   **vb** *lit:* react to, recognize, respond to; note, notice; accept, concede, grant, profess; admit, own to; greet, hail, salute; reply to, return.

acquaintance   **n** *lit:* associate, colleague, contact, friend of a friend, neighbor; association, familiarity, fellowship, relationship; introduction; *fig:* awareness, conversance, experience, knowledge, understanding.

acquire   **vb** *lit:* come into the possession of, get, obtain, pick up, procure, secure; amass, collect, gain, gather; buy, purchase; attain, win.

acquisition   **n** *lit:* possession, property; addition, gain, prize; buy, purchase; amassing, attainment, collection, gaining, procurement.

acquit vb *lit:* absolve, clear, exculpate, exonerate, vindicate; discharge, free, liberate, release; pay off, repay, settle; bear, behave, conduct, perform.

acrid adj *lit:* acid, astringent, biting, caustic, corrosive, irritant, pungent, sharp, stinging; bitter, vinegary; *fig:* acrimonious, cutting, harsh, mordant, pointed, trenchant.

across adv *lit:* to the other side; crosswise; from side to side. **prp** *lit:* over, to the other side of; on the other side of.

act n *lit:* accomplishment, achievement, deed, exploit, feat, operation, performance, stroke; decree, law, measure, ordinance, statute; routine, show, turn; affectation, dissimulation, front, pose, posture, pretense, simulation. **vb** *lit:* function, go, move, operate, perform, take effect, work; behave, conduct oneself; impersonate, play, portray, represent; counterfeit, dissimulate, feign, imitate, pose, pretend, put it on, sham.

action n *lit:* effect, functioning, movement, operation, performance, working; activity, energy, liveliness, vigor; act, deed, move, stroke; gesticulation, gesture; mechanism, mode of operation, procedure, process; battle, clash, combat, conflict, engagement, fighting; plot, scenario, story; case, lawsuit, litigation, prosecution, suit; event, happening.

activate vb *lit:* get going, mobilize, prompt, set going, set in motion, start, switch on, trigger, turn on; galvanize, impel, motivate, rouse; *spec:* catalyze (in chemistry); make radioactive (in physics); purify, treat (sewage).

active adj *lit:* busy, doing, going, engaged, occupied, working; functioning, moving, operative, running, ticking over; animated, brisk, bustling, energetic, spirited, sprightly, vigorous, vivacious; alert, lively, quick; enterprising, enthusiastic, hardworking, industrious, militant, zealous; *spec:* subjective (form of a verb, as opposed to passive).

activity n *lit:* animation, bustle, commotion, hurly-burly, life, motion, movement, stir; act, deed, work; exercise, exertion, work; hobby, interest, pastime, pursuit; endeavor, enterprise, project, scheme, venture.

actor n *lit:* artiste, performer, player, Thespian; impersonator, impostor, role-player; poseur, pretender, sham; agent, executor.

actual adj *lit:* authentic, genuine, literal, physical, positive, real, true; current, existing, present, prevailing.

acute **adj** *lit:* pointed, sharp; excruciating, fierce, intense, piercing, racking, severe, stabbing, violent; brief, short-lived, sudden; critical, dangerous, grave, serious, urgent, vital; discerning, discriminating, keen, observant, penetrating, perceptive, sensitive; astute, clever, shrewd, subtle; *fig:* at an angle, oblique; *spec:* less than a right angle (geometry).

adamant **adj** *lit:* flinty, hard, steely, stony, unbreakable, unyielding; *fig:* firm, immovable, inexorable, intransigent, obdurate, rigid, unbending, uncompromising, unshakable.

adapt **vb** *lit:* acclimatize, adjust, conform; alter, change, modify, shape, tailor; fit, match, suit.

add **vb** *lit:* compute, count up, find the sum of, reckon, total, tot up; affix (to), annex, append, increase by, put next (to), put on (to); continue, go on to say.

addict **n** *lit:* dependent, junkie, user; adherent, buff, devotee, enthusiast, fan, follower. **vb** *lit:* habituate, hook (on), make dependent; enslave.

additional **adj** *lit:* extra, further, more, other, supplementary; fresh, new; appended, attached; spare.

adequate **adj** *lit:* enough, passable, requisite, sufficient; fair, reasonable, satisfactory; commensurate, competent, suitable.

adjust **vb** *lit:* accustom, adapt, become used (to), be reconciled (with), conform, make fit; alter, change, fix, modify, reset, retune, tune; arrange, dispose, order, position, redress, regulate; accommodate, settle.

administer **vb** *lit:* control, direct, govern, manage, oversee, run, superintend, supervise; dispense, distribute, give, provide, tender; apply, execute, impose, mete out; *spec:* formally declare (an oath).

administration **n** *lit:* control, direction, management, running, superintendence, supervision; board, cabinet, government, ruling party; term of office; dispensing, distribution, provision; application, execution, imposition.

admiration **n** *lit:* appreciation, esteem, regard, respect, veneration; delight, pleasure, wonder.

admire **vb** *lit:* appreciate, esteem, hold in high regard, respect, venerate; delight in, take pleasure in, wonder at; like, love.

admission **n** *lit:* access, admittance, allowing in, entry, introduction, passage; entrance fee, ticket price; acknowledgment, confession, disclosure, revelation.

admit **vb** *lit:* acknowledge, confess, disclose, let on, own, reveal; accept, concede, grant, recognize; allow, permit; allow in, let in, receive; be large enough for, have room for; permit the possibility (of).

admittance **n** *lit:* access, admission, allowing in, entry, introduction, passage.

adopt **vb** *lit:* take on, take over, take up; assume, choose, embrace, espouse, select; become a parent to, bring up, foster.

adorable **adj** *lit:* captivating, lovable, precious; beloved, darling; alluring, attractive, charming, delightful, wonderful.

adore **vb** *lit:* dote on, idolize, love, worship; revere, venerate; be crazy about, go wild about; prostrate oneself before.

adorn **vb** *lit:* bedeck, deck, decorate, embellish, ornament; beautify, dress, garnish, grace; festoon, garland.

adulation **n** *lit:* flattery, fawning, sycophancy; blarney, bootlicking, servility; acclaim, applause, genuflection, obeisance, praise.

adult **n** *lit:* grown-up, mature person, responsible citizen. **adj** *lit:* full-grown, fully developed, grown-up, mature; ripe; *fig:* complex, erudite, intellectual; erotic, explicit, sexy.

advance **n** *lit:* development, headway, progress; betterment, breakthrough, furtherance, gain, improvement, promotion, step up; credit, loan; approach, overture, proposition. **vb** *lit:* go forward, move on, move up, proceed, progress; accelerate, further, hasten, promote, speed; bring forward, expedite; elevate, upgrade; benefit, grow, improve, thrive; credit with, lend, loan; offer, present, propose, put forward, submit, suggest. **adj** *lit:* early, prior; forward, in front.

advantage **n** *lit:* assistance, benefit, gain, good, help; profit, use; blessing, boon, convenience; ascendancy, dominance, edge, precedence, superiority, sway, upper hand.

adventure   n *lit:* enterprise, exploit, undertaking; exciting experience; chance, risk, speculation. **vb** *lit:* endanger, hazard, imperil, jeopardize, risk.

adventurous   adj *lit:* daring, enterprising, intrepid, venturesome; audacious, bold, ready for anything, temerarious; dangerous, hazardous, risky.

adverse   adj *lit:* antagonistic, hostile, inimical, opposing, unfavorable, unfriendly; contrary, negative, unfortunate, unpropitious; detrimental, harmful, injurious.

advertise   vb *lit:* display, exhibit, flaunt, hype, make known, plug, promote, promulgate, publicize, publish, push, tout; announce, emblazon, proclaim, signal; advise of, draw attention to, give notice of, inform about, warn of; put up for sale.

advertisement   n *lit:* display, hype, notice, plug, promotion, publicity; bill, circular, classified ad, commercial, poster.

advice   n *lit:* counsel, counseling, direction, feedback, guidance, instruction, recommendation, suggestion, tip; information, intelligence, notice, notification, word; caution, warning.

advise   vb *lit:* counsel, direct, give guidance to, instruct, make a recommendation to; inform, give notice of, notify; enjoin, recommend, suggest; caution, tip off, warn.

adviser   n *lit:* consultant, counselor, guide, mentor, teacher, tutor; coach, instructor, trainer; abetter, aide, assistant, henchman.

affair   n *lit:* circumstance, episode, event, happening, incident, matter, occurrence, question, subject, topic; business, concern, dealing, enterprise, transaction, undertaking; amour, relationship, romance.

affect   vb *lit:* act on, concern, influence, involve, relate to, touch; alter, change, disorder, disturb, modify, upset; impress, move, stir; adopt, assume, feign, pretend, put on, simulate.

affected   adj (pa.pt) *lit:* concerned, in question, involved; acted on, influenced, touched; distressed, impressed, moved, stimulated, stirred, upset, wounded; damaged, impaired, injured; artificial, assumed, feigned, insincere, pretended, sham, simulated, spurious, unnatural; camp, mincing, precious.

affecting **adj (pr.pt)** *lit:* distressing, emotive, moving, pitiable, pitiful, sad, touching, upsetting; inspiring, rousing, stimulating, stirring.

affection **n** *lit:* attachment, fondness, friendliness, kindness, liking, love, tenderness.

afford **vb** *lit:* have the money for, be able to buy; put up with, stand, sustain, tolerate; spare; confer, furnish, give, grant, impart, provide, render, supply.

affront **n** *lit:* insult, offense, outrage, slight; indignity, provocation; injury, wound. **vb** *lit:* insult, offend, outrage, slight; offer provocation; abuse, injure, wound.

afraid **adj** *lit:* alarmed, fearful, frightened, panicky, panic-stricken, petrified, scared, terrified; in a cold sweat, jumpy, nervous, timorous, uptight; anxious, concerned, worried; browbeaten, cowed, rattled, shaken, unnerved; cowardly, chicken, yellow.

after **adj** *lit:* later, subsequent; next, following. **adv** *lit:* behind, in the rear; afterward, later, next, subsequently, thereupon. **prp** *lit:* behind, beyond, in pursuit of, to the rear of; following, subsequent to; upon; about, concerning, with regard to; according to, copying, imitating, in the style of; identically to. **cnj** *lit:* as soon as, once, when.

again **adv** *lit:* afresh, anew, another time, once more, one more time; back, over; on the other hand, yet; also, besides, furthermore, moreover.

against **prp** *lit:* in contact with, on, touching, upon; abutting, adjacent to, bordering, contiguous with, next to; contrary to, counter to, in opposition to, versus; in contrast to; in anticipation of, in preparation for; for, in return for.

age **n** *lit:* period of existence, time of life; advanced years, elderliness, senescence; majority, maturity, ripeness; generation; century, eon, epoch, era, historical period, time; long while, years. **vb** *lit:* grow old, grow up, mature, mellow, put years on, ripen; decline, deteriorate, get old.

agenda **n** *lit:* program, schedule, timetable; layout, list, menu, plan, scheme.

aggression **n** *lit:* bellicosity, belligerence, hostility, pugnacity; force, violence; encroachment, infringement, invasion, raid; assault, attack, onslaught.

agony n *lit:* anguish, pangs, torment, torture; pain, suffering.

agree vb *lit:* be of one mind (with), concur; be consistent (with), chime, coincide, correspond, get on together, harmonize; comply, parallel, tally; assent, concede, consent, grant; *spec:* correspond in case, number, or person (in grammar).

agreement n *lit:* accord, concord, concurrence; chorus, concert, harmony, unison; correspondence, identity, match; arrangement, compact, pact, treaty, understanding; bargain, contract, deal.

agriculture n *lit:* agronomics, agronomy, cultivation, farming, plowing the soil, tillage, tilling the soil; husbandry.

ahead adv *lit:* in advance (of), in front (of); forward, on, onward, straight on; in the lead, winning.

aid n *lit:* assistance, help, support; benefit, service, use; assistant, helper, supporter; *spec:* fund, subsidy (for charities). vb *lit:* assist, benefit, be of use to, help, subsidize, sustain; abet, second, serve, support; facilitate, further, promote.

aim n *lit:* ambition, aspiration, end, goal, intention, object, objective, target; desire, intent, wish. vb *lit:* direct (at), level (at), point (at), sight (at), train (at); aspire (to), intend (to), mean (to), plan (to), purpose (to), strive (to), try (to).

air n *lit:* atmosphere, ether, waves; empyrean, heavens, sky; breeze, wind; breath, puff; ambience, aura; bearing, demeanor, feeling, flavor, impression, look, mien, tone; expression, utterance; aria, melody, melody line, tune. vb *lit:* aerate, circulate, dry, freshen, hang out, ventilate; *fig:* declare, disclose, divulge, expose, express, give vent to, make public, publicize, reveal, voice.

airfield n *lit:* airdrome; air force base; landing strip, runway.

airily adv *lit:* breezily, buoyantly, jauntily; blithely, casually, nonchalantly; ethereally, gracefully, lightly.

airless adj *lit:* close, heavy, muggy, oppressive, stifling, stuffy.

airplane n *lit:* aircraft, jet; crate, flying machine, kite; shuttle.

alarm n *lit:* apprehension, consternation, fear, fright, panic, trepidation; anxiety, nervousness, uneasiness; bell, danger signal, flare, hooter, siren, warning. **vb** *lit:* frighten, panic, put the wind up, scare; startle, unnerve; alert, signal, warn.

alert **n** *lit:* alarm; warning; lookout, watch. **vb** *lit:* alarm, warn; inform, notify, send a signal to. **adj** *lit:* attentive, awake, observant, on guard, on the ball, on the lookout, on watch, ready, vigilant, wary, watchful; brisk, lively, nimble, quick, sprightly.

alien **n** *lit:* foreigner, outsider, stranger; extraterrestrial, little green man, Martian; outcast; *spec:* hybrid (plant). **adj** *lit:* exotic, foreign, outlandish, strange, unfamiliar.

alienate **vb** *lit:* disaffect, estrange, set at odds, turn against; detach, disinterest, separate.

alike **adj** *lit:* identical, similar, uniform; akin, analogous, compatible, corresponding; equal, parallel. **adv** *lit:* identically, similarly, uniformly; compatibly, correspondingly, in the same way; equally, to the same degree.

alive **adj** *lit:* animate, breathing, conscious, living, organic; active, extant, in existence, operative, unextinguished; awake (to), sensitive (to); animated, brisk, eager, energetic, lively, spirited, sprightly, vigorous, vital, vivacious.

all **adj** *lit:* every; every one of; every bit of, every part of; as much as possible, maximum, optimum; any; nothing but, only, solely. **adv** *lit:* altogether, completely, entirely, fully, totally, utterly, wholly; exclusively. **prn** *lit:* everyone; everything; every atom, every bit, every part, every scrap.

allege **vb** *lit:* assert, aver, charge, declare, state; claim, maintain.

allegiance **n** *lit:* adherence, devotion, faithfulness, fealty, loyalty.

alley **n** *lit:* passage, passageway, pathway; corridor, gangway, walkway; lane; rink.

alliance **n** *lit:* coalition, confederacy, confederation, federation, league; marriage, partnership, union; association, combination.

allow **vb** *lit:* give permission, permit; authorize, give leave, license; bear, stand, suffer; give, grant, provide with; admit, concede, own to; keep free, leave, spare; take into account.

allowed   adj (pa.pt) *lit:* acceptable, all right, okay, permissible; authorized, licensed, permitted, sanctioned; left over, spare; provided (for).

allure   n *lit:* appeal, attraction, seductiveness, temptation; fascination; charm. **vb** *lit:* attract, captivate, charm, enchant, entice, fascinate, seduce, tempt.

ally   n *lit:* confederate, partner; acolyte, assistant, associate, collaborator, colleague, friend; helper, supporter; accomplice, cat's-paw, henchman, subordinate. **vb** *lit:* confederate (with), join forces (with), unite (with); associate (with), collaborate (with), combine (with); connect (to), relate (to).

almighty   adj *lit:* all-powerful, omnipotent; supreme; invincible, irresistible; *fig:* awesome, enormous, indescribable, tremendous, unspeakable.

alone   adj *lit:* by oneself, isolated, single, solitary, unaccompanied; apart, separate; matchless, unique; abandoned, detached, forlorn, forsaken. **adv** *lit:* by oneself, solitarily, solo; in isolation, separately; exclusively, merely, only, solely.

along   adv *lit:* forward, onward; down; as escort, in company (with), together (with); in parallel, side by side. **prp** *lit:* by the side of; down, down the length of.

already   adv *lit:* before then, by that time, previously; before now, by now, now, yet.

also   adv *lit:* additionally, in addition; likewise; besides, to boot, too; again, furthermore, moreover.

alteration   n *lit:* change, modification, reshaping; adjustment, amendment, correction, revision; difference, shift, variance; conversion, metamorphosis, transformation.

alternate   vb *lit:* happen in turns, take turns; interchange, rotate; oscillate, vary. **adj** *lit:* every other, odd; interchanging, rotating.

alternative   n *lit:* choice, option, preference; other, second; substitute. **adj** *lit:* other, second; substitute; different.

although   cnj *lit:* albeit, even though, in spite of the fact that; while.

altogether   n *fig:* birthday suit, nude. **adv** *lit:* completely, entirely, fully, quite, thoroughly, totally, utterly, wholly; all in all, all told, as a whole, collectively, generally, in general.

always adv *lit:* ever; all the time, constantly, continually, eternally, forever, perpetually, unceasingly; consistently, every time, invariably, repeatedly.

amazement n *lit:* astonishment, stupefaction, surprise; wonder.

ambassador n *lit:* emissary, envoy, plenipotentiary; diplomat, representative; consul, legate, nuncio.

ambiguous adj *lit:* equivocal, indeterminate, unclear; cryptic, Delphic, dubious, enigmatic, obscure, oracular.

ambitious adj *lit:* aspiring, eager, hopeful; desirous, driving, enterprising; audacious, bold, challenging, demanding, difficult, exacting; ostentatious, pretentious, showy.

ambivalence n *lit:* equivocation, indecision, indeterminacy, irresolution, vacillation; contradiction.

ambush n *lit:* holdup, lying in wait, stakeout, trap; mugging. **vb** *lit:* bushwhack, hold up, lie in wait for, pounce on, surprise, trap, waylay.

amend vb *lit:* correct, fix, mend, rectify, remedy, repair; ameliorate, better, improve, revise.

amends n *lit:* atonement, compensation, redress, reparation, restitution.

amid prp *lit:* among, in the middle of, surrounded by.

among prp *lit:* amid, of; along with, in with, together with; in the middle of, surrounded by; between, to each one of; throughout.

amount n *lit:* extent, magnitude, mass, measure, number, quantity, volume; entirety, lot, sum, total, whole. **vb** *lit:* add up (to), come (to).

amuse vb *lit:* be funny, divert, entertain, make laugh, tickle; keep occupied.

amusement n *lit:* diversion, divertissement; entertainment; enjoyment, fun, hilarity, laughter, merriment, mirth; game, pastime, recreation.

amusing   adj (pr.pt) *lit:* comic, diverting, droll, entertaining, funny, hilarious, humorous, merry, witty; enjoyable, interesting.

anemic   adj *lit:* ashen, bloodless, pale, pallid, wan; feeble, frail, sickly, weak; *fig:* colorless, dull, insipid; spiritless.

analysis   n *lit:* breakdown, dissection, resolution; examination, study; assay, evaluation, results of testing; finding, interpretation; reasoning.

analyze   vb *lit:* break down, dissect, resolve; consider, examine carefully, study; assay, evaluate, test; interpret.

ancestor   n *lit:* forebear, forefather, foremother, forerunner, progenitor; precursor.

ancient   adj *lit:* age-old, antediluvian, antique, archaic, hoary, old, primeval, primordial; antiquated, obsolete.

and   cnj *lit:* as well as, in addition to, plus, together with, with; furthermore, moreover; so that; in order to, to.

anger   n *lit:* choler, exasperation, fury, ire, passion, rage, spleen, strong displeasure, temper, wrath; resentment. **vb** *lit:* enrage, exasperate, incense, infuriate, madden, outrage, provoke, rile, seriously displease.

angle   n *lit:* corner, crook, elbow, hook; bend, curve; slant, slope, tilt; *fig:* approach, outlook, perspective; point of view, standpoint; plot, scheme. **vb** *lit:* bend, curve, tack, turn; fish; *fig:* bias, slant; fish (for), scheme (for), try (for).

angry   adj *lit:* beside oneself, enraged, exasperated, fuming, furious, hopping mad, incensed, infuriated, irate, livid, maddened, on the warpath, provoked, raging, riled, seething, wrathful.

anguish   n *lit:* agony, dolor, pain, suffering, torment, torture; distress, misery.

angular   adj *lit:* cornered, hooked; pointed, sharp; *fig:* bony, gaunt, lean, rangy, scrawny, skinny; awkward, clumsy, gawky, stiff.

animal   n *lit:* beast, creature; quadruped; *fig:* brute, monster, savage. **adj** *fig:* brutish, instinctual, lower, sensual.

animosity   n *lit:* antagonism, antipathy, bad blood, dislike, enmity, hatred, hostility, ill will, loathing, malevolence, rancor.

annex   vb *lit:* affix, append, attach, fasten on, join on, tack on; appropriate, arrogate, seize, take over.

announce   vb *lit:* declare, make known, proclaim; advertise, broadcast, promulgate, publish; divulge, reveal, tell; betoken, herald, portend, presage, signal.

announcement   n *lit:* declaration, proclamation, statement; broadcast, bulletin, communiqué, notice, promulgation, publication; disclosure, revelation.

annoyance   n *lit:* aggravation, displeasure, exasperation, irritation, vexation; bother, nuisance, trouble; bind, bore, pain, pain in the neck, pest.

anomaly   n *lit:* abnormality, inconsistency, oddity, peculiarity, strangeness; deviation, eccentricity, irregularity.

anonymous   adj *lit:* unattested, uncredited, unidentified, unnamed, unsigned; nameless, unknown; bland, colorless, nondescript, undistinguished, unexceptional.

answer   n *lit:* reaction, reply, response, return; comeback, defense, explanation, rejoinder, retort, riposte; solution; resolution. **vb** *lit:* react, react to, reply, reply to, respond, respond to; explain, rejoin, retort, riposte; solve; resolve.

antagonize   vb *lit:* alienate, disaffect, make an enemy of, offend, rub the wrong way; anger, annoy, irritate; counteract, neutralize, work against.

anticipate   vb *lit:* await, be prepared for, expect, foresee, foretell, look forward to, predict, see coming, wait for; antedate, be ahead of, forestall, precede.

antique   n *lit:* bygone, heirloom, relic. **adj** *lit:* antiquarian, classic, vintage; ancient, antiquated, obsolescent, obsolete, old-fashioned, outdated; aged, elderly, old.

antiseptic   n *lit:* disinfectant, germicide. **adj** *lit:* antibiotic, hygienic, sanitary, sterile, uncontaminated, unpolluted; aseptic.

apart   adj *lit:* by oneself, cut off, distant, isolated, separated; dismantled, disparate, dissected, divorced, in bits, in pieces, separate. **adv** *lit:* by oneself, independently, isolatedly, separately, to one side; asunder, to bits, to pieces.

apathy   n *lit:* disinterest, impassivity, indifference, passivity, unconcern; lethargy, sloth, torpor; coldness, insensitivity, numbness.

aperture   n *lit:* cleft, crack, fissure, gap, hole, interstice, opening, orifice, perforation, slot; chink, embrasure, eyelet, slit.

apex   n *lit:* acme, crest, crown, peak, pinnacle, point, summit, tip, top; *fig:* climax, culmination, height, zenith.

apologetic   adj *lit:* contrite, penitent, regretful, remorseful, repentant, sorry; appeasing, conciliatory.

apology   n *lit:* expression of contrition, mea culpa, regrets.

apostle   n *lit:* evangelist, missionary, preacher; advocate, champion, herald, messenger, propagandist, proselytizer; disciple.

appalling   adj (pr.pt) *lit:* awful, dire, disheartening, dreadful, fearful, grim, harrowing, horrific, horrifying, shocking, terrible.

apparent   adj *lit:* clear, evident, manifest, obvious, patent, plain, visible; conspicuous, overt; ostensible, outward, seeming, superficial; optical.

apparently   adv *lit:* ostensibly, superficially; outwardly, overtly, seemingly; evidently, obviously, patently, plainly.

appeal   n *lit:* entreaty, petition, plea, prayer, supplication; demand, request; allure, attraction, charm, fascination, interest; *spec:* referral to a higher court. vb *lit:* apply (to), make a petition (to), plead (to), pray (to); make a request (to); be alluring (to), be attractive (to), be fascinating (to); *spec:* refer to a higher court.

appear   vb *lit:* be seen, come into sight, come into view, come to light, emerge, loom, manifest oneself, materialize, surface; arise, crop up, develop, occur, show up, turn up; arrive, be present, come, enter; look, seem; be clear, be evident, be manifest, be obvious, be patent, be plain; become available, be on sale, be on show, come out; act, perform.

appearance   n *lit:* advent, arising, arrival, being present, coming, emergence, entry, manifestation, materialization, realization, surfacing; cropping up, occurrence, showing up, turn-up; availability, being on show, performance; air, bearing, demeanor, expression, figure, look, manner, mien, outward aspect; form, guise, semblance, shape; vision, visitation.

appetite n *lit:* hunger; desire, hankering, longing, yearning; relish, taste; room, space, stomach; *fig:* inclination, liking, readiness, willingness, zest.

applause n *lit:* acclaim, big hand, cheering, clapping, ovation; acclamation, accolade, plaudits, praise.

apply vb *lit:* bring to bear, employ, exercise, implement, practice, put into execution, operate, realize, use, utilize; appertain, be apposite, be pertinent, be relevant, be valid; commit (oneself to), dedicate (oneself to), give (oneself to), throw (oneself) in (to); appeal (to), make a petition (to), make a request (to), send in for information (to); address (to), introduce (to), put next (to); coat, daub on, put on, spread on.

appoint vb *lit:* assign, commission, nominate; arrange, choose, designate, determine, establish, fix, set; decree, direct, ordain, prescribe; equip, fit out, furnish, provide.

appointment n *lit:* assignation, date, engagement, meeting; consultation, interview, session; assignment, job, office, position, post situation; choice, commissioning, installation, nomination.

appreciate vb *lit:* be grateful for, be obliged for, be thankful for; cherish, enjoy, esteem, like, prize, relish, value; gain, grow, increase, rise; acknowledge, be aware of, be cognizant of, comprehend, know, perceive, realize, recognize, take account of, understand.

appreciation n *lit:* gratitude, indebtedness, obligation, thanks; admiration, enjoyment, esteem, liking, relish; gain, growth, increase, rise; acknowledgment, cognizance, comprehension, knowledge, perception, realization, recognition, understanding.

approach n *lit:* access, avenue, drive, entrance, pathway; advance, coming up, drawing near, nearing; course, means, method, mode, procedure, technique, way; attitude, way of thinking; application, overture, proposal, proposition, suggestion; approximation, likeness. **vb** *lit:* advance toward, come up to, draw near to, get close to, move toward, near; bend one's mind to, tackle; appeal to, apply to, make overtures to, sound out; approximate to, come close to, compare with, resemble.

appropriate vb *lit:* annex, arrogate, commandeer, confiscate, impound, make off with, possess oneself of, seize, take over; embezzle, pocket, steal; pilfer, thieve; allocate, apportion, assign, earmark, set aside. **adj** *lit:*

applicable, apposite, apt, fit, fitting, suitable, suited, to the purpose, well-suited; appertaining, correct, germane, pertinent, relevant, right, timely, to the point.

approval n *lit:* acclaim, applause, appreciation, approbation, commendation, praise; admiration, esteem, favor, liking, regard, respect; agreement, blessing, consent, endorsement, okay, recommendation; authorization, leave, license, permission, sanction.

approve vb *lit:* have a high opinion (of), think well (of); agree to, commend, consent to, endorse, okay, pass, validate; authorize, give leave for, license, permit, sanction.

approximate vb *lit:* approach, be bordering on, come close (to), come near (to), verge on; be like, have the semblance of, resemble. adj *lit:* close, estimated, loose, rough, virtual; comparable, similar; adjacent, bordering, near, nearby, neighboring.

area n *lit:* breadth, compass, expanse, extent, range, scope, size, width; district, locality, neighborhood, patch, plot, region, section, sector, territory, tract, zone; department, domain, province; field, realm, sphere; arena, court, floor, space, yard.

arena n *lit:* bowl, court, field, ground, hall, park, pitch, ring, stadium, stage, theater; amphitheater, battlefield, battleground, lists; *fig:* proving ground, testing ground.

argue vb *lit:* bandy words, dispute, fall out, fight, have an altercation, have words, quarrel, remonstrate, wrangle; bicker, disagree, squabble; debate, discuss, question; assert, claim, contend, hold, maintain, plead; persuade (into), talk (into); imply, suggest; demonstrate, evince, exhibit, indicate, manifest, point to, show.

argument n *lit:* altercation, clash, dispute, falling out, fight, quarrel, remonstration, row, wrangle; bickering, disagreement, squabble; debate, discussion; assertion, case, claim, contention, line of reasoning, plea, point; gist, plot, storyline, theme.

arise vb *lit:* ascend, come up, get up, go up; get out of bed, stand up, wake up; climb, mount, soar; appear, come into sight, crop up, develop, emerge, occur, show up, surface, turn up; emanate, issue, originate, spring, stem; ensue, follow, proceed, result.

aristocrat   n *lit:* grandee, noble, patrician, titled personage; *fig:* best of its kind.

aristocratic   adj *lit:* blue-blooded, highborn, lordly, noble, patrician, titled, upper-class, well-born; pedigree; courtly, dignified, polished, refined, well-bred; arrogant, haughty, proud, snobbish.

arm   n *lit:* forelimb, upper limb; appendage, crosspiece, extension, offshoot, projection, sleeve; branch, department, division, section, sector; channel, creek, inlet, sound, strait, tributary; *fig:* authority, might, power, strength. **vb** *lit:* equip with weapons, issue with weapons, provide materiel; activate, render active, switch on; provide with the means of attack or defense; *fig:* equip (oneself with), fortify (oneself with), protect (oneself with); *spec:* put an armature on (a magnet).

armed   **adj (pa.pt)** *lit:* fortified, furnished with weapons, primed, protected; activated, active, switched on; able to attack or defend; *fig:* accoutered, equipped, fitted out, provided, strengthened.

armistice   n *lit:* cease-fire, truce; peace agreement.

armor   n *lit:* breastplate, chain mail, coat of mail, cuirass, helmet, mail, suit of mail; bulletproof vest, steel plating; protection, sheathing; shield.

army   n *lit:* military, soldiers, soldiery, troops; battalions, brigades, legions; *fig:* horde, host, multitude, throng.

aroma   n *lit:* bouquet, fragrance, perfume, scent, smell; odor, whiff; redolence; *fig:* flavor, hint, suggestion.

around   adv *lit:* all over the place, everywhere, here and there; all over, through a round of time, throughout; in a circle; by a longer way; in every direction, on all sides; in circumference; active, doing, moving. **prp** *lit:* about, encircling, enclosing, encompassing, surrounding; all over the place within, scattered in; approximately, near; on the far side of, on the other side of; so as to avoid, so as to encircle; in all directions from, to all parts of.

arrange   vb *lit:* array, dispose, form up, group, marshal, order, organize, position, range, set out; align, classify, file, line up, rank, sort; adjust, straighten, tidy; devise, fix up, plan, schedule; contrive, determine, settle; adapt, orchestrate, score, transcribe.

arrangement   n *lit:* disposition, formation, grouping, order, positioning;

organization; design, plan, scheme, system; adjustment, moving; agreement, compact, deal, terms, treaty, tryst, understanding; adaptation, interpretation, orchestration, score, setting, transcription, version.

arrest n *lit:* apprehension, capture, detention, seizure; bust, cop; blockage, check, halt, obstruction, stoppage, suppression. **vb** *lit:* apprehend, capture, catch, detain, take into custody; nab, nick, pinch, run in; block, check, halt, obstruct, stop, suppress; delay, inhibit, restrain, retard, slow; *fig:* absorb, engross, fascinate, grip, hold.

arrival n *lit:* advent, approach, coming; appearance, entrance, entry; arising, occurrence; incomer, newcomer, visitor.

arrive vb *lit:* come, show up, take one's place (at), turn up; appear, enter, make an entry, put in an appearance; *fig:* become famous, make good, make it to the top, succeed.

arrogant adj *lit:* conceited, disdainful, haughty, high-handed, imperious, overbearing, presumptuous, proud, supercilious, swaggering; blustering, impudent, insolent, pretentious.

art n *lit:* representation; drawing, painting; craft, craftsmanship, expertise, mastery, skill, virtuosity; facility, ingenuity, knack, talent; deftness, dexterity; artifice, craftiness, duplicity, wile.

article n *lit:* commodity, item, object, thing; essay, feature, piece, story; clause, division, heading, paragraph, part, section; *fig:* matter, subject, topic; *spec:* a, an, or, the (in grammar); provision (in a contract).

artificial adj *lit:* man-made, synthetic; manufactured; affected, assumed, bogus, contrived, fake, false, feigned, hollow, insincere, meretricious, mock, phony, pretended, sham, specious, spurious, unnatural.

artist n *lit:* aesthete; creator; architect, cartoonist, designer, painter, sculptor, sketcher; actor, entertainer, musician, performer; artisan, craftsman, expert, master, virtuoso.

artistic adj *lit:* aesthetic, beautiful, elegant, exquisite, graceful; cultured, stylish, tasteful; creative, imaginative, sensitive.

as adv *lit:* equally, to the same degree, to the same extent; for example, like. **prn** *lit:* a condition that, a fact that, which is what. **prp** *lit:* in the character of, in the part of, in the role of; in the manner of, like. **cnj** *lit:* during the time that, when, while; in the same way that; to the same degree, to the same extent; that the result was; because, seeing that, since; though.

ashamed **adj** *lit:* conscience-stricken, embarrassed, humbled, mortified, sheepish; chagrined, crestfallen, discomfited; guilty, remorseful, sorry; bashful, shy.

aside **n** *lit:* interpolation, parenthesis; digression. **adv** *lit:* apart, away, off, out of the way, privately, separately; in reserve.

ask **vb** *lit:* inquire, put to, quiz; seek an answer; appeal to, apply to, beg, beseech, entreat, implore, petition, request, solicit; invite; look for, demand, seek; call (for).

asleep **adj** *lit:* dead to the world, dozing, off, napping, slumbering, snoozing; dormant, hibernating; numbed; *fig:* oblivious; inactive.

aspect **n** *lit:* air, attitude, bearing, demeanor, look, mien; angle, outlook, point of view, viewpoint; facet, feature, side.

aspire **vb** *lit:* be ambitious (to), be eager (to), dream one day (to), hope, long, seek, wish, yearn.

ass **n** *lit:* donkey, jennet; burro; *fig:* blockhead, chump, dolt, fathead, fool, nincompoop, nitwit, noodle, simpleton, twit.

assassination **n** *lit:* homicide, killing, murder, slaughter, slaying; butchery, destruction, elimination, extirpation, liquidation, massacre.

assault **n** *lit:* attack, hit, onslaught; offensive, storming, strike; battery, beating, mugging, robbery with violence; sexual attack. **vb** *lit:* assail, attack, batter, beat, beat up, fall upon, hit, lay into, mug, punch, set upon, strike, thump; invade, storm.

assemble **vb** *lit:* bring together, collect, congregate, convene, round up; come together, flock, gather, muster, rally; accumulate, amass, build up; connect, fit together, piece together, put together.

assert **vb** *lit:* allege, aver, contend, declare, maintain, proclaim, state; press, stand upon, uphold, vindicate.

assertive **adj** *lit:* dogmatic, emphatic, firm, forceful, insistent, positive, self-assured, strong-willed.

assess vb *lit:* appraise, estimate, evaluate, gauge, judge, rate, size up, value; levy, tax; fix the value (at).

asset n *lit:* fund, goods, holding, possession, reserve, resource; aid, benefit, boon, help.

assign vb *lit:* allocate, apportion, distribute, dole out, give out; make over (to); determine, fix, pose, set; appoint, delegate, nominate, select; accredit (to), ascribe (to), attribute (to).

assignment n *lit:* charge, commission, duty, job, mission, task; allocation, apportionment, distribution; appointment, delegation, nomination, selection; accreditation, ascription, attribution.

assist vb *lit:* abet, aid, help, serve; back, further, second, support; cooperate with.

assistance n *lit:* aid, help, succor; backing, furtherance, support; collaboration, cooperation.

assistant n *lit:* aide, helper; abettor, accessory, accomplice, henchman; backer, partner, second, supporter; collaborator, confederate. **adj** *lit:* associate, auxiliary, backup, deputy, subordinate.

associate n *lit:* ally, collaborator, confederate, friend, partner; colleague, fellow worker; companion, mate. **vb** *lit:* ally, combine, confederate, join, league, unite; consort (with), fraternize (with), go around (with), mix (with); *fig:* connect (with), identify (with), link (with), relate (with).

association n *lit:* alliance, combination, confederation, federation, league; club, company, group, syndicate, union; companionship, fellowship, friendship, partnership, relationship; connection, identification, link, relation.

assorted adj *lit:* diverse, mixed, sundry, various; arranged, classified, graded, grouped, ranged, sorted.

assortment n *lit:* diversity, medley, mixture, selection, variety; arrangement, grouping, range, selection; classification, grading, sorting.

assume vb *lit:* don, put on, wear; accept, acquire, shoulder, take on, undertake; appropriate, arrogate, expropriate, seize, take over, usurp;

adopt, affect, feign, simulate; *fig:* believe, guess, imagine, infer, presume, suppose, surmise, think.

assurance   n *lit:* affirmation, guarantee, oath, pledge, promise, word, word of honor; certitude, confidence, conviction, poise, positivity, self-confidence; audacity, boldness, courage; insurance.

astonish   vb *lit:* amaze, astound, bowl over, dumbfound, flabbergast, stagger, startle, stun.

astonishment   n *lit:* amazement, disbelief, shock, speechlessness, stupefaction, wonderment.

astute   adj *lit:* bright, canny, clever, discerning, keen, penetrating, perceptive, sharp, shrewd; cunning, subtle, wily.

asylum   n *lit:* refuge, retreat, sanctuary, shelter; mental institution, psychiatric hospital; funny farm, madhouse.

atheist   n *lit:* skeptic, unbeliever; heathen, pagan; infidel.

athlete   n *lit:* sportsman, sportswoman; gymnast, runner; competitor, contender, contestant, player.

athletic   adj *lit:* agile, energetic, fit, limber, lithe, muscular, nimble, powerful, sinewy, strong, vigorous.

atmosphere   n *lit:* air; airiness, space; *fig:* climate, conditions; ambience, environment, feeling, mood, spirit, surroundings, tone.

attach   vb *lit:* affix, append, connect, couple, fasten, fix, glue, join on, link, secure, stick, tie, unite; affiliate (oneself with), associate (oneself with); ascribe, assign; allocate, appoint, place, put, send.

attack   n *lit:* assault, charge, invasion, offensive, onset, onslaught, raid, strike; bout, fit, paroxysm, seizure, spasm; calumny, criticism, denigration, spleen, vilification, vituperation. **vb** *lit:* assail, assault, charge, fall upon, invade, set upon, storm; criticize, denigrate, insult, vilify.

attain   vb *lit:* accomplish, arrive at, bring off, fulfill, get to, obtain, reach, realize, win.

attainment   n *lit:* accomplishment, achievement, feat, fulfillment, realization, triumph, victory, win; gift, skill, talent.

attempt   n *lit:* bash, bid, crack, effort, go, shot, try, venture. **vb** *lit:* endeavor (to), make an effort (to), seek (to), strive (to), try (to), venture (to).

attend   vb *lit:* be at, be present at, frequent, go to, show up at, turn up at, visit; accompany, chaperon, escort, guard, usher; serve, wait (upon); care for, look after, nurse, take care of, tend; be attached to, be connected with, follow, result from; listen (to), pay attention (to), pay heed (to); look (to), see (to).

attention   n *lit:* awareness, concentration, consciousness, mind, notice, observation; heed; care, concern, consideration, thoughtfulness; civility, compliment(s), courtesy, gallantry, regard(s), respect(s).

attitude   n *lit:* pose, position, posture, stance; bearing, demeanor, manner, mien; disposition, mood; approach, outlook, perspective, viewpoint.

attract   vb *lit:* draw, induce, pull; allure, entice, lure; appeal to, charm, enchant, fascinate.

attraction   n *lit:* draw, inducement, magnetism, pull; allure, enticement, lure; appeal, charm, enchantment, fascination.

attractive   adj *lit:* magnetic, mesmeric; alluring, captivating, enticing, luring, seductive; appealing, charming, enchanting, fascinating; beautiful, gorgeous, handsome, lovely.

attune   vb *lit:* acclimatize (to), accustom (to), adjust (to), regulate (to), set (to).

audience   n *lit:* congregation, crowd, fans, gallery, gate, house, onlookers, spectators, turnout, viewers; market, public; consultation, interview, reception.

authentic   adj *lit:* actual, genuine, original, real, true, valid, veritable.

author   n *lit:* writer; creator, founder, generator, inventor, maker, originator, parent, prime mover, producer.

authoritarian   n *lit:* autocrat, despot, dictator, martinet, tyrant. **adj** *lit:* autocratic, despotic, dictatorial, doctrinaire, tyrannical.

authoritative   adj *lit:* authentic, official, sanctioned; commanding, confident, decisive, definite, imperative, masterful, self-assured;

dogmatic, imperious, peremptory; confirmed, factual, reliable, trustworthy, valid.

authority n *lit:* government, power, rule, supremacy; administration, board, council, local government, powers that be; connoisseur, expert, master, specialist; command, control, dominion, influence, jurisdiction, prerogative; license, permission, sanction, say-so, testimony, warrant, word; example, precedent.

authorize vb *lit:* commission, empower, entitle, license, permit, sanction, warrant; approve, confirm, ratify, vouch for.

automatic adj *lit:* mechanical, robot, self-activating, self-propelling, self-regulating; instinctual, involuntary, reflex, spontaneous, unconscious; inescapable, inevitable, unavoidable; *fig:* habitual, routine.

autonomous adj *lit:* independent, sovereign; self-determining, self-governing.

available adj *lit:* at one's disposal, on hand, on tap, to hand, usable; free, vacant; accessible, within reach; valid.

avenge vb *lit:* repay, retaliate; get even for, take vengeance on behalf of; revenge (oneself on).

avenue n *lit:* approach, driveway, pathway, walk; boulevard; road, street, thoroughfare.

average n *lit:* mean, medium, norm, par, run of the mill, standard. **adj** *lit:* intermediate, medium, middle; commonplace, middling, normal, ordinary, run-of-the-mill, so-so, standard, typical, unexceptional, usual.

averse adv *lit:* antipathetic (to), indisposed (to), reluctant (to), unwilling (to); hostile (to), inimical (to), opposed (to).

aversion n *lit:* antipathy, disinclination, indisposition, reluctance, unwillingness; animosity, hostility, opposition.

avert vb *lit:* turn away; fend off, stave off, ward off; forestall, preclude, prevent.

await vb *lit:* attend on, wait for; anticipate, be prepared for, be ready for, look for, look forward to.

awake adj *lit:* aroused, aware, conscious; alert, vigilant, watchful.

award n *lit:* conferral, endowment, presentation; gift, grant; prize, trophy. **vb** *lit:* bestow, confer, endow, give, grant, present.

aware adj *lit:* appreciative (of), apprised (of), conscious (of), informed (of), knowledgeable (of), mindful (of), sensible (of).

awareness n *lit:* appreciation, consciousness, discerning, knowledge, perception, realization, recognition, sensibility, understanding.

away adj *lit:* abroad, absent, not here, out; gone, off, started; distant, far. **adv** *lit:* abroad, elsewhere, out; apart, aside; afar, hence, into the distance, off; *fig:* continuously, doggedly, incessantly, on and on, persistently, relentlessly, repeatedly.

awful adj *lit:* appalling, distressing, ghastly, horrible, nasty, ugly, unpleasant; bad, deplorable, dreadful, terrible; inadequate, poor, shoddy, wretched.

awkward adj *lit:* blundering, clumsy, gawky, inelegant, inept, lumbering, ungainly; cumbersome, unmanageable, unwieldy; difficult, inconvenient, untimely; dangerous, hazardous, perilous, sticky, thorny, ticklish; compromising, embarrassing, inopportune, painful, trying, uncomfortable; disobliging, perverse, prickly, troublesome, unhelpful, unpredictable.

B

baby n *lit:* babe, infant, neonate, newborn; bairn, child; *fig:* idea, invention, pet project, plan, responsibility, scheme. **vb** *lit:* coddle, cosset, mollycoddle, pamper, pet, spoil; *fig:* humor, indulge, spoon-feed. **adj** *lit:* infant, newborn, young; *fig:* diminutive, little, miniature, minute, small, tiny; dwarf, midget, pygmy; childish, infantile.

back n *lit:* spine, vertebrae; hind part, hindquarters, posterior, rear; end, stern, tail; far end, other side, reverse; *fig:* effort, energy, power; *spec:* keel, keelson (of a ship, boat); top, surface (of a river, the sea; of a vein of ore; of a bow in archery). **vb** *lit:* go backwards, regress, retreat, reverse; encourage, endorse, favor, finance, second, sponsor, subsidize, support, underwrite; abet, aid, assist, come to the help of, help; bet on, gamble on; be behind, line, reinforce, strengthen; *spec:* turn, veer (of the wind). **adj** *lit:* hind, posterior, rearward; end, hindmost, rear; distant, outlying, remote; earlier, former, old, past, previous; reverse. **adv** *lit:* retrogressively, retrospectively; again, once more; ago, in the past.

background n *lit:* context, environment, milieu, scenario, scenery, setting, surroundings; distance, obscurity, shadow; breeding, circumstances, culture, history, past, record, track record, upbringing; credentials, experience, qualifications. **adj** *lit:* environmental, residual, surrounding; accompanying, incidental, secondary.

backing n *lit:* encouragement, endorsement, favor, seconding, support; financing, funding, investment, patronage, sponsorship, subsidizing, underwriting; aid, assistance, help; confirmation, corroboration, substantiation, verification; lining, reinforcement, strengthening; accompaniment, context, setting.

backward adv *lit:* rearward, retrogressively; *fig:* completely, fully, thoroughly.

bacterium n *lit:* bug, germ, microbe, micro-organism; bacillus, coccus, schizomycete, spirochete.

bad adj *lit:* evil, immoral, sinful, wicked, wrong; disobedient, naughty, unruly; damaged, defective, deficient, faulty, imperfect, inadequate, inferior, poor, unfavorable, unfortunate, unskillful, unsatisfactory, worthless; erroneous, fallacious, incorrect, invalid, spurious; dangerous, distressing, gloomy, grave, grim, harmful, injurious, offensive, painful, serious, severe, unpleasant; decayed, fetid, moldy, off, putrescent, rancid, rotten, sour, spoiled; adverse, damaging, disastrous, ruinous; ailing, ill, sick, unwell; guilty, melancholy, remorseful, sad, sorry; distressed, upset, wretched.

badly **adv** *lit:* carelessly, deficiently, imperfectly, inadequately, incorrectly, poorly, shoddily, unfavorably, unfortunately, unskillfully, unsatisfactorily; evilly, immorally, sinfully, wickedly; disobediently, improperly, naughtily, outrageously, shamefully; acutely, extremely, greatly, intensely, seriously; deeply, desperately, gravely, severely.

balance **n** *lit:* pair of scales, scales, weighing machine; equilibrium, equipoise; equality, equivalence, evenness, parity; composure, equanimity, poise, self-possession; stability, steadiness; difference, remainder, residue, rest; *spec:* regulator (in a timepiece). **vb** *lit:* be poised, be stable, be steady; achieve parity, be equivalent, correspond, equal, level, match, parallel; compensate for, counterpoise, counterweight, equalize, offset; assess, calculate, compute, compare, estimate, evaluate, total, weigh, weigh up; settle, square, tally.

balcony **n** *lit:* stoep, verandah; gallery, upper circle.

bald **adj** *lit:* hairless; depilated, glabrous; unfledged; barren, exposed, treeless; *fig:* bare, blunt, direct, forthright, naked, plain, simple, stark, unadorned, undisguised, unvarnished.

ball **n** *lit:* globe, orb, sphere; bead, drop, globule, spheroid; bullet, pellet, shot, slug; dance. **vb** *lit:* form a sphere, roll into a sphere; clog, entangle.

ban **n** *lit:* boycott, embargo, forbidding, interdiction, prohibition, proscription; banishment, deportation, exile; anathematization, curse, excommunication; outlawry. **vb** *lit:* bar, debar, disallow, embargo, forbid, interdict, outlaw, prohibit, proscribe, suppress; banish, deport, exile; blacklist, veto; anathematize, excommunicate.

banal **adj** *lit:* cliché-ridden, corny, hackneyed, pedestrian, platitudinous, stale, stereotyped, stock, tired, trite, unoriginal, vapid; commonplace, everyday, mundane, ordinary, trivial, unimaginative.

band **n** *lit:* binding, ribbon, strap, strip; belt, tape; line, streak, stripe, vein; channel, frequency range, track, wavelength range; body, company, crew, gang, group, party, troop; ensemble, orchestra. **vb** *lit:* affiliate, ally, assemble, associate, federate, group, join, league, merge, unite.

bandit n *lit:* brigand, desperado, footpad, highwayman, marauder, outlaw, pirate, robber; crook, gangster, gunman, hijacker, kidnaper, kidnapper, thief; con artist, exploiter, extortioner, swindler; *fig:* enemy.

bang n *lit:* detonation, explosion, report, shot; boom, clap, clash, crash, pop, thud; blow, box, cuff, hit, knock, punch, slam, smack, thump, wallop, whack; *fig:* impetus, vigor, zest; buzz, kick, stimulus, thrill. **vb** *lit:* bash, beat, hammer, knock, pound, pummel, rap, slam, strike, thump; clash, clatter, crash; detonate, explode, resound, thunder. **adv** *lit:* abruptly, all at once, suddenly; hard, noisily, smack, violently; absolutely, directly, exactly, headlong, precisely, quite, right, squarely, straight.

bank n *lit:* border, brink, edge, rim, riverside, shore, side, towpath; acclivity, embankment, mound, pile, rampart, ridge, rise, shelf; accumulation, heap, mass; depository, hoard, repository, reserve, reservoir, stock, store; funds, kitty, money exchange, pool, savings; bar, reef, shallows, shoal; camber, incline, lean, slant, slope, tilt; array, file, line, rank, row, tier; bench, settle, workbench, worktable; *spec:* flock (of birds); manual (on an organ). **vb** *lit:* deposit, put into the kitty, save; amass, gather, heap up, pile up, stack; count, depend, lean, rely; camber, cant, incline, lean, pitch, slant, slope, tilt, tip; embank, enclose, surround; close over, cover, extinguish.

bankrupt n *lit:* debtor, defaulter. **vb** *lit:* break, ruin; beggar, impoverish; liquidate, put into liquidation, put in the hands of a receiver. **adj** *lit:* broke, flat broke, indebted, insolvent, ruined; destitute, failed, impoverished; bust, on the rocks, washed up; *fig:* deficient, lacking, poor.

banner n *lit:* standard; coat of arms, colors, crest, escutcheon, insignia; burgee, gonfalon, pennant, pennon; ensign, flag.

bar n *lit:* baton, batten, boom, paling, pole, rail, rod, shaft, stake, stick; handle, key, lever; bolt, latch; barrier, obstruction; counter; canteen, inn, pub, saloon, taproom, tavern; bench, court, courtroom, dock, tribunal; advocates, barristers, lawyers; band, chevron, strip, stripe; block, cake, ingot, piece; bank, reef, sandbank, shallows, shoal; ridge; *fig:* ban, embargo, prohibition, proscription; deterrent, impediment, obstacle; *spec:* measure, unit of rhythm (in musical notation); unit of pressure (in meteorology). **vb** *lit:* bolt, latch, lock, put a bar across, secure; barricade,

block, exclude, keep out, obstruct, prevent; ban, forbid, prohibit; preclude.
prp *lit:* but (for), except (for), excluding, save.

barbarian **n** *lit:* brute, savage; foreigner, native; hooligan, lout, ruffian, thug, vandal; *fig:* Philistine; illiterate. **adj** *lit:* brutish, savage, uncivilized; foreign; lowbrow, Philistine; crude, primitive, uncouth, uncultured, uneducated, unsophisticated; *fig:* low, uncultivated, vulgar.

barbaric **adj** *lit:* barbarous, brutal, cruel, inhuman, ruthless; Neanderthal, primitive, savage, uncivilized; fierce, harsh, wild; coarse, crude, rough, rude, uncouth; *fig:* tasteless, vulgar.

barber **n** *lit:* coiffeur, coiffeuse, haircutter, hairdresser, hair stylist.

bare **vb** *lit:* unclothe, uncover, undress, unsheathe; disclose, expose, open, reveal; denude, strip. **adj** *lit:* denuded, exposed, naked, nude, stripped, unclothed, uncovered, undressed, unsheathed; peeled, shorn; austere, basic, cold, hard, mere, plain, severe, simple, stark, unadorned, unvarnished; literal, sheer, unembellished; blank, empty, open, vacant, void; lacking, mean, poor; barren, featureless, scrubby, treeless; abraded, worn.

bargain **n** *lit:* agreement, arrangement, compact, contract, deal, pact, transaction, treaty, understanding; cheap buy, giveaway, good deal, snip, steal. **vb** *lit:* beat down, haggle, negotiate, wheel and deal; barter, exchange, swap, trade, traffic; *fig:* bank, count, depend, rely; look (for), make allowance (for), plan (for).

barrage **n** *lit:* bar, barrier, boom, dam; bombardment, cannonade, fusillade, salvo, volley; *fig:* deluge, hail, onslaught, rain, storm, torrent.

barrel **n** *lit:* butt, cask, drum, keg, tun, vat; firkin, hogshead; cylinder, revolving drum, shaft, tube; chamber, piston chamber. **vb** *fig:* drive fast, hurtle, race, speed.

barren **adj** *lit:* desert, desolate, empty, unfruitful, unproductive, waste; childless, impotent, infertile, sterile; fruitless, uninformative, unprofitable, unresponsive, unrewarding, wasted; boring, dull, flat, jejune, stale, trite, unattractive, uninspiring, useless, vapid.

barrier **n** *lit:* bar, boom, paling, pole, rail; barricade, blockage, obstacle, obstruction; boundary, ditch, fence, wall; fortification, palisade, rampart, stockade; *fig:* check, difficulty, hindrance, hurdle, impediment, restriction, stumbling block; defense, protection.

base   n *lit:* bottom, foot, foundation; bed, dais, pedestal, plinth, podium, rest, stand; basis, bedrock, core, essence, floor, grounding, heart, origin, root, source; camp, headquarters, post, station; center, focal point, home, starting point; standard; *fig:* support; least, lowest, minimum; *spec:* alkali (in chemistry); basis of a number system (mathematics), stem (in botany, etymology, phonetics). **vb** *lit:* build, construct, establish, found, set up; locate, place, station; derive, ground. **adj** *lit:* basic, core, essential, original, root; central, focal, home, main, primary, principal; standard; first, starting; least, lowest, minimum; humble, inferior, lowly, menial, paltry, poor, servile, shabby, subservient, vulgar, wretched; contemptible, degraded, despicable, dishonorable, ignoble, low, mean, sordid, worthless; counterfeit, fake, forged, fraudulent; adulterated, debased, impure.

bashful   adj *lit:* coy, diffident, nervous, self-conscious, self-effacing, shrinking, shy, timid, timorous; embarrassed, sheepish; reserved, retiring; reticent.

basic   adj *lit:* core, fundamental, inherent, intrinsic, original, residual, root, underlying; standard; elementary, first, starting; least, lowest, minimum; central, essential, focal, key, main, primary, principal, vital; *spec:* alkaline (in chemistry).

basically   adv *lit:* firstly, fundamentally, inherently, intrinsically, originally, residually; at a minimum, at bottom, at least, at the lowest; essentially, mainly, mostly, primarily, principally.

basin   n *lit:* bowl, washbasin, washbowl, washstand; bidet; dock, harbor, haven, marina, pool; delta, drainage area, flats, valley; *spec:* synclinal area (in geology).

basis   n *lit:* base, bottom, footing, foundation; bedrock, core, essence, floor, grounding, groundwork, heart, origin, root, source; center, focal point, starting point; standard; essentials, fundamentals, grounds, precept, premise, principle, rationale, reason, substance.

bat   n *lit:* club, paddle, stick; lath, plank; *fig:* binge, carousal, drunken spree; *spec:* disc (of clay); lump, piece (of building materials); sheet (of insulation material). **vb** *lit:* hit, rap, smack, strike, swat, whack; blink, wink.

bath **n** *lit:* tub, washtub; Jacuzzi, pool, sink; ablution, dip, douche, dousing, immersion, rinse, scrub, scrubbing, soak, sponging, wash; steeping.

bathe **vb** *lit:* take a bath, swim; cleanse, dunk, drench, immerse, rinse, soak, steep, wash; dampen, moisten, wet; be immersed, be steeped; *fig:* cover, surround; bask, be covered.

batter **n** *lit:* cake mixture, sponge mixture; paste; striker; tapering slope. **vb** *lit:* assault, beat, belabor, buffet, dash against, lash, paste, pelt, pound, pummel, wallop; bruise, crush, injure, mangle, maul; slope upward.

battle **n** *lit:* action, combat, duel, engagement, fight, fighting, fray, skirmish, war, warfare; clash, conflict, contest, dispute, encounter, struggle. **vb** *lit:* contend, fight, make war, struggle, wage war; clash, contest, dispute.

bawl **n** *lit:* bellow, holler, roar; cry, howl, shout, shriek, wail, yell; blubbering, crying, sobbing, wailing; caterwauling, clamor, squalling. **vb** *lit:* bellow, holler, roar; howl, shout, shriek, yell; blubber, cry, sob, wail; caterwaul, clamor, squall.

bay **n** *lit:* bight, cove, gulf, inlet, sound; alcove, embrasure, niche, nook, recess; concavity, hanging valley, indentation; platform, stall, station; area, compartment, space, ward; barking, call, howl, ululation; *spec:* chestnut (horse); laurel (bush, tree). **vb** *lit:* bark (at), bell, cry, howl, ululate; corner, trap. **adj** *lit:* concave, recessed, semicircular; *spec:* chestnut, reddish-brown (horse); laurel (bush, tree).

be **vb** *lit:* exist, live; abide, continue, remain, stay; last, persist, subsist, survive; befall, come about, happen, occur, take place, transpire; become, equal, represent.

beach **n** *lit:* bank, littoral, shore, strand; sand, sands, seaside, shingle. **vb** *lit:* drive on shore, go aground, pull on shore, run ashore; *fig:* maroon, strand.

beacon **n** *lit:* fire, flare, lamp, light, signal, signal fire; light buoy, lighthouse, navigation light; watchtower; radio guide beam, radio mast; flashing light; *fig:* guiding light, indicator, landmark, pointer, sign, signpost; warning.

beam n *lit:* girder, joist, plank, spar, timber, trunk; ray, shaft, stream; emission, transmission; gleam; *fig:* broad smile, glow, grin, radiance; *spec:* bar, crosspiece, lever (on a pair of scales); breadth, side, width (of a ship); cylinder, roller (on a loom); shank, stem (of an anchor, a plow). **vb** *lit:* broadcast, emit, radiate, transmit; gleam, shine; aim, direct, point; *fig:* grin, smile, smile broadly.

bear n *lit:* bruin, grizzly; koala, panda; *fig:* hairy giant, shaggy person; *spec:* pessimist, seller (on the stock exchange). **vb** *lit:* bring, carry, take; convey, fetch, move, transport; drive, press, push, thrust; have, hold, possess, sustain; assume, take on; behave, conduct; entertain, harbor, support; endure, put up with, stomach, tolerate; abide, brook; admit, afford, allow, permit; experience, suffer, undergo; bring forth, bring to birth, engender, give birth to, produce, yield; affect, be pertinent, be relevant; go, move, tend, turn, veer; give out, render; exercise; *spec:* sell (shares).

beard n *lit:* bristles, full set, stubble, whiskers; awn, tuft; *spec:* barbel (on a fish). **vb** *lit:* brave, confront, defy, face.

bearer n *lit:* bringer, carrier, conveyor, messenger, porter, runner; agent, servant; holder, presenter.

bearing n *lit:* air, attitude, carriage, demeanor, deportment, manner, mien, posture; compass point, direction; application, connection, import, reference, relation, relevance, significance; endurance, stomaching, toleration; *spec:* charge, device (on a coat of arms)

beast n *lit:* animal, brute; creature; fiend, monster, ogre, savage.

beat n *lit:* pulse, throb, vibration; drumming, percussion; accent, stress; measure, meter, rhythm, time; circuit, course, patrol, round; *spec:* interference pattern (in music and wave physics). **vb** *lit:* bang, batter, buffet, cane, drub, flog, hit, lash, pound, strike, thrash, whip, whack; pulsate, pulse, throb, vibrate; drum, hammer, roar, thunder; fashion, forge, work; *fig:* best, conquer, defeat, overcome, vanquish; outdo, outstrip, overtake, overwhelm, surpass.

beautiful adj *lit:* bewitching, enchanting, exquisite, fair, gorgeous, graceful, handsome, lovely, magnificent, radiant, ravishing, stunning.

beauty n *lit:* attractiveness, charm, good looks, grace, loveliness, prettiness, pulchritude; advantage, benefit, good feature, major attraction; charmer, dreamboat, good-looker, stunner.

because   **cnj** *lit:* by reason (of), on account (of); for the reason that, in that, since.

become   **vb** *lit:* change into, develop into, grow into, turn into; come to be, get, turn; be appropriate to, be fitting to, behoove, suit; adorn, grace, set off; be the fate (of).

bed   **n** *lit:* berth, bunk; mattress, pallet; litter, pailliasse; resting place; bottom, floor, foundation, stratum, substratum, vein; border, garden, patch, plot, row; *fig:* sexual relations; *spec:* layer (of farmed oysters). **vb** *lit:* be accommodated, lodge, put up, settle (down); hit the sack, lie, sleep; have sex with, make love with, sleep with; stratify; lay down, set down; implant, insert, plant, plant out, put in.

before   **adv** *lit:* ahead, in front; earlier, in the past, previously; by now, sooner. **prp** *lit:* ahead of, in front of; in the sight of; earlier than, prior to; sooner than; in preference to; superior to.

beg   **vb** *lit:* beseech, entreat, implore, petition, plead with; ask for alms, ask for charity; *fig:* cry (off); evade, sidestep (the question).

beggar   **n** *lit:* mendicant, tramp, vagrant; suppliant; bankrupt, pauper.

begin   **vb** *lit:* commence, start; inaugurate, initiate, launch, open, set about; embark on, set out on; create, found, institute, originate; appear, come into being, emerge, spring.

beginning   **n** *lit:* commencement, onset, start; inauguration, initiation, launch, opening; outset; birth, creation, foundation, institution, origination, root(s); appearance, arising, dawn, emergence; fountainhead, source. **adj (pr.pt)** *lit:* first, inaugural, initial, leading, opening, original, primary; incipient, rudimentary.

behalf   **n** *lit:* account, part, side.

behave   **vb** *lit:* act, conduct oneself, handle, operate, perform, work; act properly, be mannerly, be polite; react.

behavior   **n** *lit:* activity, comportment, conduct, manners; action, handling, operation, performance; reaction, responsiveness.

behind n *lit:* backside, bottom, derriere, posterior, rear, seat, stern. **adv** *lit:* at the back, in the rear; afterwards, farther back, following, subsequently; in detention, in reserve; late, overdue, slow; in arrears, in debt. **prp** *lit:* at the back of, beyond, to the back of; after, following, subsequent to; later than, slower than; responsible for; backing, supporting.

being n *lit:* existence, life, living; entity, essence, substance; constitution, nature; attendance, presence; creature, individual, organism. **adj (pr.pt)** *lit:* existent; contemporaneous, continuing, present.

belief n *lit:* confession, credo, creed, doctrine, faith, persuasion, tenet; conviction, feeling, impression, opinion, understanding, view; reliance, trust; (beyond) acceptance, (beyond) credence.

believe vb *lit:* confess, have faith (in); credit; be convinced (that), hold (that); place one's trust (in), trust; consider, deem, think; conjecture, guess, imagine, presume, reckon, suppose.

believer n *lit:* adherent, devotee, disciple, proselyte.

belong vb *lit:* appertain (to), attach (to), pertain (to), relate (to); be affiliated (to); be connected (with), go together (with).

belongings n *lit:* gear, effects, junk, paraphernalia, possessions, stuff, things.

below adj *lit:* beneath, underneath; downstairs, lower; later, subsequent; inferior, lesser. **adv** *lit:* beneath, under, underneath; down, downstairs, lower; downstream; hereafter, later. **prp** *lit:* beneath, lower than, under, underneath; inferior to, less than, subordinate to, unworthy of.

bench n *lit:* pew, seat; counter, worktable; frame, platform; judiciary, magistracy, tribunal.

bend n *lit:* buckle, fold, warp; angle, corner, curve, turn; stoop; fastening, knot. **vb** *lit:* bow, buckle, fold, warp; curve, swerve, turn, veer; lean over, stoop; flex, mold, shape; *fig:* influence, persuade, sway.

beneath adv *lit:* below, under, underneath; lower. **prp** *lit:* below, lower than, under, underneath; inferior to, less than, subordinate to, unworthy of.

benefit n *lit:* advantage, gain, good, help, improvement, profit, use; dole, grant, unemployment grant, welfare; charity performance. **vb** *lit:* be good for, do good to; advantage, aid, further, serve; be advantaged, be assisted, gain, profit.

benevolent **adj** *lit:* beneficent, benign, charitable, considerate, generous, humane, kindly, philanthropic, well-disposed.

bent n *lit:* bias, inclination, leaning, penchant, preference, propensity; tendency, trend; flexion, torque; ability, endurance. **adj** *lit:* bowed, buckled, folded, twisted, warped; angled, curved; crooked, hunched, leaning, stooping; *fig:* determined (on), insistent (on), intent (on), resolved (on); criminal, dishonest, fraudulent, unscrupulous; deviant, kinky, perverted.

berth n *lit:* bed, bunk, cabin, couchette, place, seat; sleeping place; anchorage, dock, mooring, quay, wharf; *fig:* job, position, post, situation; leeway, room, space.

beside **adv** *lit:* additionally, also, further, furthermore, in addition, moreover, too. **prp** *lit:* adjoining, alongside, bordering, by the side of, contiguous with, next to; *fig:* compared to/with, in comparison with; not pertinent to, unrelated to (the point).

besides **adv** *lit:* additionally, also, further, furthermore, in addition, moreover, too; likewise, similarly; else, otherwise. **prp** *lit:* as well as, in addition to, over and above; apart from, barring, excepting, other than, save.

best n *lit:* finest, greatest, number one, optimum, supreme, top; elite, favorite, flower, pick; champion, first, victor, winner; utmost. **vb** *lit:* beat, conquer, defeat, outdo, surpass; outwit. **adj** *lit:* finest, foremost, greatest, highest, optimum, supreme, top; favorite; champion, first, leading, victorious, winning; most advantageous; most fitting. **adv** *lit:* most, supremely; most correctly, most efficiently, most thoroughly; most advantageously; most attractively, most fittingly.

bet n *lit:* gamble, risk, speculation, wager; ante, pledge, stake; *fig:* alternative, choice, course of action, route; belief, guess, opinion, supposition. **vb** *lit:* gamble, punt, risk, speculate (on), stake (on), wager; *fig:* be certain, be sure.

betray **vb** *lit:* double-cross, sell out; divulge, give away, reveal; inform on, tell on, unmask; ensnare, entrap, seduce, undo; be disloyal to, deceive; desert, forsake, leave in the lurch; *fig:* let slip, manifest, show signs of.

betrayal   n *lit:* double cross, giveaway, sellout; disclosure, divulgence, unmasking; entrapment, seduction; violation; disloyalty, deception, duplicity, perfidy, treachery, treason; desertion, forsaking, ratting.

better   vb *lit:* ameliorate, enhance, forward, further, improve; amend, correct, rectify; beat, cap, defeat, outdo, top. **adj** *lit:* finer, greater, higher, preferable, superior; more useful, more valuable; more apt, more suitable; more expert, more skilled; more intense; cured, healthier, progressing, recovering, stronger, well again. **adv** *lit:* more (than); in a superior way, more advantageously, more usefully, more valuably; more aptly, more suitably; more expertly, more skillfully; more fully, more intensely.

between   prp *lit:* betwixt, intermediate to, in the middle of, within the range separating; connecting, joining, linking; through the combined action of; in the joint possession of.

beware   vb *lit:* be careful (of), be wary (of); be on one's guard (lest/that).

beyond   adv *lit:* at a distance, behind, farther away; past. **prp** *lit:* across, behind, on the farther side of, over, to the farther side of; later than, past; above, besides, more than, outside; *fig:* out of the reach of, too much for the comprehension of.

bias   n *lit:* leaning, partiality, predilection, predisposition, prejudice; diagonal, oblique; weighting. **vb** *lit:* influence, predispose, prejudice, slant, weight.

bid   n *lit:* offer, proposition, tender; *fig:* attempt, effort, endeavor, try. **vb** *lit:* make an offer, tender; call; greet, say, wish; ask, invite; command (to), direct (to), order (to), tell (to).

big   adj *lit:* colossal, enormous, gigantic, great, huge, hulking, immense, large, massive, sizable, substantial, tremendous; adult, elder, grown-up; full, loud; pregnant (with); *fig:* important, influential, powerful, prominent, valuable; altruistic, benevolent, generous, liberal, magnanimous, noble, princely; arrogant, boastful, conceited, pompous, pretentious.

bill   n *lit:* account, check, invoice, reckoning, score, slate, tally; advertisement, broadside, broadsheet, circular, handout, leaflet, poster;

inventory, list, program, schedule; law, measure, proposal; banknote, note; beak, neb. **vb** *lit:* charge, invoice, put on the slate; advertise, announce, give advance warning of, place posters up over.

binding n *lit:* casing, cover, covering, jacket; border, edging, trimming; ski fastening. **adj** *lit:* indelible, irrevocable; compulsory, obligatory.

bird n *lit:* feathered friend, fowl; *fig:* chap, person; booing, raspberry.

birth n *lit:* accouchement, delivery, labor, parturition; nativity; ancestry, blood, breeding, family, lineage, parentage; *fig:* beginning, creation, dawn, emergence, genesis, inauguration, origination.

bit n *lit:* bite, chip, crumb, fragment, morsel, scrap, slice; part, piece, section, segment, small amount; coin; bore, drill; curb, mouthpiece; *fig:* little, minute, moment, second, while.

bite n *lit:* dentition, occlusion; grasp, grip; nip, prick, puncture, sting; morsel, mouthful, nibble, snack; *fig:* acidity, corrosiveness; kick, piquancy, punch, spice; attempt, bash, go, try; answer, reaction, response. **vb** *lit:* chew, chomp, clench, gnaw, masticate, munch, nibble, nip; grind, grip, puncture, rend, seize, sting, tear; corrode, eat into, erode, wear away; cut, pierce; be caught, take the bait; *fig:* be effective, take effect; react, respond, snap (at); annoy, bother.

bitter adj *lit:* acescent, acid, acrid, astringent, harsh, sour, tart; *fig:* acrimonious, hostile, rancorous, resentful, sulky, sullen; caustic, fierce, sharp, stinging, virulent; biting, freezing, intense, piercing; distressing, galling, grievous, heartrending, painful.

black adj *lit:* dusky, ebony-colored, jet, swarthy; dark, raven, sable; dim, inky, murky, Stygian; dirty, filthy, foul, grimy, soiled; *fig:* depressing, foreboding, funereal, hopeless, mournful, ominous, somber; evil, malignant, villainous, wicked; lowering, morose, resentful, sullen, sulky; aggressive, hostile, menacing, threatening; banned, boycotted, embargoed.

blackout n *lit:* dizzy spell, faint, loss of consciousness, swoon; epileptic fit; electricity cut, power failure; *fig:* censorship, silence, suppression.

blame n *lit:* accusation, censure, charge, recrimination; culpability, guilt; *fig:* fault, liability, responsibility. **vb** *lit:* condemn (for), find fault with (for), hold responsible (for), rebuke (for), reproach (for).

blank **n** *lit:* emptiness, space, tabula rasa, vacuity, vacuum, void; gap, hiatus; empty sheet, white page; *spec:* bull's-eye, inner, white (on a target). **adj** *lit:* bare, empty, plain, pristine, unmarked, unused, white; uncut, unformed, unshaped; *fig:* bewildered, confounded, dumbfounded, nonplused; deadpan, expressionless, impassive, lifeless, uncomprehending, vacuous.

blanket **n** *lit:* coverlet, rug; *fig:* carpet, coat, covering, film, layer, sheet. **vb** *lit:* carpet, coat, cover, envelop, spread oneself over; cloak, mask, obscure, veil. **adj** *lit:* all-inclusive, comprehensive, general, universal.

blast **n** *lit:* gust, squall, storm, wind; blare, honk, hoot, peal, wail; blow, jet; bang, crash, detonation, eruption, explosion; *fig:* outburst. **vb** *lit:* blare, blow, hoot; blow up, detonate, explode, shatter; demolish, destroy, smash, wreck, zap; kill, ruin, shrivel, wither; *fig:* be scathing about, flay, pan, slate; abuse, curse, swear at, vilify.

blatant **adj** *lit:* brazen, flagrant, glaring; conspicuous, obvious, overt, pronounced; clamorous, loudmouthed, noisy; garish, gaudy, loud, ostentatious.

bleak **adj** *lit:* bare, barren, exposed, gaunt, open, windswept; chilly, cold, raw, windy; cheerless, colorless, depressing, discouraging, gloomy, somber.

bleed **vb** *lit:* lose blood, shed blood; lose sap; leak, ooze, seep, trickle; draw blood from; draw sap from; catheterize, drain, leech, siphon off, squeeze; *fig:* blackmail from, extort from; ache (for), feel (for), have pity (for); *spec:* extend to the edge of the page (of illustrations).

blend **n** *lit:* amalgam, combination, compound, fusion, mixture, synthesis; merging, shading; harmonization. **vb** *lit:* amalgamate, combine, compound, fuse, mingle, mix; synthesize; merge (with); go well (with), harmonize (with).

bless **vb** *lit:* consecrate, hallow, make holy, sanctify; commend to God's grace, invoke divine favor upon, make the sign of the cross over; make fruitful, make happy, make joyful, make prosperous; adore, extol, glorify, praise, worship.

blessing **n** *lit:* benediction, benison; consecration, invocation; grace, thanksgiving; *fig:* approval, backing, encouragement, favor, sanction, support; benefit, gift, possession, present; boon, godsend, help, piece of luck, stroke of good fortune.

blind   **n** *lit:* louvers, shutter, slats; canopy, shade; *fig:* cover, device, facade, feint, front, mask, ploy, pretext, pretense, ruse, screen, stratagem. **vb** *lit:* put out the eyes of; be too bright for, dazzle; *fig:* keep in the dark, render oblivious (to), stop from seeing. **adj** *lit:* sightless, unseeing; *fig:* dead-end; inattentive (to), indifferent (to), insensitive (to), oblivious (to); dark, dim, hidden, obscured; unreasoning, unthinking. **adv** *lit:* ad lib, extempory, off the cuff, straight off, unseen; through instrumentation only.

block   **n** *lit:* barrier, blockage, impediment, obstacle, obstruction, stoppage; bar, brick, cube, ingot, piece; building, site, square; anvil, base, platform, support, table; pulley; *fig:* group, row, set; book, pad, ream; head. **vb** *lit:* bar, check, halt, impede, obstruct, stop; bung, choke, clog, plug up, stuff up.

blockade   **n** *lit:* barricade, barrier, obstruction; encirclement, investment, siege. **vb** *lit:* barricade, fortify, obstruct, secure; besiege, cut off, encircle, isolate.

blood   **n** *lit:* gore; plasma, serum; ancestry, birth, descent, extraction, family, genealogy, lineage, pedigree, stock, strain; kindred, relations, relatives; *fig:* juice, sap; anger, passion, temper; death, murder; disposition, feeling, temperament; buck, blade, dandy, spark; aristocracy, nobility, royal family. **vb** *lit:* smear with gore; *fig:* initiate (into), introduce (into).

bloom   **n** *lit:* blossom, flower; blossoming, flowering, opening; powdery surface; cloudiness, milkiness; *fig:* fragrance, freshness, perfection, prime, radiance; blush, flush, rosiness; *spec:* aggregation, mass (of plankton). **vb** *lit:* blossom, burgeon, flower, open; *fig:* flourish, prosper, succeed, thrive; be fragrant, be radiant.

blossom   **n** *lit:* bloom, flower; flowers, scented petals. **vb** *lit:* bloom, burgeon, flower; *fig:* come into one's own, flourish, lose one's reserve, mature, show what one can do.

blow   **n** *lit:* blast, gale, gust, wind; bang, belt, buffet, clip, clout, clump, knock, punch, smack, sock, thump, thwack, wallop, whack; *fig:* calamity, catastrophe, disappointment, disaster, setback, upset; (at a) stroke. **vb** *lit:*

fan, gust, puff, waft, whirl, whistle; blast, buffet, sweep, whisk; breathe hard, exhale, pant; pipe, play; blare, hoot, sound; *fig:* exhaust, spend, squander, use up; divulge, reveal, tell; *spec:* lose, miss (one's chance); burn out (a fuse); spout (of whales).

blue vb *lit:* bleach, dye white; *fig:* exhaust, spend, squander, use up. **adj** *lit:* aquamarine, azure, cerulean, cyan, indigo, turquoise, ultramarine; cold, frozen, numb; *fig:* dejected, depressed, downcast, doleful, glum, melancholy; depressing, dismal, unpromising; bawdy, erotic, indecent, obscene, smutty; *spec:* flattened, seventh (note in music).

blunt vb *lit:* dull, take the edge off; *fig:* dampen, deaden, muffle, soften, weaken. **adj** *lit:* dull, flat; *fig:* bluff, forthright, frank, plainspoken, outspoken, straightforward; explicit, forceful.

blur n *lit:* blot, smear, smudge, splotch; blear, fog, haze, mist, vagueness; streak. **vb** *lit:* blemish, blot, smear, smudge; cloud, darken, obscure, soften; flash, streak.

blush n *lit:* flush, glow, reddening, suffusion; bloom, rosiness. **vb** *lit:* color, crimson, flush, redden, suffuse; be ashamed (at), be mortified (at).

board n *lit:* joist, panel, plank, timber; lath, slat; table; catering, food, meals, provisions; committee, council, directors, trustees; arena, platform, stage, surface. **vb** *lit:* plank (over), shutter, timber (over); cater for, feed, provide meals for; billet, lodge, put up, quarter; enter, get on, mount.

boast n *lit:* brag, vaunt; joy, pride, pride and joy, treasure. **vb** *lit:* brag, talk big; blow one's own trumpet, crow, vaunt; be proud of, flatter oneself; *fig:* exhibit, have, own, possess.

boastful adj *lit:* big-headed, bragging, conceited, egotistical, vaunting.

boat n *lit:* craft, ship, vessel; canoe, cutter, dinghy, ketch, launch, sloop, yacht, yawl; cruiser, liner, ferry.

body n *lit:* figure, form, frame; build, physique; being, human, mortal, person, soul; cadaver, corpse, mortal remains; torso, trunk; fuselage, nave; *fig:* bulk, core, main part, majority, mass; essence, matter, substance; density, firmness, fullness, opacity, solidity; band, collection, company, group, set.

bog n *lit:* fen, marsh, morass, moss, quagmire, slough, swamp.

boil n *lit:* abscess, carbuncle, furuncle, pimple, pustule, spot, sty. **vb** *lit:* steam, vaporize; cook, poach; evaporate; agitate, bubble, churn, foam, seethe; *fig:* be incensed, fulminate, fume, hit the roof, rage, rant.

bold adj *lit:* audacious, brave, courageous, daring, fearless, intrepid, valiant; flirtatious, forward, shameless; brash, cheeky, impudent, saucy; *fig:* bright, conspicuous, loud, showy, striking, vivid; forceful, lively, spirited.

bolt n *lit:* bar, catch, latch, peg, pin, rod, slide; arrow, dart, quarrel; dash, runner, sprint; stroke of lightning, thunderflash; *spec:* roll (of cloth). **vb** *lit:* bar, fasten, latch, lock, peg, pin, secure; dash, flee, fly, run for it, sprint; gobble, gorge, guzzle, stuff, wolf.

bomb n *lit:* explosive device, mine, shell; *fig:* nasty shock, unwelcome surprise; fortune, lot of money; success, treat. **vb** *lit:* blitz, blow up, bombard, detonate, shell; *fig:* fly, hurtle, race, rocket, speed.

bond n *lit:* adhesion, adhesiveness, stickiness, tackiness; cement, glue, gum, mortar; binding, chain, cord, fastening, fetter, manacle, rope, shackle; molecular force; affinity, attachment, link, tie; agreement, contract, covenant, pledge, promise; guarantee, security, surety; debenture, promissory note. **vb** *lit:* cement, fasten (together), fix (together), fuse, glue, gum.

bonus n *lit:* bounty, commission, dividend, extra, gratuity, honorarium, premium, reward; perk; share of profits; prize, winnings; windfall.

book n *lit:* publication, tome, volume; work; archive, chronicle, ledger, log, record; libretto, script. **vb** *lit:* enter, insert, log, post, put down, record, register, write down; engage, line up, reserve, schedule; take the name of; check (in).

boost n *lit:* encouragement, furtherance, help; expansion, hike, hoist, improvement, increase, lift. **vb** *lit:* advance, encourage, foster, further, help; add to, enlarge, expand, hike up, hoist, improve, increase, lift, promote, support.

boot n *lit:* overshoe, heavy shoe; kick, punt. **vb** *lit:* shoe; kick, punt; chuck (out), kick (out), throw (out); avail, be of use, profit; *spec:* access, insert (a computer program).

border n *lit:* boundary, brink, edge, frontier, limit, margin, rim; flower bed; edging, fringe, hem, trimming; outskirts. **vb** *lit:* adjoin, be adjacent to, bound, delimit, front on, march with; edge, fringe.

bore **n** *lit:* hole, shaft; barrel, caliber; *fig:* drag, nuisance, pain, pest; chore, thankless task. **vb** *lit:* drill, mine, penetrate (into), pierce (into), sink a shaft (into), tunnel (into); *fig:* bother, fatigue, tire, weary.

boredom **n** *lit:* ennui, having nothing to do, listlessness, monotony, tedium, tediousness, tiresomeness.

boring **adj (pr.pt)** *lit:* dismal, dull, flat, humdrum, insipid, monotonous, mundane, numbing, ordinary, soporific, stale, stultifying, tedious, tiresome, uninteresting, wearisome.

borrow **vb** *lit:* have the use of; have, use, utilize; adopt, appropriate, copy, derive, imitate, pilfer, pirate, plagiarize.

bosom **n** *lit:* breast(s), bust; chest; *fig:* emotions, feelings, heart, sentiments; center, midst. **adj** *lit:* close, dear, intimate.

boss **n** *lit:* knob, ornament, stud; chief, employer, foreman, gaffer, leader, manager, master, overseer, supervisor.

bother **n** *lit:* annoyance, inconvenience, irritation, nuisance, problem, vexation; commotion, disturbance, fuss, to-do. **vb** *lit:* annoy, be a nuisance, inconvenience, irritate, pester, plague, vex; go to the trouble (to), make the effort (to); blast, damn.

bottom **n** *lit:* base, basis, floor, foundation; underneath, underside; backside, behind, posterior, rear, rump, seat; hull, keel; *fig:* core, heart, root, source. **adj** *lit:* base, fundamental, ground, lowest, ultimate.

bough **n** *lit:* branch, offshoot; shoot, stem; twig.

boundary **n** *lit:* border, edge, extremity, fringe, frontier, limit, line, margin, termination.

bountiful **adj** *lit:* beneficent, generous, liberal, munificent; ample, copious, plenteous, plentiful, prolific, unstinting.

bout **n** *lit:* contest, encounter, fight, round; period, session, spell, stint, time.

bow **n** *lit:* bend, bob, inclination, kowtow, nod; curve, distortion, warp; fore, front, prow, sharp end; looped knot. **vb** *lit:* bend (low), bob, incline, kowtow, nod; curve, distort, hunch, warp; play the violin; *fig:* defer (to), give in (to), surrender (to), yield (to); crush, oppress, subdue, weigh down.

bowl   **n** *lit:* basin, dish; container, pot, vessel; hurl, pitch, throw; ball, wood. **vb** *lit:* fling, hurl, pitch, throw; roll.

box   **n** *lit:* carton, case, package; chest, crate, trunk; receptacle; bang, blow, buffet, clip, clout, punch, wallop; *fig:* inset, rectangle; goal area, penalty area; cabin, hut, lodge; jock, protector. **vb** *lit:* enclose, insert, pack into; confine, pen; fight, spar, trade punches; bang, buffet, clip, clout, punch, thump, wallop.

boy   **n** *lit:* adolescent, lad, son, stripling, young man, youth; chap, fellow, guy.

brain   **n** *lit:* central nervous system, cerebral hemispheres, cerebrum, gray matter; intellect, mind; common sense, intelligence, nous, wit; *fig:* genius, mastermind, prodigy; expert; highbrow, scholar; control system, guidance system.

brake   **n** *lit:* check, constraint, curb, decelerator, rein; bracken, ferns, thicket, undergrowth. **vb** *lit:* check, constrain, curb, decelerate, halt, rein in, slow, stop.

branch   **n** *lit:* bough, offshoot; shoot, stem; twig; arm, limb; *fig:* ramification; department, office, part, section, subdivision, subsidiary. **vb** *lit:* diversify, divide, fork, ramify, spread (out); develop, expand, increase, proliferate.

brand   **n** *lit:* colophon, hallmark, label, logo, mark, sign, stamp, symbol; class, kind, make, sort, type, variety; *fig:* imputation, slur, stigma, taint. **vb** *lit:* label, mark, sign, stamp; *fig:* call, mark down as, stigmatize as.

brandish   **vb** *lit:* flourish, swing, wave about, whirl, wield; display, exhibit, flaunt, hold (in front of).

brawn   **n** *lit:* beef, muscle, muscularity, robustness, strength, vigor.

breach   **n** *lit:* break, cleft, fissure, gap, hole, rift, split; infraction, infringement, transgression, violation; alienation, difference, division, estrangement, separation, variance; breaking of the waves, surf. **vb** *lit:* break, crack, fracture, make an opening, rend, split; infringe, transgress against, violate.

bread n *lit:* loaf; *fig:* food, livelihood, nourishment, provisions, sustenance; cash, funds, money.

breadth n *lit:* latitude, span, width; beam; area, compass, extent, measure, range, scale, scope, size, spread, sweep; liberality, openness; integrity, totality.

break n *lit:* crack, fracture, rupture, snap; breach, cleft, fissure, gap, hole, rent, rip, tear; alienation, divergence, estrangement, separation, split; division, parting, severance; breather, halt, intermission, interval, pause, recess, rest, stop; *fig:* chance, opportunity; piece of luck, stroke of good fortune; alteration, change, difference; dawn (of day); *spec:* ad lib, cadenza (in a musical performance); run (of points in billiards); spin (on a ball). **vb** *lit:* come apart, crack, fracture, rupture, snap; crush, fragment, powder, shatter; breach, leave a gap in, make a hole in, rend, rip, tear; interpose, separate, split up; divide, part, sever; be intermittent; disconnect; discontinue, leave (off), stop, take a breather, take time (off); interrupt; interpolate (in), put one's oar (in); infract, infringe, transgress against; overwhelm, subdue, tame, undermine; degrade, demote, dismiss, ruin; *fig:* disclose, divulge, impart, let out, reveal, tell; appear, emerge, erupt forth; beat, better, exceed, outdo, top (a record); cure (a habit); cushion, soften (a fall); *spec:* escape from (prison); leave (cover); run (for it); spin (of a ball on bouncing); unfurl (a flag); violate (a promise, one's parole).

breast n *lit:* bosom, bust, chest; mammary gland; mound, rounded hill; *fig:* conscience, heart, mind, soul. **vb** *lit:* reach with the chest; *fig:* confront, engage with, meet, oppose.

breath n *lit:* animation, life; exhalation, inhalation, respiration; gasp, pant; breeze, flutter, puff, waft; aroma, odor, perfume, scent; *fig:* hint, suggestion, suspicion, whisper.

breathe **vb** *lit:* exhale, inhale, respire; blow, gasp, pant, puff; *fig:* murmur, say softly, sigh, whisper; infuse (into), inject (into).

breed n *lit:* family, lineage, pedigree, stock; class, kind, race, sort, species, type, variety. **vb** *lit:* multiply, proliferate, procreate, propagate, reproduce; cultivate, farm, raise, rear; bring up, educate, train; *fig:* beget, cause, create, generate, occasion, produce.

bribe **n** *lit:* bait, carrot, enticement, greased palm, inducement, kickback. **vb** *lit:* buy, get at, grease the palm of, pay off, suborn.

bridge **n** *lit:* crossover, span, viaduct; flyover, overpass; catwalk, gantry; bond, connection, link; *spec:* navigation center (on a ship); support (for the strings on a violin, for a cue, for a pair of spectacles); top (of the nose). **vb** *lit:* go over, lie across, span, straddle; connect, join, link.

brief **n** *lit:* outline, précis, summary, synopsis; argument, contention; case, statement; summons, writ; *spec:* epistle (papal). **vb** *lit:* advise, bring up to date, fill in, give a rundown, inform; instruct, prime; précis, summarize. **adj** *lit:* concise, short, succinct; outline, thumbnail; brusque, curt, sharp, terse; fleeting, momentary, short-lived, transitory.

bright **adj** *lit:* brilliant, dazzling, effulgent, glittering, glowing, intense, luminous, resplendent, scintillating, shimmering, shining, vivid, white; clear, pellucid, translucent, transparent; blazing, cloudless, fair, sunny; *fig:* astute, clever, ingenious, intelligent, imaginative, inventive, practical, quick-witted, shrewd; cheerful, encouraging, favorable, happy, jolly, optimistic, promising; animated, lively, vivacious; glorious, illustrious, magnificent.

brilliant **adj** *lit:* bright, dazzling, effulgent, intense, luminous, lustrous, radiant, resplendent, shining, very white; coruscating, glittering, scintillating, twinkling; glamorous, grand, magnificent, splendid; *fig:* excellent, expert, extremely intelligent, highly gifted, masterly, very talented; glorious, illustrious, magnificent.

bring **vb** *lit:* carry, convey, deliver, fetch, take, transport; advance, forward, present, proffer; conduct, escort, guide, lead, steer; turn (about); cut (down), shoot (down); *fig:* induce (to), persuade (to), prevail upon (to); compel (to), force (to), oblige (to); carry (off), pull (it off); command, earn, net, sell for.

brink **n** *lit:* cliff top, edge, sheer edge; bank, brim, verge; *fig:* point, threshold.

brisk **adj** *lit:* bustling, busy, energetic, lively, sprightly, spry, vigorous; bracing, exhilarating, invigorating, keen, sharp; piquant.

bristle **n** *lit:* hair, whisker; prickle, spine, thorn. **vb** *lit:* prickle, rise, stand on end; *fig:* bridle, flare up, recoil; crawl (with), swarm (with), teem (with).

brittle adj *lit:* crisp, rigid, taut, tense; fragile, friable; *fig:* edgy, nervous, stiff; cool, stilted; unstable.

broad adj *lit:* thick, wide; ample, free, generous, extensive, large; capacious, open, roomy, spacious; *fig:* comprehensive, encyclopedic, sweeping, universal; liberal, permissive, progressive; uninhibited, unrestrained; blue, coarse, indecent, indelicate, vulgar; full (daylight); *spec:* accented (dialect).

broadcast n *lit:* program, transmission. vb *lit:* air, radio, relay, televise, transmit; announce, circulate, noise abroad, proclaim, publish; disperse, disseminate, scatter, sow, seed, spread.

brown vb *lit:* fry, roast, sauté. adj *lit:* bister, dun, sepia, tan, umber; auburn, brunette, chestnut, hazel; dark, dusky, tawny; bronzed, tanned; chocolate-colored, coffee-colored.

bruise n *lit:* contusion, discoloration; sore spot, tenderness; dent, indentation. vb *lit:* contuse, discolor; damage, injure, wound; crush, pound, powder.

brush n *lit:* besom, broom; bristles, hair; bushy tail; bushes, scrub, thicket, undergrowth; abrasion, bump, contact, friction, glance, graze, scrape; *fig:* confrontation, encounter, skirmish, tussle; *spec:* contact (electrical). vb *lit:* clean, dust, sweep; paint; bump, make contact with, glance off, scrape; caress, flick, stroke, touch.

brutal adj *lit:* bestial, callous, cruel, inhuman, merciless, relentless, ruthless, savage, unfeeling; harsh, repressive, rigorous, severe, stern, strict, tyrannical; coarse, gross, rude.

brute n *lit:* animal, beast; *fig:* bully, ruffian, sadist, savage, thug; barbarian, boor, lout.

bubble n *lit:* bead, drop, globule; blister, vesicle; *fig:* speculative venture. vb *lit:* boil, effervesce, fizz, seethe; babble, gurgle, murmur, ripple.

buckle n *lit:* catch, clasp, hasp; bend, bow, distortion, fold, kink, warp. vb *lit:* do up, fasten, lace up, latch, tie up; bend, bow, crumple, distort, fold, kink, warp.

budget n *lit:* finances, funds, resources; allocation, amount set aside, cost specification, estimate; financial program. **vb** *lit:* allocate, cost, estimate; set aside an amount (for); plan one's fiscal affairs.

bug n *lit:* beetle, creepy-crawly, insect, midge; bacterium, germ, micro-organism, virus; infection; concealed microphone; *fig:* defect, fault, gremlin, snag; craze, fad, rage. **vb** *lit:* plant a microphone on; tap; *fig:* annoy, disturb, irk, pester, plague.

build n *lit:* body shape, figure, frame, physique. **vb** *lit:* construct, erect, make, put up; create, form, fashion, mold; amass, assemble, collect, put together; base, establish, found; augment, develop, expand, extend, increase.

building n *lit:* construction, edifice, erection, structure; block, house.

bulge n *lit:* lump, protuberance, swelling; dilation, distension; blister, bump, cyst, wen; broadening, expansion, thickening; corporation, eminence, overhang, protrusion; *fig:* fluctuation, temporary increase, rise. **vb** *lit:* dilate, distend, expand, project, protrude, stick out, swell.

bulk n *lit:* immensity, magnitude, size, volume; body, majority, major proportion, mass, most part; cargo, hold. **vb** *lit:* expand, swell (up); amass, pile (up); broaden (out), thicken (out); loom (large).

bulky adj *lit:* big, hulking, immense, large, massive; cumbersome, heavy, ponderous, unwieldy, weighty.

bull n *lit:* ox; *fig:* buyer, speculator; bunkum, humbug, nonsense, rubbish, twaddle, bull's-eye, inner target; *spec:* full-grown male (elephant, moose, seal, walrus, whale, etc.); decree, edict (papal); optimist, buyer (on the stock exchange).

bullet n *lit:* ball, pellet, shot, slug; cartridge, casing.

bully n *lit:* blackmailer, intimidator, persecutor; oppressor; ruffian, thug, troublemaker. **vb** *lit:* browbeat, bulldoze, domineer, intimidate, oppress, push around, terrorize.

bump n *lit:* bang, blow, collision, crash, impact, jolt, shock, thump; contusion, knob, lump, nodule; bulge, swelling. **vb** *lit:* bang into, collide with, crash into, jolt, knock into, strike, thump; bounce, jar, rattle, shake; *fig:* run (into); kill (off).

bun n *lit:* cake, muffin, roll, pastry, scone; coil, knot, mass.

bunch n *lit:* bouquet, bundle, clump, cluster, handful, parcel, posy, sheaf, spray; batch, collection, pile; knot, tuft; band, crowd, gang, group, mob, party, team. **vb** *lit:* assemble, cluster, concentrate, congregate, crowd together, group, pack together; clench, contract, knot.

bundle n *lit:* batch, bunch, collection, group, pile, stack; bale, bolt, mass, package, parcel, roll; knot, node; *fig:* lot. **vb** *lit:* batch up, collect together, group, pile up, stack; bale, pack up, parcel together, roll up, tie up; *fig:* hurry, hustle, push, shove, thrust.

bunk n *lit:* bed, berth, cot, sleeping place; balderdash, claptrap, hooey, humbug, junk, nonsense, piffle, rubbish, stuff and nonsense, twaddle.

burden n *lit:* encumbrance, fardel, load, weight; cargo, freight; *fig:* millstone, onus, responsibility, strain, stress, worry. **vb** *lit:* encumber, load, weigh down; saddle (with); *fig:* handicap, make difficult for, oppress, penalize, worry.

burglar n *lit:* housebreaker, raider, sneak thief; intruder, trespasser, robber.

burglary n *lit:* breaking and entering, housebreaking, larceny, theft; break-in, robbery.

burial n *lit:* interment; funeral, obsequies.

burn n *lit:* brand, scorch, singe; firing, launch, lift-off, thrust; fast ride. **vb** *lit:* be on fire, blaze; ignite, kindle, light, set alight; glow, smoke; brand, char, cremate, incinerate, singe; oxidize; *fig:* consume, expend, use; hurt, smart, sting; be inflamed, be passionate, smolder with desire (for), yearn (for).

burst n *lit:* emission, outpouring, transmission; eruption, gust, rush, surge; acceleration, sprint, spurt; breach, break, rupture, split; blast, discharge, explosion, salvo, volley; display, shower. **vb** *lit:* blow up, explode, fly apart, puncture, rupture, shatter; barge (in), rush (in); break (into), snap (into); break (out), erupt; flood, gush, overflow, spout; implode. **adj** **(pa.pt)** *lit:* flat, punctured, ruptured; blown up, exploded, shattered; breached, broken, holed.

bury vb *lit:* inhume, inter, lay to rest; dig in, embed, plant, sink; *fig:* conceal, cover up, hide away; engross, immerse, preoccupy.

bus n *lit:* coach, streetcar, tram; *fig:* automobile, car; airplane; *spec:* distributor (electrical).

bush n *lit:* hedge, shrub, woody plant; forest, jungle, thicket, wilds; outback, scrub, veldt.

business n *lit:* commerce, industry, manufacturing, marketing, trading; company, concern, firm, organization; craft, job, line, métier, occupation, profession, trade, work; deals, transactions; assignment, duty, function, responsibility; affair, issue, matter, topic.

bust n *lit:* bosom, breasts, chest, figure; head and shoulders, statue; arrest, cop, raid. **vb** *lit:* break, burst, rupture, shatter; bankrupt, impoverish, ruin; arrest, catch, cop, raid. **adj (pa.pt)** *lit:* broken, burst, ruptured, shattered; bankrupt, broke, impoverished, ruined; arrested, caught, raided.

busy adj *lit:* active, exacting, full, strenuous; engaged, engrossed, fully employed, occupied, preoccupied; hard at it, industrious, laboring, toiling away; *fig:* fussy, officious; interfering, meddlesome, prying; *spec:* overdetailed, restless (in art).

but cnj *lit:* however, nevertheless, on the other hand, still, yet; except (for/that), save (for/that); unless. **adv** *lit:* just, merely, no more than, only, simply.

butcher n *lit:* slaughterer; killer, slayer; sadist, torturer. **vb** *lit:* slaughter; carve, cut up, dress, joint; cut down, kill, slay; *fig:* botch, make an utter hash of, mutilate, travesty.

button n *lit:* boss, knop, rivet, roundel, stud; bell push, disk, key, knob, pad; bud.

buy n *lit:* purchase; acquisition; bargain. **vb** *lit:* pay for, purchase; invest in; acquire, procure, secure; bribe, pay (off), square; *fig:* accept, believe, credit, grant.

buyer n *lit:* emptor, purchaser; client, customer, habitué, patron; agent, purchasing manager, stock manager, supplier.

by adv *lit:* at hand; beyond, past; aside, away. **prp** *lit:* along, alongside, beside, close to, near; past, through, via; on, over; because of, through the means of, through the use of; the invention of, the work of; in proportion to, in relation to, with respect to; times; before, prior to; according to; to the extent of; *spec:* called, of, under (the name).

C

cabin   n *lit:* chalet, cottage, hovel, hut, lodge, shack, shanty, shed; berth, deckhouse, quarters, room.

cabinet   n *lit:* case, closet, commode, cupboard, dresser, locker; administration, assembly, council, ministry; apartment, boudoir, chamber.

cable   n *lit:* chain, cord, flex, line, wire; hawser, rope; telegram.

cafe   n *lit:* cafeteria, coffee bar, lunchroom, restaurant, snack bar.

cage   n *lit:* enclosure, pen, pound. **vb** *lit:* confine, coop up, fence in, immure, impound, incarcerate, lock up, restrain, shut up.

cake   n *lit:* bar, block, cube, loaf, mass, slab. **vb** *lit:* bake, cement, coagulate, congeal, consolidate, dry, encrust, harden, ossify, solidify, thicken.

calculate   vb *lit:* adjust, compute, consider, count, determine, estimate, figure, gauge, judge, rate, reckon, value, weigh, work out; design, intend, plan.

calculation   n *lit:* computation, estimate, estimation, figuring, forecast, judgment, reckoning; caution, circumspection, contrivance, deliberation, discretion, foresight, forethought, planning, precaution.

call   n *lit:* cry, hail, shout, signal, whoop, yell; announcement, appeal, demand, invitation, notice, plea, request, ring, summons, supplication, visit; cause, grounds, justification, occasion, reason, urge. **vb** *lit:* announce, arouse, cry, hail, rouse, shout, waken, yell; assemble, bid, contact, convene, gather, invite, muster, phone, rally, ring up, summon; christen, describe as, designate, dub, label, name, style, term; appoint, declare, decree, ordain, order, proclaim, set apart; consider, estimate, regard, think.

calling   n *lit:* career, line, mission, occupation, profession, province, pursuit, trade, vocation, walk of life, work.

callous   adj *lit:* apathetic, cold, hard-boiled, hardhearted, heartless, indifferent, insensitive, inured, obdurate, thick-skinned, torpid, uncaring, unfeeling, unsusceptible, unsympathetic.

calm   n *lit:* calmness, hush, peace, quiet, repose, serenity, stillness, tranquility. **vb** *lit:* hush, mollify, placate, relax, soothe. **adj** *lit:* halcyon, mild, pacific, peaceful, placid, quiet, restful, serene, smooth, still, tranquil, windless; collected, composed, cool, dispassionate, equable, impassive, imperturbable, relaxed, undisturbed, unemotional, unexcited, unflappable, unruffled.

camp   n *lit:* bivouac, camp site, encampment, tents. **adj** *lit:* affected, artificial, effeminate, mannered, ostentatious, posturing.

can   n *lit:* canister, container, cylinder, tin, tube.

cancel   vb *lit:* abolish, abrogate, annul, call off, countermand, delete, do away with, efface, eliminate, erase, expunge, obliterate, quash, repeal, repudiate, revoke; compensate for, counterbalance, make up for, neutralize, nullify, offset.

cancellation   n *lit:* abandonment, abolition, annulment, deletion, elimination, quashing, repeal, revocation.

candidate   n *lit:* applicant, claimant, competitor, contender, contestant, entrant, nominee, runner, solicitant.

canopy   n *lit:* awning, covering, shade, tester.

canteen   n *lit:* bar, cafe, dining hall, mess, refectory, restaurant; cutlery drawer; flask, water container.

cap   n *lit:* cover, lid, seal, top; detonator; hat, headdress. **vb** *lit:* beat, better, complete, cover, crown, exceed, excel, finish, outdo, surpass, top, transcend.

capable   adj *lit:* able, accomplished, adept, adequate, apt, competent, efficient, experienced, gifted, proficient, qualified, skillful, susceptible.

capacity   n *lit:* amplitude, compass, extent, range, room, scope, size, space, volume; ability, aptitude, brains, capability, efficiency, faculty, power, strength; appointment, function, office, position, post, role, service, sphere.

cape   n *lit:* cloak; headland, peninsula, point, promontory.

capital   n *lit:* assets, cash, finances, funds, investment(s), means, money, property, resources, stock, wealth, wherewithal. **adj** *lit:* cardinal, central, chief, controlling, foremost, important, leading, main, overruling, paramount, preeminent, prime, principal, vital; excellent, fine, first-rate, splendid, superb.

capsize   vb *lit:* invert, keel over, overturn, tip over, turn turtle, upset.

capsule   n *lit:* lozenge, pill, tablet; case, pericarp, pod, receptacle, sheath, shell, vessel.

captain   n *lit:* boss, chief, commander, leader, master, number one, officer, (senior) pilot, skipper.

captivate   vb *lit:* allure, attract, beguile, charm, dazzle, enamor, enchant, enthrall, fascinate, infatuate, lure, mesmerize, win.

captive   n *lit:* convict, detainee, hostage, internee, prisoner, slave. **adj** *lit:* caged, confined, enslaved, imprisoned, incarcerated, locked up, restricted, subjugated.

capture   n *lit:* apprehension, arrest, imprisonment, seizure, taking captive, trapping. **vb** *lit:* apprehend, arrest, bag, catch, secure, seize, take prisoner.

car   n *lit:* automobile, motor, motorcar, vehicle; cable car, coach, railway carriage, van.

carafe   n *lit:* decanter, flagon, flask, jug, pitcher.

card   n *lit:* playing card, postcard, visiting card; wire brush; *fig:* means, plan; character, crank, joker.

care   n *lit:* affliction, anxiety, concern, disquiet, hardship, pressure, responsibility, stress, tribulation, trouble, vexation, worry; attention, caution, circumspection, consideration, forethought, heed, meticulousness, pains, prudence, regard, vigilance; charge, custody, guardianship, management, ministration, protection, supervision, ward. **vb** *lit:* be concerned, feel interest; like, want, wish; mind.

career   n *lit:* calling, life work, occupation, pursuit, vocation; course, passage, path, procedure, progress, race. **vb** *lit:* bolt, dash, hurtle, race, rush, speed, tear.

careful   adj *lit:* accurate, cautious, circumspect, conscientious, discreet, fastidious, painstaking, precise, prudent, punctilious, scrupulous, thoughtful, thrifty; alert, attentive, concerned, mindful, particular, solicitous, vigilant, wary.

careless *adj lit:* absentminded, cursory, forgetful, heedless, incautious, indiscreet, negligent, perfunctory, remiss, thoughtless, unconcerned, unmindful, unthinking; inaccurate, irresponsible, lackadaisical, neglectful, offhand, slipshod, sloppy; artless, casual, nonchalant.

caretaker *n lit:* concierge, curator, custodian, janitor, keeper, superintendent, warden. *adj lit:* holding, interim, temporary.

carnage *n lit:* bloodbath, butchery, havoc, holocaust, killing, massacre, mass murder, shambles, slaughter.

carnival *n lit:* celebration, fair, festival, fete, fiesta, holiday, jamboree, jubilee, merrymaking, revelry.

carpenter *n lit:* cabinetmaker, joiner, woodworker.

carpet *n lit:* floor covering, rug. *vb lit:* cover (wall to wall); *fig:* call to account, rebuke, reprimand, reprehend, summon, tell off.

carriage *n lit:* conveyance, delivery, freight, transport; cab, coach, vehicle; *fig:* bearing, behavior, conduct, demeanor, deportment, gait, manner, mien, posture.

carry *vb lit:* bear, bring, convey, haul, lift, lug, move, relay, take, transport; accomplish, effect, gain, win; drive, impel, influence, motivate, spur, urge; hold up, maintain, shoulder, stand, support, sustain, uphold; broadcast, communicate, display, stock.

cart *n lit:* dray, tumbrel, vehicle, wagon. *vb lit:* bear, carry, heave, haul, lug.

carton *n lit:* box, case, container, pack, packet.

carve *vb lit:* chip, chisel, cut, engrave, etch, fashion, grave, incise, indent, mold, sculpt, slice, whittle.

case *n lit:* box, cabinet, canister, capsule, carton, cartridge, casket, chest, container, crate, holder, receptacle, suitcase, trunk; casing, cover, envelope, folder, jacket, sheath; circumstance(s), context, contingency, dilemma, event, plight, predicament, situation, state; example, instance, occasion, occurrence; *spec:* action, dispute, lawsuit, proceedings, process, suit, trial.

cash n *lit:* banknotes, bullion, coinage, currency, dough, funds, money, ready money, resources, wherewithal. **vb** *lit:* give cash, obtain cash.

cashier n *lit:* accountant, bank clerk, bursar, purser, teller, treasurer. **vb** *lit:* break, cast off, discard, discharge, dismiss, expel.

cask n *lit:* barrel, keg, wooden vessel.

casket n *lit:* box, case, chest, coffer, coffin.

castle n *lit:* chateau, citadel, donjon, fastness, fortress, keep, peel, stronghold, tower.

casual adj *lit:* accidental, chance, contingent, incidental, irregular, occasional, random, unexpected, unforeseen, unintentional; apathetic, blasé, cursory, informal, lackadaisical, nonchalant, offhand, perfunctory, unconcerned.

casualty n *lit:* loss, sufferer, victim; accident, calamity, catastrophe, contingency, disaster, misadventure, misfortune, mishap.

cat n *lit:* feline, grimalkin, kitty, mouser, puss, pussy, tabby.

catalog n *lit:* directory, index, inventory, list, record, roll, roster, schedule. **vb** *lit:* alphabetize, classify, file, index, list, register.

catastrophe n *lit:* adversity, affliction, blow, calamity, devastation, disaster, fiasco, mischance, misfortune, mishap, reverse, tragedy, trial, trouble.

catch n *lit:* bolt, clasp, clip, fastener, hook, latch; disadvantage, drawback, hitch, snag, stumbling block, trap, trick. **vb** *lit:* apprehend, arrest, capture, clutch, ensnare, entangle, entrap, grab, grasp, grip, seize, snare, take; detect, discover, expose, find out, surprise, take unawares; contract, develop; discern, hear, perceive, sense.

category n *lit:* class, classification, department, division, grade, grouping, heading, list, rank, section, type.

cause n *lit:* agent, creator, genesis, mainspring, maker, originator, producer, root, source; agency, aim, basis, consideration, end, grounds, incentive, inducement, motivation, object, purpose, reason; attempt, conviction, enterprise, ideal, movement, undertaking. **vb** *lit:* begin, bring about, create, effect, generate, incite, induce, lead to, motivate, occasion, precipitate, provoke, result in.

caution   **n** *lit:* alertness, care, circumspection, deliberation, discretion, forethought, heed, prudence, vigilance; admonition, advice, counsel, injunction, warning. **vb** *lit:* admonish, advise, tip off, urge, warn.

cautious   **adj** *lit:* alert, cagey, careful, circumspect, discreet, guarded, judicious, tentative, vigilant, wary, watchful.

cave   **n** *lit:* cavern, cavity, den, grotto, hollow. **vb** *lit:* hollow out, make into a cave.

cavity   **n** *lit:* crater, dent, gap, hole, hollow, pit.

cease   **vb** *lit:* break off, come to an end, conclude, culminate, discontinue, end, fail, finish, halt, leave off, refrain, stay, stop.

ceiling   **n** *lit:* roof; maximum altitude; peak, summit, top, upper limit.

celebrate   **vb** *lit:* commemorate, commend, eulogize, exalt, extol, honor, laud, observe, praise, proclaim, rejoice, reverence, toast.

celebration   **n** *lit:* carousel, festival, festivity, fete, jollification, jubilee, merrymaking, party, revelry; anniversary, commemoration, honoring, observance, remembrance, solemnization.

celebrity   **n** *lit:* bigwig, dignitary, luminary, name, personage, personality, superstar, VIP; distinction, fame, glory, notability, preeminence, prominence, renown, repute.

cell   **n** *lit:* cavity, chamber, cubicle, cytoplasm, dungeon, stall; caucus, group, nucleus, unit.

cellar   **n** *lit:* basement, bunker, crypt, vault; salt container.

cement   **n** *lit:* adhesive, binder, concrete, glue, gum, paste, plaster, sealant. **vb** *lit:* attach, bind, bond, combine, glue, gum, join, plaster, seal, solder, stick together, weld.

cemetery   **n** *lit:* burial ground, churchyard, graveyard, necropolis.

center   **n** *lit:* bull's-eye, crux, epicenter, focus, fulcrum, hub, middle, midpoint, nub, nucleus, pivot. **vb** *lit:* cluster, concentrate, converge, focus.

ceramics   n *lit:* earthenware, porcelain, pottery, terra-cotta.

ceremony   n *lit:* commemoration, function, observance, parade, service, show, solemnities; ceremonial, decorum, etiquette, form, niceties, pomp, protocol.

certain   adj *lit:* assured, confident, convinced, positive, satisfied, sure; conclusive, irrefutable, plain, true, undeniable, unequivocal, unmistakable, valid; bound, definite, destined, inescapable, inevitable, inexorable; decided, established, fixed, settled; constant, dependable, reliable, stable, steady, trustworthy, unquestionable; express, particular, precise, specific.

certificate   n *lit:* authorization, credential(s), diploma, license, voucher, warrant.

certify   vb *lit:* ascertain, assure, authenticate, confirm, corroborate, endorse, guarantee, notify, testify, validate, verify, vouch.

chain   n *lit:* bond, coupling, fetter, link, manacle, union; progression, sequence, series, set, string, succession, train. vb *lit:* bind, confine, enslave, fetter, handcuff, manacle, shackle, tether, trammel, unite.

chair   n *lit:* bench, seat, sedan, throne; authority, chairperson, office.

chairperson   n *lit:* chair, director, presider, speaker, toastmaster.

challenge   n *lit:* confrontation, dare, defiance, provocation, test, trial, ultimatum. vb *lit:* accost, arouse, brave, call out, confront, dare, defy, demand, dispute, object to, provoke, question, require, summon, tax, test.

champion   n *lit:* challenger, conqueror, defender, nonpareil, patron, protector, title holder, victor, vindicator, warrior, winner. vb *lit:* advocate, back, defend, fight for, support, uphold.

chance   n *lit:* likelihood, occasion, odds, opening, opportunity, possibility, probability, prospect, scope; accident, coincidence, contingency, fate, fortuity, luck, misfortune, providence; gamble, hazard, jeopardy, risk, speculation, uncertainty. vb *lit:* befall, betide, come to pass, happen, occur; endanger, gamble, hazard, jeopardize, risk, stake, venture, wager. adj *lit:* accidental, casual, contingent, fortuitous, incidental, random, unforeseen, unintentional.

change   n *lit:* alteration, difference, innovation, modification, permutation, revolution, transition, vicissitude; conversion, exchange, substitution; break, diversion, novelty, variety. **vb** *lit:* alter, convert, fluctuate, modify, reform, reorganize, shift, transform, vacillate, vary, veer; alternate, barter, exchange, remove, substitute, swap, trade.

channel n *lit:* canal, conduit, duct, furrow, groove, gutter, main, passage, strait; *fig:* approach, avenue, course, means, path, route, way. **vb** *lit:* conduct, convey, direct, guide.

chapel n *lit:* church, meeting house, mission, oratory, place of worship.

chapter n *lit:* clause, episode, period, phase, section, stage.

character n *lit:* attributes, caliber, complexion, disposition, individuality, nature, personality, quality, reputation, temperament, type; honor, integrity, rectitude, uprightness; eccentric, oddity, original; cipher, emblem, figure, glyph, hieroglyph, letter, pictograph, logo, rune, sign, symbol; part, portrayal, role; fellow, guy, individual, sort, type.

characteristic n *lit:* attribute, feature, idiosyncrasy, peculiarity, quality, trait. **adj** *lit:* distinctive, distinguishing, idiosyncratic, individual, singular, specific, symptomatic, typical.

characterize vb *lit:* brand, distinguish, identify, indicate, mark, represent, stamp, typify.

charge n *lit:* accusation, allegation, indictment; assault, attack, onslaught, rush, sortie; burden, care, custody, duty, responsibility, trust, ward; amount, cost, expenditure, expense, fee, payment, price, rate; command, direction, exhortation, injunction, mandate, order, precept. **vb** *lit:* accuse, blame, impeach, incriminate, indict; assail, assault, attack, rush, storm; afflict, burden, commit, entrust; fill, instill, load, suffuse; bid, command, enjoin, exhort, instruct, require.

charitable adj *lit:* benevolent, generous, lavish, philanthropic; considerate, favorable, humane, kindly, lenient, magnanimous, sympathetic, understanding.

charm n *lit:* allure, appeal, attraction, enchantment, fascination, magnetism, spell; amulet, fetish, talisman, trinket. **vb** *lit:* allure, attract, beguile, cajole, captivate, enamor, enchant, enrapture, fascinate, please, win over.

chart

60

chart n *lit:* blueprint, diagram, graph, plan, table. **vb** *lit:* draft, graph, outline, plot, sketch.

chase n *lit:* hunt, pursuit, race. **vb** *lit:* drive, expel, hound, hunt, pursue, run after, track.

chasm n *lit:* abyss, breach, cleft, crater, crevasse, fissure, gorge, hiatus, hollow, ravine, rift, void.

chat n *lit:* chatter, gossip, heart-to-heart, talk. **vb** *lit:* chatter, gossip, jaw, prate, talk.

cheap adj *lit:* bargain, cut-price, economical, inexpensive, low-cost, reasonable, sale; common, inferior, paltry, shoddy, tatty; contemptible, despicable, mean, scurvy, vulgar.

cheat n *lit:* deceit, deception, fraud, rip-off, swindle, trickery; charlatan, con artist, dodger, double-crosser, impostor, rogue, shark, trickster. **vb** *lit:* bamboozle, beguile, con, deceive, defraud, do, dupe, fleece, hoax, hoodwink, rip off, swindle, take in, trick; baffle, check, deprive, foil, frustrate, prevent, thwart.

check n *lit:* examination, investigation, scrutiny, test; control, curb, hindrance, impediment, limitation, obstruction, restraint; blow, disappointment, frustration, reverse, setback. **vb** *lit:* compare, enquire into, examine, inspect, look at, make sure, note, probe, scrutinize, test, verify; arrest, bar, control, curb, delay, halt, hinder, impede, limit, obstruct, restrain, stop, thwart; blame, chide, rebuff, rebuke, reprimand, scold, tell off.

cheerful adj *lit:* animated, blithe, buoyant, cheery, contented, enthusiastic, happy, jaunty, jolly, merry, sparkling, sprightly, sunny.

chemist n *lit:* apothecary, dispenser, druggist, pharmacist.

chest n *lit:* thorax; case, casket, coffer, crate, strongbox.

chew vb *lit:* bite, crunch, gnaw, grind, munch; *fig:* mull over, ponder, reflect upon, ruminate, weigh.

chic adj *lit:* elegant, fashionable, modish, smart, sophisticated, stylish.

chicken n *lit:* fowl, hen, rooster; coward, sissy; challenge, dare. **vb** *fig:* cowardly, frightened, pusillanimous, scared, timid.

chief   **n** *lit:* boss, chieftain, commander, head, leader, manager, master, ringleader, ruler, superintendent. **adj** *lit:* capital, cardinal, especial, foremost, highest, key, leading, main, paramount, predominant, preeminent, prevailing, primary, principal, supreme, uppermost, vital.

child   **n** *lit:* baby, brat, infant, issue, juvenile, kid, minor, nipper, offspring, progeny, toddler, tot, youngster.

childhood   **n** *lit:* immaturity, infancy, minority, youth.

childish   **adj** *lit:* immature, infantile, juvenile, puerile, simple, young.

china   **n** *lit:* ceramics, crockery, porcelain, pottery, service, tableware.

choice   **n** *lit:* alternative, option, pick, preference, say, selection, variety. **adj** *lit:* best, dainty, elite, exclusive, exquisite, hand-picked, precious, prime, prize, rare, special, superior, uncommon, valuable.

choose   **vb** *lit:* adopt, designate, desire, fix on, opt for, pick, prefer, see fit, settle upon, single out, take, wish.

chop   **n** *lit:* dismissal, sacking, the axe, the boot, the sack. **vb** *lit:* axe, cut, fell, hack, hew, lop, sever, truncate.

chorus   **n** *lit:* choir, choristers, ensemble, singers; refrain, response, strain; accord, concert, harmony.

chronic   **adj** *lit:* deep-seated, incessant, incurable, ineradicable, ingrained, persistent.

church   **n** *lit:* abbey, cathedral, chapel, meeting house, minster, mission, shrine, synagogue, temple; congregation, denomination, sect.

cinema   **n** *lit:* films, motion pictures, movies, picture palace, pictures, picture show.

circle   **n** *lit:* band, circumference, cordon, cycle, disc, lap, loop, orb, perimeter, revolution, ring, sphere; area, bounds, circuit, compass, enclosure, orbit, range, region, scene; assembly, clique, company, fraternity, group, set, society. **vb** *lit:* belt, circumnavigate, coil, compass, encircle, enclose, envelop, gird, revolve, ring, rotate, surround, whirl.

circulation   **n** *lit:* currency, distribution, spread, transmission; circling, flow, rotation.

circumstance n *lit:* condition, contingency, detail, event, fact, factor, incident, occurrence, particular, position, situation.

citizen n *lit:* burgher, denizen, dweller, inhabitant, resident.

city n *lit:* conurbation, metropolis, municipality.

civic adj *lit:* communal, community, local, municipal.

civil adj *lit:* civic, domestic, home, municipal, political; accommodating, affable, courteous, courtly, obliging, polite, refined, urbane, well-mannered.

civilization n *lit:* advancement, cultivation, culture, enlightenment, progress, refinement, sophistication; community, people, society; customs, mores, way of life.

civilized adj *lit:* cultured, enlightened, humane, polite, sophisticated, urbane.

claim n *lit:* affirmation, allegation, assertion, call, petition, pretension, privilege, request, requirement, right. **vb** *lit:* allege, assert, call for, demand, exact, insist, maintain, profess, require, uphold.

clarify vb *lit:* clear up, elucidate, explain, resolve, simplify; cleanse, purify, refine.

clarity n *lit:* clearness, definition, explicitness, intelligibility, lucidity, precision, simplicity.

class n *lit:* caste, category, classification, department, division, genre, grade, group, kind, order, rank, set, sort, species, status, type, value. **vb** *lit:* categorize, classify, codify, designate, grade, rank, rate.

classify vb *lit:* arrange, catalog, categorize, codify, file, grade, rank, sort, systematize.

clause n *lit:* article, chapter, paragraph, part, section; heading, item, point, provision, specification, stipulation.

claw n *lit:* nail, nipper, pincer, talon, unguis. **vb** *lit:* dig, lacerate, mangle, maul, rip, scrape, scratch.

clean vb *lit:* cleanse, disinfect, dust, launder, mop, purify, rinse, scrub, sponge, sweep, wash, wipe. **adj** *lit:* flawless, fresh, hygienic, immaculate, laundered, pure, sanitary, spotless, unblemished, unsoiled, washed;

antiseptic, clarified, decontaminated, purified, sterilized, unadulterated, unpolluted; chaste, decent, good, guiltless, innocent, moral, respectable, undefiled, upright, virtuous; delicate, elegant, neat, simple, tidy, uncluttered; complete, conclusive, decisive, entire, perfect, thorough, total, unimpaired, whole.

clear **vb** *lit:* clean, erase, purify, refine, tidy (up), wipe; break up, clarify, brighten; absolve, acquit, excuse, exonerate, vindicate; free, liberate, set free; disengage, disentangle, extricate, loosen, open, rid, unblock, unload; jump, leap, miss, pass over; earn, gain, make, reap. **adj** *lit:* bright, cloudless, fine, halcyon, light, shining, sunny, unclouded; apparent, audible, coherent, comprehensible, conspicuous, evident, explicit, intelligible, manifest, obvious, palpable, plain, pronounced, recognizable, unambiguous, unmistakable; empty, free, open, smooth, unhindered, unimpeded, unobstructed; crystalline, glassy, pellucid, see-through, transparent; certain, decided, definite, positive, resolved, sure; clean, innocent, pure, stainless, unblemished, undefiled, untarnished.

clearly **adv** *lit:* beyond doubt, distinctly, evidently, markedly, obviously, seemingly, undeniably.

cleft **n** *lit:* crack, crevice, chink, fissure, split; dimple.

clergyman **n** *lit:* chaplain, cleric, curate, father, minister, padre, parson, pastor, priest, rabbi, rector, reverend, vicar.

clever **adj** *lit:* able, adroit, astute, bright, canny, capable, dexterous, gifted, intelligent, keen, knowledgeable, quick-witted, resourceful, shrewd, skillful, smart, talented.

client **n** *lit:* applicant, buyer, customer, patient, shopper.

clientele **n** *lit:* business, clients, customers, market, regulars, trade.

cliff **n** *lit:* crag, face, overhang, precipice, rock face, scarp.

climate **n** *lit:* clime, region, temperature, weather; disposition, feeling, mood, temper, tendency.

climax **n** *lit:* acme, culmination, head, height, highlight, orgasm, peak, summit, zenith. **vb** *lit:* culminate, peak.

climb **n** *lit:* ascent, rise, slope, steep part; increase, progression. **vb** *lit:* ascend, clamber, mount, scale; increase, soar, top.

clinic   n *lit:* hospital, infirmary, medical center, ward; seminar, tutorial.

cling   vb *lit:* adhere, attach, be true to, clutch, embrace, fasten, grip, stick, twine around.

clip   n *lit:* blow, box, clout, punch, smack, whack; rate, speed, velocity; fastener, holder, pin, staple. **vb** *lit:* crop, cut, pare, prune, shear, shorten, trim; blow, box, cuff, knock, punch, smack, thump, wallop; attach, fasten, fix, hold, staple.

cloak   n *lit:* cape, coat, cover, mantle, wrap; blind, front, mask, pretext, shield. **vb** *lit:* camouflage, cover, disguise, hide, mask, screen, veil.

clock   n *lit:* chronometer, repeater, timepiece, watch; dial, gauge, meter, speedometer; odometer. **vb** *lit:* pace, rate, time; report (in), sign (on); knock (off), sign (off).

cloister   n *lit:* covered walk; convent, monastery; den, retreat.

close   vb *lit:* bar, block, clog, cork, lock, plug, seal, secure, shut, stop up; cease, complete, conclude, discontinue, finish, terminate, wind up; grapple (with), wrestle (with); connect, join. **adj** *lit:* adjacent, approaching, handy, imminent, impending, near, neighboring; compact, congested, cramped, dense, impenetrable, packed, short, thick, tight; accurate, conscientious, exact, literal, precise; alert, assiduous, careful, detailed, dogged, earnest, intense, intent, keen, minute, painstaking, rigorous, searching, thorough; attached, devoted, familiar, intimate, loving; airless, heavy, oppressive, stale, stifling, stuffy, suffocating, unventilated; hidden, private, reticent, secluded, secretive, taciturn, unforthcoming; mean, miserly, niggardly, parsimonious, stingy, ungenerous. **adv** *lit:* near.

closet   n *lit:* cabinet, cupboard, locker; private room. **vb** *lit:* admit, shut.

cloth   n *lit:* fabric, material, textile.

clothe   vb *lit:* accouter, attire, cover, drape, dress, equip, fit out, garb, outfit, rig, robe.

clothes/clothing   n *lit:* apparel, attire, costume, dress, garb, garments, gear, outfit, vesture, wardrobe, wear.

cloud   n *lit:* billow, gloom, haze, mist, murk, nebula, vapor; dense mass, horde, multitude, swarm, throng. **vb** *lit:* darken, dim, eclipse, obscure, overcast, shade, shadow, veil; confuse, disorient, distort, impair, muddle.

club n *lit:* bat, bludgeon, cudgel, stick, truncheon; association, circle, clique, fraternity, group, guild, lodge, order, set, society, union. **vb** *lit:* bash, batter, beat, bludgeon, clobber, clout, pummel, strike.

clue n *lit:* hint, indication, inkling, intimation, lead, sign, suspicion, tip-off, trace.

clumsy adj *lit:* awkward, blundering, bungling, clownish, gauche, gawky, inept, lumbering, maladroit, uncoordinated, uncouth, ungainly, unskillful.

coach n *lit:* bus, carriage, vehicle; instructor, trainer, tutor. **vb** *lit:* cram, drill, instruct, train, tutor.

coarse adj *lit:* boorish, brute, gruff, loutish, rough, rude, uncivil; bawdy, earthy, improper, indelicate, offensive, ribald, smutty, vulgar; coarse-grained, crude, homespun, unpolished, unrefined.

coarseness n *lit:* bawdiness, boorishness, indelicacy, offensiveness, ribaldry, roughness, smut, uncouthness.

coast n *lit:* beach, coastline, littoral, seaside, shore, strand. **vb** *lit:* cruise, drift, freewheel, get by, sail, taxi.

coat n *lit:* fleece, fur, hair, hide, skin, wool; coating, covering, overlay. **vb** *lit:* apply, cover, smear, spread.

coin n *lit:* cash, change, copper, money, silver. **vb** *lit:* issue, mint, mold; conceive, create, forge, formulate, invent, make up, think up.

coincide vb *lit:* be concurrent, occur simultaneously, synchronize; accord, harmonize, match, tally; acquiesce, concur, correspond.

coincidental adj *lit:* accidental, chance, unintentional; coincident, concurrent, simultaneous, synchronous.

cold n *lit:* chill, coldness, frigidity, frostiness, inclemency; catarrh, coryza, flu, influenza, rheum, rhinitis. **adj** *lit:* arctic, biting, bitter, bleak, boreal, chilly, freezing, frosty, gelid, raw, wintry; chilled, numbed, shivery; aloof, dead, distant, frigid, indifferent, phlegmatic, reserved, standoffish, stony, unmoved, unsympathetic.

collaborate vb *lit:* cooperate, join forces, participate, team up, work together; collude, conspire, fraternize.

collapse n *lit:* breakdown, cave-in, disintegration, downfall, subsidence; exhaustion, failure, faint, flop. **vb** *lit:* break down, cave in, crack up, crumble, fail, faint, fold, founder, give way, subside.

colleague n *lit:* ally, associate, companion, comrade, confederate, partner, teammate.

collect vb *lit:* accumulate, aggregate, amass, gather, heap, hoard, stockpile; assemble, cluster, congregate, convene, converge, rally; acquire, obtain, raise, secure.

collection n *lit:* accumulation, anthology, coacervation, compilation, heap, hoard, mass, set, stockpile, store; assembly, assortment, company, congregation, crowd, gathering, group; contribution, offering.

college n *lit:* body of colleagues; academy, campus, institute, polytechnic, seminary, university.

collide vb *lit:* clash, conflict, crash, meet head-on.

color n *lit:* coloration, dye, hue, paint, pigment, shade, tincture, tinge, tint; bloom, blush, brilliance, flush, glow, vividness; *fig:* appearance, disguise, facade, guise, pretense, pretext, semblance. **vb** *lit:* dye, paint, stain, tinge, tint; *fig:* disguise, distort, embroider, exaggerate, falsify, garble, misrepresent, prejudice, slant, taint; blush, flush, redden.

colorful adj *lit:* bright, brilliant, intense, motley, multicolored, psychedelic, variegated, vibrant, vivid; distinctive, lively, picturesque, rich, stimulating, unusual.

combination n *lit:* amalgamation, blend, composite, mixture; alliance, association, cartel, coalition, compound, confederation, consortium, merger, syndicate, union.

combine vb *lit:* amalgamate, associate, bind, blend, compound, connect, fuse, incorporate, integrate, link, merge, put together, synthesize, unify.

come vb *lit:* appear, approach, arrive, enter, move towards, near, occur, show up, turn up; attain, materialize, reach; fall, happen, take place; emanate, emerge, flow, issue, result, turn out; be available, be made, be produced.

comedian n *lit:* clown, comic, jester, joker, wit.

comedy n *lit:* drollery, farce, hilarity, humor, joking, light entertainment, slapstick, wisecracking.

comfort n *lit:* alleviation, cheer, consolation, ease, enjoyment, help, relief, succor, support; coziness, opulence, snugness, well-being. **vb** *lit:* alleviate, assuage, cheer, commiserate with, console, ease, enliven, hearten, reassure, relieve, soothe, strengthen.

comfortable adj *lit:* adequate, agreeable, ample, convenient, cozy, homely, loose-fitting, pleasant, restful, snug; contented, happy, relaxed; affluent, prosperous, well-off, well-to-do.

comical adj *lit:* absurd, amusing, diverting, droll, entertaining, farcical, funny, hilarious, ludicrous, ridiculous, side-splitting.

coming n *lit:* accession, advent, arrival. **adj** *lit:* approaching, due, forthcoming, imminent, impending, near, next; aspiring, future, promising, up-and-coming.

command n *lit:* behest, bidding, commandment, directive, edict, injunction, instruction, order, precept, requirement, ultimatum; authority, control, domination, government, grasp, management, power, rule, supervision, sway. **vb** *lit:* bid, charge, compel, demand, enjoin, require; control, dominate, govern, head, manage, rule, supervise, sway.

comment n *lit:* observation, remark, statement; annotation, commentary, criticism, explanation, exposition, note. **vb** *lit:* interpose, mention, note, observe, point out, remark, say; annotate, criticize, elucidate, explain, interpret.

commission n *lit:* appointment, charge, duty, employment, errand, function, mandate, task, warrant; allowance, brokerage, compensation, cut, fee, percentage; board, commissioners, committee, delegation, representative. **vb** *lit:* appoint, authorize, contract, delegate, empower, nominate, order, send.

commitment n *lit:* duty, liability, obligation, responsibility; dedication, devotion, involvement, loyalty; assurance, guarantee, pledge, undertaking, word.

common adj *lit:* average, commonplace, customary, daily, familiar, frequent, habitual, humdrum, ordinary, plain, routine, standard, stock, usual; accepted, general, popular, prevailing, universal, widespread;

communal, community, public, social; coarse, hackneyed, inferior, low, pedestrian, stale, undistinguished, vulgar.

communal adj *lit:* collective, community, general, joint, neighborhood, public.

communicate vb *lit:* acquaint, be in contact, be in touch, call, convey, disclose, divulge, inform, make known, pass on, publish, report, reveal, spread, transmit, unfold.

communication n *lit:* connection, contact, conversation, correspondence, link, transmission; announcement, disclosure, dispatch, intelligence, message, news, report, statement.

community n *lit:* commonwealth, general public, neighborhood, people, residents, society; affinity, identity, likeness, similarity.

companion n *lit:* accomplice, ally, associate, colleague, comrade, crony, mate, partner; aide, assistant, attendant, chaperon, escort; counterpart, match.

company n *lit:* assembly, band, body, circle, group, party, set, troop; association, business, concern, corporation, firm, house, partnership, syndicate; callers, guests, presence, visitors.

compare vb *lit:* balance (with), collate (with), contrast, juxtapose; equate, liken, parallel (to); approach, approximate, come up to, equal, match.

comparison n *lit:* collation, contrast, distinction, juxtaposition; analogy, comparability, correlation, resemblance, similarity.

compartment n *lit:* alcove, berth, booth, carriage, chamber, cubicle, niche, pigeonhole; category, department, section, subdivision.

compassion n *lit:* charity, commiseration, compunction, condolence, humanity, kindness, mercy, pity, sympathy, tenderness.

compensate vb *lit:* atone, indemnify, make good, recompense, refund, reimburse, remunerate, repay, requite, satisfy; balance, cancel (out), counteract, make amends, make up for, offset.

compensation n *lit:* amends, atonement, damages, indemnity, payment, recompense, reimbursement, remuneration, reparation, restitution, satisfaction.

competent adj *lit:* able, adequate, capable, endowed, fit, proficient, qualified, sufficient, suitable.

competition n *lit:* contention, contest, one-upmanship, opposition, rivalry, strife; championship, event, quiz, tournament; challengers, field, rivals.

competitor n *lit:* adversary, antagonist, challenger, competition, contestant, emulator, opponent, rival.

compilation n *lit:* anthology, collection, compendium, compiling, miscellany, selection.

complacent adj *lit:* contented, gratified, pleased with oneself, satisfied, self-righteous, smug, unconcerned.

complain vb *lit:* bemoan, beef, carp, deplore, find fault, gripe, groan, growl, grumble, kick up a fuss, moan, whine.

complaint n *lit:* accusation, criticism, dissatisfaction, fault-finding, grievance, grumble, moan, remonstrance; affliction, ailment, disease, disorder, illness, indisposition, sickness.

complete vb *lit:* accomplish, achieve, cap, conclude, discharge, do, execute, finalize, finish, realize, round off, settle, wrap up. adj *lit:* all, entire, full, integral, unabridged, undivided, whole; accomplished, achieved, concluded, finished; absolute, consummate, perfect, thorough, total, utter.

completely adv *lit:* absolutely, altogether, entirely, from beginning to end, fully, in full, quite, solidly, thoroughly, totally, utterly, wholly.

complex n *lit:* network, organization, scheme, structure, system; fixation, obsession, phobia, preoccupation. adj *lit:* circuitous, complicated, intricate, involved, knotty, labyrinthine, mingled, tangled, tortuous; composite, compound, heterogeneous, manifold, multiple.

complicate vb *lit:* confuse, entangle, involve, muddle, snarl up.

complicated adj *lit:* complex, elaborate, interlaced, intricate, involved, labyrinthine; difficult, perplexing, problematic, puzzling.

compliment n *lit:* admiration, commendation, congratulations, courtesy, eulogy, flattery, honor, praise, tribute. vb *lit:* commend, congratulate, extol, felicitate, laud, praise, salute, speak highly of.

comply **vb** *lit:* abide by, accord, acquiesce, adhere to, agree to, consent to, defer, discharge, follow, observe, respect, satisfy, submit.

component **n** *lit:* constituent, element, ingredient, part, unit. **adj** *lit:* composing, inherent, intrinsic.

composition **n** *lit:* arrangement, configuration, design, form, layout, makeup, organization, structure; compilation, creation, fashioning, formulation, invention, making, production; essay, exercise, opus, piece, study, work, writing; balance, concord, harmony, proportion, symmetry.

compound **n** *lit:* alloy, blend, combination, composite, conglomerate, fusion, medley, mixture. **vb** *lit:* amalgamate, blend, combine, concoct, fuse, intermingle, mix, unite; add to, aggravate, complicate, exacerbate, intensify, magnify, worsen; adjust, settle a dispute. **adj** *lit:* complex, composite, intricate, multiple.

comprehension **n** *lit:* conception, discernment, grasp, intelligence, perception, realization, understanding; compass, field, limits, range, reach, scope.

comprehensive **adj** *lit:* all-inclusive, blanket, broad, complete, exhaustive, extensive, inclusive, sweeping, thorough, wide.

compromise **n** *lit:* accord, adjustment, agreement, concession, middle ground, settlement, trade-off. **vb** *lit:* adjust, agree, arbitrate, compound, concede, meet halfway, settle; discredit, embarrass, expose, implicate, jeopardize, prejudice.

compulsory **adj** *lit:* binding, imperative, mandatory, obligatory, requisite.

conceal **vb** *lit:* camouflage, cover, disguise, hide, keep secret, mask, obscure, screen, secrete.

conceited **adj** *lit:* arrogant, bigheaded, cocky, egotistical, immodest, puffed up, swollen-headed, vainglorious.

conceive **vb** *lit:* appreciate, apprehend, comprehend, fancy, grasp, imagine, suppose, understand; contrive, create, design, develop, formulate, produce, think up; become pregnant.

concentrate **n** *lit:* distillate, essence, extract. **vb** *lit:* be engrossed in, focus attention on, put one's mind to, rack one's brains; center, cluster, converge, focus; accumulate, collect, congregate, gather.

concentration   n *lit:* absorption, application, single-mindedness; centralization, compression, consolidation, convergence, intensification; accumulation, aggregation, collection, horde, mass.

concern   n *lit:* affair, business, field, interest, involvement, matter, mission, responsibility, task; bearing, importance, reference, relevance; anxiety, apprehension, attention, consideration, disquiet, distress, heed, worry; company, corporation, enterprise, firm, organization. **vb** *lit:* affect, apply to, be relevant to, involve, pertain to, regard; bother, disquiet, disturb, make uneasy, perturb, trouble, worry.

concerned   adj *lit:* active, implicated, involved, mixed up, privy to; anxious, bothered, distressed, troubled, uneasy, upset, worried; attentive, caring, interested, solicitous.

concerning   prp *lit:* about, apropos of, as to, in the matter of, on the subject of, regarding, relating to, touching, with reference to.

concert   n *lit:* accord, agreement, concordance, harmony, unanimity, unison; in collaboration, in league; performance.

concise   adj *lit:* brief, compact, compressed, condensed, laconic, pithy, summary, terse, to the point.

conclude   vb *lit:* cease, come to an end, complete, draw to a close, finish, round off, wind up; assume, deduce, gather, infer, reckon, sum up, suppose; accomplish, carry out, decide, determine, effect, fix, pull off, settle, work out.

conclusion   n *lit:* close, completion, end, finish, result; consequence, culmination, issue, outcome, upshot; agreement, conviction, deduction, judgment, opinion, resolution, settlement.

condemn   vb *lit:* blame, denounce, reprehend, reproach, upbraid; convict, damn, doom, sentence.

condescending   adj *lit:* disdainful, lofty, patronizing, snooty, supercilious.

condition   n *lit:* circumstances, plight, predicament, situation, state of affairs; demand, limitation, modification, prerequisite, provision, qualification, requirement, restriction, stipulation, terms; fettle, fitness, health, shape, trim; ailment, complaint, malady, problem; class, grade, order, position, rank, status. vb *lit:* accustom, adapt, prepare, ready, tone up, train, work out.

conditional adj *lit:* contingent, dependent, provisional, qualified, subject to.

conduct n *lit:* administration, direction, leadership, management, organization, running; attitude, bearing, behavior, demeanor, manners, ways. vb *lit:* administer, control, direct, handle, lead, manage, preside over, regulate, supervise; accompany, attend, convey, escort, guide, steer, usher; acquit, act, behave, carry.

confer vb *lit:* accord, award, bestow, give, grant, present; consult, converse, deliberate, discourse, parley.

conference n *lit:* congress, convention, discussion, meeting, seminar, symposium.

confess vb *lit:* acknowledge, admit, blurt out, come clean, confide, disclose, divulge, get off one's chest, grant, own up, reveal; affirm, assert, confirm, declare, profess, prove.

confession n *lit:* acknowledgment, admission, disclosure, exposure, revelation.

confidence n *lit:* belief, faith, reliance, trust; assurance, boldness, courage, nerve, self-reliance.

confident adj *lit:* certain, convinced, counting on, secure, sure; assured, bold, dauntless, positive, self-assured.

confidential adj *lit:* classified, hush-hush, intimate, off-the-record, private, secret; faithful, trusted, trustworthy.

confirm vb *lit:* assure, clinch, fix, fortify, reinforce, strengthen; approve, authenticate, bear out, corroborate, endorse, ratify, sanction, substantiate, verify.

confirmation n *lit:* authentication, corroboration, proof, substantiation, validation, verification; acceptance, approval, assent, endorsement, ratification, sanction.

conflict n *lit:* battle, clash, collision, combat, contention, contest, encounter, fight, fracas, strife, warfare; antagonism, disagreement, discord, dissension, friction, hostility, opposition. **vb** *lit:* clash, collide, combat, contend, contest, disagree, interfere, strife, struggle.

confuse **vb** *lit:* baffle, bemuse, bewilder, mystify, perplex, puzzle; confound, disarrange, disorder, mingle, mistake, mix up, muddle, tangle; abash, addle, demoralize, discompose, disconcert, discountenance, disorient, embarrass, fluster, mortify, rattle, upset.

confusion **n** *lit:* befuddlement, bewilderment, disorientation, perplexity, puzzlement; bustle, chaos, clutter, commotion, disorder, jumble, mess, muddle, shambles, tangle, turmoil, upheaval; abashment, chagrin, discomfiture, distraction, embarrassment, fluster.

congratulate **vb** *lit:* compliment, felicitate, wish joy to.

congratulations **n** *lit:* best wishes, compliments, good wishes, greetings.

congregate **vb** *lit:* assemble, come together, concentrate, convene, converge, flock, gather, mass, muster, rally, throng.

congregation **n** *lit:* assembly, brethren, flock, host, multitude, parishioners.

connect **vb** *lit:* affix, ally, associate, combine, join, link, unite.

connection **n** *lit:* alliance, association, attachment, junction, link, tie, union; affinity, bond, communication, correlation, correspondence, intercourse, relationship, relevance; context, reference; acquaintance, ally, associate, contact, friend, sponsor; kin, kindred, relation, relative.

conquer **vb** *lit:* beat, crush, defeat, humble, master, overcome, prevail, quell, rout, subdue, subjugate, surmount, vanquish; acquire, annex, occupy, seize, win.

conquest **n** *lit:* defeat, overthrow, rout, triumph, victory; acquisition, annexation, appropriation, invasion, occupation, subjection, takeover; captivation, enchantment, enthrallment, enticement; admirer, catch, fan, prize, supporter, worshiper.

conscience **n** *lit:* moral sense, principles, scruples.

conscientious **adj** *lit:* careful, diligent, exact, meticulous, painstaking, particular, punctilious, thorough; high-minded, honorable, incorruptible, just, scrupulous, strict, upright.

conscious n *lit:* awareness, perception; ego, mind. **adj** *lit:* alert, alive to, awake, aware, responsive; calculated, deliberate, intentional, rational, reasoning, responsible, wailful.

consecutive **adj** *lit:* chronological, following, running, succeeding, successive, uninterrupted.

consequence n *lit:* effect, issue, outcome, repercussion, result; account, importance, note, portent, significance, value, weight; distinction, eminence, repute, standing, status.

consequently **adv** *lit:* accordingly, hence, subsequently, therefore, thus.

conservative n *lit:* middle-of-the-road, moderate, right-winger, traditionalist. **adj** *lit:* cautious, conventional, die-hard, moderate, quiet, sober, traditional.

consider **vb** *lit:* cogitate, contemplate, deliberate, examine, meditate, mull over, ponder, reflect, ruminate, study, weigh; believe, deem, judge, rate, think; bear in mind, care for, reckon with, regard, remember, take into account.

considerable **adj** *lit:* abundant, ample, comfortable, goodly, large, lavish, noticeable, plentiful, sizable, substantial, tidy; noteworthy, significant.

considerate **adj** *lit:* attentive, concerned, kind, mindful, obliging, tactful, thoughtful, unselfish.

considering **prp** *lit:* all in all, insomuch as, in view of.

consignment n *lit:* assignment, committal, dispatch, distribution, entrusting, handing over, sending, transmittal; batch, delivery, shipment.

consistent **adj** *lit:* constant, dependable, persistent, regular, steady, undeviating; accordant, coherent, compatible, congruous, harmonious, logical.

conspiracy n *lit:* confederacy, frame-up, intrigue, machination, plot, treason.

conspire vb *lit:* confederate, contrive, devise, intrigue, machinate, plot, scheme; combine, contribute, cooperate, tend.

constant adj *lit:* continual, even, fixed, habitual, invariable, permanent, regular, stable, steady, unbroken, unvarying; ceaseless, continuous, endless, everlasting, incessant, interminable, never-ending, nonstop, persistent, relentless, sustained, uninterrupted, unrelenting; determined, dogged, persevering, resolute, unwavering; attached, devoted, faithful, staunch, true, trustworthy, unfailing.

constitution n *lit:* charter, statute; composition, establishment, formation; build, character, disposition, form, health, makeup, nature, physique, structure, temperament.

construct vb *lit:* assemble, build, create, design, engineer, erect, fabricate, formulate, found, make, manufacture, organize, raise, set up.

construction n *lit:* building, composition, edifice, erection, fabrication, formation, shape, structure; explanation, inference, interpretation, rendering.

constructive adj *lit:* helpful, practical, productive, useful.

consult vb *lit:* ask advice of, consider, debate, deliberate, question, refer to, turn to; have regard for, respect, take account of.

consultation n *lit:* conference, council, deliberation, dialogue, examination, interview, meeting, session.

consume vb *lit:* absorb, deplete, drain, exhaust, expend, fritter away, lavish, spend, squander, use, vanish, waste; devour, eat up, gobble, guzzle, polish off, put away; decay, demolish, destroy, devastate, ravage.

contact n *lit:* association, communication; approximation, contiguity, junction, union; acquaintance, connection. vb *lit:* approach, call, communicate with, get in touch with, phone, speak to, write to.

contain vb *lit:* accommodate, hold, seat; comprise, include, involve; curb, hold back, repress, restrain, stifle.

contemplative adj *lit:* deep in thought, meditative, musing, pensive, rapt, reflective, thoughtful.

contemporary n *lit:* compeer. adj *lit:* coexisting, concurrent, synchronous; current, latest, modern, newfangled, present-day, up-to-date, with it.

contempt n *lit:* derision, disdain, disregard, disrespect, hauteur, mockery, scorn, slight.

content n *lit:* comfort, contentment, ease, pleasure, satisfaction; essence, gist, meaning, substance, thoughts; capacity, size, volume. **vb** *lit:* delight, gratify, humor, placate, please, satisfy, suffice. **adj** *lit:* agreeable, comfortable, contented, fulfilled, satisfied.

contest n *lit:* competition, game, match, tournament, trial; affray, battle, combat, conflict, discord, dispute, fight, struggle. **vb** *lit:* compete, contend, fight, strive; argue, challenge, debate, dispute, object to, oppose.

context n *lit:* background, connection, framework; ambience, circumstances, situation.

continual adj *lit:* constant, continuous, endless, frequent, incessant, perpetual, repetitive, uninterrupted.

continue vb *lit:* carry on, endure, last, persist, remain, stay on, survive; go on, keep at, maintain, persevere, pursue, stick to, sustain; extend, lengthen, prolong; proceed, resume, take up.

continuous adj *lit:* constant, continued, extended, prolonged, unceasing, uninterrupted.

contract n *lit:* agreement, arrangement, commission, compact, covenant, deal, engagement, treaty, understanding. **vb** *lit:* compress, condense, constrict, lessen, narrow, reduce, shrink, tighten, wither; agree, arrange, clinch, engage, enter into, negotiate, pledge; catch, develop.

contradict vb *lit:* contravene, counteract, deny, dispute, negate, oppose.

contradictory adj *lit:* antagonistic, conflicting, discrepant, incompatible, inconsistent, irreconcilable, opposite, paradoxical.

contrast n *lit:* comparison, difference, disparity, dissimilarity, divergence, foil, opposition. **vb** *lit:* compare, differentiate, distinguish, oppose, set off.

contribute vb *lit:* add, bestow, chip in, donate, give, provide; be instrumental, conduce, help, tend.

control n *lit:* authority, charge, command, discipline, guidance, management, oversight, rule, supervision; check, curb, limitation, restraint. vb *lit:* command, conduct, direct, manage, oversee, rule, supervise; check, constrain, curb, hold back, limit, master, restrain, subdue.

controversial adj *lit:* contended, debatable, disputable, disputed.

convenient adj *lit:* beneficial, commodious, handy, helpful, labor-saving, opportune, suitable, useful, well-timed; accessible, at hand, nearby, within reach.

conventional adj *lit:* common, customary, formal, habitual, normal, proper, regular, standard, traditional, usual; bourgeois, commonplace, hackneyed, pedestrian, routine, stereotyped.

conversation n *lit:* chat, communication, dialogue, discourse, discussion, gossip, talk.

convert n *lit:* disciple, proselyte. vb *lit:* alter, change, transform, turn; adapt, apply, modify, reorganize, revise; baptize, convince, proselytize, regenerate.

convict n *lit:* criminal, culprit, felon, prisoner. vb *lit:* condemn, find guilty, imprison, sentence.

conviction n *lit:* assurance, certainty, confidence, firmness, reliance; belief, creed, faith, opinion, persuasion, view.

convince vb *lit:* assure, persuade, prevail upon, prove to, sway.

cool n *lit:* calmness, composure, poise, self-control, temper. vb *lit:* chill, freeze, refrigerate; abate, allay, calm (down), dampen, lessen, moderate, quiet. adj *lit:* chilled, chilling, nippy, refreshing; calm, collected, composed, level-headed, placid, unemotional, unruffled; aloof, apathetic, indifferent, lukewarm, reserved, unconcerned, uninterested; bold, brazen, cheeky, impertinent, impudent; *fig:* cosmopolitan, sophisticated, urbane.

cooperate vb *lit:* aid, assist, collaborate, contribute, coordinate, help, join forces, work together.

coordination n *lit:* balance, coherence, integration, organization, synchronization.

copy n *lit:* counterfeit, duplicate, imitation, replica, reproduction, transcription. **vb** *lit:* counterfeit, duplicate, photocopy, reproduce, transcribe; ape, emulate, follow, imitate, mimic, repeat, simulate.

core n *lit:* center, gist, heart, kernel, medulla, nub, pith.

corner n *lit:* angle, bend, joint; cavity, cranny, niche, nook, recess; pickle, predicament, tight spot. **vb** *lit:* bring to bay, trap.

corpse n *lit:* body, cadaver, carcass, remains.

correspond **vb** *lit:* accord, agree, compare, conform, correlate, harmonize, tally; exchange letters (with), keep in touch (with).

correspondence n *lit:* agreement, comparability, conformity, congruity, correlation, harmony, similarity; letters, mail, mailbag.

corrupt **vb** *lit:* debauch, deprave, pervert; bribe, fix, square, suborn, subvert; contaminate, debase, defile, doctor, interfere with, spoil, tamper with; decay, putrefy, rot. **adj** *lit:* debased, degenerate, depraved; bent, crooked, dishonest, unprincipled, unscrupulous; contaminated, defiled, polluted, spoiled, tainted; decayed, decaying, putrescent, putrid, rotten, rotting.

cost n *lit:* charge, expense, outlay, price; damage; harm, injury, loss, penalty, sacrifice. **vb** *lit:* sell at; *fig:* necessitate the loss of.

cottage n *lit:* cabin, chalet, hut, shack; thatched house.

couch n *lit:* bed, divan, settee, settle, sofa; chaise; chaise longue; bench, seat. **vb** *lit:* express, frame, phrase, word.

cough n *lit:* bark, hack, wheeze; chill, hoarseness, huskiness. **vb** *lit:* bark, hack, wheeze; gob (up), spew (up), vomit (up); *fig:* pay (up); give (up).

council n *lit:* assembly, board, chamber, committee, conference, congress, panel, tribunal; conclave, diet, synod.

counsel n *lit:* advice, direction, guidance, information, recommendations, suggestions; advocate, barrister, lawyer; adviser, consultant. **vb** *lit:* advise, advocate, recommend, urge.

counselor n *lit:* adviser, barrister, consultant; doctor, specialist, therapist.

count n *lit:* calculation, computation, reckoning; amount, sum, total; poll; charge, item, unit. **vb** *lit:* add (up), calculate, compute, number, reckon (up), score, tally, total (up); consider, deem, judge, regard as, think; include (among); *fig:* be of account, matter, signify.

country   n *lit:* kingdom, land, nation, state, territory; area, region, zone; geography, terrain; countryside, farmland, provinces, rural areas; *fig:* electorate, populace, voters.

couple   n *lit:* brace, duet, duo, pair, twosome; few. vb *lit:* clasp, connect, hitch, join, link, yoke; marry, unite; copulate, have intercourse, mate.

courage   n *lit:* audacity, boldness, bottle, bravery, daring, gallantry, grit, guts, nerve, pluck, valor.

course   n *lit:* bearing, channel, direction, heading, line, path, route, track, trajectory, way; advancement, progress, progression, sequence, succession; manner, mode, policy, procedure; duration, elapsing, passing, term, time; classes, curriculum, lectures, program, studies; circuit, lap, links, track; layer, stratum. vb *lit:* dash, flow, race, scud, scurry, stream, surge; chase, hunt, pursue.

court   n *lit:* cloister, quadrangle, square, yard; hall, manor; bar, bench, law court, tribunal; attendants, cortege, entourage, retinue, suite; homage. vb *lit:* date, go steady with, take out, woo; attract, draw upon oneself, invite, provoke; curry favor with, fawn upon, flatter, solicit.

cover   n *lit:* canopy, cap, coating, dress, envelope, jacket, lid, sheath, top, wrapper; camouflage, concealment, protection, shelter; cloak, disguise, mask, screen, veil; *fig:* indemnity, insurance. vb *lit:* clothe, coat, dress, envelop, wrap up; camouflage, cloak, conceal, enshroud, hide, house, mask, obscure, screen, veil; defend, protect, shelter, shield; engulf, flood, immerse, submerge; *fig:* guarantee, indemnify, insure; comprehend, contain, embrace, encompass, include, incorporate, involve, take account of; describe, detail, recount, relate; double for, stand in for, substitute for; counterbalance, make up for; pass through, travel over.

cowardly   adj *lit:* chickenhearted, craven, fainthearted, gutless, lily-livered, pusillanimous, spineless, timid, timorous, weak.

crack   n *lit:* chink, cleft, cranny, crevice, fissure, rift, split; defect, flaw, weakness; detonation, firing, report, shot; bang, blow, clip, thump, whack; *fig:* jape, lark, laugh; gag, joke, quip; dig, gibe, sneer; attempt, bash, go, try; *spec:* cocaine; first light (of dawn). vb *lit:* chip, fracture, split; crash, make a sharp noise, snap; bang, buffet, clip, thump, whack; *fig:* give way, yield; break down, collapse, go to pieces; decipher, resolve, solve, work out; become shrill, break, falter; *spec:* break open (a safe).

craft   n *lit:* art, artistry, dexterity, expertise, know-how, skill, workmanship; handiwork, work; calling, line, occupation, trade, vocation; cunning, guile, subterfuge, subtlety, trickery; airplane, aircraft, airship, boat, ship, spaceship, vessel.

crane   n *lit:* boom, derrick, hoist, winch; outlet pipe; egret, heron, stork; *spec:* (camera) platform. vb *lit:* raise, stretch.

crash   n *lit:* bang, detonation, explosion, loud noise, thud; accident, collision, pile-up, smash; collapse, depression, disaster, failure, fiasco. vb *lit:* bang, clash, detonate, explode, make a loud noise, thunder; break, fracture, shatter, shiver, smash; fall headlong (into), hurtle (into), pitch (into), plunge (into); drive (into), have an accident, plow (into), wreck; smash (through); collapse, fold up, go bust, go under; *fig:* flop (on a bed).

crate   n *lit:* box, case, packing case; *fig:* heap, jalopy, rust-bucket. vb *lit:* box (up), encase, pack (up).

craving   n *lit:* desire, hunger, longing, lust, thirst, yearning.

crawl   n *lit:* shuffle, slither, wriggle; dawdle, plod; *spec:* freestyle (swimming stroke). vb *lit:* creep, move on all fours, shuffle, slither, wriggle; dawdle, inch along, move at a snail's pace; move furtively, move stealthily; swarm (with), teem (with); abase oneself, grovel, toady.

crazy   adj *lit:* demented, deranged, insane, lunatic, mad, mental, unbalanced, unhinged; absurd, asinine, bird-brained, cockeyed, half-baked, idiotic, inane, irresponsible, ludicrous, nonsensical, preposterous, scatterbrained, senseless, unworkable; bizarre, eccentric, odd, outrageous, peculiar, weird; *fig:* fanatical (about), wild (about); berserk (about), hysterical (about); *spec:* asymmetrical, irregular (paving).

crease   n *lit:* fold, tuck; furrow, groove, wrinkle; corrugation; *spec:* goal area (hockey or lacrosse). vb *lit:* crinkle, crumple, fold, ruck, rumple, wrinkle; *spec:* fold (with laughter); graze (with a bullet).

create   vb *lit:* bring about, bring into existence, cause, devise, dream up, form, generate, invent, make, originate, produce; constitute, dub, establish, found, set up; coin, initiate.

creation   n *lit:* cosmos, life, nature, universe, world; formation, generation, making, origination, production; constitution, establishing, foundation, laying down, setting up; achievement, invention, mode, piece, style, work.

creative *adj lit:* fertile, imaginative, ingenious, inventive, original, productive.

creature n *lit:* being, living thing, organism; animal, beast, brute.

credit n *lit:* belief, confidence, faith, trust; clout, influence, position, prestige, standing; esteem, regard, repute; acclaim, acknowledgment, approval, commendation, honor, merit, thanks; source of pride (to); (on) account; plus balance, (in) the black. **vb** *lit:* accept, believe, buy, fall for, swallow; acknowledge (as being), honor (with being); ascribe (to), attribute (to), chalk up (to).

creditor n *lit:* investor, lender, mortgagee.

crew n *lit:* company, complement, hands; rowers; personnel, staff; band, gang, squad, team; bunch, crowd, horde, lot, mob, pack.

crime n *lit:* felony, malfeasance, misdeed, misdemeanor, offense, transgression; lawbreaking, misconduct, villainy; evil, sin, wickedness, wrong.

criminal n *lit:* crook, felon, lawbreaker, offender, transgressor, villain; con, convict, jailbird. **adj** *lit:* bent, crooked, felonious, illegal, unlawful; *fig:* deplorable, outrageous, scandalous.

crisis n *lit:* climax, crunch, crux, culmination, point of no return, turning point; situation, emergency, exigency, extremity, plight, predicament, straits.

critic n *lit:* commentator, pundit, reviewer; authority, connoisseur, expert; detractor, faultfinder.

critical adj *lit:* climactic, dire, emergency, exigent, extreme, grave, hairy, precarious, urgent; crucial, decisive, pivotal, psychological, vital; analytical, diagnostic; derogatory, disparaging.

criticism n *lit:* analysis, appreciation, assessment, commentary, critique, notice, review; censure, flak, knocking, strictures.

criticize vb *lit:* analyze, appreciate, assess, comment upon, pass

criticize 82

judgment on, review; censure, disparage, find fault with, knock, pan, pick to pieces.

croak n *lit:* caw, squawk, wheeze. **vb** *lit:* caw, grunt, squawk, wheeze; *fig:* complain, grouse, grumble, moan; die, expire, kick the bucket, pass over.

crooked adj *lit:* bent, curved, hooked, looped, meandering, tortuous, winding; bowed, crippled, hunched; deformed, disfigured, distorted, misshapen, warped; askew, at an angle, awry, lopsided, slanting, uneven; *fig:* deceitful, dishonest, fraudulent, treacherous, underhand, unscrupulous.

crop n *lit:* fruits, harvest, produce, yield; riding whip; *spec:* craw (of certain birds); handle (of a whip). **vb** *lit:* clip, cut, lop, mow, shear, shorten, snip, trim; browse on, graze; *fig:* come (up), pop (up), turn (up).

cross n *lit:* crucifix, rood; crossing, intersection, junction; hybrid, mixture, mongrel; *fig:* affliction, burden, grief, trial. **vb** *lit:* intersect, meet; bridge, extend over, pass over, span; ford, go over, get over, traverse; hybridize, interbreed, mix; foil, frustrate, impede, oppose, thwart. **adj** *lit:* oblique, transverse; adverse, opposing; *fig:* angry, annoyed, grumpy, ill-humored, impatient, peeved, snappish, sullen, surly, testy, waspish.

crowbar n *lit:* hook, jimmy, lever.

crowd n *lit:* army, flock, herd, host, mass, mob, multitude, pack, press, swarm, throng; bunch, clique, group, set; attendance, gate, spectators; masses, populace, public; plebians, plebs, proletariat, rabble. **vb** *lit:* assemble, cluster, congregate, flock, muster, swarm, throng; cram, huddle, mass, press, push, surge; congest, pack, pile into, squeeze into; elbow, jostle, shove.

crucial adj *lit:* critical, decisive, pivotal, psychological, vital.

cruel adj *lit:* barbarous, bloodthirsty, brutal, callous, fierce, hard-hearted, harsh, heartless, implacable, inhuman, inhumane, merciless, pitiless, relentless, ruthless, sadistic, savage, unfeeling, unnatural, vicious.

cruelty n *lit:* barbarity, bloodthirstiness, brutality, callousness, ferocity, fiendishness, harshness, heartlessness, inhumanity, murderousness, ruthlessness, sadism, savagery, viciousness.

crumb n *lit:* morsel, scrap; bit, shred, snippet.

crumble vb *lit:* break up, decompose, disintegrate, fall apart; crush, fragment, grind; *fig:* collapse, go to pieces.

crumple vb *lit:* crease, rumple, wrinkle; break, collapse, give way; *fig:* cave in, yield; break down, go to pieces.

crush n *lit:* crowd, jam, press, squash, surge, throng. vb *lit:* compact, compress, crumble, crumple, grind, mangle, mash, mill, pound, squeeze; embrace, hug, press; conquer, overpower, overwhelm, rout, trounce; oppress, put down, quell, subdue, suppress; *fig:* abash, chagrin, humiliate, mortify, shame.

crust n *lit:* coating, covering, skin, surface; scab; mantle; dough, pastry; *fig:* effrontery, gall, impudence, nerve.

cry n *lit:* bellow, holler, scream, screech, shout, shriek, whoop, yell; bawl, weep; petition, prayer, supplication; proclamation; slogan, watchword; *spec:* call, sound (of an animal). vb *lit:* bellow, call out, holler, scream, screech, shout, shriek, sing out, ululate, whoop, yell; advertise, announce, broadcast, hawk, proclaim, publish, trumpet; bawl, blubber, greet, shed tears, weep.

cuddle n *lit:* embrace, hug, kiss. vb *lit:* embrace, hug; nestle, snuggle; grope, fondle, pet, smooch.

cuff n *lit:* wristband; box on the ear, clip, smack; *fig:* bracelet, handcuff(s). vb *lit:* box the ears of, clip on the ear, smack one's head.

culprit n *lit:* guilty party, malefactor, miscreant, offender, transgressor.

cultivate vb *lit:* farm, tend, till, work; grow, plant; *fig:* civilize, develop, elevate, enrich, foster, improve, refine, train; associate with, consort with, court.

culture n *lit:* civilization, life-style, society, way of life; arts; education, enlightenment, erudition, polish, refinement, taste; agronomy, cultivation, farming, tillage; *spec:* growth (of bacteria for experiment).

cultured adj *lit:* civilized, enlightened, genteel, lettered, polished, refined; erudite, highbrow, scholarly, well-read, well-versed.

cunning   adj *lit:* artful, canny, crafty, devious, foxy, sharp, shrewd, smart, subtle, wily; clever, deft, dexterous, ingenious.

cup   n *lit:* beaker, glass, mug, teacup; chalice, goblet; trophy, vase; bra, support.

cupboard   n *lit:* cabinet, closet, dresser, press.

cure   n *lit:* antidote, medicine, remedy, specific, treatment; spiritual care; *spec:* preservation (of meats). **vb** *lit:* correct, heal, mend, remedy, restore; *spec:* dry, pickle, salt, smoke.

curious   adj *lit:* inquiring, inquisitive, questioning, searching; meddling, nosy, prying; novel, quaint; bizarre, extraordinary, odd, peculiar, singular, strange, unorthodox, unusual.

current   n *lit:* draught, drift, flow, stream, tide; *fig:* mood, tendency, trend. **adj** *lit:* contemporary, ongoing, popular, present, present-day, up-to-the-minute; in, in fashion, trendy; circulating; common knowledge.

curse   n *lit:* execration, expletive, oath, obscenity, swearword; anathema, evil eye, hex, jinx, malediction; affliction, calamity, disaster, misfortune, plague. **vb** *lit:* blaspheme; cuss, swear; anathematize, damn, excommunicate; *fig:* blight, burden, plague, torment.

curved   adj (pa.pt) *lit:* bent, bowed, hooked, humped, looping, rounded, sinuous, tortuous, winding.

custody   n *lit:* care, charge, guardianship, keeping, preservation, protection, ward; confinement, detention, remand; ownership, possession.

custom   n *lit:* convention, fashion, form, observance, practice, rule, usage; habit, routine, wont; clientele, goodwill, patrons, trade.

customary   adj *lit:* accepted, common, conventional, established, general, normal, ordinary, regular, routine, usual.

customer   n *lit:* buyer, client, patron, purchaser, shopper; habitué, regular; *fig:* character, individual.

cut   n *lit:* gash, incision, laceration, nick, rip, slash, slit; chop, joint, steak; blow, knock, hit, slice; fashion, mode, shape, style; percentage, portion, rake-off, ration, share; decrease, economy, reduction, saving; *fig:* dig, gibe, slight; *spec:* (short) way. **vb** *lit:* gash, incise, lacerate, nick, rip, slash, slit; chop, dice; carve, chisel, engrave, saw, sculpt, whittle; clip, dock, hack, hew, lop, mow, reap, shear, trim; divide, sever, slice (through), split (off); axe, decrease, economize on, reduce, save on; abbreviate, curtail, edit out, shorten, truncate; *fig:* cold-shoulder, ignore, ostracize, snub. **adj (pa.pt)** *lit:* incised, lacerated, ripped, slit; chopped; carved, engraved, sculpted, whittled; clipped, docked, lopped, shorn, trimmed; culled, harvested, mown, reaped; cleft, divided, severed, sliced, split; axed, decreased, reduced; abridged, curtailed, edited, shortened, truncated; *fig:* cold-shouldered, ostracized, slighted, snubbed.

cut off **vb** *lit:* excise, remove, sever; amputate; isolate, separate; disconnect, interrupt, obstruct; bring to a halt, discontinue, suspend; *fig:* disinherit, disown.

cylinder **n** *lit:* pipe, tube; drum, revolving chamber, roller; piston chamber.

cynic **n** *lit:* misanthrope; disbeliever, skeptic; pessimist.

cynical **adj** *lit:* misanthropic; disbelieving, distrustful, skeptical; ironic, sarcastic, sardonic, scornful; pessimistic.

D

dad   n *lit:* daddy, father, old man, pa, papa.

dam   n *lit:* barrage, barrier, dike, embankment, wall; reservoir, water supply. **vb** *lit:* barricade, block up, hold back, hold in, restrain, restrict, stem.

damage   n *lit:* harm, hurt, impairment, injury; destruction, devastation; *fig:* cost, expense, price, sum; reparation(s). **vb** *lit:* harm, hurt, impair, injure; mutilate, ruin, spoil, vandalize, wreck.

damp   n *lit:* clamminess, dankness, humidity, moisture; dew; *fig:* chill, gloom, restraint. **vb** *lit:* moisten, wet; water (down); *fig:* chill, deject, depress, dispirit, inhibit, restrain, stifle. **adj** *lit:* clammy, dank, humid, moist, muggy, wet; dewy, soggy.

dance   n *lit:* ball, dinner, disco, hop, party, social; measure, step; ballet. **vb** *lit:* take the floor, trip the light fantastic; boogie, bop, jive, rock, shimmy; cavort, jig, leap, pirouette, prance, spin, sway, swing; *fig:* dart, flicker, flit, twinkle.

danger   n *lit:* peril; hazard, jeopardy, risk; menace, threat.

dangerous   adj *lit:* dicey, perilous; hairy, hazardous, precarious, risky; menacing, nasty, threatening, ugly.

daring   n *lit:* audacity, boldness, bravery, courage, dauntlessness, derring-do, grit, guts, intrepidity, nerve, spirit, temerity, valor. **adj (pr.pt)** *lit:* audacious, bold, brave, courageous, dauntless, gritty, gutsy, intrepid, nerveless, spirited, temerarious, venturesome.

dark   adj *lit:* brunette, dusky, ebony, swarthy; black, nighttime, nocturnal, unlit; dim, dingy, murky, threatening; gloomy, grim, somber; *fig:* doleful, morbid, mournful; cryptic, deep, enigmatic, mysterious, obscure, occult; diabolical, evil, foul, hellish, infernal, satanic, sinister, wicked; forbidding, glowering, ominous; ignorant, unenlightened, untaught.

darken   vb *lit:* blacken, cloud over, dim; shadow; eclipse; *fig:* cast a pall over, depress, sadden; become harsh.

darling   n *lit:* adored, apple of one's eye, angel, beloved, dearest, light of one's life, love, precious, sweetheart, treasure; favorite, pet.

dash   n *lit:* élan, flair, panache, style; dart, race, run, sprint; hint, pinch, smack, suggestion, touch. **vb** *lit:* fling, hurl, sling, throw; dart, fly, race, run, speed, sprint; shatter, shiver, smash; *fig:* blight, confound, disappoint, foil, frustrate, spoil, thwart.

data   n *lit:* facts, figures, information, statistics.

dawn   n *lit:* daybreak, sunrise, sunup; morning; *fig:* advent, birth, genesis, origin, outset, rise. **vb** *lit:* break, brighten, lighten; *fig:* begin, develop, emerge, originate, rise; hit, strike.

day   n *lit:* date, hours of daylight, time; age, era, generation, period.

dead   n *lit:* deceased, defunct, departed; *spec:* middle (of night, of winter). **adj** *lit:* deceased, defunct, departed, perished; inanimate, lifeless, still; extinct, past; barren, inactive, obsolete, sterile; *fig:* inoperative, unproductive, useless; apathetic, indifferent, numb, paralyzed, soulless, wooden; shattered, spent, worn out; empty; not in play; dull, flat, uninteresting; absolute, complete, total; certain, sure.

deadly   adj *lit:* deathly, fatal, lethal, mortal; destructive, pernicious, poisonous, venomous; *fig:* grim, implacable, relentless, ruthless; accurate, precise, unerring; boring, tedious, uninteresting.

deaf   adj *lit:* hard of hearing, unable to hear; *fig:* indifferent (to), oblivious (to), unresponsive (to).

deal   n *lit:* agreement, arrangement, contract, transaction, understanding; amount, degree, extent, portion, proportion, share; distribution. **vb** *lit:* bargain, do business (with), trade (in), traffic (in); allot, dispense, distribute, divide, give (out), share (out); cope (with), have to do (with).

dealer   n *lit:* merchant, trader, wholesaler; peddler, pusher; dispenser, distributor.

dear   n *lit:* angel, beloved, darling, love, precious, sweetheart, treasure. **adj** *lit:* beloved, cherished, darling, precious, treasured; close, familiar, intimate; esteemed, respected, valued; costly, expensive. **adv** *lit:* at a high price; considerably, very much.

death n *lit:* decease, demise, departure, expiration, passing, release; bereavement, loss; mortality; grim reaper; *fig:* annihilation, destruction, end, extermination, extinction, ruination, undoing.

debate n *lit:* consideration, deliberation; dialogue, discussion, talk; argument, contention, dispute. **vb** *lit:* consider, deliberate; discuss, talk over; argue, contend, dispute, wrangle over.

debt n *lit:* arrears, due, liability, obligation, owed amount; debit, overdraft; (in) the red.

decay n *lit:* atrophy, wasting, withering; decomposition, mortification, putrefaction, putrescence, rot, rotting; caries; mold; decadence, decline, degeneracy, degeneration, deterioration, disintegration. **vb** *lit:* atrophy, waste, wither; corrode, decompose, mortify, putrefy, putresce, rot; crumble, decline, degenerate, deteriorate, disintegrate, molder.

deceitful adj *lit:* crafty, cunning, deceptive, dishonest, dissimulating, duplicitous, false, fraudulent, sly, treacherous, underhand, untrustworthy.

deceive vb *lit:* bamboozle, cheat, con, double-cross, dupe, fool, hoax, swindle, take in, trick.

deception n *lit:* cheating, chicanery, dissimulation, duplicity, fraudulence, legerdemain, swindling, treachery, trickery; artifice, fake, feint, fraud, hoax, imposture, lie, pretense, ruse, stratagem, subterfuge, swindle, trick.

deceptive adj *lit:* ambiguous, ambivalent, fallacious, illusory, misleading, specious, unreliable, untrustworthy.

decide vb *lit:* conclude, determine, make up one's mind, resolve; adjudicate, arbitrate, choose, elect, settle.

decision n *lit:* conclusion, resolution; arbitration, choice, judgment, settlement; ruling, verdict; firmness, finality, resolve, strength of purpose.

decisive adj *lit:* conclusive, definite, definitive, final, positive; firm, forceful, resolute, strong; critical, crucial, fateful.

declare vb *lit:* affirm, announce, assert, depone, proclaim, pronounce, state, testify.

decline n *lit:* declivity, depression, downward slope; *fig:* decrease, diminution, downturn, falling off, recession, reduction; decay, degeneration, deterioration, weakening, worsening. **vb** *lit:* descend, dip, sink, slope downwards; *fig:* decrease, diminish, fall off, lessen, shrink, take a downturn; decay, degenerate, deteriorate, weaken, worsen; forgo, reject, say no to, turn down.

decoration   n *lit:* adornment, elaboration, embellishment, garnish, ornamentation, tinsel, trimmings; bauble, flourish, frill, ornament; award, colors, medal, order, ribbon.

decrease   n *lit:* abatement, decline, diminution, drop, easing, falling off, lessening, reduction, shrinking, slackening, subsidence, waning. **vb** *lit:* abate, decline, diminish, drop, ease, fall off, lessen, shrink, slacken, subside, wane; make less, reduce.

deduce   vb *lit:* conclude, derive, gather, infer, understand; extrapolate.

deduction   n *lit:* conclusion, corollary, extrapolation, inference, reasoning, rider; debit, decrease, reduction, subtraction, withdrawal.

deep   adj *lit:* abyssal, yawning; broad, wide; *fig:* extreme, great, intense, profound; abstruse, cryptic, esoteric, mysterious, obscure; absorbed, engrossed, immersed, rapt; discerning, penetrating, sagacious, wise; erudite, learned; artful, canny, cunning, devious, knowing, shrewd; *spec:* bass, low, resonant (voice); dark, rich, strong (color).

defeat   n *lit:* beating, overthrow, rout, thrashing, trouncing; discomfiture, failure, rebuff, repulse, reverse, setback; strategic withdrawal. **vb** *lit:* beat, crush, overthrow, rout, thrash, trounce; confound, discomfit, foil, stop, thwart.

defect   n *lit:* blemish, fault, flaw, imperfection; error, inaccuracy, mistake; absence, deficiency, inadequacy, lack, weakness. **vb** *lit:* change sides, desert, go over (to), run (to).

defective   adj *lit:* broken, faulty, imperfect, incomplete, inoperative, out of order; lacking, scant, short; retarded, subnormal.

defend   vb *lit:* barricade, fortify; cover, guard, keep safe, preserve, protect, shelter, shield; champion, justify, speak up for, support, uphold, vindicate.

defense   n *lit:* barricade, bastion, bulwark, fortification; cover, guard, protection, security, shelter, shield; alibi, denial, excuse, explanation, justification, rebuttal, refutation, vindication.

defensive adj *lit:* covering, guarding, preserving, protective, sheltering, shielding; precautionary; hunted, wary; apologetic, explanatory, justificatory.

defiant adj *lit:* contumacious, disobedient, insubordinate, mutinous, rebellious, recalcitrant, refractory, truculent, willful; bold, challenging, daring.

deficiency n *lit:* absence, deficit, inadequacy, incompleteness, insufficiency, lack, scarcity, shortage; failing, shortcoming, weakness.

deficit n *lit:* shortage, shortfall; overdraft; arrears.

define vb *lit:* describe, designate, explain, gloss, interpret, specify, spell out; circumscribe, delineate, limit, mark, set the parameters of.

definite adj *lit:* clear, exact, explicit, express, fixed, precise; certain, positive, settled, sure.

deflect vb *lit:* avert, edge, fend off, parry, ward off; glance off, ricochet; slew, swerve, turn, veer.

deformity n *lit:* abnormality, defect, disfigurement, malformation; distortion, mutilation; ugliness.

defy vb *lit:* brave, challenge, confront, face; baffle, defeat, foil, frustrate, resist, thwart; be contumacious towards, be recalcitrant towards, be refractory towards, be truculent towards, disobey, flout, mutiny against, rebel against.

degree n *lit:* extent, intensity, level, measure, quality, quantity, rate, scale, standard; division, gradation, grade, mark, point, rung, step, unit; class, position, rank, standing, status; *spec:* academic title.

delay n *lit:* adjournment, deferment, postponement; stay, suspension; hold-up, interval, stoppage, wait. vb *lit:* adjourn, defer, postpone, put off, suspend; check, detain, hold up, retard, slow, stop; dally, dawdle, linger, tarry.

delete vb *lit:* cut out, edit out, erase, expunge, rub out; cancel, cross out, obliterate, strike out; leave out, omit.

deliberate vb *lit:* consider, debate, meditate (over), mull (over), ponder (over), think (over). adj *lit:* calculated, conscious, considered, intentional, premeditated, studied, voluntary; measured, methodical, prudent, unhurried.

delicacy   n *lit:* daintiness, elegance, lightness; fastidiousness, finesse, precision; subtlety; fragility, frailty, infirmity; refinement, sensibility, taste; cake, dainty, savory, sweet, tidbit.

delicate   adj *lit:* dainty, elegant, exquisite, fine, graceful, light; deft, expert, fastidious, precise; diplomatic, discreet, subtle, tactful; fragile, frail, sickly, squeamish, weak; discriminating, prudish, refined, sensitive; critical, difficult, ticklish, touchy; faint, muted, soft, subdued.

delicious   adj *lit:* appetizing, delectable, luscious, mouthwatering, scrumptious, tasty; delightful, exquisite, pleasing, pleasurable.

delight   n *lit:* gratification, happiness, pleasure, rapture; gem, joy, prize, treasure. vb *lit:* captivate, charm, enchant, gratify, make happy, please, ravish; amuse, divert, entertain.

delightful   adj *lit:* agreeable, captivating, charming, enchanting, gratifying, pleasant, pleasing, pleasurable; amusing, diverting, entertaining.

deliver   vb *lit:* bear, bring, carry, convey, transport; provide, supply; dispense, distribute, give out; give (to), hand over, transfer, turn over (to); cede (to), grant (to), yield (to); administer, deal, inflict; liberate, loose, release, save, set free; present, proclaim, publish, read; strike, throw.

delivery   n *lit:* consignment, dispatch, distribution; conveyance, transmittal; supply, transmission; ceding, surrender; liberation, release, rescue; elocution, enunciation, intonation; birth, childbirth, labor; bowl, pitch.

delusion   n *lit:* hallucination, misapprehension, misbelief, misconception, self-deception.

demand   n *lit:* call, need, request, requirement; charge, claim, order, requisition. vb *lit:* claim, exact, insist on, request, require; call for, necessitate, need; entail, involve.

demolish   vb *lit:* bulldoze, destroy, flatten, level, pull down, raze, tear down; *fig:* annihilate, defeat, drub, thrash, trounce; confound, overturn, totally disprove, undo; devour, gobble up, put away, stuff away.

demolition n *lit:* bulldozing, destruction, leveling, pulling down, wrecking.

demonstrate vb *lit:* illustrate, show, teach by example; display, evince, exhibit, make clear, manifest; march, picket, rally.

demonstration n *lit:* display, exhibition, illustration, exposition, manifestation, presentation; evidence, proof, testimony; march, parade, protest.

density n *lit:* consistency; body, compactness, homogeneity; bulk, solidity, thickness; *fig:* imbecility, obtuseness, slowness, stupidity; *spec:* specific gravity.

deny vb *lit:* disclaim, disown, renounce, repudiate; contradict, gainsay, rebuff, refute; forbid, refuse; begrudge; negate.

depart vb *lit:* blow, evaporate, exit, go, go away, leave, move out, set out, take one's leave, vamoose; disappear, vanish; retire, withdraw; deviate, diverge, stray; swerve (from), veer (from).

department n *lit:* bureau, division, office, section; *fig:* business, domain, line, province, responsibility, sphere.

departure n *lit:* exit, going, leaving, moving out, setting out; retiring, withdrawal; deviation, divergence, straying; change, difference, innovation, novelty; *fig:* death, decease, demise; *spec:* latitudinal distance.

depend vb *lit:* bank (on), count (on), lean (on), rely (on); calculate (on), reckon (on); be based (on), be contingent (upon), hinge (upon).

dependent adj *lit:* conditional (on), contingent (on); based (on), calculated (on); reliant.

deposit n *lit:* alluvium, dregs, lees, sediment; precipitate; loess, silt; down payment, premium, retainer, stake. vb *lit:* lay, place, put, set; drop, settle; bank, lodge, pay in, put in.

depravity n *lit:* amorality, debauchery, degeneracy, lasciviousness, licentiousness, perversion, vice, wickedness.

depress vb *lit:* lower, press down, push down; cast down, desolate, grieve, sadden; daunt, discourage, dispirit, put off; hinder, retard, slow, weaken; cheapen, debase, devalue, downgrade, reduce.

depression n *lit:* basin, bowl, concavity, dell, dip, hollow, indentation; dejection, desolation, despair, despondency, hopelessness, melancholia, sadness; decline, recession, slump, stagnation.

deprivation n *lit:* bereavement, confiscation, dispossession, lack, loss, removal, withdrawal; destitution, hardship, need, privation.

deprive vb *lit:* bereave, dispossess, divest; rob, strip; withhold the benefit (of), withhold the use (of).

depth n *lit:* breadth, drop, profundity, vertical measure, width; *fig:* intensity, strength; complexity, intricacy, involvement; insight, penetration, perception, sagacity, wisdom; erudition, learning, scholarship; (in the) middle (of), (in the) midst (of); *spec:* low pitch, profundo (of voice); darkness, richness, vibrancy (of color).

deputy n *lit:* agent, delegate, locum tenens, proxy, representative; assistant, lieutenant, second-in-command; relief, stand-in, substitute, understudy; *spec:* legislator, member of the assembly (in certain countries).

derelict n *lit:* down-and-out, tramp, vagrant; hulk, skeleton, wreck; abandoned vessel. adj *lit:* abandoned, deserted, forsaken; dilapidated, skeletal, ruined, wrecked; failing, lax, negligent, remiss.

descend vb *lit:* go down, sink, subside; drop, fall, plummet, plunge; alight, climb down, dismount; pounce (upon), swoop (upon); dip, slant down, slope down; decrease, diminish, lessen, reduce; *fig:* be handed down, be passed on; be derived (from), originate (from), spring (from); lower oneself (to), stoop (to); degenerate, deteriorate.

descendants n *lit:* children, grandchildren, heirs, inheritors, issue, offspring, posterity, progeny, scions, successors.

describe vb *lit:* delineate, draw, limn, mark out, outline; characterize, depict, detail, portray, represent; give an account of, relate, tell.

description n *lit:* characterization, depiction, portrayal, representation, verbal sketch; account, narration, report, story; appearance, character, look, manner, mien, type, variety.

desert n *lit:* waste, wasteland; dunes, sand; outback, pampas, scrub, veldt, wilderness; tundra; isolation, remoteness, solitude. vb *lit:* abandon, forsake, walk out on; jilt, leave in the lurch, maroon, rat on, strand; leave, quit, vacate; abscond, defect, run away.

deserve vb *lit:* be worthy of, justify, merit, rate, warrant.

design n *lit:* draft, drawing, elevation, outline, plan, sketch; blueprint, pattern, template; configuration, figure, form, motif; architecture, graphics, technical drawing; *fig:* aim, end, goal, intention, object, objective, target; enterprise, project, scheme; intrigue(s), machination(s). vb *lit:* draft, draw, outline, plan, sketch; contrive, devise, fashion, invent; aim, intend, mean, propose, purpose.

desirable adj *lit:* alluring, seductive, sexy, tempting; advantageous, beneficial, good, preferable, profitable, useful, welcome.

desire n *lit:* ambition, aspiration, hope, wish; craving, hunger, longing, yearning; lechery, libido, lust, sex drive. vb *lit:* entreat, petition, request, solicit; aspire to, hope for, wish for; fancy, set one's heart on, want; crave, hunger for, long for, yearn for; lust after.

desk n *lit:* bureau, escritoire, secretary, writing table; lectern, pulpit; counter, department, kiosk, office, stall; stand.

despair n *lit:* depression, hopelessness, futility, misery, utter dejection, wretchedness; great disappointment. vb *lit:* be depressed, be suicidal; abandon hope (of), give up, lose hope (of).

desperate adj *lit:* forlorn, hopeless, suicidal, wretched; critical, dire, drastic, urgent, dangerous, daring, hazardous, risky, wild; determined; frantic.

desperately adv *lit:* forlornly, hopelessly, suicidally, wretchedly; critically, direly, drastically, urgently; dangerously, gravely, seriously, severely; *fig:* extremely, very.

despise vb *lit:* deride, disdain, look down on, look upon with contempt, scorn, spurn.

despite prp *lit:* in spite of, notwithstanding, regardless of.

dessert n *lit:* confection, pudding, sweet, treat, trifle; last course.

destination n *lit:* journey's end, goal, stop, target; *fig:* aim, end, object, objective, purpose.

destroy vb *lit:* abolish, annihilate, dash to pieces, demolish, dismantle, do away with, exterminate, extirpate, kill, pull down, put an end to, ravage, raze, ruin, shatter, smash, tear down, wipe out, wreck.

destruction n *lit:* abolition, annihilation, demolition, dismantling, eradication, extermination, extinction, extirpation, killing, massacre, pulling down, ruin, shattering, slaughter, smashing, tearing down, undoing, wreckage.

detach vb *lit:* disconnect, disengage, disunite, free, loosen, separate, sever, tear off, unfasten, unhitch; demarcate, designate, pick out, single out.

detachment n *lit:* disconnection, disengagement, separation, unfastening; distance, noninvolvement; aloofness, remoteness, unconcern; impartiality, neutrality, objectivity; demarcation, designation, selection; *spec:* detail, party, squad, unit (of the armed forces).

detail n *lit:* particular(s), small point(s), specific(s), technicality; component, element, factor, item; nicety, trivium; *spec:* detachment, party, squad, unit (of the armed forces). **vb** *lit:* catalog, enumerate, itemize, list, specify; describe, give an account, narrate, recount; designate, detach, pick out, single out.

detect vb *lit:* discern, distinguish, identify, make out, notice, perceive, scent, spot, spy; discover, find, find out, track down, uncover.

deterioration n *lit:* decline, degeneration, degradation, detriment, downturn, fall, impairment, regression, slide, worsening.

determine vb *lit:* decide, make up one's mind, purpose, resolve; ascertain, calculate, discover, establish, find out, learn, work out; condition, control, dictate, govern, regulate, rule; conclude, end, finish, settle, terminate.

detour n *lit:* deviation, diversion; circumnavigation, digression, excursion, roundabout way. **vb** *lit:* circumnavigate, deviate round, digress, find a way round, make a diversion.

devalue vb *lit:* cheapen, debase, degrade; depreciate, weaken; inflate, make worthless.

develop vb *lit:* begin, commence, establish, generate, invent, originate, start; evolve, form, grow, mature, progress; breed, cultivate, foster, promote, rear; contract; *spec:* elaborate on, take further (a musical theme, a chess maneuver); print (a photograph).

development n *lit:* advance, evolution, growth, increase, maturation, progress; circumstance, event, happening, occurrence, situation; serial expression.

device n *lit:* apparatus, appliance, contraption, gadget, instrument, tool; artifice, contrivance, dodge, gambit, maneuver, ploy, stratagem, strategy, wile; badge, colophon, emblem, logo, motif, trademark.

devious adj *lit:* artful, calculating, cunning, indirect, scheming, sly, underhand, wily; circuitous, erratic, rambling, roundabout, twisting, winding.

devise vb *lit:* contrive, design, dream up, frame, invent, plan, think up, work out; compose, write; bequeath, leave.

devoted adj (pa.pt) *lit:* committed, consecrated, dedicated, pledged; ardent, caring, loving, loyal, true.

devout adj *lit:* ardent, devoted, earnest, fervent, passionate, sincere, zealous; godly, holy, pious, religious; solemn.

diagram n *lit:* artwork, chart, graphic, layout, outline, plan; cross section, exploded view, representation.

dialogue n *lit:* conversation, discourse, discussion; two-way communication; *fig:* lines, script, words.

dictator n *lit:* absolute ruler, autocrat; despot, tyrant.

dictatorial adj *lit:* autocratic, despotic, tyrannical; authoritarian, disciplinarian, imperious, magisterial, oppressive, totalitarian.

die n *lit:* mold, stamp, template; dice. vb *lit:* breathe one's last, depart this life, expire, fall asleep, give up the ghost, pass away, pass over; cash in one's chips, croak, kick the bucket, snuff it; be killed, be slain, fall, lay down one's life, perish; *fig:* decline, dwindle, ebb, fade, fizzle out, lapse, pass, peter out, run down, sink, stop, subside, wane, wilt, wither; ache (for), hunger (for), long (for).

diet n *lit:* fare, food, nourishment, nutrient, subsistence; controlled intake, course of regulated meals, fast, regimen. vb *lit:* fast, lose weight, slim.

differ   **vb** *lit:* be distinct (from), depart (from), diverge (from), vary (from); contend (with), contrast (with), demur (with), take issue (with).

difference   **n** *lit:* contrast, disparity, dissimilarity, variation; change, discrepancy, divergence; distinction, exception, particularity, singularity; clash, conflict, contention; contretemps, disagreement, dispute, squabble; balance, remainder, rest.

different   **adj** *lit:* at odds, at variance, contrasting, disparate, diverse, miscellaneous, varied, various; changed, divergent; atypical, distinctive, exceptional, particular, singular, uncommon, unique; clashing, contentious, conflicting, opposed, opposite; additional, distinct, individual, new, other, separate.

difficult   **adj** *lit:* complicated, demanding, intricate, involved, problematical, taxing; arduous, burdensome, hard, laborious, painstaking, strenuous; knotty, thorny, ticklish, uphill; awkward, grim, straitened, trying; fractious, obstreperous, refractory, troublesome, unmanageable; fastidious, fussy, hard to please, pedantic, tiresome.

difficulty   **n** *lit:* burden, hardship, labor, strenuousness, toil; complication, hurdle, impediment, obstacle, pitfall, stumbling block; dilemma, enigma, intricacy, problem, predicament, quandary; fix, jam, mess, pickle, plight, spot of trouble; danger, distress, jeopardy, peril.

dig   **n** *lit:* archaeological site, excavation; jab, poke, prod, thrust; *fig:* gibe, sarcastic remark, sneer, taunt, wisecrack. **vb** *lit:* burrow, delve, excavate, mine, quarry, scoop, tunnel; break up, fork, hoe, spade over, till, turn over; jab, poke, prod, thrust; *fig:* go (into), probe (into), research (into); find (out), root (out); appreciate, enjoy, like, understand.

digest   **n** *lit:* abstract, condensation, paraphrase, précis, résumé, summary, synopsis. **vb** *lit:* absorb, assimilate, metabolize; abridge, condense, paraphrase, reduce, shorten, summarize; *fig:* consider, contemplate, meditate over, ponder, take in, understand; bear, brook, endure, stand, stomach, tolerate.

digestion   **n** *lit:* absorption, assimilation, incorporation, metabolism; *fig:* consideration, contemplation, meditation, pondering; stomach.

dignified   **adj (pa.pt)** *lit:* august, decorous, formal, grave, imposing, noble, solemn, stately; lofty, lordly; exalted.

dignity n *lit:* decorum, grandeur, majesty, nobility, solemnity, stateliness; hauteur, loftiness; eminence, honor, importance, rank, standing, status; pride, self-esteem.

dilute vb *lit:* thin, water down; adulterate, cut, weaken; *fig:* attenuate, mitigate, temper; decrease, lessen, reduce. adj *lit:* thin, watered down, watery; adulterated, cut, weakened; *fig:* attenuated, mitigated, tempered; decreased, lessened, reduced.

dim vb *lit:* dull, fade out, turn down; become obscure, blur, darken, obscure; tarnish. adj *lit:* cloudy, gray, overcast, shadowy; blurred, dark, fuzzy, indistinct, obscure; dingy, dull, opaque, tarnished; pale, weak; *fig:* confused, hazy, vague; depressing, discouraging, gloomy, somber; dense, obtuse, slow, stupid, thick.

dine vb *lit:* eat, feed; have dinner, have lunch, have supper; banquet, feast.

dinner n *lit:* lunch, supper; banquet, feast, spread; meal, repast.

diploma n *lit:* certificate, charter, document; degree, doctorate; honor.

diplomat n *lit:* ambassador, attaché, chargé d'affaires, consul, envoy, foreign office official, government spokesperson, legate, representative, statesman; mediator, negotiator.

diplomatic adj *lit:* ambassadorial, consular, governmental, official, state; politic, prudent; discreet, subtle, tactful.

direct vb *lit:* guide, indicate how to get (to), lead, point the way (to), show (toward), usher; administer, conduct, control, govern, manage, oversee, rule, run, superintend; command, instruct, order; address, aim, level, point, train; route, send. adj *lit:* straight, undeviating; face-to-face, head-on, immediate; nonstop, through; blunt, explicit, outspoken, plain, straightforward, unambiguous, unequivocal; candid, frank, honest, open, sincere; *spec:* quoted, verbatim (speech, words).

direction n *lit:* bearing, compass point, course, line, orientation; guidance, indication, lead; administration, control, governing, management, ruling, running, superintending, supervision; commands, instruction, orders; address, destination.

directly adv *lit:* straight, without deviation; face-to-face, in person; at once, immediately, instantly, promptly, right away, straight away; bluntly, plainly, straightforwardly, unambiguously, unequivocally; candidly, frankly, honestly, openly, sincerely.

director   **n** *lit:* administrator, governor, manager, member of the board, organizer, supervisor; boss, chief, controller, head, leader.

dirt   **n** *lit:* filth, grime, mud, slime; excrement, feces, muck, prurience, scatology; earth, soil; foreign body, impurity; *fig:* concupiscence, obscenity, pornography, salacity, smut; gossip, low-down, scandal.

dirty   **vb** *lit:* befoul, defile, mess up, soil, stain. **adj** *lit:* filthy, foul, grimy, grubby, mucky, muddy, polluted, slimy, soiled; dingy, discolored, dusty, murky, shabby, squalid, tarnished; *fig:* blue, fecal, indecent, obscene, pornographic, prurient, salacious, scabrous, scatological, smutty; corrupt, dishonest, fraudulent, illegal; mean, treacherous.

disable   **vb** *lit:* cripple, debilitate, hamstring, handicap, incapacitate, put out of action, render incapable; paralyze; disqualify, invalidate.

disabled   **adj (pa.pt)** *lit:* bedridden, crippled, debilitated, hamstrung, handicapped, incapacitated, out of action, paralyzed; disqualified, invalidated.

disadvantage   **n** *lit:* burden, handicap, hardship, impediment, inconvenience, liability; flaw, minus, trouble, weakness; detriment, loss. **vb** *lit:* burden, create problems for, handicap, hinder, impede, inconvenience.

disagree   **vb** *lit:* be opposed, clash, conflict, contradict, differ, diverge; argue, bicker, dispute, dissent, quarrel, wrangle; cause trouble, cause problems; be different, be unequal.

disagreeable   **adj** *lit:* bad-tempered, churlish, cross, difficult, ill-natured, peevish, unfriendly, unlikable; disgusting, distasteful, nasty, obnoxious, offensive, repellent, repulsive.

disappear   **vb** *lit:* evanesce, fade out, melt away, vanish; be lost to view, go, leave, pass from one's sight; escape, flee, fly; be lost; die, ebb, peter out, taper off, wane.

disappearance   **n** *lit:* evanescence, evaporation, vanishing; departure, desertion, going, leaving; escape, flight; absence, eclipse, loss; end, passing, petering out, tapering off, waning.

disappoint vb *lit:* chagrin, dash, dismay; fail, let one down; foil, frustrate, thwart.

disappointment n *lit:* chagrin, dismay; dejection, discouragement; disillusion, letdown; frustration, misfortune, setback.

disaster n *lit:* calamity, cataclysm, catastrophe, ruination, tragedy; blow, misfortune, reverse, trouble.

disastrous adj *lit:* calamitous, cataclysmic, catastrophic, ruinous, tragic; devastating, dire; ill-starred, unlucky.

discard vb *lit:* chuck out, dispense with, dispose of, ditch, drop, dump, get rid of, jettison, throw away.

discern vb *lit:* distinguish, make out, observe, perceive, recognize, see, sense; discriminate (between), judge (between), tell.

discharge n *lit:* emission, flux, oozing, secretion, seepage, suppuration; emptying, evacuation, unburdening, unloading; demobilization, dismissal, ejection, release; acquittal, freeing, liberation, remission; payment, settlement; accomplishment, execution, fulfillment, observance; blast, detonation, firing, shooting. **vb** *lit:* emit, exude, give off, leak, ooze, secrete, seep, suppurate; empty, evacuate, unburden, unload; demobilize, dismiss, eject, expel, release, remove, sack; acquit, clear, free, liberate, remit; pay, settle; accomplish, do, execute, fulfill, observe, perform; blast, detonate, fire, set off, shoot.

discipline n *lit:* control, order, regulation; practice, regimen, training; chastisement, correction, punishment, strictness; area, branch, field, specialism, specialty; *spec:* (sports) event. **vb** *lit:* chastise, correct, punish; be strict with, break in, control, drill, educate, exercise, regulate, train.

discolor vb *lit:* soil, stain, tarnish; bleach, etiolate, fade, lighten, pale, yellow; darken.

disconnect vb *lit:* detach, disengage, put asunder, separate, take apart, uncouple, undo; free, loosen, release; cut off, switch off, turn off.

discount n *lit:* concession, cut, price cut, rebate, reduction. **vb** *lit:* disbelieve, disregard, ignore, let pass, take with a pinch of salt; give a reduction, mark down, reduce.

discover vb *lit:* come across, find, light upon; bring to light, dig up, reveal, turn up, uncover, unearth; ascertain, detect, discern, find out, learn; notice, perceive, realize, see, spot; conceive, devise, invent, make, originate.

discovery n *lit:* digging up, finding, turning up, unearthing; ascertaining, detection, discerning, learning; noticing, perceiving, realization, seeing, spotting; conception, creation, introduction, invention, origination.

discreet adj *lit:* diplomatic, tactful; judicious, politic, sensible; cautious, guarded, prudent, wary.

discriminate vb *lit:* differentiate (between), distinguish (between), draw a distinction (between); act unjustly (against), be biased (against), be prejudiced (against).

discuss vb *lit:* confer about, consult about, converse about, debate, go into, talk over.

discussion n *lit:* conference, consultation, conversation, debate, talk; dialogue, exchange of views; negotiation, talks.

disease n *lit:* ailment, complaint, disorder, illness, malady, sickness; blight, contagion, infection, infestation; condition; *fig:* failing, vice, weakness.

disfigurement n *lit:* blemish, deformity, malformation, mutilation, scar; blot, blotch, mark, spot, stain.

disgrace n *lit:* dishonor, ignominy, odium, opprobrium; humiliation, shame; degradation; aspersion, reproach, slur, stain, stigma. vb *lit:* bring shame upon, discredit, dishonor, sully; humiliate, mortify, shame; expose, show up.

disgraceful adj *lit:* appalling, contemptible, detestable, disgusting, infamous, outrageous, scandalous, shameful, shocking; dishonorable, ignominious, opprobrious, unworthy.

disguise n *lit:* facade, front, imposture, semblance, simulation; costume; camouflage, cover. vb *lit:* dress up (as), make up (as); camouflage, hide, mask, screen, veil; dissimulate, falsify.

disgust n *lit:* abhorrence, aversion, detestation, distaste, loathing, nausea, repugnance, revulsion. **vb** *lit:* fill with loathing, nauseate, offend, outrage, repel, revolt, sicken, turn one's stomach.

dish n *lit:* bowl, plate, platter, saucer, tableware; course, preparation, recipe. **vb** *lit:* present, serve.

dishonest adj *lit:* bent, corrupt, crooked, false, lying, mendacious, perfidious, treacherous, unscrupulous, untrustworthy, untruthful; deceitful, dissimulating, economical with the truth, sham.

disillusion n *lit:* disappointment, disenchantment; true perception; anticlimax. **vb** *lit:* bring down to earth, disabuse, disenchant, open one's eyes, undeceive; disappoint, fail, let down.

disintegration n *lit:* breakup, collapse, crumbling, decomposition, destruction, falling apart, fission, fragmentation, shattering; *spec:* (radioactive) decay.

dislike n *lit:* antipathy, aversion, disapproval, disfavor, distaste. **vb** *lit:* be antipathetic toward, be averse to, be disinclined to, disapprove of, disfavor, have a distaste for, object to.

dismal adj *lit:* bleak, cheerless, dark, depressing, discouraging, gloomy, lowering, lugubrious, somber; boring, dreary, dull, tedious.

dismiss vb *lit:* discharge, give one's leave, send away; axe, cashier, chuck out, expel, fire, give the boot, give the sack, lay off, make redundant, remove, sack, send down, send packing; banish, dispel, shelve.

dismissal n *lit:* discharge, dispatch, leave to go, marching orders, release; expulsion, laying off, notice, redundancy, removal, sacking.

disorder n *lit:* chaos, confusion, disarray, disorganization, disruption, untidiness; anarchy, lawlessness; derangement, dishevelment, dislocation.

disperse vb *lit:* broadcast, diffuse, disseminate, scatter, spread, strew; break up, separate; dispel, dissipate, dissolve.

display n *lit:* exhibition, parade, show; array, presentation, spectacle; facade, imposture, ostentation, pretense. **vb** *lit:* demonstrate, evince, exhibit, parade, present, reveal, show; betray, disclose; boast, flaunt, flourish, vaunt.

displease   vb *lit:* annoy, be disagreeable to, exasperate, gall, irk, irritate, offend, put out, upset, vex.

dispose   vb *lit:* adjust, arrange, group, marshal, order, place, put, set, stand; bias (toward), condition (to), incline (to), influence (towards), move (to), prompt (to); make an end (of), free oneself (of); get rid (of), rid oneself (of).

dispute   n *lit:* argument, contention, debate, disagreement, dissension; altercation, conflict, discord, friction, quarrel, wrangle. vb *lit:* argue with, contend with, challenge, contradict, debate, disagree with, dissent to, quarrel with, question; clash with, squabble with, wrangle with.

disqualification   n *lit:* disbarment, elimination, exclusion, expulsion; incapacitation, ineligibility.

disregard   n *lit:* heedlessness, ignoring, neglect, negligence; disdain, disrespect, indifference. vb *lit:* discount, ignore, neglect, pass over, pay no attention to, take no notice of, turn a blind eye to; brush aside, laugh off, make light of; cut dead, snub, walk straight past.

disrespectful   adj *lit:* cheeky, discourteous, impertinent, impudent, insolent, irreverent, rude; irreverent, sacrilegious.

disruptive   adj *lit:* anarchic, destructive, disorderly, distracting, obstreperous, troublesome, unruly, upsetting.

dissolve   vb *lit:* deliquesce, liquefy, melt, thaw; break down, break up, crumble, decompose, disintegrate, disperse, dissipate, evaporate, fade away, vanish; dismantle, dismember, disunite, loose, separate; *fig:* adjourn, discontinue, suspend; annul, cancel, conclude, end, finish, terminate.

dissuade   vb *lit:* deter, disincline, put off; discourage.

distance   n *lit:* extent, range, reach, remove, separation, space, stretch; gap, interval; *fig:* coldness, coolness, reserve, restraint. vb *lit:* leave behind, outrun, outstrip; dissociate (oneself from), separate (oneself from).

distant   adj *lit:* faraway, far-flung, far-removed, remote; apart, disparate, distinct, outlying, scattered, separate; faint, indistinct, obscure; *fig:* cold, cool, formal, reserved, restrained, reticent, withdrawn.

distinct   adj *lit:* detached, discrete, separate, unconnected; different, individual; apparent, clear, evident, manifest, marked, noticeable, patent, plain, recognizable, unmistakable, well-defined.

distinction n *lit:* contrast, difference; differentiation, discernment, discrimination, separation; characteristic, idiosyncrasy, individuality, particularity, peculiarity, singularity, uniqueness; celebrity, credit, eminence, fame, honor, note, prominence, worth; award, prize.

distinctive adj *lit:* different, distinguishable, extraordinary, individual, original, particular, peculiar, singular, unique.

distinguish vb *lit:* differentiate, discriminate, tell apart; discern, make out, perceive, pick out, recognize, see; individualize, label, mark out, separate, single out; glorify, make famous.

distort vb *lit:* bend, bow, buckle, deform, twist, warp; *fig:* misrepresent, pervert, slant.

distress n *lit:* discomfort, misery, suffering, wretchedness; anguish, grief, pain, torment, woe; blow, calamity, difficulty, hardship, misfortune, privation, trial. vb *lit:* pain, torment, trouble, upset; bother, disturb, harass, worry; grieve, sadden, wound.

distribution n *lit:* allocation, allotment, apportionment, dispensing, dispersion, dissemination, division, doling out, giving out, handing out, measuring out, scattering, spreading; dispersal, extent, range, scope, spread; arrangement, disposition, grouping; delivery, dispatch, handling, transportation.

distrust n *lit:* chariness, doubt, skepticism, suspicion, wariness. vb *lit:* be suspicious of, be wary of, have doubts about, suspect.

disturb vb *lit:* bother, disrupt, distract, inconvenience, interrupt, intrude on; trouble; annoy, harass, pester, plague, worry; discompose, distress, fluster, perturb, ruffle, shake, unsettle; derange, disorder, interfere with, touch.

disturbance n *lit:* agitation, disorder, distraction, upset; interruption, intrusion, interference; bother, broil, commotion, demo, fracas, hubbub, ruckus, ruction, rumble, rumpus, tumult, uproar.

ditch n *lit:* channel, drain, dike, fosse, gully, trench, verge. vb *lit:* dig a channel in, drain, excavate, irrigate; land on water; *fig:* discard, drop, dump, get rid of, jettison; abandon, maroon, leave in the lurch.

diversion n *lit:* detour, deviation, digression; amusement, delectation, enjoyment, entertainment, gratification, pleasure, recreation, sport.

divert vb *lit:* avert, deflect, fend off, parry, redirect, turn aside, ward off; distract (from), draw away (from), lead away (from), sidetrack; *fig:* amuse, delight, entertain, gratify.

divide n *lit:* border, division, margin, partition; *spec:* border hills, watershed. vb *lit:* bisect, halve, split in two; cut (up), disconnect, part, segregate, separate, sever, sunder; arrange, order, sort; allot, dispense, distribute, measure out, share; alienate, break up, come between, disrupt, estrange, interpose between.

divine n *lit:* cleric, member of the clergy, minister, priest, reverend; doctor of divinity, theologian. vb *lit:* apprehend, deduce, discern, infer, perceive, understand; conjecture, foretell, predict; dowse. adj *lit:* godly, hallowed, holy, religious, sacred, spiritual; celestial, godlike, heavenly; beatific, mystic, numinous, transcendental; *fig:* angelic, beautiful, lovely, perfect, wonderful.

division n *lit:* bisection, halving, splitting in two; disconnection, parting, segregation, separation, severing, sundering; ordering, sorting; allocation, dispensing, distribution, measuring out, sharing; alienation, breakup, disruption, divorce, estrangement, interruption.

divorce n *lit:* break, disunion, estrangement, parting, rupture, separation, splitting, sundering; annulment. vb *lit:* dissociate, disunite, divide, part, separate, sever, split up, sunder; be separated from; have one's marriage dissolved.

do n *lit:* celebration, banquet, dance, event, feast, function, occasion, party. vb *lit:* accomplish, carry out, execute, perform, render, undertake, work at; bring about, cause, effect; create, make, produce; achieve, complete, conclude, empty, exhaust, finish; cover, go, proceed, travel; journey through, look at, tour, visit; act, behave, conduct oneself; mount, play, present, put on; arrange, deal with, fix, look after, organize, prepare, see to; be responsible for, take over; bestow on, confer on, give, grant; be, get on, make out, manage; answer, be adequate, be usable, be useful, serve, suffice; figure out, resolve, solve, sort out; cook; *fig:* cheat, con, dupe, swindle, take for a ride; raid, rob; beat up, thrash; *spec:* spend time (in prison).

dock n *lit:* basin, channel, harbor, quay, wharf; stump; accused's enclosure. **vb** *lit:* berth, moor, put in, tie up; couple, hook up, join, link up; amputate, cut off; *fig:* abridge, curtail, cut short, reduce, subtract from.

doctor n *lit:* consultant, general practitioner, GP, physician, specialist, surgeon; father of the Church, theologian. **vb** *lit:* apply treatment to, treat; mend, patch up, repair; alter, change, falsify, tamper with; adulterate, dilute, spike.

dog n *lit:* hound, mutt, pooch, pup; *fig:* blackguard, cur, scoundrel, villain. **vb** *lit:* follow, hound, pursue, shadow, tail, track, trail.

domestic adj *lit:* indigenous, internal, national, state; domiciliary, residential; family, household, private; house, pet, trained.

dominate **vb** *lit:* control, have the ascendancy over, lead by the nose, monopolize, prevail over, rule; be predominant in, loom over, overshadow, tower above; eclipse, outshine, upstage.

domination n *lit:* ascendancy, authority, control, mastery, power, supremacy; oppression, repression, subjection, tyranny.

donate **vb** *lit:* contribute, gift, give, present; bequeath, leave.

donation n *lit:* alms, contribution, gift, present; gratuity; collection, offering.

donor n *lit:* contributor, giver; benefactor, philanthropist; *spec:* source of organ(s) for transplant surgery.

doom n *lit:* decree, destiny, fate, judgment, lot, verdict; catastrophe, condemnation, death, destruction, disaster, ruination; end of the world, last trump. **vb** *lit:* destine (to be), foreordain (to be); condemn (to), consign (to), damn (to), sentence (to).

door n *lit:* entrance, entry, way in; egress, exit, ingress, way out; flap, gate, lintel, opening, port, portal, threshold, trap.

dose n *lit:* dosage; amount, measure, quantity; medication, medicament, medicine, placebo, tincture, treatment; *fig:* bout, session.

dot n *lit:* jot, point, spot, stop; fleck, mark, speck. **vb** *lit:* dab, fleck, spot, stipple. stud; *fig:* hit, smack; disperse, scatter, spread.

doubt n *lit:* distrust, dubiety, lack of faith, mistrust, suspicion, uncertainty, vacillation; misgiving, qualm, reservation; ambiguity, confusion, perplexity; hesitancy, indecision, irresolution, wavering. **vb** *lit:* be uncertain, distrust, have little faith in, mistrust, suspect; query, question; be hesitant, be irresolute, vacillate, waver.

doubtful   **adj** *lit:* distrustful, dubious, hesitant, irresolute, suspicious, uncertain, unconvinced, unsure; ambiguous, debatable, indeterminate, obscure, problematical, questionable, vague; disreputable, shady, suspect.

down   **n** *lit:* descent, drop, fall; dejection, depression, mood; failure, reversal, setback; knockdown, tackle; scrimmage; dune, grassy undulation, hill, knoll, mound; feathers, fluff, hair. **vb** *lit:* fell, floor, knock down, tackle, trip; drink, gulp, knock back, quaff, put away, toss off. **adv** *lit:* to a lower position, below; to the ground; on the ground; downstairs; to the present time; to a smaller state; to a defeated state; at a disadvantage, behind; in black and white, on record; in cash, on the spot; to leeward. **prp** *lit:* in a descent along/by/through; on/to a lower position in/on; along, with the current of.

draft   **n** *lit:* breeze, current, gust, wind; drawing, haul, pull, traction; drink, swallow, swig; dose, measure; catch, trawl; *spec:* displacement (of a ship).

drag   **n** *lit:* bore, bother, burden, chore, effort, nuisance, pain; friction, resistance; trawl; scent; inhalation, pull. **vb** *lit:* draw, haul, heave (along), pull, tow, tug; crawl, creep, dawdle, go slowly; draw (out), spin (out), stretch (out); get left behind, lag behind, straggle; *spec:* dredge, trawl (underwater).

drain   **n** *lit:* conduit, culvert, ditch, outlet, sewer; drag (on), strain (on). **vb** *lit:* draw off, empty, evacuate, pump out; milk, tap; discharge, exude, flow (out), ooze (out), seep (out); deplete, exhaust, sap, strain, use up.

dramatic   **adj** *lit:* histrionic, theatrical, Thespian; affecting, moving, powerful, striking; expressive, forceful, vivid; climactic, electrifying, exciting, sensational, tense, thrilling.

drape   **n** *lit:* curtain, hanging; cloth, fold. **vb** *lit:* cover, curtain, enfold, hang; arrange in folds, pleat.

draw   **n** *lit:* attraction, enticement, lure; dead heat, stalemate, tie; choosing, picking, selection. **vb** *lit:* drag, haul, pull, tow; approach, come, get; allure, attract, elicit, entice, induce, invite, seduce, tempt; infuse;

extract, pull out, unsheathe; disembowel, eviscerate; extend (out),
lengthen (out), spin (out), stretch (out); deduce, infer, make; breathe in,
inhale, take a pull; delineate, depict, design, map out, outline, portray,
sketch; choose, pick, select; *spec:* extrude (plastics, wire); pull away, pull
together (curtains); pull back (a bowstring); shed, spill (blood); write out
(a check).

drawer n *lit:* shelf; box, chest; bartender, tapster; artist, draughtsman;
spec: person who signs a check.

drawing n *lit:* delineation, outline; illustration, representation; pencil
sketch.

dreadful adj *lit:* alarming, formidable, frightening, ghastly, shocking,
tragic; *fig:* abysmal, appalling, awful, terrible, useless, worthless.

dream n *lit:* delusion, fantasy, illusion, reverie, vision; ambition,
aspiration, hope, wish; *fig:* beauty, gem, joy, treasure. vb *lit:* fantasize,
imagine; *fig:* conceive (of), think (of).

dreamy adj *lit:* calming, lulling, relaxing, soothing; absent,
abstracted, faraway, preoccupied; fanciful, impractical, quixotic, vague;
fantastic, intangible, misty, unreal; *fig:* attractive, exciting.

dress n *lit:* apparel, attire, clothes, clothing, costume, garb, garments,
getup, outfit, raiment, rig; frock, gown, robe. vb *lit:* change, put one's
clothes on; clothe, put clothes on; drape, furbish, rig out; do (up); comb,
groom; align, arrange, set, straighten; bandage, plaster, put medication
on; garnish, season.

dressmaker n *lit:* couturier, modiste, seamstress.

drill n *lit:* auger, bit, borer, gimlet; ridge of soil; discipline, exercise,
training; *fig:* method, procedure, routine. vb *lit:* bore, make a hole in,
pierce; sow in rows; discipline, exercise, instruct, train; rehearse (in),
teach (in).

drink n *lit:* beverage, liquid refreshment; bumper, draft, gulp, sip,
snort, swallow, swig; cup, dram, glass, mouthful, mug, tot; alcohol, liquor,
spirits; booze, hard stuff, hooch, plonk, rotgut, vino; cocktail, brew,
infusion, tipple, poison; *fig:* briny, ocean, sea. vb *lit:* down, imbibe,
partake of, quaff, sip, sup, swallow; gulp, guzzle, knock back, swig, swill

down, toss off; booze, carouse, drown one's sorrows, hit the bottle, tope; absorb, suck up.

drive   n *lit:* avenue, entrance, pathway; excursion, jaunt, outing, run, spin, trip; campaign, crusade, effort, push; hit, stroke; power, transmission; *fig:* ambition, dynamism, energy, enterprise, initiative, motivation, pep, vigor, zip. **vb** *lit:* herd, impel; compel, constrain, force, hammer, oblige, prod, spur; plunge, ram, stab; power, propel, push; hit, strike; control, direct, operate, steer; go, travel; cause to become, make, send; *fig:* aim (at), get (at).

driver   n *lit:* chauffeur, motorman, navigator, pilot, steersman; cowboy, drover, herder, herdsman, shepherd; *spec:* golf club.

drop   n *lit:* bead, drip, globule; mouthful, nip, pinch, sip, taste, trace; abyss, chasm, height, precipice; fall, lowering; *fig:* decline, decrease, deterioration, downturn, reduction, slump. **vb** *lit:* dive, fall, plummet, plunge, sink; bag, shoot; descend, droop, tumble; lay; decline, diminish; abandon, deposit, desert, disown, omit, reject, relinquish, renounce, throw over; let (off), set down; cease, forsake, give up, quit; *spec:* send (a line, a note).

drought   n *lit:* dry spell; aridity, dehydration; *fig:* deficiency, inadequacy, scarcity, shortage.

drum   n *lit:* percussion instrument, tambour; tympanum; barrel, cylinder; pad, residence. **vb** *lit:* beat rhythmically, tattoo, throb; *fig:* drive (into), instill (into).

drunk   adj *lit:* inebriated, intoxicated, maudlin; blotto, boozed up, canned, legless, paralytic, pickled, pie-eyed, plastered, stewed, stoned, tight, well-oiled.

drunkard   n *lit:* alcoholic, dipsomaniac, drunk, lush, soak, sot, toper, wino.

dry   vb *lit:* dehydrate, desiccate; parch; shrivel (up), wizen (up). **adj** *lit:* arid, brut, dehydrated, desiccated, moistureless, parched, torrid; *fig:* formal, official; dull, monotonous, tedious; deadpan, laconic, sardonic, sharp.

duck   n *lit:* drake, waterfowl; dip, plunge; dodge. **vb** *lit:* bob down, dodge, drop; dive, plunge, submerge; dunk, immerse; avoid, elude, evade, sidestep.

due n *lit:* deserts, merits; privilege, right. **adj** *lit:* appropriate, deserved, fitting, just, merited, rightful; adequate, enough, sufficient; outstanding, owed, payable; awaited, expected, scheduled.

dull **vb** *lit:* cloud, dim, obscure; sully, tarnish; *fig:* alleviate, assuage, blunt, mitigate, palliate, soften; dampen, depress. **adj** *lit:* blunt, unhoned; cloudy, dim, gloomy, overcast; drab, faded, indistinct, murky, somber, uninteresting; dense, dim, slow, stolid, thick; apathetic, blank, indifferent, insensitive, lifeless, sluggish; boring, dreary, flat, monotonous, plain, tedious, tiresome, unimaginative.

durable **adj** *lit:* hard-wearing, long-lasting, permanent, resistant, strong, substantial, tough; lasting, sound, stable; dogged, hardy, persevering.

duration n *lit:* continuance, continuation, existence, length, persistence; period, term, time.

during **prp** *lit:* throughout, through the entire time of; at some time in, in the course of.

dusk n *lit:* eventide, gloaming, nightfall, twilight; gloom, murk, shadiness, shadow.

dust n *lit:* ash, fluff, grains, grit, particles, powder; dirt, earth, ground, soil; cloud, fumes. **vb** *lit:* brush, brush off, clean, clear, polish, wipe; *fig:* powder, scatter, sprinkle.

dusty **adj** *lit:* dirty, grimy, grubby; unpolished, unswept; crumbly, gritty, powdery.

duty n *lit:* allegiance, loyalty, obedience; deference, homage; charge, obligation, office, responsibility, service; assignment, function, mission, role, task; operations, work; *fig:* effectiveness, utility; *spec:* excise, tax (customs).

dye n *lit:* colorant, coloring, pigment, stain. **vb** *lit:* color, pigment, stain, tint.

dying **adj (pr.pt)** *lit:* declining, expiring, fading, going, passing, sinking; final, last.

dynasty n *lit:* family, house, line, succession.

E

each adj *lit:* every, every single. **adv** *lit:* apiece, individually, per capita, per person. **prn** *lit:* every one, one and all.

earnest n *lit:* gravity, seriousness, sincerity, solemnity; collateral, guarantee, pledge, security, surety. **adj** *lit:* grave, serious, sincere, solemn; determined, fixed, intent, resolute, steady; ardent, devoted, eager, fervent, passionate, vehement, zealous.

earth n *lit:* globe, planet, world; clay, loam, mold, soil; clod, sod.

easy adj *lit:* effortless, light, painless, simple, smooth, undemanding; gentle, leisurely, unhurried; carefree, comfortable, cushy, peaceful, relaxed, tranquil; affable, amiable, casual, genial, informal, natural, sociable, unpretentious; flexible, indulgent, liberal, tolerant; amenable, biddable, docile, pliant, submissive, tractable.

eat vb *lit:* consume, devour, digest, ingest, swallow; bolt, chomp, masticate, munch, scoff; dine, feed; abrade (away), corrode, dissolve, erode, wear (away); *fig:* take back (one's words).

economic adj *lit:* lucrative, profitable, solvent, viable; budgetary, fiscal, monetary, pecuniary; commercial, financial, mercantile, trade; cheap, inexpensive, low-priced.

economy n *lit:* budgetary management, finance, financial organization, profit-and-loss margin, turnover; cost-efficiency, frugality, parsimony, thrift; saving.

edict n *lit:* command, decree, law, mandate, order, ordinance, proclamation, regulation, rule, statute.

edition n *lit:* impression, issue, printing; copy, volume; program.

educate vb *lit:* bring up, civilize, cultivate, enlighten, inform, rear; coach, drill, instruct, school, teach, train, tutor.

education n *lit:* civilizing, culture, enlightenment, informing; coaching, drill, instruction, learning, schooling, teaching, training, tuition, tutelage.

effect n *lit:* aftermath, consequence, outcome, result; impact, importance, meaning, significance; action, force, implementation, operation; clout, influence, power, weight; (in) fact, (in) reality. **vb** *lit:* accomplish, achieve, bring about, cause, create, make, perform, produce.

effective adj *lit:* active, causative, operative, productive; compelling, consequential, efficacious, emphatic, forceful, important, impressive, influential, powerful, significant, striking, telling; able, competent, energetic, useful, vigorous; contemporary, current, in force, in operation.

efficient adj *lit:* able, businesslike, competent, effective, productive, proficient, skilled; deft, dexterous, neat, tidy.

effort n *lit:* energy, exertion, force, pains, power, work; strain, stress, struggle, travail; attempt, bash, endeavor, go, shot, stab, try.

electric adj *lit:* charged, live; power; *fig:* sparkling, stimulating, stirring, tense, thrilling.

element n *lit:* component, constituent, factor, ingredient, item, member, part, unit; domain, field, habitat, medium; coil, filament, resistance, wire; electrode; rudiment(s).

else adv *lit:* additionally, also, as well, besides, in addition; if not, instead, otherwise.

embarrassment n *lit:* awkwardness, bashfulness, chagrin, discomfiture, humiliation, mortification, shame; excess, superabundance, surfeit, surplus; *fig:* difficulty, predicament, problem.

embassy n *lit:* legation, mission; ambassador's residence, consulate; agency, ministry.

embrace n *lit:* clasp, clinch, hug, squeeze. **vb** *lit:* clasp, cuddle, enfold, hold, hug, squeeze; comprehend, contain, enclose, encompass, include, take in; accept, receive; *fig:* adopt, espouse, take up.

emergency n *lit:* crisis, crunch, crux, exigency, extremity, matter of life and death; danger, urgency, vicissitude.

emission n *lit:* discharge, ejaculation, emanation, exudation, issue, radiation, transmission; escape, leak; secretion.

emit vb *lit:* broadcast, diffuse, discharge, eject, ejaculate, emanate, exhale, exude, give off, give out, issue, radiate, scatter, secrete, send out, shed, throw out, transmit.

emotion n *lit:* disposition, feeling, mood, sensation, sentiment; ardor, fervor, passion, vehemence.

emphasize vb *lit:* accent, accentuate, give priority to, highlight, play on, stress, underline.

employee n *lit:* hand, staff member, wage earner, worker.

enamored adj (pa.pt) *lit:* bewitched, captivated, enraptured, fascinated, infatuated, in love, smitten.

enclose vb *lit:* comprehend, contain, embrace, hold, include; circumscribe, encircle, encompass, hedge in, hem in, shut in; add in, insert, put in.

end n *lit:* cessation, close, closure, completion, conclusion, denouement, expiry, finale, finish, halt, resolution, stop, termination, winding up; boundary, edge, extremity, limit, terminus, tip; death, decease, demise; abolition, annihilation, cancellation, destruction, dissolution, downfall, extinction, scrapping; aim, aspiration, goal, intention, objective, purpose; leftover, remainder, remnant, scrap; behind, bottom, posterior, rear, stern; final blow, last straw, worst. vb *lit:* cease, close, come to a halt, conclude, expire, finish, halt, stop, terminate, wind up; bound; decease, die, pass away; be canceled, be destroyed, be extinguished, be scrapped; abolish, cancel, destroy, extinguish, kill, scrap.

endanger vb *lit:* compromise, hazard, imperil, jeopardize, put at risk.

endure vb *lit:* bear, brook, put up with, stand, stomach, swallow, take, tolerate, withstand; experience, go through, suffer, undergo; abide, continue, last, live on, persist, remain, survive.

enemy n *lit:* adversary, antagonist, foe; competitor, rival; opposition.

energy n *lit:* animation, drive, fire, force, life, liveliness, power, stamina, strength, verve, vigor, vim, vivacity, zest, zip.

engagement n *lit:* betrothal; agreement, bond, contract, oath, pledge, understanding, vow; appointment, date, meeting, rendezvous, tryst; commission, employment, gig, job, post, situation; action, battle, conflict, encounter, fight, skirmish.

engineer n *lit:* mechanic, physicist, technician, technologist; designer, inventor, planner.

enjoy vb *lit:* appreciate, delight in, like, relish, revel in, take pleasure in; experience, have, own, possess, use.

enjoyable adj *lit:* amusing, delightful, entertaining, gratifying, pleasant, pleasurable.

enough adj *lit:* adequate, satisfactory, sufficient. **adv** *lit:* adequately, satisfactorily, sufficiently.

ensure vb *lit:* confirm, guarantee, make sure.

enter vb *lit:* come in, go in, pass into, penetrate, pierce; enlist, enroll, join, sign up for; list, log, note, record, register, take down; put forward, submit, tender.

entrance n *lit:* door, doorway, ingress, way in; gate, opening, port, trap; mouth; admittance, entry; access, avenue; appearance, arrival, introduction. **vb** *lit:* bewitch, captivate, charm, enchant, enrapture, enthrall, fascinate, infatuate; hypnotize, mesmerize, spellbind.

entry n *lit:* appearance, entrance, introduction; door, doorway, ingress, way in; avenue; access, admission, admittance, entree; candidate, competitor, contestant, entrant, player; item, minute, note, record; plea, submission.

envious adj *lit:* covetous, green, jealous.

environment n *lit:* background, context, milieu, setting, surroundings; countryside, landscape, nature; domain, habitat.

episode n *lit:* adventure, affair, event, happening, incident, occurrence; chapter, installment, part.

equal n *lit:* compeer, counterpart, equivalent, fellow, match, peer. **vb** *lit:* agree with, balance with, be level with, equate with, match, parallel, rival, tie with; amount to, come to, total. **adj** *lit:* alike, balanced, commensurate, corresponding, even, level, like, uniform; up (to).

equally adv *lit:* alike, evenly, identically, proportionately, regularly, symmetrically, uniformly; fairly, impartially, justly, squarely.

equivalent   n *lit:* counterpart, equal, opposite number, parallel. **adj** *lit:* comparable (to), equal (to), tantamount (to).

erect   vb *lit:* build, construct, pitch, put up, raise, set up; establish, found, institute; harden, stiffen. **adj** *lit:* perpendicular, upright, vertical; haughty, proud; hard, ithyphallic, rigid, standing, stiff, tumescent.

error   n *lit:* blooper, corrigendum, erratum, fault, inaccuracy, literal, mistake, slip.

especially   adv *lit:* expressly, mainly, markedly, notably, outstandingly, particularly, peculiarly, principally, singularly, specifically, unusually.

essay   n *lit:* article, composition, dissertation, paper, piece. **vb** *lit:* attempt, have a go at, try; gauge, test, try out.

estate   n *lit:* domain, holdings, lands, property; assets, effects, possessions, wealth; condition, position, rank, standing, station, status; caste, class, order.

ethics   n *lit:* conscience, integrity, morality, moral values, principles, scruples, standards.

evaporate   vb *lit:* vaporize; desiccate, dry up; *fig:* disappear, dissipate, dissolve, fade away, vanish.

even   vb *lit:* balance (up), equal (up), level (out), match (up), square (up); settle (the score). **adj** *lit:* flat, flush, level, parallel, steady, uniform; balanced, drawn, equal, tied; constant, regular, unbroken, unwavering; calm, composed, cool, placid, serene, stable, tranquil, unruffled; **adv** *lit:* evenly; exactly (as), just (as); indeed, nay, veritably; fully, quite, right; surprisingly; still, yet.

ever   adv *lit:* at all, at any time, on any occasion; always, constantly, continually, eternally, incessantly, perpetually, unceasingly.

everybody   prn *lit:* each one, each person, the world; everyone.

evil   n *lit:* badness, immorality, iniquity, malevolence, malice, malignity, sin, sinfulness, vice, wickedness, wrongdoing; blasphemy, sacrilege, ungodliness; calamity, catastrophe, disaster, injury, misfortune, pain, suffering. **adj** *lit:* bad, immoral, iniquitous, malicious, malignant, sinful, wicked; blasphemous, sacrilegious, ungodly; calamitous, catastrophic, disastrous, injurious; foul, noxious, offensive, putrescent, vile.

evolve vb *lit:* advance, develop, form, grow, metamorphose, progress, transform.

exactly adv *lit:* accurately, carefully, faithfully, faultlessly, meticulously, precisely, punctiliously, rigorously, scrupulously, specifically, unerringly.

exaggerate vb *lit:* amplify, embellish, emphasize, enlarge, inflate, magnify, overstate.

exaggeration n *lit:* amplification, embellishment, emphasis, enlargement, inflation, overstatement.

except vb *lit:* bar, exclude, leave out, omit, pass over; absolve, exempt. **prp** *lit:* apart from, bar, barring, but, excluding, omitting, other than, save, saving; absolving, exempting, not including.

exceptional adj *lit:* abnormal, atypical, extraordinary, singular, special, strange, uncommon, unusual; excellent, outstanding, prodigious.

excitement n *lit:* activity, ado, agitation, commotion, flurry, furor; animation, elation, exaltation, fever, heat, passion; kick, thrill; impulse, stimulation, urge.

exciting adj *lit:* electrifying, exhilarating, galvanizing, rousing, sensational, stimulating, thrilling.

exclamation n *lit:* cry, ejaculation, interjection.

exclusive adj *lit:* private, sole, unshared; chic, classy, fashionable, posh, restricted, select.

executive n *lit:* administrator, manager, official; administration, directorate, government, leadership, management.

exemption n *lit:* absolution, dispensation, exception, immunity.

exercise n *lit:* activity, effort, exertion, movement; discipline, drill, training, workout; employment, practice, use, utilization; problem, task, work. **vb** *lit:* discipline, drill, practice, train, work out; apply, employ, exert, use, utilize; burden, preoccupy

exhaust n *lit:* emission, waste; carbon monoxide. **vb** *lit:* be emitted, discharge, escape; consume, dissipate, finish, run through, spend, use up;

drain, empty, void; bankrupt, disable, fatigue, sap, tire out, weaken, wear out.

exhaustion   n *lit:* debilitation, fatigue, prostration, tiredness.

existence   n *lit:* actuality, being, life, reality; creation.

expect   vb *lit:* anticipate, forecast, foresee, foretell, predict; contemplate, hope for, look for, watch for; demand, insist on, rely upon.

expenditure   n *lit:* costs, expenses, outgoings, outlay, payment; application, consumption.

expense   n *lit:* cost, disbursement, expenditure, outlay, payment; sacrifice.

expensive   adj *lit:* costly, dear, exorbitant, extortionate, extravagant, overpriced, steep.

experience   n *lit:* familiarity, involvement, knowledge, observation, practice, trial, understanding; adventure, affair, episode, event, incident, occurrence. vb *lit:* encounter, face, go through, know, meet, observe, sample, suffer, taste, try, undergo.

experienced   adj *lit:* adept, competent, expert, knowledgeable, practiced, qualified, seasoned, trained, veteran; mature, sophisticated, worldly-wise.

explain   vb *lit:* clarify, elucidate, illustrate, interpret, resolve; account for, excuse, justify; rationalize.

explanation   n *lit:* clarification, elucidation, illustration, interpretation, resolution, solution; account, answer, excuse, justification, reason; rationalization.

explore   vb *lit:* inquire into, examine, investigate, look into, probe, research, search; reconnoitre, scout; sightsee, tour, travel.

expose   vb *lit:* disclose, display, exhibit, present, reveal, show, uncover; betray, denounce, divulge, lay bare, make known, unmask; endanger, imperil, jeopardize, leave open (to).

expressive   adj *lit:* eloquent, forceful, lively, moving, poignant, telling, vivid; allusive (of), indicative (of), meaningful (of), suggestive (of); pointed, pregnant, significant.

external   **adj** *lit:* exterior, outer, outward; apparent, surface, visible; alien, exotic, foreign.

extra   **adj** *lit:* accessory, additional, ancillary, auxiliary, fresh, more, new, supplementary; excess, redundant, spare, superfluous, surplus, unneeded, unused.

extract   **vb** *lit:* cull, draw, pluck out, pull out, take out, uproot; bring out, elicit, evoke; gather, glean, reap; distill, express, press out, squeeze out; abstract, cite, quote.

extravagant   **adj** *lit:* excessive, lavish, profligate, wasteful; exaggerated, extreme, fanciful, fantastic, immoderate, inordinate, unreasonable, wild; flamboyant, flashy, garish, gaudy, ostentatious; costly, exorbitant, expensive, extortionate, steep.

eye   **n** *lit:* orb; optic, peeper; *fig:* appreciation, discernment, discrimination, perception, vision; (keep a) watch (on). **vb** *lit:* contemplate, gaze at, look at, regard, stare at, study, watch; leer at, ogle.

F

fable n *lit:* story, tale, yarn; legend, myth; allegory, parable; fabrication, fiction, invention.

face n *lit:* countenance, features, physiognomy; air, appearance, expression, look; frown, grin, grimace, pout, scowl; exterior, front, obverse, outside, surface, top; facade, outward appearance; character, disposition, physical form; font, print, type; cliff edge, edge, sheer side, wall; aspect, facet, plane; *fig:* audacity, cheek, effrontery, gall, nerve; dignity, image, prestige, status. **vb** *lit:* look toward, turn to; front on to, give on to, overlook; anticipate, be confronted by, have to cope with, look forward to; encounter, experience, present oneself to, stand before; brave, confront, defy, overcome, stare (down); clad, coat, cover, laminate, sheathe, veneer; edge, line, trim; *spec:* dress (stone).

facilities n *lit:* amenities, equipment, services; accommodation, buildings, rooms; arrangements, means, opportunities, resources; aid, assistance.

facility n *lit:* adroitness, dexterity, ease, efficiency, effortlessness, fluency, skill, smoothness; docility, pliancy.

fact n *lit:* actuality, reality, truth; act, action, circumstance, event, happening, incident, occurrence; factor.

factor n *lit:* component, consideration, constituent, element, ingredient, part, unit; multiplicand; agent, bailiff, estate manager, steward.

factory n *lit:* plant, works; depot, warehouse; assembly line.

factual adj *lit:* accurate, actual, authentic, detailed, exact, faithful, objective, real.

fade vb *lit:* blanch, dim, discolor, dull, pale; bleach, etiolate, wash out; decline, die, dwindle, ebb, fail, flag, wane, wilt, wither; disappear, vanish.

fail vb *lit:* be unable (to), be unsuccessful (in); flub, flunk; neglect (to); be useless to; be in vain, come to nothing, fall through, flop, go wrong, miscarry; be absent, be lacking, be missing; decline, deteriorate, fade, sink, wane; break down, cease, conk out, die, disappear, give out, give up, go out, peter out, stop; go bankrupt.

failure n *lit:* unsuccessful attempt; inability; absence, breakdown, deficiency, deterioration, lack, loss, negligence, omission; defeat, disaster, fiasco; collapse, disintegration; bankruptcy, crash, ruin; dud, flop, incompetent, lame duck, loser, washout.

faint n *lit:* blackout, dizzy spell, swoon, syncope. **vb** *lit:* become dizzy, black out, keel over, lose consciousness, pass out, swoon. **adj** *lit:* dizzy, giddy, lightheaded, woozy; exhausted, fatigued, worn to a frazzle; feeble, halfhearted, slight, weak; fearful, timid, timorous; dim, dull, faded, hazy, indistinct, light, soft, vague; distant, faltering, low, muffled, subdued.

fair n *lit:* amusement park, carnival; bazaar, market; exhibition, show. **adj** *lit:* blond, blonde, flaxen, light, yellow; bright, clear, cloudless, dry, sunny; beautiful, bonny, handsome, lovely, pretty; error-free, fine, legible, presentable; civil, courteous, gentle, polite; favorable, likely, promising; adequate, all right, average, moderate, not bad, okay, passable, reasonable, satisfactory; aboveboard, equitable, honest, impartial, judicial, judicious, just, square, unbiased, unprejudiced; open, unobstructed.

fairy n *lit:* brownie, fay, peri, pixie, sprite; leprechaun.

faith n *lit:* belief, confidence, conviction, reliance, trust; communion, creed, religion, theology; allegiance, constancy, fidelity, loyalty.

faithful n *lit:* adherents, believers, devotees, followers; communicants, congregation. **adj** *lit:* devoted, loyal, steadfast, true; dependable, reliable, trusty; accurate, actual, authentic, detailed, exact, factual, precise, truthful.

faithfulness n *lit:* constancy, devotion, fidelity, loyalty; dependability, reliability; accuracy, authenticity, exactness, precision, truth.

fake n *lit:* copy, counterfeit, forgery, imitation, reproduction, sham, simulation; fraud, impostor; charlatan, mountebank. **vb** *lit:* copy, counterfeit, forge, reproduce; feign, rig, sham, simulate. **adj** *lit:* copied, counterfeit, forged, phony, reproduced, sham, simulated; affected, assumed, false, feigned, imitation, pretended.

fall n *lit:* dive, drop, plunge, slip, tumble; collapse, defeat, destruction, overthrow, ruin, surrender; death; descent, incline, slant, slope;

precipitation; depth, height; *fig:* decline, decrease, dip, lessening, lowering, reduction, slump; lapse, sin, transgression; *spec:* hold, throw (in wrestling). **vb** *lit:* dive, drop, plunge, slip, tumble; keel over, topple, trip; be defeated, be destroyed, be overthrown, collapse, surrender, yield; be lost, die, perish; descend, incline downward, slant, slope; be precipitated, cascade, rain, shower down; *fig:* abate, be reduced, decline, decrease, diminish, dip, flag, go down, lessen, lower, slump; backslide, lapse, transgress; become, get, happen, occur, turn; be drawn (into); *spec:* be thrown (in wrestling).

false **adj** *lit:* erroneous, fallacious, inaccurate, incorrect, invalid, untrue, wrong; lying, mendacious, untruthful; deceitful, dishonest, disloyal, faithless, perfidious, traitorous, unfaithful, unreliable, untrustworthy; deceiving, deceptive, misleading; artificial, counterfeit, fake, feigned, forged, sham, simulated, synthetic, trumped up; ersatz, imitation, substitute; ill-founded, misconceived; off, out of tune.

fame **n** *lit:* celebrity, distinction, eminence, illustriousness, name, note, renown, reputation, repute, stardom; infamy, notoriety.

family **n** *lit:* folks, household, people, relations, relatives; clan, kin, kindred, kinsmen, tribe; children, issue, offspring, progeny; ancestry, blood, descent, genealogy, house, line, lineage, parentage, pedigree; class, genre, group, kind.

famous **adj** *lit:* celebrated, distinguished, eminent, illustrious, legendary, noted, renowned, reputed, well-known; infamous, notorious.

fan **n** *lit:* air conditioner, blower, vane, ventilator; aficionado, buff, devotee, enthusiast, supporter. **vb** *lit:* air-condition, blow, ventilate; *fig:* arouse, excite, kindle, provoke, stir up; *spec:* spread out (cards).

fanatic **n** *lit:* activist, extremist, militant, zealot; addict, devotee, enthusiast.

fantasy **n** *lit:* daydream, dream, image, mental picture, vision; nightmare; fairy story; fancy, imagination; invention, originality; fiction, lie, untruth.

far **adj** *lit:* distant, remote; outlying; farther, hinder, other. **adv** *lit:* a long way, deep, distantly, remotely; considerably, definitely, much, positively.

fare n *lit:* passenger, pickup, traveler; fee, price, ticket money, transportation cost; food, provisions, rations, sustenance. **vb** *lit:* be, do, go, get along, make out, proceed, turn out, work out; be fed, eat, feed.

farewell n *lit:* adieu, goodbye, valediction; leave-taking, parting, send-off, well-wishing.

farm n *lit:* homestead, plantation, ranch; acreage, fields; battery, breeding station, stud. **vb** *lit:* cultivate, till, work; breed, raise, rear, tend; contract (out), subcontract (out).

farmer n *lit:* homesteader, rancher; agriculturalist, agronomist; grower, planter, producer; breeder, shepherd; contractor, subcontractor.

fascinate vb *lit:* allure, attract, bewitch, captivate, enchant, enrapture, enthrall, entrance, infatuate, mesmerize, put a spell on, ravish, spellbind; intrigue.

fascination n *lit:* allure, attraction, charm, enchantment, magic, magnetism, spell; captivation, infatuation.

fashion n *lit:* convention, custom, usage; craze, fad, rage, trend, vogue; creation, cut, form, line, make, mode, pattern, shape; manner, style, way; appearance, description, kind, sort, type; high society, jet set. **vb** *lit:* build, create, form, make, mold, knead, shape, work.

fashionable adj *lit:* à la mode, chic, modish, snappy, snazzy, stylish, trendy; current, in, in vogue, latest, popular, up-to-the-minute.

fast n *lit:* abstinence; period of abstinence; hunger strike. **vb** *lit:* abstain, go hungry, refrain from eating, take no food. **adj** *lit:* brisk, fleet, hasty, hurried, quick, rapid, swift; fixed, secure, tight; *fig:* close, firm, loyal, steadfast; dissolute, licentious, loose, promiscuous; intemperate, rash, reckless, wild; *spec:* before time, early (of a clock); permanent, unfading (colors); sound (sleep). **adv** *lit:* briskly, hastily, hurriedly, quickly, rapidly, speedily, swiftly; fixedly, securely, tightly; *fig:* firmly, loyally, steadfastly, unflinchingly; close (by), near (by); *spec:* sound, soundly (asleep).

fasten vb *lit:* attach, connect, join, link, secure, unite; bind, chain, tie; affix, bond, cement, glue; nail, rivet, tack, weld; buckle, button, do up, hook up, lace, pin (on), zip; *fig:* aim (on), concentrate (on), focus (on); latch (on to), seize (on); push (on to).

fat n *lit:* adipose tissue, carbohydrate; blubber, flab; grease, oil; butter, lard, margarine, polyunsaturates; *fig:* body, fullness, richness, substance. **adj** *lit:* adipose; blubbery, corpulent, flabby, fleshy, obese, overweight, plump, portly, roly-poly, rotund, stout, tubby; greasy, oily, oleaginous; broad, bulky, enormous, great, huge, jumbo, massive, vast, wide; *fig:* fertile, fruitful, lush, rich.

fatal adj *lit:* deadly, lethal, mortal; incurable, terminal; *fig:* calamitous, catastrophic, disastrous; critical, decisive, fateful, portentous.

fate n *lit:* destiny, predestination, providence; lot, portion; forecast, future, horoscope, stars; luck, fortune.

father n *lit:* begetter, progenitor, sire; dad, daddy, old man, pa, papa, pop; elder, senator; abbot, confessor, priest, prior, vicar; *fig:* author, creator, discoverer, founder, inventor, maker. **vb** *lit:* beget, sire; engender, generate; adopt, foster; *fig:* establish, found, institute, originate.

fault n *lit:* defect, deficiency, flaw; blunder, error, inaccuracy, lapse, mistake, slip; omission; blemish, imperfection; blame, culpability, guilt, responsibility; offense, sin, transgression, trespass. **vb** *lit:* find a flaw in, pick holes in; blame.

faultless adj *lit:* exemplary, flawless, immaculate, impeccable, irreproachable, perfect, spotless, unblemished.

faulty adj *lit:* blemished, broken, defective, deficient, flawed, imperfect; inaccurate, incorrect, invalid, wrong; malfunctioning.

favor n *lit:* approbation, approval, esteem, good looks, goodwill, patronage, support; bias, partiality; good turn, kindness, service; keepsake, kerchief, ribbon, token. **vb** *lit:* approve of, commend, fancy, support; be biased toward, have a soft spot for, prefer, side with; grace (with), oblige (with); *fig:* look like, resemble, take after.

favorable adj *lit:* approving, encouraging, positive, welcoming, well-disposed; advantageous, beneficial, good, helpful, opportune, propitious; clement, suitable.

favorite n *lit:* best, choice, pick, preference; certainty, cinch, hot tip, sure thing, tip.

fear n *lit:* anxiety, apprehension, dread, foreboding, fright, misgiving, panic, terror, timidity, trepidation, unease; horror, phobia; reverence, veneration. **vb** *lit:* apprehend, be afraid, be apprehensive, be frightened, be terrified, dread; suspect; be anxious, tremble; respect, revere, reverence, venerate.

fearless **adj** *lit:* bold, daring, dauntless, heroic, indomitable, intrepid, unafraid, unflinching.

feasible **adj** *lit:* achievable, possible, practicable, realizable, viable, workable.

feast **n** *lit:* banquet, blowout, spread; meal, repast; celebration, festival, saint's day; *fig:* delight, pleasure, treat. **vb** *lit:* banquet, gorge (on), stuff, wine and dine; entertain sumptuously; *fig:* delight, gladden, gratify.

federation **n** *lit:* alliance, association, combination, confederacy, league, syndicate, syndication.

fee **n** *lit:* charge, cost, hire, payment, price, toll; emolument, remuneration.

feeble **adj** *lit:* debilitated, doddering, failing, frail, puny, sickly, skinny, slight, thin, weak; delicate, effete, faint, indecisive, ineffectual, insignificant; *fig:* flimsy, inadequate, lame, poor, tame, threadbare.

feed **vb** *lit:* cater for, provision, seat, victual; provide for, supply to; exist (on), live (on), subsist (on); devour, eat; crop, graze; *fig:* foster, fuel, nourish, strengthen; channel, duct, pipe, supply.

feel **vb** *lit:* caress, finger, fondle, fumble over, grasp, grope, handle, paw, stroke, touch; be aware of, experience, notice, perceive, sense; test (out), try (out); believe, consider, hold, think; agonize, be sorry, bleed; have great sympathy.

feeling **n** *lit:* consciousness, impression, perception, presentiment, sensation, sense; air, atmosphere, aura, mood; idea, notion, suspicion; consensus, opinion, view; affection, fondness, sentimentality, warmth; emotion, fervor, passion; compassion, empathy, sympathy, understanding.

feminine **adj** *lit:* female, girlish, ladylike, maidenly, matronly, womanly.

fence **n** *lit:* barrier, hedge, hurdle, palings, palisade, railings, stockade, wire, wire netting; receiver of stolen property. **vb** *lit:* barricade, hedge (in), pen (in); fortify, secure, shield; dispose of stolen property; *spec.* fight (with swords).

ferry **vb** *lit:* chauffeur, convey, drive, escort, run, see (to), ship, transport.

fertile **adj** *lit:* fecund, fruitful; arable, cultivable; abundant, luxuriant, productive, prolific, rich, teeming.

fertilize **vb** *lit:* impregnate, inseminate, make pregnant; pollinate; compost, dress, manure, mulch.

festival **n** *lit:* feast, saint's day; anniversary; celebration, gala, party.

festive **adj** *lit:* celebratory, convivial, festal, happy, holiday, jolly, joyous, merry; bright, colorful, decorative, gay.

fetch **vb** *lit:* bring, carry, convey, deliver, get, obtain, recover, retrieve, take; escort, guide, lead; draw out, elicit; bring in, earn, make, produce, sell for.

fever **n** *lit:* heat, high temperature; *fig:* delirium, ferment, flush, frenzy, passion.

feverish **adj** *lit:* burning, febrile, flushed, hectic, hot, inflamed; *fig:* delirious, frenetic, frenzied, impassioned, passionate.

few **n** *lit:* couple, handful, scattering. **adj** *lit:* hardly any, not many; meager, scanty, scarce, sparse.

fiancé(e) **n** *lit:* affianced, betrothed, engaged, intended.

fiasco **n** *lit:* catastrophe, debacle, disaster, rout, ruin.

fiber **n** *lit:* filament, strand, thread; nap, pile, texture; *fig:* being, nature, spirit, soul; (moral) strength.

fiction **n** *lit:* narrative, story, tale, yarn; fantasy, imagination, invention; fabrication, fib, imposture, lie, simulation, untruth.

fictitious **adj** *lit:* imaginary, invented, made-up, unreal, untrue; imagined, make-believe; affected, assumed, counterfeit, feigned, sham, simulated.

fiddle **n** *lit:* violin; *fig:* con, fraud, graft, rip-off, swindle. **vb** *lit:* play the violin, scrape the strings; *fig:* fidget (with), mess about (with), play (with), tamper (with), toy (with); cheat, con, rip off, swindle.

field n *lit:* lea, meadow, pasture; acreage; *fig:* area, confines, domain, province, territory; line, sphere; bounds, limits, range, scope; department, discipline, specialty; competitors, contestants, entrants, runners; applicants, candidates. **vb** *lit:* catch, retrieve, throw back; *fig:* cope with, deal with, handle; deflect, parry, turn aside.

fierce adj *lit:* dangerous, fell, feral, ferocious, murderous, predatory, savage, tigerish, untamed, wild; furious, raging, tempestuous, violent; *fig:* blazing, fiery, hot; cutthroat, intense, strong.

fight n *lit:* affray, altercation, brawl, clash, conflict, fracas, free-for-all, melee, riot, row, scrap, scrimmage, scuffle, set-to, struggle, tussle; bout, boxing match, contest; action, battle, engagement, skirmish, war; *fig:* aggression, belligerence, militancy; gameness, mettle, spirit. **vb** *lit:* brawl, clash, come to blows, cross swords, do battle, scrap, scuffle, tussle, wrestle; box, spar; combat, engage, skirmish, struggle against, wage war against; bicker, squabble, wrangle; contest, dispute, oppose, resist against.

fill vb *lit:* cram, crowd, pack; charge (up), replenish, restock; suffuse; supply; sate, satiate, satisfy, stuff; saturate; bung, cork, plug, seal, stop; cover, occupy, take up; *fig:* discharge, execute, fulfill; belly out, extend, inflate.

film n *lit:* coating, integument, layer; membrane, skin, tissue; dusting, powder; blur, cloud, haze, mist; celluloid, feature, movie, tape, video. **vb** *lit:* photograph, shoot, take; blur (over), cloud (over), haze (over), mist (over).

final adj *lit:* closing, concluding, last, terminal, terminating, ultimate; conclusive, decisive, definitive, irrevocable.

finally adv *lit:* in conclusion, lastly, to end with; at last, eventually, in the end, ultimately; conclusively, decisively, definitively, irrevocably, once and for all.

finance n *lit:* banking, commerce, economics, investment; bourse, money market, stock market; asset(s), backing, capital, fund(s), funding, money, resource(s). **vb** *lit:* back, bankroll, float, fund, guarantee, put up the money for, sponsor, support, underwrite.

financial adj *lit:* commercial, economic, fiscal, monetary.

find   n *lit:* catch, discovery; acquisition, bargain. **vb** *lit:* chance upon, come across, discover, encounter, light upon, meet, stumble on; acquire, gain, get hold of, lay one's hands on, locate, obtain, procure, run down, spot, track down, turn up, uncover; recover, regain, retrieve; bring to light, detect, reveal; furnish, provide, supply; *fig:* become aware, note, notice, observe, perceive, realize; declare, proclaim, pronounce.

finding   n *lit:* detection, discovery, location, recovery, retrieval, tracking down; conclusion, decision, judgment, verdict; answer, result, total.

fine   n *lit:* forfeit, penalty; fee, price, toll. **vb** *lit:* mulct, penalize; compel to pay. **adj** *lit:* admirable, attractive, beautiful, excellent, exquisite, magnificent, smart, splendid, striking, stylish; dainty, delicate, elegant, fragile, slender; slight, thin, tenuous; diaphanous, gauzy, gossamer, light, sheer; crushed, powdery, pulverized, refined; clear, pure, unadulterated, unalloyed; bright, dry, fair, sunny; agreeable, all right, good, okay, suitable; critical, discriminating, fastidious, keen, precise, sensitive, sharp; cutting, razor-edged; brilliant, polished.

finish   n *lit:* close, completion, conclusion, culmination, end, ending, stop, termination, windup; bankruptcy, liquidation, ruin; death, demolition, destruction; defeat; luster, patina, polish, shine, surface texture; *fig:* culture, refinement, sophistication. **vb** *lit:* accomplish, achieve, cease, close, complete, conclude, culminate (in), do, end, round off, stop, terminate, wind up; drain (off), drink (up), eat (up), use (up); destroy, ruin; kill (off); defeat; coat, face, lacquer, polish, texture, wax; *fig:* perfect, refine.

fire   n *lit:* combustion; blaze, conflagration, inferno; coals, embers, flames, sparks; barbecue, beacon, brazier, grate, hob, oven, stove; bombardment, fusillade, shelling, sniping; *fig:* brightness, brilliance, flare, intensity, luster, radiance, scintillation, sparkle; ardor, fervor, force, heat, passion, zeal; animation, dash, eagerness, enthusiasm, excitement, life, spirit, verve, vigor, vivacity; creativity, inspiration; danger, hardship, ordeal, trial, tribulation. **vb** *lit:* ignite, kindle, light, set ablaze, set alight to, set on fire; bake; cauterize; detonate, explode, touch off; discharge, let off, shoot; *fig:* arouse, electrify, galvanize, inflame, inspire, rouse, stir; fuel; boot out, cashier, dismiss, give the sack, lay off; *spec:* catch, start (of an engine).

firm   n *lit:* business, company, organization, outfit. **adj** *lit:* fast, fixed, immovable, rooted, secure, solid, stable, steady, strong, sturdy, unshakable; compact, dense, hard, rigid, stiff; *fig:* adamant, inflexible, obdurate, resolute, steadfast, unfaltering, unflinching, unswerving.

firmness n *lit:* fixity, immobility, security, solidity, stability, steadiness, strength, sturdiness; compactness, density, hardness, rigidity, stiffness, tensile strength; *fig:* inflexibility, obduracy, resolve, steadfastness, strength of purpose.

first adj *lit:* dawn, earliest, initial, opening, original, primary, primeval; foremost, leading; chief, head, highest, prime, principal, top; basic, cardinal, elementary. **adv** *lit:* at the outset, beforehand, initially, in the beginning, to start with; rather, sooner.

fish n *fig:* character, individual, person, type; bracket, plate, stay. **vb** *lit:* angle (for), bait a line (for), net, trawl (for); dive (for); *fig:* be on the lookout (for), try (for); fumble (for), search (for).

fit n *lit:* dimensions, shape, size; appropriateness, aptitude, rightness, suitability; attack, bout, convulsion, seizure, spasm; outbreak, spell; humor, mood. **vb** *lit:* be appropriate for, be apt for, be right for, conform to, correspond to, match, suit, tally; equip, rig; slot, sort; frame. **adj** *lit:* able, adequate, competent, deserving, equipped, good enough, qualified, right, suitable, well-suited; athletic, hale, healthy, in condition, in good shape, robust, trim, well.

fitness n *lit:* appropriateness, aptitude, aptness, correspondence, eligibility, match, suitability; athleticism, good condition, health, shape.

flag n *lit:* arms, banner, colors, ensign, jack, standard; burgee, gonfalon, pennant. **vb** *lit:* be fatigued, droop, ebb, fade, fail, sag, slump, taper off, tire, wane, weary, wilt, wither; label, mark, tab; hail, salute, wave (down).

flair n *lit:* ability, aptitude, feel, genius, gift, knack, talent; dash, elegance, panache, savoir faire, style, virtuosity.

flamboyant adj *lit:* extravagant, florid, grandiose, ornate, ostentatious, swaggering, theatrical; garish, gaudy, loud, showy.

flame n *lit:* fire; light; *fig:* amour, boyfriend, girlfriend, love, sweetheart; ardor, fervency, intensity, passion. **vb** *lit:* blaze, burn, flare, flash, glow, shine; blush, flush, suffuse.

flap n *lit:* apron, cover, fold, lappet, lid, tab; airfoil, aileron; *fig:*

commotion, fluster, fuss, panic, state, tizzy. **vb** *lit:* bang, beat, flail, flutter, swing, thresh, wave; *fig:* be flustered, get into a state, panic.

flash   n *lit:* beam, blaze, burst, flare, flicker, gleam, glow, glint, glistening, scintillation, spark, sparkle; cascade, deluge, flood, spurt; *fig:* blur, streak; instant, moment, second, trice, twinkling; display, exposure, show; news headline. **vb** *lit:* beam, blaze, burst, flare, flicker, gleam, glow, glint, glisten, scintillate, spark, sparkle; *fig:* blur, shoot, streak; dash, speed, sprint, zip; display, expose, let one see, show.

flashy   adj *lit:* garish, gaudy, loud, ostentatious, showy; cheap, tasteless, vulgar.

flask   n *lit:* bottle, canteen, carafe, decanter; powder horn; retort.

flat   n *lit:* apartment, room, story; lowland, plain; marsh, swamp; backdrop, prop. **adj** *lit:* horizontal, level, plane, uniform; at full length, prone, prostrate, recumbent, supine; burst, collapsed, deflated, empty, punctured; *fig:* boring, colorless, dead, insipid, lifeless, stale, vapid, watery; blue, dejected, depressed, morose; absolute, categorical, fixed, positive, unequivocal, unqualified; *spec:* back, short (vowel, diphthong); below the right (musical) pitch; deflated (tire). **adv** *lit:* horizontal, in a heap, to the ground; *fig:* absolutely, categorically, positively, unequivocally, utterly.

flatter   vb *lit:* be sycophantic toward, butter up, crawl to, fawn over, soft-soap, toady; overcompliment, overpraise; humor (into), wheedle (into); become, enhance, set off, show to good advantage.

flattery   n *lit:* fawning, obsequiousness, servility, soft soap, sycophancy, toadying.

flavor   n *lit:* essence, piquancy, savor, smack, tang, taste; *fig:* character, feel, quality, stamp, tone; hint, suggestion, tinge, touch. **vb** *lit:* imbue (with), infuse (with); season, spice; *fig:* add interest to, ginger up.

flee   vb *lit:* beat it, bolt, fly, make off, run away, run for it, scram, split, take a powder, take off; abscond, escape, get away; hurtle, race, speed, sprint; disappear, fade away, vanish.

fleet   n *lit:* armada, flotilla, navy; company, force, team. **adj** *lit:* fast, nimble, rapid, speedy, swift; ephemeral, evanescent, fast-fading, transient.

flesh   n *lit:* meat, muscle; brawn, fat, gristle, tissue; food; *fig:* body, physical self; carnality, physical urges; humanity, humankind, human nature, humans.

flexible   adj *lit:* elastic, plastic, pliable, pliant, springy, tensile; ductile, moldable; agile, limber, lithe, loose-limbed, nimble, supple; *fig:* adaptable, adjustable, variable; amenable, compliant, responsive, tractable.

flight   n *lit:* aircraft, airplane; journey; flying; air travel, flying time; collection, flock, swarm; squadron, wing; aeronautics, aviation; escape, fleeing, getaway; rout, scattering, stampede; *fig:* digression, foray, sally; staircase; salvo, volley; hurdle, jump.

flimsy   adj *lit:* delicate, frail, insubstantial, slight, chiffon, diaphanous, gauzy, gossamer, light, sheer, thin; rickety, shaky, unsteady; *fig:* feeble, implausible, shallow, trivial, unconvincing, weak.

flippant   adj *lit:* disrespectful, facetious, frivolous, impertinent, impudent, irreverent, pert, saucy, smart-alecky.

flirt   n *lit:* coquette, gadabout, minx, tease; philanderer, rake. **vb** *lit:* be coquettish (with); *fig:* play (with), toy (with), trifle (with).

float   n *lit:* bobber, cork, quill; pontoon, raft; ball cock; blade, paddle; spatula, trowel; cash in hand, petty cash, small change; parade vehicle. **vb** *lit:* be buoyant, stay up; bob, drift, glide, slide; hover, levitate; *fig:* establish, launch, set up; circulate, divulge, publish; sell shares in.

flock   n *lit:* nap, pile, tuft, wool; colony, flight, rookery, skein; *fig:* collection, company, crowd, group, herd, mass, throng; assembly, congregation. **vb** *lit:* assemble, collect, congregate, crowd, gather, mass, throng.

flood   n *lit:* deluge, inundation, spate, tide, torrent; immersion, overflow, submersion; *fig:* glut, plethora, profusion, rush. **vb** *lit:* drown, engulf, immerse, inundate, overflow, submerge, swamp; drench, saturate, soak; flow, gush, rush, surge; *fig:* fill, glut.

floor   n *lit:* base, bed, bottom, ground, surface; level, story, tier. **vb** *lit:* fell, flatten, knock down, level, raze; put down, set down; *fig:* confound, defeat, discomfit, nonplus, perplex, puzzle, stump, throw.

flourish   n *lit:* gesticulation, gesture, wave; display, parade, show; fanfare, tucket; decoration, embellishment, ornamentation; curlicue, kern, loop, sweep. **vb** *lit:* bloom, blossom, burgeon, flower, grow, thrive; do well, get on, increase, prosper; brandish, gesture with, swish, wave, wield; display, parade, show, vaunt.

flow   **n** *lit:* circulation, current, drift, spate, stream, tide; bleeding, dripping, oozing, trickling; effusion, emanation, emission, escape, leak; cascade, deluge. **vb** *lit:* circulate, course, gush, pour, run, surge; bleed, drip, ooze, trickle; be emitted, emanate, emerge, escape, issue, leak; cascade, deluge, flood, inundate, stream, teem.

flower   **n** *lit:* bloom, blossom, efflorescence; *fig:* best, cream, elite, pick. **vb** *lit:* bloom, blossom, burgeon, effloresce, open; mature, ripen; flourish, prosper, thrive.

fluctuate   **vb** *lit:* alternate, go up and down, oscillate, seesaw, swing, undulate, vary; vacillate, waver.

fluid   **n** *lit:* liquid; liquor. **adj** *lit:* flowing, gaseous, liquid; melted, runny; aqueous, watery; *fig:* mellifluous, smooth, soft, tender; changeable, fluctuating, mercurial, volatile; elegant, graceful, sinuous.

flush   **n** *lit:* blush, reddening, ruddiness; freshness, prime; *spec:* hand with all one suit (cards). **vb** *lit:* blush, burn, color hotly, crimson, go red, redden, suffuse; douche, flood, rinse out, wash; *fig:* beat (out), hunt (out), nose (out), sniff (out). **adj** *lit:* even, flat, level, parallel, square; abundant, overflowing; rich, wealthy, well off. **adv** *lit:* evenly (with), level (with), parallel (with), squarely (against).

flustered   **adj (pa.pt)** *lit:* agitated, bothered, disturbed, excited, hurried, nervous, perturbed, rattled, upset.

flute   **n** *lit:* fife, pipe, whistle; groove; *spec:* shuttle (in weaving). **vb** *lit:* pipe, whistle; sing shrilly; carve a groove in.

fly   **n** *lit:* aphid, aphis, bluebottle, gnat, housefly, insect, midge; fishhook. **vb** *lit:* flutter, glide, hover, sail, soar, take wing; control, operate, pilot; have at the masthead, hoist, raise, wave; *fig:* bolt, dart, dash, race, shoot, speed, sprint, tear, zip; go (at), hurl oneself (at), rush (at); elapse, pass rapidly, roll past, vanish. **adj** *lit:* canny, knowing, sharp, shrewd, smart.

fold   **n** *lit:* crease, pleat, turnover, turnup; furrow, wrinkle; flock of sheep; *fig:* congregation, parish. **vb** *lit:* bend over, crease, double, pleat, tuck, turn tuck, turn under; envelop (in), wrap (in); collapse, crumple, drop in a heap, fall over, keel over; *fig:* crash, fail, go bankrupt, go bust.

follow vb *lit:* dog, pursue, shadow, stalk, track, trail; be after, look for, search for; be next, come after, succeed, supersede, tag on behind; develop, ensue, issue (from), proceed (from), result; *fig:* copy, emulate, imitate, model oneself on; adhere to, be a devotee of; conform to, keep, obey, observe; catch on, comprehend, fathom, get, grasp, see, understand; appreciate, keep up with.

follower n *lit:* adherent, believer, devotee, disciple, fan, supporter, worshiper; attendant, henchman, retainer; hanger-on, sidekick.

following n *lit:* acolytes, adherents, aficionados, disciples, devotees, fans, neophytes, public, supporters; crew, entourage, retinue, staff, suite. **adj (pr.pt)** *lit:* ensuing, later, next, subsequent, succeeding, successive.

fond adj *lit:* enamored (of); adoring, devoted, doting, indulgent, loving; cherished, favorite, pet.

fondness n *lit:* affection, devotion, love; liking, partiality, predilection, soft spot, taste, weakness.

food n *lit:* chow, diet, fare, grub, nosh, nourishment, pabulum, provisions, rations, sustenance, tuck, victuals; cooking, cuisine, menu; feed, fodder, provender; *fig:* energy source, fuel.

fool n *lit:* ass, blockhead, chump, clod, cretin, dolt, dunce, fathead, idiot, imbecile, moron, nincompoop, nitwit, numskull, simpleton, twit; butt, dupe, gull, mark, mug, sucker; clown, comic, jester. **vb** *lit:* bamboozle, deceive, dupe, gull, have on, hoodwink, put one over on, take in, trick; antic (about), lark (about), mess (about); play (about with), toy (with), trifle (with).

foolish adj *lit:* asinine, brainless, cretinous, daft, fatheaded, fatuous, half-baked, idiotic, imbecile, inane, mad, moronic, senseless, stupid; absurd, illadvised, imprudent, indiscreet, injudicious, unintelligent.

foot n *lit:* base, bottom, end, leg, podium, stanchion; 12 inches; *fig:* infantry, infantrymen; *spec:* metrical unit (in verse). **vb** *lit:* pace (out), stride (out), walk; *fig:* pay, settle.

forbid vb *lit:* ban, interdict, outlaw, prohibit, proscribe, rule out, veto.

forbidden adj (pa.pt) *lit:* banned, interdicted, outlawed, out of bounds, prohibited, proscribed, ruled out, taboo, vetoed.

force n *lit:* army, body, brigade, corps, patrol, service, squad, troop; dynamism, energy, impulse, life, momentum, power, strength, vigor; coercion, compulsion, duress, pressure, violence; emphasis, fervor, intensity, vehemence; effectiveness, efficacy, punch, weight. **vb** *lit:* compel, constrain, drive, impose (upon), oblige, pressurize; break open, prize apart, strong-arm, wrench open; extort (from), wring (from).

forceful adj *lit:* dynamic, effective, effectual, potent, powerful, weighty; cogent, compelling, telling.

forcible adj *lit:* aggressive, armed, forceful, violent; *fig:* compelling, potent, powerful.

forecast n *lit:* prediction, prognosis, projection, prophecy. **vb** *lit:* augur, foresee, foretell, predict, prognosticate, prophesy.

foreign adj *lit:* alien, exotic, imported, outlandish, strange, unfamiliar; extraneous (to), irrelevant (to), unrelated (to).

foreigner n *lit:* alien, immigrant, outlander, stranger.

foreman n *lit:* gaffer, governor, overseer, straw boss, superintendent, supervisor; convener, spokesman.

foresee vb *lit:* anticipate, forecast, foretell, predict, prognosticate, prophesy.

foresight n *lit:* anticipation, farsightedness, forethought, preparedness, prescience.

forest n *lit:* woodland, woods; copse, coppice, heath, moor, scrub, thicket, undergrowth, wilderness; national park, nature reserve, parkland.

forestry n *lit:* arboriculture, silviculture, woodcraft; dendrology.

forever adv *lit:* eternally, evermore, permanently; always, continually, incessantly, perpetually.

forfeit n *lit:* fine, penalty; loss, surrendering. **vb** *lit:* be obliged to give up, have to relinquish, lose, surrender.

forgery n *lit:* copy, counterfeit, fake, phony, sham; copying, counterfeiting, faking.

forget vb *lit:* fail to think of, neglect, omit, overlook; leave behind; dismiss from one's mind, put behind one.

forgetful adj *lit:* absentminded, inattentive, neglectful, oblivious, unmindful.

forgive vb *lit:* absolve, pardon, remit; excuse, overlook; grant pardon.

forgiveness n *lit:* absolution, pardon, remission; grace, mercy.

forgotten adj (pa.pt) *lit:* neglected, omitted, overlooked; forlorn, forsaken, left behind; behind one, dismissed from one's mind.

fork n *lit:* pronged instrument; rake, trident; branch, prong, tine; bifurcation, divergence, divide, division, ramification, split; zigzag. vb *lit:* impale, prong, stab; dig up, rake, turn over; bifurcate, branch, diverge, divide, ramify, split; zigzag.

form n *lit:* mold, template; configuration, outline, pattern, shape; body, build, construction, figure, frame, physique, structure; framework, order, organization, plan, system; character, description, guise, mode, sort, style; fashion, manner, method, way; application, blank, document, schedule, slip; bench, seat, settle; *fig:* condition, health, spirits, trim; behavior, conduct, etiquette, manners, protocol. vb *lit:* create, fashion, forge, make, model, mold, shape; build, construct; establish, found, set up; appear, come into being, emerge, evolve, manifest oneself, materialize, take shape; arrange, dispose, draw up, organize; *fig:* contract, cultivate, develop.

formal adj *lit:* approved, conventional, correct, decorous, prescribed, punctilious, set, solemn; ceremonial, official.

formality n *lit:* convention, correctness, decorum, etiquette, punctiliousness, solemnity; ceremony, protocol; custom, matter of form, observance.

formation n *lit:* compilation, composition, creation, fashioning, modeling, molding, shaping; building, construction; development, establishment, foundation; evolution, manifestation, materialization; arrangement, configuration, disposition, form, grouping, organization.

former adj *lit:* earlier, erstwhile, one-time, past, previous, prior, quondam; above, above-mentioned, aforesaid, preceding; ancient, bygone, old.

fortunate   adj *lit:* favored, lucky; convenient, opportune, timely; advantageous, favorable, felicitous.

fortune   n *lit:* chance, destiny, fate, luck, providence; circumstance(s), event(s), happening(s), occurrence(s); prosperity, riches, success, treasure, wealth.

forward   vb *lit:* dispatch, freight, remit, send, send on, ship; advance, aid, expedite, further, promote, speed on, support. **adj** *lit:* advance, first, foremost, leading; early, precocious, premature; bold, brazen, cheeky, familiar, fresh, impudent, officious, pert, presumptuous, pushy. **adv** *lit:* ahead, on, onward; into the open, into view, out; in the open, on the table.

foul   n *lit:* breach of the rules, illegality, misdemeanor, villainy. **vb** *lit:* contaminate, defile, dirty, pollute, smear, soil, stain; catch on, choke up, clog, entangle in, jam, obstruct, snarl up in; break the rules, commit an illegality. **adj** *lit:* contaminated, defiled, dirty, polluted, soiled, stained; disgusting, filthy, noisome, offensive, putrescent, revolting, scabrous, squalid, stinking; disgraceful, dishonorable, iniquitous, scandalous, wicked; underhand, against the rules, illegal, unfair, unscrupulous, unsportsmanlike; blasphemous, blue, coarse, gross, indecent, obscene, scatological; blustery, rough, stormy, unfavorable, wild.

found   vb *lit:* base, ground, support; establish, inaugurate, institute, originate, set up, start. **adj (pa.pt)** *lit:* discovered, located, situated; brought to light, detected, spotted, tracked down; acquired, obtained, procured, run down.

foundation   n *lit:* base, basis, footing, grounding; establishment, institution, origination, setting up.

founder   n *lit:* initiator, originator, patriarch. **vb** *lit:* go to the bottom, sink; collapse, lurch, subside; go lame, stumble, trip; *fig:* break down, come to nothing, fall through.

fraction   n *lit:* bit, fragment, part, section; chip, particle, scrap, shred, sliver; factor, multiplicand; division, sector, segment.

fragile   adj *lit:* breakable, brittle, delicate, fine, slight, weak; *fig:* feverish, hungover, ill, nauseous, sick.

fragment   n *lit:* bit, fraction, part, section; chip, particle, scrap, shard, sherd, shred, sliver. **vb** *lit:* break up, come apart, disintegrate, shatter, shiver, splinter, split up; disperse, divide, separate, sever.

fragrance **n** *lit:* aroma, bouquet, perfume, scent; *fig:* beauty, radiance, sweetness.

fragrant **adj** *lit:* aromatic, perfumed, scented, sweet-smelling; *fig:* beautiful, radiant.

frail **adj** *lit:* decrepit, delicate, feeble, flimsy, infirm, rickety, slight, unsteady, weak.

frame **n** *lit:* form, shell, skeleton, struts, system; casing, mounting, setting, surround; cradle, support, trestle; body, build, figure, morphology, physique, shape. **vb** *lit:* build, construct, fashion, form, invent, make, model, put together; case, mount, set, surround; codify, compose, couch, define, draft, express, formulate; *fig:* fit (up), fix the blame on.

frank **vb** *lit:* postmark, stamp. **adj** *lit:* blunt, candid, forthright, honest, open, outspoken, plainspoken, sincere, straightforward, uninhibited.

frankly **adv** *lit:* bluntly, candidly, forthrightly, honestly, openly, outspokenly, plainspokenly, sincerely, straightforwardly, uninhibitedly.

fraud **n** *lit:* chicanery, con, deceit, deception, duplicity, forgery, hoax, swindle, trick, trickery; charlatan, con artist, counterfeit, crook, fake, forger, impostor, mountebank, phony, quack, sham, swindler.

fraudulent **adj** *lit:* counterfeit, crooked, deceitful, deceptive, dishonest, duplicitous, phony, sham, spurious, swindling.

free **vb** *lit:* emancipate, let go, let out, liberate, loose, redeem, release, turn loose, unleash, untie; disentangle, extricate, relieve, rescue; clear (of), rid (of). **adj** *lit:* complimentary, for nothing, gratis, gratuitous, on the house; at large, loose, on the loose; at leisure, available, idle, spare, uncommitted, unrestricted; empty, unengaged, uninhabited, unused, vacant; casual, easy, familiar, informal, laid-back, liberal, relaxed, uninhibited; generous, lavish, munificent, openhanded, unsparing; open, unimpeded, unobstructed, unrestrained; allowed, permitted; at liberty, emancipated; autonomous, democratic, independent.

freedom **n** *lit:* autonomy, independence; emancipation, liberty; release; ease, familiarity, frankness, informality, openness; laxity, licence, presumption; exemption, immunity; ability, facility, latitude, leeway, opportunity, power, scope.

freely adv *lit:* cleanly, easily, readily, smoothly; candidly, frankly, openly, sincerely, straightforwardly, uninhibitedly; of one's own volition, spontaneously, voluntarily; unchallenged, unrestrainedly, unrestrictedly; abundantly, copiously, lavishly, liberally, openhandedly.

freeze vb *lit:* chill, frost, ice, ice over, refrigerate; numb; *fig:* fix, stiffen, stop dead, stop in one's tracks, suspend, transfix.

freight n *lit:* cargo, consignment, goods, load, payload, shipment; carriage, transportation.

frequent vb *lit:* be a regular at, hang out at, haunt, patronize, visit often; be most often found at. **adj** *lit:* constant, continual, customary, familiar, habitual, persistent, recurrent, repeated.

fresh adj *lit:* green, handpicked, natural, new, verdant; raw, uncured, unprocessed; latest, modern, novel, recent, up-to-date; additional, auxiliary, different, further, supplementary; bracing, brisk, clean, crisp, invigorating, pure, spanking; blooming, glowing, healthy, rosy, wholesome; *fig:* alert, bright, energetic, invigorated, keen, lively, revived, spry, young; callow, inexperienced, untrained, youthful; bold, brazen, cheeky, familiar, impudent, pert, presumptuous, saucy.

friend n *lit:* confidant, confidante, crony, intimate; buddy, chum, mate, pal; ally, associate, colleague, companion, comrade, partner.

friendly adj *lit:* affable, amiable, amicable, companionable, cordial, genial, kindly, neighborly, sociable, well-disposed; affectionate, attached, chummy, close, familiar, fond, intimate; benevolent, benign, generous, good, helpful, kind, sympathetic.

friendship n *lit:* amity, concord, rapport, regard; affection, attachment, fondness, goodwill, love; alliance, association, companionship, comradeship, partnership.

fright n *lit:* alarm, apprehension, dread, fear, panic, terror, trepidation; start, scare, shock; *fig:* apparition, eyesore, mess, scarecrow, sight.

frighten vb *lit:* alarm, petrify, put the wind up, scare, startle, terrify, unnerve; cow, daunt, intimidate, menace, threaten.

frightening **adj (pr.pt)** *lit:* alarming, dreadful, fearsome, horrendous, petrifying, scary, startling, terrifying, unnerving; daunting, intimidatory, menacing, threatening; creepy, dark, eerie, ghastly, macabre, sinister, spooky.

frightful **adj** *lit:* awful, dreadful, ghastly, grim, horrible, lurid, terrible; *fig:* appalling, insufferable, unpleasant, very bad.

fringe **n** *lit:* border, edging, trimming; tassel; edge, freeze, limits, margin, periphery, rim. **vb** *lit:* border, edge, hem, march on, skirt. **adj** *lit:* alternative, unconventional, unorthodox.

frivolous **adj** *lit:* dizzy, flighty, fun-loving, irresponsible, nonsensical, silly, trivial; childish, insignificant, juvenile, minor, paltry, shallow, trifling, unimportant.

from **prp** *lit:* off, out of; out of the possession of; beginning at, starting at; because of, by reason of; caused by; in comparison with.

frost **n** *lit:* freezing, hoar, rime; *fig:* chill, coldness, frigidity, hauteur; failure, flop.

frosty **adj** *lit:* chilly, frozen, gelid, hoary, icy, wintry; *fig:* gray, white; cold, frigid, unfriendly, unapproachable.

frown **vb** *lit:* glare, glower, scowl; *fig:* look askance (upon).

fruit **n** *lit:* produce, product; berry, drupe, pome; grain, nut, pod, seed; crop, harvest, yield; *fig:* issue, offspring, progeny, young; advantage, benefit, profit, return; consequence, effect, outcome, result.

frustrate **vb** *lit:* baffle, block, bring to nothing, counter, defeat, foil, forestall, nullify, prevent, stymie, thwart; discourage, dishearten; leave unsatisfied.

frustration **n** *lit:* bafflement, blocking, bringing to nothing, countering, defeating, foiling, forestalling, nullification, prevention, thwarting; discouragement; dissatisfaction.

fuel **n** *lit:* kindling, tinder; fodder, food, nourishment; ammunition, materiel; *fig:* encouragement, support; incitement, provocation. **vb** *lit:* arm, charge, feed, fill up, load, prime, stoke; *fig:* encourage, intensify, provoke.

fulfill vb *lit:* accomplish, achieve, attain, complete, conclude, execute, keep, observe, perform, realize, satisfy.

full adj *lit:* brimming, filled, loaded; chock-a-block, crammed, crowded, jammed, packed; gorged, replete, sated, satiated, satisfied; complete, entire, intact; broad, comprehensive, detailed, extensive; exhaustive, maximum, thorough; abundant, copious, plentiful; baggy, capacious, voluminous; buxom, curvaceous, rounded; deep, loud, resonant, rich. adv *lit:* completely, entirely, thoroughly; to the brim; directly, straight; perfectly, very.

fully adv *lit:* abundantly, amply, comprehensively, sufficiently; absolutely, completely, entirely, thoroughly, totally, utterly; altogether, perfectly.

fume n *lit:* gas, smoke, vapor; *fig:* fury, heat, passion, rage. vb *lit:* exude, smoke; *fig:* chafe, fret, rage, seethe, smolder.

fun n *lit:* amusement, diversion, enjoyment, entertainment, excitement, pleasure, recreation, sport; high jinks, japes, jocularity, jollity, larks, skylarking; buffoonery, clowning, teasing; horseplay, playfulness; (in) jest; (make) game (of), (make) sport (of). adj *lit:* amusing, enjoyable, entertaining, exciting, pleasurable.

function n *lit:* business, charge, duty, employment, job, mission, office, post, responsibility, role, task; activity, faculty, operation, purpose, service; equation; *fig:* affair, do, gala, reception, party. vb *lit:* go, operate, run, work.

fund n *lit:* capital, finance(s), resource(s), saving(s), treasury; kitty, pool, reserve, stock, store, vein. vb *lit:* bankroll, endow, finance, float, pay for, stake.

fundamental adj *lit:* basic, elementary, essential, indispensable, key, primary, underlying.

funeral n *lit:* memorial service, obsequies, requiem; burial, cremation, interment.

funnel n *lit:* chimney, smokestack; cone, filter; channel, cylinder, tube. vb *lit:* channel, convey, duct, pass; filter, stream.

funny adj *lit:* amusing, choice, comic, delirious, farcical, hilarious, humorous, killing, rib-tickling, riotous, sidesplitting, waggish; curious, odd, peculiar, queer, strange, suspicious, weird; eccentric, quirky; devious, tricky, underhand.

furious adj *lit:* angry, beside oneself, boiling, enraged, fuming, incensed, livid, maddened, raging; fierce, stormy, tempestuous, tumultuous, turbulent, violent; boisterous, frenzied, unrestrained, wild.

furniture n *lit:* appliances, equipment, fittings, household effects; accessories, accouterments, decor, decoration, trappings.

further vb *lit:* advance, aid, assist, expedite, farther, forward, foster, promote, speed. adj *lit:* additional, extra, more, supplementary; hinder, more distant, remoter. adv *lit:* additionally, again, more, more deeply; at a greater distance, to a greater distance; also, besides, moreover.

fury n *lit:* anger, ire, passion, rage; ferocity, storminess, tempestuousness, turbulence, violence; frenzy, wildness.

fuss n *lit:* bother, bustle, commotion, dust, flap, flurry, fluster, furor, stir, tumult. vb *lit:* be flustered, fidget, flap, fret, worry; bustle (about); create a scene (about), make a song and dance (about).

fussy adj *lit:* choosy, discriminating, finicky, particular, pernickety, picky, selective; difficult, exacting, hard to please; delicate, nice, squeamish; busy, overdetailed, overelaborate.

future n *lit:* days to come, hereafter; outlook, way ahead. adj *lit:* coming, prospective; later, subsequent; destined, eventual; unborn.

G

gain   n *lit:* accretion, enlargement, growth, increase, rise; acquisition, earnings, emolument, increment, profit, return, winnings, yield; advance, advantage, benefit, headway, improvement, progress, victory, win. **vb** *lit:* build up, enlarge, grow, increase, rise; acquire, be paid, bring in, capture, earn, get, glean, make, net, obtain, pick up, profit by, receive, secure, take, win; advance, arrive at, attain to, catch up (on), improve, make headway, progress; *spec:* stall for (time).

gale   n *lit:* cyclone, hurricane, storm, tempest, tornado, typhoon; *fig:* burst, explosion, howl, outburst, peal.

gallant   n *lit:* adventurer, cavalier, daredevil, hero, buck, gentleman; admirer, beau, escort, suitor. **adj** *lit:* audacious, bold, brave, daring, dashing, dauntless, fearless, heroic, intrepid, manly, noble, valiant; chivalrous, courteous, gentlemanly, gracious; grand, imposing, magnificent, splendid.

gallop   vb *lit:* hurry, race, run, speed; dash, fly, sprint.

gamble   n *lit:* bet, speculation, wager; chance, lottery, risk, venture. **vb** *lit:* bet (on), play (at), stake, wager; chance, risk, venture.

game   n *lit:* competition, contest, match, tournament; leisure activity, pastime, recreation, sport; diversion, joke, lark, romp; chase, prey, quarry; *fig:* plan, ploy, scheme, stratagem, tactic; business, line, métier; fun, sport. **adj** *lit:* brave, dogged, fearless, intrepid, persistent, spirited; prepared (for), ready (for), willing (for).

gang   n *lit:* band, clique, crew, group, party, ring, set, squad, team. **vb** *lit:* combine (together), come (together), team (up).

gangster   n *lit:* bandit, brigand, desperado, hood, hoodlum, mobster, racketeer.

gap   n *lit:* break, discontinuity, hiatus, intermission, interstice, interval, lacuna, pause, space, vacuum, void; chink, crack, crevice, hole, opening, recess, rent, rift; *fig:* difference, disparity, divergence.

gape   vb *lit:* open, widen, yawn; goggle, stare.

gardening n *lit:* cultivation, horticulture; growing, planting, sowing; landscaping.

garnish n *lit:* adornment, decoration, embellishment, ornament, trimming; relish. **vb** *lit:* adorn, bedeck, decorate, embellish, ornament, trim; flavor, spice.

gate n *lit:* barrier, boom, grille, wicket; doorway, entrance, exit, portal; channel, passage; lock, sluice, valve; *fig:* attendance, spectators; frame, framework. **vb** *lit:* confine, curfew, detain, keep in, restrict.

gather **vb** *lit:* accumulate, amass, assemble, coacervate, expand, grow, heap up, increase, rise, thicken; collect, convene, group, hoard, muster, pile up, stack up, stockpile; clasp, embrace, enfold, hug; fold, pleat, ruffle, tuck; crop, cull, garner, harvest, pick, pluck, reap; *fig:* conclude, deduce, infer, presume, surmise, understand.

gauge n *lit:* dial, indicator, measure, meter; criterion, example, exemplar, guideline, model, pattern, sample, standard, touchstone, yardstick; bore, caliber, magnitude, span, thickness, width. **vb** *lit:* ascertain, assess, compute, count, determine, evaluate, judge; measure, value, weigh; estimate, guess.

gay n *lit:* homosexual, lesbian. **adj** *lit:* carefree, cheerful, festive, frolicsome, fun-loving, happy, jovial, joyous, light-hearted, merry, sportive, sunny; bright, colorful, flamboyant, gaudy, showy; homosexual, lesbian, Sapphic.

gaze n *lit:* gape, look, regard, stare. **vb** *lit:* gape, look, regard, stare.

gear n *lit:* cog, cogwheel; linkage, machinery, mechanism, transmission, work(s); accessories, apparatus, equipment, implements, instruments, tackle, tools; accouterments, paraphernalia, rigging, supplies, trappings; belongings, effects, kit, stuff, things; attire, clothes, clothing, garments. **vb** *lit:* connect, link, mesh; equip, fit (up), harness (up), rig; adapt (to), adjust (to).

gem n *lit:* jewel, precious stone, stone; *fig:* flower, masterpiece, prize, treasure.

general n *lit:* head, leader, officer; common, ordinary, usual. **adj** *lit:* accepted, accustomed, common, conventional, customary, everyday, habitual, ordinary, popular, prevailing, regular, typical, universal, usual, widespread; all-inclusive, blanket, catholic, collective, comprehensive, sweeping, total; ill-defined, imprecise, indefinite, inexact, unspecific, vague.

generally **adv** *lit:* as a rule, commonly, conventionally, customarily, habitually, largely, mainly, mostly, normally, ordinarily, predominantly, regularly, typically, usually; extensively, popularly, universally, widely.

generate **vb** *lit:* breed, cause, create, engender, initiate, make for, originate, produce, stir up.

generation **n** *lit:* creation, engendering, genesis, origination, procreation, production, propagation; age group, family group; *fig:* age, day, era, period, time.

generosity **n** *lit:* beneficence, bounty, charity, kindness, liberality, munificence; altruism, unselfishness; leniency, magnanimity.

generous **adj** *lit:* beneficent, bounteous, bountiful, charitable, free, kind, lavish, liberal, munificent, openhanded, unstinting; abundant, ample, copious, full, rich; altruistic, unselfish; lenient, magnanimous.

genius **n** *lit:* brain, intellect, mastermind; expert, master, natural, virtuoso; brilliance, flair; faculty, gift, knack, talent.

gentle **adj** *lit:* benign, bland, meek, mild, moderate, peaceable, placid, quiet, temperate; biddable, docile, manageable, tame, tractable; compassionate, humane, lenient, merciful; calm, easy, light, low, serene, slight, soft, tender; gradual, imperceptible, muted, slow; aristocratic, noble, patrician, refined.

genuine **adj** *lit:* authentic, bona fide, legitimate, real, true, veritable; honest, sound, sterling; natural, original, pure, unadulterated; heartfelt, sincere, unaffected, unfeigned.

germ **n** *lit:* bacterium, bug, microbe, micro-organism, virus; bud, corm, seed, spore; egg, gamete, nucleus, ovum; *fig:* beginning, origination.

gesture **n** *lit:* gesticulation, motion, signal; action, deed, demonstration. **vb** *lit:* beckon, gesticulate, motion, signal.

get **vb** *lit:* acquire, come by, come into possession of, inherit, obtain, pick up, receive, succeed to; bring, fetch, procure, secure, win; earn, gain, make, net, realize; arrest, collar, entrap, grab, seize, take; hit, shoot, strike; become, come to be, grow, turn; catch, come down with, contract; contact, reach; *fig:* comprehend, follow, hear, learn, perceive, see, understand; arrange, contrive, fix, organize, wangle; induce, influence, persuade, prevail upon; arrive, come to; affect, stimulate; annoy, irritate; confound, mystify, stump; begin, start; go, leave.

ghost n *lit:* phantom, specter, wraith; spirit; apparition, spook; pseudonymous author; *fig:* glimmer, hint, merest possibility, shadow, suggestion. **vb** *lit:* appear suddenly, flit; author, pen, write for somebody else.

giant n *lit:* colossus, titan, ogre; enormous being; *spec:* large star. **adj** *lit:* colossal, enormous, gargantuan, huge, immense, mammoth, titanic, vast.

gift n *lit:* contribution, donation, present; gratuity, tip; bequest, legacy; oblation, offering, sacrifice; *fig:* attribute, faculty, flair, genius, talent.

gifted adj (pa.pt) *lit:* brilliant, clever, expert, masterly, superb, talented.

girl n *lit:* damsel, gal, lass, maid, maiden; daughter; miss.

give n *lit:* bend, elasticity, flexibility, resilience, resistance. **vb** *lit:* bestow, confer, donate, hand over, impart, issue, present; bring, deliver, fetch, let have, provide with, supply; award, contribute, pay, return; accord, cause, create, grant; administer, deal, dole out, mete out; emit, render, transmit, utter, vent; devote, entrust with, lend; demonstrate, display, evidence, furnish, manifest, show; carry out, do, make, perform; cede, relinquish, surrender, throw (in) the towel, yield; be elastic, bend; open (on to), lead (out to).

glad adj *lit:* delighted, gratified, happy, pleased; willing; cheerful, cheering, gratifying, pleasing.

glamour n *lit:* allure, charisma, enchantment, fascination, magnetism, mysterious quality, spell; gloss, luminescence, radiance.

glare n *lit:* dirty look, frown, gaze, glower, scowl; blaze, brilliance, brightness, dazzle; *fig:* garishness, gaudiness, loudness, showiness. **vb** *lit:* frown, give a dirty look, gaze, glower, lower, scowl; blaze, dazzle, flare, shine brightly.

glaze n *lit:* gloss, lacquer, varnish; slip; finish, luster, polish, shine. **vb**

lit: gloss, lacquer, varnish; coat, laminate; fit windows, glass; *fig:* become vacant, dull, glass over, go blank.

glide   **vb** *lit:* plane, skate, skim, slide, slip; drift, float, sail; coast, freewheel, roll.

glimpse   **n** *lit:* glance, look, peek, peep; flash, sight, view. **vb** *lit:* glance, look quickly, peek, peep, squint; catch sight of, espy, sight, spot.

gloom   **n** *lit:* darkness, dimness, dusk, murk, obscurity, shadow, umbra; *fig:* dejection, depression, despair, despondency, hopelessness, low spirits, unhappiness.

gloomy   **adj** *lit:* cloudy, crepuscular, dark, dim, dusky, murky, obscure, shadowy, somber; *fig:* blue, dejected, depressed, despondent, downcast, glum, in low spirits, morose, unhappy; black, depressing, dismal, dispiriting, doleful, joyless, pessimistic.

glorious   **adj** *lit:* beautiful, bright, brilliant, divine, excellent, fine, gorgeous, great, heavenly, marvelous, radiant, resplendent, splendid, superb, wonderful; celebrated, distinguished, eminent, honored, illustrious, magnificent, noted, triumphant.

glory   **n** *lit:* adoration, beatification, blessing, eulogy, homage, honor, praise, reverence, veneration, worship; magnificence, majesty, pomp, splendor; distinction, eminence, illustriousness, renown; beauty, brightness, brilliance, radiance, resplendence; *fig:* aura, halo. **vb** *lit:* delight (in), exult (in), pride oneself (in), rejoice (in), revel (in).

glow   **n** *lit:* brightness, gleam, glimmer, lambency, light, phosphorescence, radiance; *fig:* blush, flush, reddening; ardor, fervor, heat, passion, warmth. **vb** *lit:* gleam, glimmer, light, radiate, shine; be red-hot, be white-hot, burn, smolder; be suffused, blush, color, flush, redden, tingle.

glue   **n** *lit:* adhesive, gum, tack; cement. **vb** *lit:* gum, paste; affix, cement, stick, tack.

glum   **adj** *lit:* blue, dejected, depressed, despondent, doleful, downcast, gloomy, in low spirits, morose, unhappy; dismal, joyless, pessimistic.

go   **n** *lit:* attempt, bash, crack, shot, stab, try, turn, whirl; drive, dynamism, energy, life, spirit, verve, vigor, vivacity. **vb** *lit:* advance, fare, move, pass, proceed, repair, travel; depart, leave, set off, withdraw; be spent, elapse, flow, lapse, slip away; die, expire, pass away, perish; break down, fail, give way; function, operate, perform, run, work; be, become; attend, be present; develop, fall out, happen, result, turn out; be acceptable, be permitted; extend (between), lead (to), reach (to), span (over), spread (over), stretch (to); refer (to), take (to); contribute (toward), serve (to), tend (toward); blend (together), chime (together), fit (together), harmonize (together).

goal n *lit:* mark, net, target; objective; *fig:* aim, end, object; design, intention, purpose.

god n *lit:* deity, divinity; fetish, idol, image; *fig:* celebrity, hero.

gold(en) adj *lit:* aureate, gilded, gilt, yellow; blond, blonde, flaxen; *fig:* best, glorious, happy, prosperous, rich, successful; excellent, favorable, promising, propitious.

gone adj (pa.pt) *lit:* absent, away, departed, vanished; lost, missing; elapsed, finished, over, past; dead, deceased, done; exhausted, spent, used.

good n *lit:* merit, morality, probity, righteousness, virtue; advantage, benefit, gain, profit, use, usefulness, well-being. adj *lit:* acceptable, capital, commendable, fine, first-rate, great, pleasing, satisfactory, valuable, worthy; fair, halcyon, pleasant, sunny; admirable, beneficent, benevolent, charitable, estimable, humane, honorable, kindly, praiseworthy, upright, virtuous; dutiful, mannerly, obedient, polite, proper, well-behaved; agreeable, congenial, convivial, enjoyable, gratifying; authentic, bona fide, genuine, legitimate, real, true, valid; accomplished, adept, adroit, clever, competent, dexterous, efficient, expert, proficient, skilled, useful; advantageous, beneficial, favorable, helpful, opportune, propitious; healthy, nonpoisonous, salubrious, sound, untainted, wholesome; adequate, ample, considerable, extensive, large, long, solid, substantial; (for) ever.

goods n *lit:* commodities, merchandise, stock, wares; belongings, chattels, effects, gear, paraphernalia, possessions, property, things.

gossip n *lit:* busybody, chatterbox, scandalmonger; chitchat, hearsay, idle talk, scandal, tittle-tattle. vb *lit:* chat, mind other people's business, prattle, tattle, tell tales.

govern vb *lit:* administer, command, control, direct, manage, oversee, pilot, rule, steer; decide, determine, influence; check, contain, curb, discipline, master, restrain, tame.

government n *lit:* administration, authority, execution, rule; assembly, congress, diet, parliament, senate; regime; command, control, direction, management.

grab n *lit:* clutch, grasp, snatch; seizure, sequestration; scoop. **vb** *lit:* capture, catch, clutch, grasp, grip, nab, seize, snatch.

grace n *lit:* ease, elegance, finesse, panache, poise, polish, style, taste; attractiveness, charm; benevolence, charity, favor, goodwill, kindness; clemency, forgiveness, lenience, mercy, pardon; benediction, prayer, thanksgiving; divine influence, salvation; allowance, amnesty, interval, time in hand. **vb** *lit:* adorn, bedeck, decorate, dignify, distinguish, embellish, enhance, honor, ornament.

graceful adj *lit:* elegant, fine, flowing, gracile, natural, smooth, symmetrical.

gradual n *lit:* antiphon, canticle, processional; antiphonal, missal. **adj** *lit:* continuous, gentle, progressive, slow, steady.

grand adj *lit:* august, dignified, elevated, exalted, glorious, imposing, impressive, lofty, lordly, luxurious, magnificent, majestic, opulent, palatial, splendid, stately, sumptuous; highest, main, principal, supreme.

grant n *lit:* allowance, award, endowment, subsidy; allocation, donation. **vb** *lit:* accede to, agree to, cede, concede, consent to; accord, assign, bestow, confer, convey, give, transfer, vouchsafe, yield; acknowledge, admit.

grasp n *lit:* clasp, clutch, grip, hold, possession; *fig:* control, range, reach, scope; comprehension, perception, realization, understanding. **vb** *lit:* catch, clasp, clutch, grab, grip, hold, seize; *fig:* comprehend, get, realize, see, understand.

grass n *lit:* greenery, herbage, pasture, verdure; sward, lawn, turf; cannabis, ganja, hemp, marijuana, pot. **vb** *lit:* lay out a lawn, turf.

grate n *lit:* bars, griddle, grill, grille; fireplace; mesh, screen. **vb** *lit:* mince, shred; abrade, file, grind, rasp, rub, scrape, scratch; *fig:* chafe (on), get (on) one's nerves, jar (on).

grateful adj *lit:* appreciative, thankful; obliged (to).

grave n *lit:* last resting place; crypt, tomb, vault; headstone. **adj** *lit:*

grim, sedate, serious, sober, solemn, somber; critical, dangerous, perilous, severe, threatening, urgent, weighty.

gravity n *lit:* force, weight; *fig:* dignity, earnestness, sobriety, seriousness, solemnity, thoughtfulness; grimness, perilousness, severity; consequence, importance, moment, significance.

gray adj *lit:* cloudy, dark, dim, dismal, drab, gloomy, murky, overcast; ashen, bloodless, pale, pallid, sallow, wan; elderly, hoary, old; *fig:* colorless, dull, neutral; indistinct, misty, vague.

graze n *lit:* abrasion, scrape; scratch; cannon, glance, kiss. vb *lit:* abrade, brush, chafe, scrape; cannon off, glance off, shave, skim, touch.

grease n *lit:* fat, lard; lubricant, oil; lanolin. vb *lit:* lard, lubricate, oil, rub fat over, smear; *fig:* bribe, put money in (one's palm).

greasy adj *lit:* fatty, oily; slick, slippery; *fig:* fawning, ingratiating, slimy, smarmy, unctuous.

great adj *lit:* big, bulky, expansive, extensive, immense, large, long, protracted, vast; considerable, decided, extreme, high, pronounced, strong; critical, crucial, grave, heavy, momentous, serious, significant, solemn; absolute, complete, positive, total; chief, grand, leading, main, principal; august, dignified, idealistic, impressive, lofty, noble; celebrated, distinguished, eminent, illustrious, notable, outstanding, prominent, remarkable; active, enthusiastic, keen; adept, adroit, expert, skilled; excellent, marvelous, terrific, tremendous, wonderful.

greed n *lit:* appetite, covetousness, cupidity, desire, hunger, longing, rapacity, selfishness; esurience, gluttony, insatiability, voracity.

green n *lit:* common, heath; lawn, turf; putting area. vb *lit:* blooming, flourishing, grassy, leafy, verdant; immature, unripe; pliable, supple, tender, unseasoned; ill, nauseous, pallid, sick, unhealthy; environmental, environmentalist; *fig:* callow, inexperienced, new, raw, unpracticed, untrained; credulous, gullible, innocent, naive, unsophisticated; envious, jealous.

greet vb *lit:* address, hail, salute, welcome; *fig:* meet (with), react to (with), respond to (with).

greeting n *lit:* hail, salutation, salute, welcome; compliment(s), regard(s), respect(s).

grief   n *lit:* mourning, sadness, sorrow; heartache, heartbreak, misery, wretchedness; (come to) nothing, (come to) ruin.

grievance   n *lit:* beef, complaint, gripe, moan; grounds for complaint, hardship, wrong.

grieve   vb *lit:* keen, lament, mourn, sorrow, weep (for); distress, hurt, pain, sadden, wound.

grill   n *lit:* grate, grid, gridiron, griddle, rack; barbecue; dining room, kitchen, restaurant; bars, lattice, mesh. vb *lit:* barbecue, broil, fry, roast, toast; *fig:* interrogate, pump, quiz.

grim   adj *lit:* fierce, forbidding, formidable, sinister, terrible; frightful, ghastly, gruesome, hideous, horrible; harsh, implacable, merciless, ruthless, unrelenting; dark, gloomy, menacing, sullen, threatening.

grip   n *lit:* clasp, clutch, grasp, hold, possession; footing, leverage, purchase; traveling bag; clip; handle, haft, shaft; *fig:* clutches, control, influence, mastery, power; comprehension, perception, understanding. vb *lit:* clasp, clutch, grasp, hold, latch on to, seize; *fig:* absorb, engross, enthrall, entrance, fascinate, rivet.

groan   n *lit:* moan, sigh. vb *lit:* moan, sigh; call painfully, utter despairingly; *fig:* be burdened, be laden.

groove   n *lit:* channel, cutting, furrow, rift, score, trench; *fig:* routine, rut. vb *lit:* channel, flute, furrow, rifle, score.

gross   n *lit:* bulk, entirety, whole; twelve dozen, 144. vb *lit:* bring in, earn, make, take. adj *lit:* bulky, corpulent, fat, hulking, massive, thick; coarse, crude, improper, indecent, indelicate, offensive, ribald, rude, vulgar; boorish, crass, ignorant, insensitive, unfeeling, unsophisticated; blatant, flagrant, glaring, manifest, plain, utter; outrageous, shocking; *spec:* (earnings, income) before tax, weight (of goods) including container.

ground   n *lit:* earth, land, soil, terra firma; arena, field, park, pitch; floor; *spec:* (electrical) earth, earthing. vb *lit:* lay down, put down; base, establish, pitch, set; coach (in), educate (in), initiate (in), instruct (in), teach (in), tutor (in). adj **(pa.pt)** *lit:* crushed, milled, powdered, pulverized; filed (down), sanded (down); eroded (away); *fig:* oppressed.

group   n *lit:* band, bunch, cluster, collection, company, gang, gathering, pack, party, set; class, category. vb *lit:* assemble, associate, cluster, collect, gather, get together; arrange, assort, bracket together, classify, marshal, order, put together, sort.

grow **vb** *lit:* develop, germinate, shoot, sprout; breed, cultivate, farm, produce, propagate; arise (from), spring (from), stem (from); augment, enlarge, expand, extend, get bigger, increase, spread, stretch, swell; advance, flourish, multiply, progress; *fig:* become, come to be, get, turn.

growth **n** *lit:* development, germination, shoot, sprout; cultivation, propagation; evolution; augmentation, enlargement, expansion, extension, increase, spread, stretching, swelling; cancer, lump, tumor; advance, flourishing, multiplication, progress, proliferation.

grueling **adj** *lit:* arduous, backbreaking, demanding, exhausting, grinding, laborious, punishing, stiff, taxing.

gruesome **adj** *lit:* bloody, ghastly, gory, grim, grisly, horrible, horrific, macabre, sickening, terrible.

guarantee **n** *lit:* assurance, collateral, pledge, security, warranty. **vb** *lit:* answer for, insure, pledge, promise, stand behind, vouch for, warrant.

guard **n** *lit:* defender, lookout, sentinel, sentry, warder, watchman; custodian, jailer, screw; escort; buffer, bumper, pad, safety screen, shield; vigilance, wariness, watchfulness. **vb** *lit:* defend, patrol, police, protect, secure, watch over; escort, mind, tend.

guardian **n** *lit:* keeper, protector, trustee, warden; curator, custodian, escort, guard, warder.

guess **n** *lit:* conjecture, hypothesis, speculation, supposition, surmise, theory. **vb** *lit:* conjecture, estimate, fancy, hazard, hypothesize, imagine, reckon, surmise.

guest **n** *lit:* caller, visitor; boarder, lodger.

guide **n** *lit:* beacon, key, landmark, pointer, sign, signal, signpost; directory, handbook, manual; chaperon, conductor, escort, leader, pilot, usher; *fig:* master, paradigm; example, inspiration. **vb** *lit:* control, direct, handle, maneuver, steer; conduct, escort, lead, shepherd, usher; advise, counsel.

guilt **n** *lit:* blameworthiness, culpability; misconduct, wrongdoing; bad conscience, self-condemnation, shame; dishonor.

guilty adj *lit:* culpable, responsible, wrong; ashamed, contrite, hangdog, remorseful, rueful, sorry.

gun n *lit:* firearm; cannon, gat, piece, rod, shooter; pistol, revolver, rifle, shotgun; starting pistol; *fig:* nozzle, spray, syringe; accelerator, throttle. **vb** *lit:* hunt (down), shoot (down); *fig:* hunt (for), look (for); accelerate, race.

gutter n *lit:* conduit, drain, pipe; ditch, groove, scupper, trench, trough. **vb** *lit:* flicker, smoke.

guts n *lit:* bowels, intestines; entrails, tripe, viscera; *fig:* backbone, bravery, courage, fortitude, nerve, pluck, spunk; insides, machinery, works.

guy n *lit:* man; chap, fellow, lad. **vb** *lit:* caricature, make fun of, send up, take off.

gypsy n *lit:* tinker, traveler; rover; vagrant.

H

habit n *lit:* custom, fashion, practice, routine, rule, tendency, way; idiosyncrasy, mannerism, proclivity, trait, wont; consuetude, usage; addiction, dependence; composition, constitution, frame, makeup, nature, structure; apparel, costume, dress, garb, garment.

hail n *lit:* call, cheer, greeting, shout, yell; greetings, salutation; bombardment, rain, shower, volley; *fig:* shouting distance; *spec:* frozen rain, ice. **vb** *lit:* address, call to, greet, shout to, yell at; accost, flag down, wave down; acclaim, applaud, glorify, honor, salute; cascade (down), pelt, pour (down), rain; come (from), have started (from), originate (from).

hair n *lit:* locks, mane, mop, tresses; filament, strand, thread, villus; down, fluff, fur; *fig:* fraction, narrow margin, whisker; split second.

hairy adj *lit:* hirsute, shaggy, woolly; bearded, stubbly, unshaven, whiskered, whiskery; downy, fleecy, flocculent, furry; awned, tufted; *fig:* chancy, hair-raising, hazardous, risky.

hall n *lit:* corridor, passageway; entrance, entry, foyer, lobby, vestibule; auditorium, chamber, meeting place, nave, salon; dormitory, residence; manor house, mansion.

halt n *lit:* pause, standstill, stop; impasse; close, end, termination. **vb** *lit:* draw up, hold still, pause, pull up, stop; break off, cease, desist, take a rest; arrest, check, curb, terminate; block, obstruct.

hammer n *lit:* gavel, mallet, striking head; clapper. **vb** *lit:* bang, beat, hit, strike; drive; fashion, forge, make, shape; *fig:* clobber, defeat, drub, thrash, trounce; din (into), drum (into), grind (into); drudge (away at), keep (on at), plug (on away at), work (away at).

hamper n *lit:* basket. **vb** *lit:* delay, encumber, handicap, hinder, hold back, hold up, impede, obstruct.

hand n *lit:* mitt, paw; assistance, help, support; influence, part, role, share; crewman, employee, laborer, operative, sailor, worker; clap, ovation, round of applause; artistry, deftness, dexterity, skill; calligraphy, handwriting, longhand, script, writing; *fig:* (in) order, (in) progress; (in) readiness, (in) reserve; (at) one's command, (on) tap. **vb** *lit:* deliver, give, pass; assist, help.

handicap   **n** *lit:* defect, disability, impairment; disadvantage, difficulty, drawback, encumbrance, hindrance, impediment, limitation, penalty, restriction, stumbling block; edge, head start. **vb** *lit:* encumber, hamper, hinder, hold back, hold up, impede, limit, restrain, restrict, retard.

handle   **n** *lit:* grip, haft, hilt, knob, lever, stock, switch; *fig:* agnomen, cognomen, name, nickname, praenomen, title. **vb** *lit:* feel, grasp, hold, pick up, touch; control, direct, manage, manipulate, maneuver, use, wield; cope with, deal with, take care of, treat; deal in, trade in, traffic in.

handsome   **adj** *lit:* attractive, becoming, comely, fine, good-looking, personable; ample, bountiful, large; generous, liberal, magnanimous.

happen   **vb** *lit:* befall, come about, come to pass, eventuate, occur, pass, take place; fall out, turn out; be done (to), transpire (to); appear, arise, crop up, materialize.

happily   **adv** *lit:* cheerfully, contentedly, delightedly, gaily, gladly, joyfully, pleasurably, willingly; appropriately, suitably; felicitously, harmoniously, successfully; fortunately, luckily, providentially; blithely, casually, unwittingly.

happiness   **n** *lit:* cheerfulness, contentment, delight, enjoyment, gaiety, gladness, harmony, joy, joyfulness, joyousness, lightheartedness, pleasure; beatitude, blessedness, jubilation; bliss, ecstasy.

happy   **adj** *lit:* cheerful, contented, delighted, gay, glad, gratified, joyful, joyous, pleased, sunny; blissful, ecstatic, elated, exultant, overjoyed, rapturous; over the moon, thrilled, walking on air; beatific, blessed, rapt; appropriate, apt, opportune, timely; favorable, felicitous, promising, successful; fortunate, lucky, providential; blithe, casual, unwitting.

harass   **vb** *lit:* badger, beleaguer, chivy, harry, hassle, hound, pester, plague, trouble, vex, worry; annoy, bug, exasperate, torment.

harassment   **n** *lit:* badgering, chivying, harrying, hassling, hounding, pestering; molestation, persecution.

harbor   **n** *lit:* anchorage, marina, port, quay, wharf, yacht basin; *fig:* haven, mooring, shelter; asylum, refuge, retreat, sanctuary. **vb** *lit:*

accommodate, lodge, provide refuge for, shelter; conceal, hide, protect, shield; entertain, foster, hold, nurse, retain.

hard **adj** *lit:* compact, firm, inflexible, rigid, solid, stiff, strong, tough, unyielding; bare, indisputable, physical, plain, practical, real, unvarnished; arduous, backbreaking, complex, complicated, difficult, formidable, intricate, involved, knotty, laborious, rigorous, strenuous, thorny, uphill; bad, disagreeable, distressing, grievous, harsh, painful, ugly, unpleasant; fierce, forceful, powerful, violent; cold, grim, implacable, mean, near, obdurate, pitiless, ruthless, stern, strict, stingy, unfeeling, unsparing; acrimonious, bitter, hostile, rancorous; *spec:* alcoholic (drinks); calciferous (water); penetrative (rays). **adv** *lit:* assiduously, determinedly, diligently, energetically, forcefully, industriously, intensely, intently, keenly, persistently, powerfully, strenuously, strongly, vigorously, violently; badly, harshly, laboriously, painfully, roughly, slowly, with difficulty; completely, fully; firmly, solidly, tightly; close, near; *spec:* frozen, solid; (hold) tight.

harden **vb** *lit:* set, solidify, stiffen; cake, congeal, freeze, jell; anneal, temper; *fig:* brace, fortify, nerve, steel, strengthen; accustom, habituate, inure, season, train; brutalize, toughen.

hardly **adv** *lit:* barely, just, only just, scarcely; probably not, surely not; with difficulty.

hardship **n** *lit:* burden, difficulty, encumbrance, labor, oppression, privation, suffering, trial, tribulation, trouble.

harm **n** *lit:* damage, hurt, ill, impairment, injury; detriment, disservice, mischief. **vb** *lit:* damage, hurt, ill-treat, ill-use, impair, injure, maltreat, spoil.

harmful **adj** *lit:* damaging, hurtful, impairing, injurious, noxious; baneful, deleterious, detrimental, malignant, mischievous, pernicious; destructive, ruinous.

harmless **adj** *lit:* innocuous; not poisonous, safe; gentle, inoffensive, mild.

harmony **n** *lit:* euphony, mellifluousness, musicality; arrangement, chord structure, part writing; *fig:* accord, agreement, balance, compatibility, concord, consonance, correspondence, rapport, unanimity, unity; amicability, friendship, sympathy, understanding.

harsh adj *lit:* discordant, dissonant, strident; grating, jarring, rasping, raucous, rough; brutal, cruel, dour, draconian, hard, pitiless, relentless, ruthless, stern, strict, unfeeling, unpleasant; austere, grim, severe, Spartan; bleak, cold, sharp, unrelenting; acrid, astringent, bitter, pungent, sour.

harvest n *lit:* gathering, gleaning, reaping; crop, produce, yield; *fig:* fruits, result, return; effect, product. **vb** *lit:* gather, glean, reap; pick, pluck; mow; *fig:* accumulate, amass, collect, garner, take in.

haste n *lit:* dispatch, expedition, hurrying, urgency; hustle, impetuosity, rush.

hasty adj *lit:* impetuous, impulsive, precipitate, rash, thoughtless; cursory, fleeting, perfunctory, short, superficial; brusque, fiery, impatient, irascible, quick-tempered.

hate n *lit:* abhorrence, detestation, loathing, odium, repugnance, revulsion; animosity, antagonism, antipathy, dislike. **vb** *lit:* abhor, be repelled by, detest, have an aversion to, loathe; be antagonistic toward, dislike intensely; be loath (to), be sorry (to), be unwilling (to).

haul n *lit:* drag, heave, pull; distance, journey, trip; catch, harvest, yield; *fig:* booty, loot, spoils, swag, takings. **vb** *lit:* drag, heave, pull, tug; draw, tow, trail; carry, hump, lug; cart, convey, move, transport; *spec:* turn, veer (of a sailing ship, of the wind).

haunt n *lit:* base, habitat, hangout, patch, stamping ground, territory; den, hidey-hole, lair, refuge, retreat, sanctum. **vb** *lit:* come back, frequent, return, visit; beset, obsess, prey on, weigh on.

have vb *lit:* hold, keep, own, possess, retain; carry, stock, store; comprehend, contain, include, take in; accept, get, obtain, receive, secure, take; acquire, gain; enjoy, experience, feel, meet with, suffer, sustain, undergo; allow, consider, endure, entertain, permit, put up with, tolerate; be a parent of, bear, bring forth, deliver, give birth to; be a relative of; assert, declare, maintain; engage in, carry on; cheat, deceive, fool, hoax, outwit, swindle, trick; be compelled (to), be forced (to), be obliged (to), be required (to), ought (to); cause to, force to, oblige to, require to; cause to be, require to be.

head n *lit:* braincase, cranium, skull; block, loaf, noddle, nut, poll; apex, crest, crown, peak, summit, tip, top; climax, crisis, culmination, denouement, turning point; cape, foreland, promontory; boss, captain, chief, commander, director, leader, manager, master, principal; fore, forefront, front, van; beginning, origin, rise, source, start; ability, aptitude, brains, flair, intelligence, mentality, mind, understanding; capacity, faculty; division, section, subject, topic; bathroom, lavatory, men's room, ladies' room, toilet, water closet; individual, person, soul; *spec:* chuck (on a drill, a lathe); cluster (of flowers); froth (on beer); pickup (on a tape head); pressure (of steam in a steam engine); (lose one's) self-control; striking end (of a hammer). **vb** *lit:* be on top of, cap, crown, top; go first of, lead; excel, outdo, outstrip; be in charge of, command, control, direct, govern, manage, rule, run; aim (for), make (for), set off (for), steer (for); go, move, travel, turn; decapitate, lop, poll; butt; cut (off), fend (off), ward (off).

heading   n *lit:* headline, rubric, title; division, section; bearing, compass-point, direction; *spec:* drift, exploratory tunnel (in a mine), hitting a ball with one's head (soccer), leading (a group, revolt, etc.).

headquarters   n *lit:* base, barracks, camp, command center, home, living quarters, main office, offices, post, residence, station.

heal   vb *lit:* cure, remedy, restore; knit, mend, regenerate; *fig:* patch up, reconcile, settle, smooth over.

healing   n *lit:* curing, officinal, remedying, restoration; knitting, mending, regeneration; *fig:* reconciliation, smoothing things over. **adj (pr.pt)** *lit:* curative, medicinal, remedial, restorative, therapeutic; comforting, soothing.

health   n *lit:* condition, fitness, shape, soundness, well-being.

healthy   adj *lit:* fit, hale and hearty, in fine fettle, in good condition, in the pink, sound, well; active, flourishing, robust, strong, sturdy; beneficial, bracing, invigorating, nourishing, wholesome; hygienic, sanitary.

hear   vb *lit:* listen to; attend to, hearken to, heed, take in; catch, pick up; be informed, be told, find, gather, learn, understand; examine, judge, try.

heart   n *lit:* cardiac muscle; center, core, hub, kernel, middle, nucleus; *fig:* mind, soul; affection, love; feeling, sentiment, sympathy; disposition, nature, temperament; bottle, courage, fortitude, guts, nerve;

determination, resolution, spirit; energy, enthusiasm; crux, essence, marrow, pith, root; (by) memory, (by) rote.

heartless adj *lit:* brutal, callous, cold, cruel, harsh, merciless, pitiless, unfeeling.

heat n *lit:* high temperature, temperature, warmth; torridity; febrility, fever, feverishness; blaze, fire, flame; *fig:* intensity, fervor, vehemence; agitation, excitement, passion; pressure; *spec:* estrus (in female mammals); eliminator, preliminary race, qualifier. vb *lit:* keep warm, make hot, warm (up); cook, microwave, put on the boil; *fig:* excite, inflame, rouse, stimulate.

heave n *lit:* haul, pull, tow, tug; fling, pitch, throw; convulsion, surge, swell; *spec:* dislocation, displacement (of a geological stratum). vb *lit:* drag, haul, pull, tow, tug; hoist (up), lift (up); fling, hurl, pitch, throw, toss; billow, convulse, rise, surge, swell; breathe heavily, give vent to, pant, utter, wheeze; gag, retch.

heaven n *lit:* garden of Eden, paradise; life to come, next world, Nirvana; Elysian fields, happy hunting ground, place of the dead, Valhalla; firmament, sky; *fig:* bliss, ecstasy, joy, rapture.

hectic adj *lit:* excited, feverish, frantic, frenetic, frenzied; flushed, rosy; fevered; atrophied, consumptive, painfully thin, wasted.

height n *lit:* altitude, elevation; tallness; crag, fell, rocky point; hill, mountain, peak, summit; apex, crest, crown, pinnacle, top, zenith; climax, culmination, limit, maximum, ultimate; acme, embodiment, epitome; eminence, grandeur.

hell n *lit:* Gehenna, Hades, infernal regions, netherworld, Tartarus, underworld; abyss, bottomless pit, eternal fires, fire and brimstone, weeping and wailing and gnashing of teeth; purgatory; *fig:* agony, martyrdom, nightmare, ordeal, torment; commotion, din, uproar; deuce, dickens, heck.

help n *lit:* aid, assistance, succor, support; avail, benefit, use; collaboration, cooperation; amelioration, facilitation, improvement; balm, relief, remedy; assistant, worker. vb *lit:* aid, assist, lend a hand, succor, support; abet, be with, collaborate with, cooperate with; serve; ameliorate, facilitate, improve; alleviate, cure, remedy; avoid, prevent oneself from; abstain from, keep from, refrain from, resist.

helpful

helpful   adj *lit:* accommodating, considerate, cooperative, kind, neighborly; beneficial, profitable, serviceable, useful; constructive, practical, productive, supportive, timely.

helpless   adj *lit:* defenseless, exposed, unprotected, vulnerable; feeble, incapable, weak; impotent, powerless; incompetent.

hence   adv *lit:* and so, ergo, for which reason, therefore; from now, from this time; from here, from this place; from that source.

herald   n *lit:* announcer, crier, messenger; forerunner, harbinger, precursor, token. **vb** *lit:* pave the way, precede, presage, usher in; announce, broadcast, proclaim, publish, trumpet.

hereditary   adj *lit:* congenital, genetic, inheritable, transmissible; ancestral, bequeathed, family, handed down, inherited, patrimonial.

hero   n *lit:* popular figure; conqueror, victor; celebrity, demigod, idol, star, superstar; champion; lead, principal character, protagonist.

heroic   adj *lit:* audacious, bold, brave, courageous, daring, fearless, gallant, intrepid, valiant; epic, legendary, mythological; *fig:* elaborate, exaggerated, extravagant, grandiose, inflated.

hesitant   adj *lit:* reluctant, unwilling; diffident, halting, irresolute, timid, uncertain, vacillating, wavering.

hesitate   vb *lit:* be reluctant (to), be unwilling (to), scruple (to); delay, pause, wait; dither, falter, shilly-shally, vacillate, waver.

hidden   adj (pa.pt) *lit:* cloaked, concealed, covert, masked, shrouded, veiled; cryptic, occult, secret; dark, obscure; ulterior, clandestine, furtive, underhand.

hide   n *lit:* concealment, hiding place. **vb** *lit:* conceal, cover, mask, screen, shroud, veil; bury, cache; hush up, keep secret, suppress; camouflage, disguise; go to ground, go underground, hole up, lie low.

hideous   adj *lit:* frightful, grotesque, gruesome, horrible, monstrous, ugly, unsightly; appalling, awful, dreadful, repulsive, sickening, terrible.

high   adj *lit:* lofty, tall; elevated, soaring, towering; chief, eminent, exalted, important, main, noble, prominent, ruling, superior; capital, grave, serious; extreme, great, powerful; dear, expensive, steep, stiff; extravagant, grand, lavish, rich; arrogant, domineering, haughty, lofty, overbearing, proud; latest, most advanced; acute, piercing, sharp, shrill, soprano, treble; gamy, putrescent, rancid; elated, exhilarated, merry, tipsy; euphoric, inebriated, intoxicated, spaced out, stoned, turned on. **adv** *lit:* aloft, far up, way above.

hill   n *lit:* down, fell, tor; hummock, knoll, kop, kopje, mound; gradient, incline, rise, slope.

hindrance   n *lit:* check, encumbrance, handicap, impediment, limitation, restriction; barrier, hurdle, obstacle, obstruction, stumbling block; difficulty, drawback, snag.

hint   n *lit:* clue, intimation, pointer, suggestion, tip, whisper, word, wrinkle; implication, innuendo, insinuation; allusion, mention; dash, speck, suspicion, taste, tinge, trace, whiff. **vb** *lit:* give a clue, suggest, tip off; imply, insinuate; allude, mention.

hire   n *lit:* rent, rental; charge, fee, payment, price, wages. **vb** *lit:* charter, lease, rent; lease out, let, rent out; employ, engage, sign up, take on.

historic   adj *lit:* earth-shattering, epoch-making; great, important, momentous, significant; consequential, seminal; famous, illustrious.

historical   adj *lit:* chronicled, documented, recorded; attested, authentic, factual, verified; antiquated, archaic, old-fashioned, outmoded; of olden days.

history   n *lit:* ancient days, antiquity, olden days, past, yesterday; annals, archives, chronicles, records; account, recital, story; autobiography, biography.

hit   n *lit:* blow, buffet, impact, knock; clout, cuff, punch, rap, slap, smack, swipe, tap, thump, thwack, wallop, whack; cannon, collision; shot, stroke; *fig:* fluke, lucky chance; sensation, smash, success, triumph, winner; dig, sarcasm, thrust, witticism; assassination, murder. **vb** *lit:* bang, bash, beat, belt, buffet, clobber, clout, cuff, knock, punch, slap, smack, strike, thump, wallop, whack; bang into, bump, cannon into, collide with, crash into, run into; damage, devastate, overwhelm; *fig:* affect, influence, leave a mark on, touch; attain, gain, reach; accomplish, achieve; come across, encounter; assassinate, murder.

hoard   n *lit:* cache, stockpile, treasure trove; heap, mass, pile, store. **vb**

lit: cache, garner, lay up, put by, stash away, stockpile; amass, heap up, pile up, store.

hobby n *lit:* avocation, leisure activity, pastime, pursuit, sideline; amusement, entertainment.

hold n *lit:* clutch, grasp, grip; footing, leverage, purchase; *fig:* dominance, influence, power, pull, sway; *spec:* cargo space (on a ship); fermata, pause (in musical dynamics). **vb** *lit:* clasp, cling to, clutch, grasp, grip; have, keep, retain; be in possession of, occupy, possess; bear, carry, support, sustain, take; accommodate, be large enough for, contain, seat; arrest, detain, restrain, stop; confine, imprison; *fig:* believe, consider, deem, judge, reckon, think; be in force, continue, exist, last, operate, persist, remain, stand; call, conduct, convene, convoke, organize, run; be enough for, satisfy; adhere (to), stick (to).

hole n *lit:* aperture, crack, fissure, opening, orifice, outlet, puncture, rent, tear; cavity, gap; excavation, hollow, pit, shaft; burrow, den, earth, lair, scrape; *fig:* dive, dump, joint; fix, jam, mess, spot; discrepancy, fallacy, fault, flaw, inconsistency. **vb** *lit:* sink.

holiday n *lit:* break, furlough, leave, leisure time, time off; feast, festival, saint's day.

hollow n *lit:* basin, bowl, concavity, crater, dell, depression, hole, pit, trough; crease, dimple; palm; channel, groove. **adj** *lit:* empty, vacant; deep-set, indented, sunken; *fig:* booming, deep, dull, resonant, sepulchral; empty, meaningless, pointless, specious, useless; artificial, false, flimsy, insincere. **adv** *fig:* dully, resonantly, sepulchrally; falsely, insincerely; completely, thoroughly, totally, utterly.

holy adj *lit:* consecrated, hallowed, sacred, sacrosanct; divine, godly, numinous; pious, religious, saintly; blessed, venerable; *fig:* awesome, dreadful, unearthly; unholy.

home n *lit:* fireside, hearth, household; abode, domicile, dwelling, habitation, place, residence; habitat, nest; base; asylum, hall of residence, institution, refuge, sanatorium; *fig:* (at) ease (in); *spec:* plate (in baseball). **vb** *lit:* be directed (in on), be guided (in on). **adj** *lit:* domiciliary, household, residential; own, private; familiar, normal, usual; national; local. **adv** *lit:* to one's domicile, to one's household, to one's residence; to one's country; *fig:* to one's destination, to one's goal, to where one belongs.

honest adj *lit:* ethical, honorable, straight, true, truthful, veracious; decent, law-abiding, reputable, upright, virtuous; reliable, trustworthy; authentic, bona fide, genuine, real; candid, frank, open, sincere; equitable, fair, good, just.

honesty n *lit:* ethics, honor, truthfulness, veracity; faithfulness, fidelity; decency, integrity, legality, morality, probity, uprightness, virtue; authenticity, genuineness, good faith, straightforwardness, trustworthiness; candor, frankness, openness, sincerity; equity, fairness, goodness, justice.

honor n *lit:* credit, esteem, fame, glory, kudos, prestige, repute; commendation, glorification, homage, recognition, reverence, veneration; dignity, high rank; decency, honesty, integrity, morality, probity, uprightness, virtue; chastity, modesty, purity, virginity; compliment, grace, privilege; decoration, distinction, title; *spec:* high trump (in cards). **vb** *lit:* acclaim, celebrate, glorify, pay homage to, venerate; adore, hallow, revere, worship; dignify, ennoble, exalt; decorate; compliment, grace; commend, praise; be faithful to, discharge, fulfill, keep, perform; acknowledge, credit; *spec:* accept, cash, clear, pass, pay (a monetary transaction).

honorable adj *lit:* decent, law-abiding, reputable, upright, virtuous; equitable, ethical, fair, good, honest, just, moral, principled, reliable, trustworthy; creditable, estimable, noble, proper, right.

hop n *lit:* jump, skip, step; twitch; leg, short flight; dance, dancing party. **vb** *lit:* jump on one leg; bound, skip, spring; fly across, take a short flight; *fig:* beat (it), get out of (it).

hope n *lit:* desire, dream, expectancy, wish; ambition; anticipation, expectation; optimism; grounds for optimism, promise. **vb** *lit:* aspire (to), long (to), look forward (to); long (for), wait (for); earnestly wish, trust.

hopeful adj *lit:* expectant, optimistic, sanguine; auspicious, encouraging, heartening, promising, propitious.

hopeless adj *lit:* irreparable, irreversible; futile, impossible, impracticable, pointless, useless, vain; incompetent, inferior, worthless; despairing, desperate.

horrible adj *lit:* awful, dreadful, frightful, ghastly, grim, gruesome, hideous, repugnant, repulsive; beastly, disagreeable, mean, nasty, unkind.

horrid *adj lit:* awful, beastly, disagreeable, malevolent, malignant, mean, nasty, offensive, spiteful, unpleasant.

horrify *vb lit:* appall, outrage, shock; disgust, nauseate, revolt, sicken.

horror *n lit:* abhorrence, disgust, nausea, repugnance, revulsion; dread, fright; *fig:* disgusting thing, loathsome creature, monster.

hospitable *adj lit:* generous, gracious, liberal, receptive, welcoming.

hospitality *n lit:* welcome; reception; generosity, liberality, kindness.

host *n lit:* innkeeper, landlord, proprietor; anchor man, master of ceremonies, presenter; parasiticized object; army, horde, mass, mob, multitude, vast number; *spec:* bread (at Communion services). *vb lit:* introduce, present; entertain.

hostage *n lit:* captive, pawn; security.

hostile *adj lit:* adverse, antagonistic, bellicose, belligerent, inimical, opposed, unfriendly.

hot *adj lit:* boiling, scorching, searing, sultry, sweltering, torrid, tropical; burning, fiery, flaming, heated, roasting, scalding; curried, peppery, spicy; *fig:* ardent, fervent, intense, passionate, vehement; fierce, fiery, impetuous, lustful, stormy; approved, popular. *adv lit:* close, immediately.

hotel *n lit:* boarding house, caravansary, guesthouse, hostel, rooming house; hospice, inn; chalet, motel.

house *n lit:* building, dwelling, edifice, residence; abode, domicile, home; clan, family, line, lineage; business, company, establishment, firm, organization. *vb lit:* accommodate, contain, cover, harbor, keep, put up, sheathe, shelter, take in.

household *n lit:* family, folks, home, ménage, people; establishment. *adj lit:* domestic, family; about the house.

however *adv lit:* by what means, how on earth, in what way; no matter how, to whatever extent. *cnj lit:* all the same, at all events, but, despite this, nevertheless, nonetheless, still, yet.

hug   n *lit:* clasp, clinch, embrace, squeeze; grip, hold. **vb** *lit:* clasp, embrace, enfold, hold, squeeze; *fig:* cleave to, skirt, stay close to; be protective toward, cling on to, guard, hang on to, nurse.

huge   adj *lit:* colossal, cyclopean, enormous, gargantuan, gigantic, immense, mammoth, massive, monumental, prodigious, titanic, tremendous, vast.

human   n *lit:* individual, man, person, woman; mortal, soul. **adj** *lit:* anthropoid; mortal; approachable, kindly, understanding; forgivable, natural, understandable; fallible, vulnerable.

humane   adj *lit:* benign, compassionate, gentle, good-natured, kindly, sympathetic, understanding; charitable, forgiving, lenient, merciful.

humanity   n *lit:* human race, mankind, people everywhere; benevolence, brotherly love, compassion, generosity, gentleness, kindliness, kindness, sisterly love, sympathy, toleration, understanding; leniency, mercy.

humble   vb *lit:* abase, degrade, demean, humiliate; bring down, chasten, disgrace, mortify, shame, subdue, take down a peg. **adj** *lit:* modest, self-effacing, unassuming; deferential, obsequious, respectful, subservient; common, lowly, obscure, ordinary, simple, undistinguished, unpretentious; commonplace, insignificant, low, mean, plebeian, poor, unimportant.

humid   adj *lit:* muggy, steamy, sticky, sultry; damp, moist.

humor   n *lit:* mood, spirits, state of mind, temper; caprice, fancy, freak, vagary, whim; comedy, drollery, jocularity, joking, pleasantries, wit, witticisms. **vb** *lit:* accommodate, gratify, indulge, pander to; acquiesce in, flatter.

humorous   adj *lit:* amusing, comical, funny, waggish, witty; droll, facetious, jocose, playful.

hunger   n *lit:* ravening, starvation; appetite; emptiness; craving, desire, longing, need, yearning. **vb** *lit:* raven (for), starve (for); have an appetite (for); crave, long, lust, pine, yearn.

hungry   adj *lit:* ravening, starved, starving; empty, famished, peckish; *fig:* eager (for), greedy (for).

hunt   n *lit:* chase, pursuit; quest; search; *spec:* pack (of hounds). **vb** *lit:*

chase, harry, hound, pursue; follow, stalk, track down; forage (for), look (for), search (for), seek.

hurricane n *lit:* cyclone, gale, storm, tempest, tornado, typhoon.

hurry n *lit:* dash, rush; flurry, haste, speed; dispatch, urgency; commotion. **vb** *lit:* dash, fly, race, run, rush; accelerate, expedite, hasten, quicken, speed; hustle, push on, spur on.

hurt n *lit:* injury, lesion, sore, trauma, wound; bruise; distress, pain; damage, mischief, wrong. **vb** *lit:* injure, wound; bruise, damage, harm, impair; ache, be sore, pain, sting, throb; *fig:* aggrieve, cut to the quick, distress, pain, sadden. **adj (pa.pt)** *lit:* injured, wounded; bruised, damaged, harmed, impaired; in pain, sore; *fig:* aggrieved, cut to the quick, distressed, miffed, offended, pained, piqued, saddened.

husband n *lit:* man, partner; hubby, old man; spouse. **vb** *lit:* conserve, garner, hoard, save, store; be steward over, be thrifty with, manage carefully.

hut n *lit:* cabin, hogan, lean-to, shack, shanty, shed.

hypnotic n *lit:* anesthetic, sedative; narcotic, opiate; drug. **adj** *lit:* mesmerizing, spellbinding, trance-inducing; narcotic, opiate; sedative, soporific.

hypocrisy n *lit:* double standards, inconsistency; cant, duplicity, insincerity, speciousness.

hypocrite n *lit:* charlatan, faker, fraud, impostor, mountebank, sham.

hypothesis n *lit:* postulate, premise, proposition, supposition, theory; conjecture, possibility, suggestion.

hypothetical adj *lit:* academic, conjectural, posited, postulated, putative, speculative, theoretical; proposed, supposed.

I

icy adj *lit:* arctic, biting, bitter, boreal, cryogenic, freezing, frosty, frozen, gelid, raw; glassy, slippery, slippy, wintry; *fig:* cold, distant, frigid, glacial, hostile, inimical, stony.

idea n *lit:* hypothesis, suggestion, supposition, theory; design, plan, scheme; concept, conception, thought; fancy, notion, whim; belief, conviction, opinion, view, viewpoint; aim, end, intention, meaning, object, objective, purpose; import, reasoning, significance; clue, hint, inkling, suspicion; feeling, impression; essence, form, gist, nub.

ideal n *lit:* paragon, perfection; example, exemplar, model, paradigm, pattern; embodiment, epitome; standard(s); principle(s), value(s). adj *lit:* consummate, optimal, perfect; exemplary, model; classic, complete, quintessential, supreme; conceptual, hypothetical, imaginary, notional, paradisical, theoretical, unattainable, utopian.

idealistic adj *lit:* optimistic, romantic; moral, principled; naive, impracticable, impractical; ambitious, hopeful; perfectionist.

identical adj *lit:* alike as two peas, congruent, duplicated, exactly the same, geminate, indistinguishable, twin; corresponding, equal, equivalent, like, matching.

identify vb *lit:* know, place, recognize; discern, diagnose, name, pick out, pinpoint, single out, tag; catalog, classify, label; associate (with), categorize (with), relate (with); empathize (with), sympathize (with).

identity n *lit:* name, particulars; individuality, particularity, singularity, uniqueness; equality, identicality, sameness, unity; empathy, rapport, sympathy, unanimity.

idiot n *lit:* cretin, duffer, dunce, half-wit, imbecile, moron, twerp; blockhead, clod, dimwit, fool, lunatic, simpleton; ass, chump, twit.

idiotic adj *lit:* asinine, blockheaded, cretinous, daft, dimwitted, fatuous, feeble-minded, half-witted, insane, lunatic, moronic, stupid, witless.

idle vb *lit:* do nothing, laze, loaf, shirk, slack, take it easy; fritter (away), while (away); dawdle, drift, tick over, vegetate. adj *lit:* indolent, lazy, loafing, shirking, slack, slothful; inactive, inoperative, out of action, stationary, unoccupied, unused; jobless, redundant, unemployed; abortive, futile, groundless, pointless, unproductive, useless, vain, worthless; frivolous, irrelevant, trivial, unnecessary.

idleness n *lit:* indolence, laziness, loafing, shirking, slacking, sloth, time-wasting; inactivity, inertia, sluggishness, torpor; joblessness, unemployment.

if cnj *lit:* in the event that; assuming, on condition that, on the assumption that, provided, supposing; whether; admitting that, although, even though; albeit, though.

ignorance n *lit:* lack of education, unknowing; inexperience, innocence, unawareness.

ignorant adj *lit:* uneducated, unlearned, unlettered, untaught, untrained; boorish, crass, gross, lumpen, uncomprehending; green, inexperienced, innocent, naive, unaware, unconscious, uninformed, unwitting.

ignore vb *lit:* be oblivious to, dismiss, disregard, neglect, take no notice of, turn one's back on; overlook, turn a blind eye to; cold-shoulder, cut dead, ostracize, shun.

ill n *lit:* affliction, misfortune, suffering, trial, tribulation, trouble; hurt, injury; evil, mischief, unkindness, wrong. adj *lit:* indisposed, infirm, off color, poorly, sick, unwell; damaging, detrimental, harmful; bad, evil, wicked, wrong; acrimonious, hostile, inimical, malevolent, unfriendly; inauspicious, ominous, sinister, unfavorable. adv *lit:* badly, hard, poorly, unfavorably; barely, hardly, only just, scarcely; insufficiently.

illegal adj *lit:* criminal, felonious, illicit, prohibited, proscribed, unlawful, wrong; bootleg, unauthorized; actionable.

illegible adj *lit:* indecipherable, undecipherable, unreadable; faint, impossible to make out, obscure.

illegitimate adj *lit:* bastard, born out of wedlock, natural; illegal, unauthorized; inconsistent, illogical, invalid, specious, spurious, unwarranted; improper, incorrect.

illness n *lit:* ailment, cachexia, complaint, disease, disorder, indisposition, infirmity, malady, sickness.

illusion n *lit:* misapprehension, misconception, mistaken impression; apparition, daydream, figment of the imagination, magic, mirage.

illusory adj *lit:* deceptive, false, unreal, untrue; figmentary, imaginary, nonexistent; erroneous, fallacious, fictitious, misleading.

illustration n *lit:* picture; artwork, chart, drawing, figure, graphic, halftone, line drawing, map, photo, plate, print; demonstration, example, instance, specimen; analogy, comparison.

image n *lit:* effigy, figure, likeness, picture, representation, statue, statuette; appearance, reflection; conception, idea, mental picture, notion, perception; *fig:* double, same.

imaginary adj *lit:* fictitious, illusory, imagined, invented, made-up; nonexistent, unreal; hypothetical, supposed, theoretical.

imagination n *lit:* conception, invention, insight, originality; creativity, ingenuity, resourcefulness, vision, wit.

imaginative adj *lit:* creative, ingenious, inventive, original; fanciful, lively, vivid, witty.

imagine vb *lit:* conceptualize, create, devise, dream up, invent, picture, plan, think up, visualize; believe, comprehend, realize, think; assume, deem, gather, infer, surmise; conjecture, fancy.

imitate vb *lit:* copy, duplicate, echo, emulate, mirror, repeat, simulate; ape, impersonate, mimic; caricature, do, parody, take off.

imitation n *lit:* copy, counterfeit, duplicate, echo, fake, forgery, impersonation, mirror image, replica, reproduction, sham; duplication, emulation, mimicry, simulation; caricature, parody, takeoff. **adj** *lit:* artificial, counterfeit, duplicate, ersatz, fake, forged, reproduction, sham, simulated, synthetic.

immediate adj *lit:* direct, instant; closest, nearest; most recent; current, present, prevailing; urgent; *spec:* intuitive, self-evident (knowledge, in philosophy).

immediately adv *lit:* at once, instantly, instantaneously, now, straight away, without delay; directly, promptly, on the spot, there and then; at first hand.

immobile adj *lit:* fixed, motionless, rigid, stationary, stiff, still, unmoving; square, stable, static, steady.

immobilize vb *lit:* freeze, halt, paralyze, stop, transfix; brace, splint; cripple, disable, put out of action; withdraw from circulation.

immoral adj *lit:* degenerate, depraved, indecent; corrupt, dishonest, evil, sinful, unethical, unprincipled, wicked, wrong; dissolute, profligate, reprobate.

immorality n *lit:* degeneracy, depravity, indecency; corruption, dishonesty, evil, sinfulness, unethical behavior, vice, wickedness; dissoluteness, profligacy.

impact n *lit:* concussion, contact, shock; bang, blow, crash, jolt, smash; force, power; momentum; *fig:* burden, impression, thrust; brunt, weight; consequences, effects, influence, repercussions, significance. vb *lit:* crash (on), hit, strike; impinge on, press together; compact, harden.

impair vb *lit:* damage, harm, injure; debilitate, hinder, mar, spoil, weaken; decrease, deteriorate, lessen, reduce, worsen.

impassable adj *lit:* impenetrable, unnavigable; insurmountable, unscalable.

impatience n *lit:* hastiness, impetuosity, intolerance; shortness of temper, snappishness; anxious expectancy, eagerness, restlessness; fretfulness, nervousness.

impatient adj *lit:* brooking no delay, hasty, impetuous, overeager, rash; short-tempered, snappish; anxiously expectant, eager, restless; fretful, nervous.

impenetrable adj *lit:* dense, impassable, impermeable, solid, thick; *fig:* baffling, incomprehensible, inexplicable, inscrutable, mysterious, unfathomable.

imperative adj *lit:* compulsory, indispensable, obligatory, vital; crucial, essential, necessary, urgent; authoritative, commanding, exigent, imperious, insistent, peremptory.

imperceptible adj *lit:* indiscernible, infinitesimal, invisible, microscopic, minute, subtle, undetectable, unnoticeable; faint, fine, tiny; gradual.

imperfect   **adj** *lit:* defective, deficient, faulty, flawed, incomplete, unfinished; broken, damaged, impaired; underdeveloped; abnormal, deformed, misshapen, subnormal.

imperil   **vb** *lit:* endanger, hazard, jeopardize, put at risk, risk.

impersonal   **adj** *lit:* detached, dispassionate, formal; bureaucratic, businesslike, disinterested, neutral; cold, inhuman.

impersonate   **vb** *lit:* imitate, masquerade as, pass oneself off as, pose as; act as, mimic, play the part of, take the role of; ape, take off.

impetuous   **adj** *lit:* hasty, impulsive, precipitate, rash, unthinking; eager, headlong, unrestrained.

implausible   **adj** *lit:* doubtful, dubious, incredible, inconceivable, suspect, suspicious, unbelievable, unconvincing, unlikely, unreasonable.

implement   **n** *lit:* instrument, piece of equipment, tool, utensil; appliance, device. **vb** *lit:* carry out, discharge, execute, perform, put into effect.

implementation   **n** *lit:* carrying out, discharge, execution, fulfillment, performance, putting into effect.

implication   **n** *lit:* conclusion, corollary, inference, meaning, ramification, significance; association, connection, entanglement, involvement.

implicit   **adj** *lit:* contained, included, inherent; inferred, tacit, understood, unspoken; absolute, complete, steadfast, total, unqualified, unreserved, unshakable; *spec:* invisible (response, in psychiatry).

imply   **vb** *lit:* hint, insinuate, intimate, suggest; connote, denote, mean, signify; entail, involve, presuppose.

impolite   **adj** *lit:* bad-mannered, discourteous, ill-mannered, rude, ungracious, unmannerly; ungentlemanly, unladylike; abusive, boorish, impudent, insolent, insulting.

importance   **n** *lit:* significance, usefulness, value; consequence, distinction, mark, note, standing; concern, influence, interest; eminence, moment, substance, weight.

importunate adj *lit:* badgering, bothersome, clamorous, demanding, insistent, pertinacious, pressing.

impose vb *lit:* apply, enforce, establish, institute, ordain; fix (on), inflict, lay (on), place (on), put (on), set (on); *fig:* butt in (upon), intrude, trespass; play (upon), presume (upon); *spec:* set up (type for printing).

imposition n *lit:* application, enforcement, establishment, institution, ordinance; fixing on, inflicting on, laying on, placing on; *fig:* burden, hardship; charge, duty, tax, toll; encroachment, intrusion, presumption.

impossible n *lit:* unattainable; inconceivable, unthinkable; insoluble, unanswerable; unendurable; unacceptable. adj *lit:* impracticable, not feasible, not viable, out of the question, unattainable; inconceivable, unthinkable; insoluble, unanswerable, unworkable; unendurable; hopelessly unsuitable, outrageous, unacceptable.

imprecise adj *lit:* approximate, inexact, rough, vague; ambiguous, equivocal, indefinite, indeterminate, loose; careless, inaccurate, sloppy.

impress vb *lit:* emboss, imprint, print, stamp; *fig:* have an effect upon, influence, make an impression on, move, reach; emphasize (on), stress (upon).

impression n *lit:* brand, dent, imprint, indentation, mark, print, stamp; edition, issue, printing; *fig:* effect, impact, influence; conviction, feeling, idea, memory, notion, opinion, reaction, recollection; *spec:* model, mold (of teeth).

impressionable adj *lit:* easily influenced, responsive, sensitive, suggestible, susceptible; gullible.

impressive adj *lit:* affecting, commanding, imposing, moving, powerful, stirring, striking.

imprison vb *lit:* confine, immure, incarcerate, intern, jail, lock up, put away, send down, shut up.

improbable adj *lit:* farfetched, implausible, unlikely; doubtful, questionable, uncertain; unforeseeable, untoward.

improper adj *lit:* erroneous, false, incorrect, wrong; inapposite, inappropriate, infelicitous, out of place, uncalled for, unsuitable, unwarranted; impolite, indelicate, unbecoming, unseemly, vulgar.

improve vb *lit:* ameliorate, better, enhance, make better; advance, develop, gain in strength, grow, increase, pick up, progress, rise; amend, correct, mend, polish up, rectify, reform; get better, rally, recover, recuperate.

improvement n *lit:* amelioration, betterment, enhancement; advance, development, gain, growth, increase, pickup, progress, rise; correction, emendation, polishing, rectification, reformation; rally, recovery.

impulse n *lit:* force, impetus, momentum, pressure; push, stimulus, thrust; *fig:* drive, motivation, urge; passion, spark, spirit; fancy, inclination, whim, wish, yen.

impunity n *lit:* immunity, licence; without punishment; without restriction.

inability n *lit:* incapacity, incompetence; helplessness, impotence, powerlessness.

inaccurate adj *lit:* erroneous, faulty, incorrect, out, wrong; imprecise, inexact; defective, unreliable.

inactive adj *lit:* immobile, inert, inoperative, out of service; idle, unoccupied, unused; dormant, in abeyance, latent; indolent, lazy, lethargic, sluggish, torpid; passive, sedentary.

inadequate adj *lit:* deficient, incomplete, insufficient, meager, scanty, sparse, too few, too little; incompetent, not up to it, unfit, unsatisfactory.

inappropriate adj *lit:* inapposite, inapt, incongruous, unfitting, unsuitable, unsuited; infelicitous, unbecoming, unseemly; untimely, wrong; disproportionate.

inattentive adj *lit:* absentminded, distrait, dreamy, preoccupied, vague; paying no heed (to).

inaudible adj *lit:* silent, unheard; incomprehensible, muffled, mumbling.

inaugurate vb *lit:* begin, commence, initiate, launch, open, usher in; commission, dedicate, induct, install.

inauspicious adj *lit:* black, ill-omened, ominous, unfortunate, unlucky, unpromising.

incapable adj *lit:* helpless, powerless, unfit; incompetent, ineffectual, inefficient, inept; not capable (of); not admitting (of).

incense n *lit:* fumes, heady aroma, scented smoke; aroma, fragrance, perfume, scent; *fig:* homage; adulation, praise. vb *lit:* anger, enrage, inflame, infuriate, madden, make one's blood boil, rile.

incentive n *lit:* inducement, motivation, stimulus; bait, carrot, enticement, lure.

inchoate adj *lit:* early, imperfect, incipient, incomplete, rudimentary, undeveloped.

incident n *lit:* circumstance, episode, event, happening, occasion, occurrence; action, clash, commotion, crime, disturbance, scene.

incidental adj *lit:* accompanying, ancillary (to), concomitant, lesser, minor, secondary (to), subordinate (to); accidental, chance, coincidental, fortuitous, random.

inclination n *lit:* angle, gradient, lean, slant, slope; heel, list; bending, bow, nod; *fig:* bent, disposition, fondness, liking, partiality, propensity, tendency.

incline n *lit:* angle, gradient, ramp, slope. vb *lit:* bend, bow, nod; lean over, stoop; heel, list, slant, slope, tilt, tip over; *fig:* be predisposed (to), tend (to); influence (to), persuade (to), sway (to).

include vb *lit:* contain, cover, embrace, enclose, encompass, incorporate, take in; comprehend, comprise, embody; add (in), enter, insert (in); count (in), reckon (in).

incognito adj *lit:* anonymous, under an assumed name, unknown; in disguise, unrecognizable. adv *lit:* anonymously, under an assumed name, without being recognized; in disguise, unrecognizably.

income n *lit:* earnings, gains, pay, proceeds, receipts, revenue, salary, stipend.

incompatible adj *lit:* conflicting, contradictory, irreconcilable, mutually antipathetic; inconsistent (with); at odds, inharmonious, unsympathetic.

inconceivable adj *lit:* unimaginable, unthinkable; incredible, mind-blowing, unbelievable; impossible.

inconclusive adj *lit:* indecisive, indeterminate; arguable, debatable, unfinished, unsettled.

inconsistent adj *lit:* changeable, fickle, inconstant, unpredictable, variable; conflicting, contradictory, contrary, different, incompatible, incongruous, irreconcilable.

inconvenience n *lit:* bother, disturbance, nuisance, upset. **vb** *lit:* bother, discommode, disrupt, disturb, put to trouble.

incorrect adj *lit:* erroneous, inaccurate, out, wrong; defective, faulty, flawed; mistaken.

increase n *lit:* addition, augmentation, extension, gain, increment; development, enlargement, expansion, growth; escalation, rise, upsurge; amplification, enhancement, intensification; multiplication, propagation. **vb** *lit:* add on to, augment, extend, prolong; develop, enlarge, expand, gain, grow, spread; escalate, rise, surge; amplify, enhance, intensify; multiply, propagate.

incredible adj *lit:* beyond belief, unbelievable, unimaginable; amazing, astonishing, astounding, mind-boggling.

incur vb *lit:* bring upon oneself, draw down, evoke, invoke, provoke; earn, gain; be liable to.

incurable adj *lit:* inoperable, irremediable; fatal, mortal, terminal; *fig:* incorrigible, inveterate.

indecision n *lit:* doubt, hesitancy, hesitation, irresolution, vacillation.

indeed adv *lit:* certainly, definitely, positively, undoubtedly, veritably; actually, in fact, really.

indefinite adj *lit:* boundless, indeterminate, limitless, unbounded, unlimited; imprecise, inexact, loose, vague.

indent n *lit:* dent, impression, notch; niche, nook, recess; demand, order, requisition; *spec:* space (at the head of a paragraph). **vb** *lit:* cut, make an impression, nick, notch, penetrate (into); serrate; leave space.

independence n *lit:* autonomy, self-determination, self-rule, sovereignty; self-reliance, self-sufficiency; freedom, liberty; impartiality, objectivity; *fig:* private income.

independent   n *spec:* non-party member, unaffiliated politician; nonconformist (cleric or congregation). **adj** *lit:* autonomous, nonaligned, self-determining, self-governing, sovereign; self-reliant, self-sufficient; free, liberated, unaffiliated; impartial, objective.

indestructible   **adj** *lit:* imperishable, incorruptible, indissoluble, permanent, unbreakable; immortal; *fig:* durable.

indicate   vb *lit:* display, point out, point to, show (to); mark, signal, single out; betoken, denote, express, reveal, signify; read, register; imply, suggest.

indication   n *lit:* mark, pointer, sign, signal, token; evidence, symptom; implication, inkling, suggestion.

indifference   n *lit:* detachment, disinterest, unconcern; apathy, inattention, negligence; insignificance, unimportance.

indignant   adj *lit:* angry, annoyed, exasperated, full of wrath.

indignation   n *lit:* anger, annoyance, exasperation, wrath; pique, resentment.

indirectly   adv *lit:* circuitously, in a roundabout way, obliquely; deviously; at second hand; by implication; fortuitously, incidentally.

indiscreet   adj *lit:* tactless, undiplomatic; ill-judged, impolitic, imprudent, incautious, injudicious; scandalous.

indiscretion   n *lit:* tactlessness; folly, impetuosity, imprudence; act of folly, gaffe, impropriety, peccadillo; betrayal, disclosure, leak.

indispensable   adj *lit:* crucial, essential, key, necessary, vital.

individual   n *lit:* one, unit; being, creature; mortal, party, person, soul; character, nonconformist, one-off, original. **adj** *lit:* discrete, distinct, particular, respective, separate, single, unique; characteristic, distinctive, idiosyncratic, peculiar, personal, singular, special.

induce   vb *lit:* get (to do), impel, influence, move, persuade, prompt; bring about, cause, effect, lead to, occasion; deduce, derive, infer; *spec:* produce (an electric current, radioactivity).

industry n *lit:* commerce, manufacturing, trade; business; hard work, labor, toil; application, diligence, effort, perseverance, zeal.

inebriated adj (pa.pt) *lit:* blind drunk, drunk, intoxicated, merry, tipsy; boozed up, high, pickled, plastered, smashed, sozzled, stoned, three sheets to the wind, under the influence.

inefficient adj *lit:* wasteful; incapable, incompetent, inept, sloppy; feeble, weak.

inequality n *lit:* difference, disparity, irregularity, variation; disproportion; unevenness, variability; deviation.

inert adj *lit:* idle, immobile, inactive, inanimate, lifeless, motionless, static, still, unconscious, unmoving; dead; passive, quiescent, unresponsive.

inertia n *lit:* immobility, inactivity; passivity, unresponsiveness; apathy, idleness, indolence, lassitude, lethargy, sloth, torpor.

inevitable adj *lit:* automatic, inescapable, inexorable, necessary, unavoidable.

inexperienced adj *lit:* callow, green, immature, raw, unpracticed, unschooled, untried, unversed.

infallible adj *lit:* inability to be wrong; dependability, reliability; omniscience.

infamous adj *lit:* disreputable, heinous, iniquitous, notorious, opprobrious, scandalous, shocking; disgraceful, dishonorable, outrageous.

infant n *lit:* babe, baby, neonate, toddler, tot.

infantile adj *lit:* babyish, childish, juvenile, puerile; *fig:* early, primary.

infect vb *lit:* blight, contaminate, poison, pollute, taint; affect, spread to.

infer vb *lit:* conclude, deduce, derive, gather, presume, reason, surmise, take as read, understand.

inference n *lit:* conclusion, corollary, deduction, presumption, reasoning, surmise, understanding.

inferior   adj *lit:* junior, lesser, secondary, subordinate, subsidiary; lower; poor, second-rate, shoddy, substandard, worse.

infiltrate   vb *lit:* filter through, into, penetrate, percolate through, pervade; get into, pass into, slip into, sneak into.

infinite   adj *lit:* boundless, endless, illimitable, immeasurable, inestimable, inexhaustible, limitless, measureless, unbounded, untold; countless, numberless; eternal, everlasting, perpetual; *fig:* immense, vast.

infirm   adj *lit:* ailing, debilitated, decrepit, frail, weak; shaky, wobbly; indecisive, irresolute, vacillating.

inflate   vb *lit:* blow up, puff out, pump up; balloon, bloat, dilate, distend, expand, swell; *fig:* aggrandize, exaggerate; be devalued, be worth less.

inflict   vb *lit:* impose, place, visit, wreak; exact.

influence   n *lit:* ascendancy, domination, spell, sway; effect, force, pressure, weight; control, direction; authority, clout, hold, leverage, power; connections, pull. vb *lit:* affect, dispose, incline, have an effect on, induce, lead (to), move, persuade, predispose, sway; have a bearing on; carry weight with, pull strings with.

influential   adj *lit:* effective, efficacious, important, significant, telling, weighty; moving, persuasive; powerful, well-connected.

inform   vb *lit:* advise, apprise, enlighten, let know, notify, tell; blab, peach, sneak, tell.

informal   adj *lit:* casual, easy, familiar, unceremonious, unofficial; colloquial, idiomatic.

information   n *lit:* data, facts, info; advice, intelligence, news, word; bulletin, message, printout, report.

ingredient   n *lit:* component, constituent, element, factor, part.

inhabit   vb *lit:* abide in, dwell in, live in, occupy, reside in; people, populate.

inhabitant   n *lit:* denizen, dweller, inmate, native, occupant, occupier, resident, tenant.

inhibit   vb *lit:* constrain, hold back, restrain; check, discourage, hinder; prevent, stop.

inhuman   adj *lit:* barbaric, barbarous, bestial, brutal, cruel, heartless, ruthless, unfeeling; diabolical, fiendish; abnormal, subhuman; superhuman.

initial   n *lit:* character, letter. **vb** *lit:* endorse, sign; countersign. **adj** *lit:* beginning, first, inaugural, introductory, opening; early, primary, rudimentary.

initiative   n *lit:* drive, dynamism, enterprise, get-up-and-go, gumption, resourcefulness; leadership; advantage, control, dominance, lead.

inject   vb *lit:* jab, syringe; mainline, shoot; immunize, inoculate; infuse; *fig:* insert, introduce; throw in, toss in; force in.

injustice   n *lit:* inequity, wrong; bias, discrimination, inequality, prejudice, unfairness.

inn   n *lit:* hospice, hostel, hostelry, public house, tavern; bar, boozer, oasis, pub, watering hole.

innocence   n *lit:* blamelessness, guiltlessness; chastity, purity, virginity, virtue; artlessness, ingenuousness, naivety, simplicity; inexperience, unsophistication, unworldliness; credulousness, gullibility; ignorance, unawareness.

innocent   adj *lit:* blameless, faultless, guiltless, not guilty; chaste, immaculate, pure, spotless, unblemished, virgin; artless, ingenuous, naive, open, simple; harmless, innocuous, inoffensive; ignorant (of), unaware (of).

inoffensive   adj *lit:* harmless, innocuous, mild, peaceable, quiet, unobtrusive, unprovocative.

inquisitive   adj *lit:* curious, inquiring, investigative; intrusive, nosy, prying, snooping.

insane   adj *lit:* certifiable, mentally disordered; crazy, demented, deranged, lunatic, mad, mental, unbalanced, unhinged.

insanity   n *lit:* dementia, mental derangement, mental illness; lunacy, madness; *fig:* folly, senselessness, stupidity; irresponsibility.

insecure   adj *lit:* defenseless, exposed, open to attack, unprotected, unsafe, vulnerable; flimsy, precarious, rickety, rocky, shaky, unreliable, unsteady, wobbly; anxious, diffident, unsure.

insensitive adj *lit:* callous, hardened, indifferent, tough, unfeeling; indifferent, uncaring, unconcerned; dull, obtuse.

insert n *lit:* additional material, inset, interpolation; addendum, corrigendum; tip-in. vb *lit:* implant, interpolate, interpose, introduce, put in, tuck in, work in.

inside n *lit:* interior; contents; bowels, entrails, guts, innards, viscera. adj *lit:* inner, interior, internal; *fig:* confidential, exclusive, private, restricted; limited, small; in prison. adv *lit:* in, indoors. prp *lit:* in, into, within.

insight n *lit:* acumen, comprehension, discernment, penetration, perspicacity, vision; understanding, wisdom; perception, realization, solution.

insignificant adj *lit:* inconsequential, meaningless, negligible, nugatory, unimportant; extraneous, irrelevant; minor, paltry, petty, trifling, trivial.

insincerity n *lit:* dissimulation, duplicity, hypocrisy, perfidy, pretense; dishonesty, mendacity, untruthfulness.

insist vb *lit:* demand; maintain, repeat; stand firm, take a stand.

insistent adj *lit:* compulsive, demanding, emphatic, importunate, persistent, pressing.

insoluble adj *lit:* undissolvable; *fig:* indecipherable, inexplicable, mystifying, unfathomable.

inspect vb *lit:* examine, go over, look over, scan, scrutinize, survey, vet.

inspiration n *lit:* creativity, insight, muse, stimulus.

inspire vb *lit:* arouse, enkindle, excite, fire, spur, stimulate, stir.

install vb *lit:* lodge, place, position, settle, set up; establish, inaugurate, institute, introduce.

instant n *lit:* flash, jiffy, moment, second, time, trice, twinkling of an eye. adj *lit:* immediate, prompt, rapid; *fig:* imperative, pressing; *spec:* convenience (food).

instead adv *lit:* alternatively, in lieu; preferably, rather; in place (of).

instinctive adj *lit:* inborn, inherent, innate, involuntary, natural, reflex, spontaneous.

institute n *lit:* academy, college, foundation, school, society; decree, doctrine, law, precept, principle, rule. **vb** *lit:* establish, found, initiate, introduce, launch, originate, set up, start.

instruct vb *lit:* coach, direct, drill, educate, school, teach, train; command, order; advise, apprise, counsel, inform, notify, tell.

instruction n *lit:* coaching, direction, drill, education, schooling, teaching, training; command, order; advice, counsel, information.

instructor n *lit:* coach, director, mentor, teacher, trainer; commander; adviser, counsel.

instrument n *lit:* device, gadget, implement, tool, utensil; appliance, mechanism; dial, meter, readout; agent, factor; channel, means, medium, vehicle; contract, deed, legal document, writ; *fig:* pawn, puppet.

insult n *lit:* affront, incivility, offense, rudeness, scurrility, slight; abuse, invective, vituperation. **vb** *lit:* abuse, affront, be rude to, be offensive to, call names, offend, outrage, slight.

insurance n *lit:* assurance, cover, guarantee, indemnity, safeguard, security, warranty; policy; premium.

integrate vb *lit:* absorb, accommodate, assimilate, blend in, fuse, harmonize, incorporate, merge, mesh, mingle; connect up, put together, unify.

integrity n *lit:* completeness, homogeneity, totality, unity, wholeness; *fig:* honesty, honor, incorruptibility, principle, probity, sincerity, virtue.

intellectual n *lit:* thinker; academic, philosopher, scholar; highbrow. **adj** *lit:* cerebral, mental, rational; academic, bookish, philosophical, scholarly.

intelligence n *lit:* brains, gray matter, mind; acumen, discernment, discrimination, intellect, perception, reason, wit; data, facts, information, knowledge, news, notification, word; secret service.

intelligent adj *lit:* brainy, bright, clever, penetrating, perceptive, quick-witted, reasoning, smart, thinking.

intelligible   **adj** *lit:* comprehensible, decipherable, legible, lucid, simple, understandable.

intend   **vb** *lit:* aim, be determined, mean, propose, purpose; destine, earmark, have in mind.

intense   **adj** *lit:* acute, concentrated, deep, extreme, great, powerful, profound, severe; burning, consuming, fanatical, fervent, impassioned, passionate, vehement; earnest, fierce, haunted, strained; bright; dense.

intention   **n** *lit:* aim, design, idea, objective, plan, purpose, target; *spec:* concept (in logic).

interest   **n** *lit:* concern, importance, moment, pertinence, relevance, significance, weight; curiosity; attention, notice, regard; activity, hobby, occupation, pastime, pursuit; claim, commitment, influence, involvement, stake; benefit, gain, profit; affair, business, matter; (in the) cause (of). **vb** *lit:* affect, concern, involve; absorb, engross, fascinate, grab the attention of, intrigue; amuse, divert, entertain.

interesting   **adj (pr.pt)** *lit:* affecting, compelling, gripping, riveting, thought-provoking; absorbing, engrossing, fascinating, intriguing, stimulating; amusing, diverting, entertaining, pleasing; curious, strange, unusual.

interfere   **vb** *lit:* butt in, intervene, intrude, meddle, stick one's oar (in); clash (with), conflict (with); react (with); take a liberty (with).

interior   **n** *lit:* inside; center, core, heart; heartland; contents; domestic scene. **adj** *lit:* inside, internal, inward; inner, mental, personal, private; domestic, home.

interlude   **n** *lit:* break, breathing space, halt, intermission, pause, respite, rest, stoppage; diversion, interim entertainment, voluntary.

intermediate   **adj** *lit:* in-between, intervening, transitional; medium, middle.

interminable   **adj** *lit:* endless, everlasting, infinite, perpetual; boring, long-drawn-out, long-winded, protracted, tedious, wearisome.

intermittent   **adj** *lit:* discontinuous, fitful, periodic, spasmodic, sporadic.

internal **adj** *lit:* inside, interior; inner, private, secret; domestic, home; company, in-house, personnel, staff.

interpret **vb** *lit:* decipher, decode, make sense of, translate; elucidate, explain; bring out the meaning of, render; read, understand.

interpretation **n** *lit:* decipherment, decoding, translation; elucidation, exegesis, explanation; analysis, diagnosis, reading, understanding; performance, rendition, version; meaning.

interrogate **vb** *lit:* cross-examine, grill, pump, question, quiz; ask.

interrupt **vb** *lit:* break into, butt into, cut off, disturb, hold up, intrude into, punctuate; check, cut short, stop; break off, discontinue, suspend; interfere with, obstruct.

interval **n** *lit:* break, distance, gap, hiatus, period, space, term, time; intermission, pause; interim, meantime, meanwhile.

interview **n** *lit:* audience, consultation, meeting, talk; examination, interrogation. **vb** *lit:* examine, interrogate, question, quiz.

intestines **n** *lit:* guts, tripe, viscera; bowels, entrails, innards.

intimidate **vb** *lit:* browbeat, bully, cow, lean on, menace, terrorize, threaten; daunt, dishearten, frighten, overawe, scare, terrify.

intolerance **n** *lit:* impatience; dogmatism, fanaticism, illiberality, narrow-mindedness; discrimination, prejudice; chauvinism.

intolerant **adj** *lit:* impatient, uncharitable; dogmatic, fanatical, illiberal, narrow-minded; discriminating, prejudiced; chauvinistic.

intone **vb** *lit:* chant, recite, warble; sing.

intoxication **n** *lit:* drunkenness, inebriety; poisoning; *fig:* delirium, euphoria, exaltation, exhilaration.

intransigent **adj** *lit:* intractable, obdurate, obstinate, stubborn, tenacious, uncompromising, unyielding.

intrepid **adj** *lit:* audacious, bold, brave, daring, dauntless, fearless, heroic, nerveless, stouthearted, undaunted, valiant.

intricate **adj** *lit:* complex, complicated, elaborate, involved, labyrinthine, tangled, tortuous.

intrigue n *lit:* complot, conspiracy, machination, plot, scheme, stratagem, trick; amour, liaison, romance. **vb** *lit:* fascinate, interest; perplex, puzzle; connive, conspire, plot, scheme.

intriguing **adj (pr.pt)** *lit:* fascinating, interesting; perplexing, puzzling.

introduce **vb** *lit:* acquaint, make known, present; bring in, establish, inaugurate, institute, launch, pioneer, usher in; announce, bring up, broach, lead off, preface, put forward; add, insert, interpolate, put in; put next to.

introduction n *lit:* presentation; debut, establishment, inauguration, institution, launching, pioneering; foreword, opening statement, overture, preamble, preface, prelude, prologue; addition, insertion, interpolation.

introverted **adj** *lit:* indrawn, introspective; reserved, withdrawn; self-contained; self-centered.

intruder n *lit:* burglar, prowler, raider; gate-crasher, interloper, trespasser; invader.

intuition n *lit:* awareness, feeling, hunch, instinct, presentiment, sense.

intuitive **adj** *lit:* instinctive; penetrative, percipient; innate, instinctual, involuntary, natural, reflex, spontaneous.

invade **vb** *lit:* burst in, encroach upon, infringe, occupy, raid; infect, infest, overrun, penetrate, permeate; assault, attack.

invalid n *lit:* convalescent, patient. **adj** *lit:* bedridden, disabled, frail, ill, sick, sickly; inoperative, not in service, null, void; fallacious, false, incorrect, irrational, untrue.

invaluable **adj** *lit:* precious, priceless; *fig:* essential, indispensable, necessary, vital.

invariably **adv** *lit:* always, consistently, every time, regularly, rigidly, unfailingly.

invasion n *lit:* encroachment, infringement, intrusion, occupation, penetration, permeation; infestation; assault, attack, incursion, raid.

invent **vb** *lit:* come up with, create, construct, devise, formulate, originate; conceive, imagine, make up, think up; concoct, cook up, fabricate.

invention   n *lit:* creativity, genius, imagination, ingenuity, originality; construction, devising, formulation, origination; brainchild, creation, discovery, innovation, novelty; fabrication, fantasy, fiction, story; falsehood, lie, untruth.

inventive   adj *lit:* creative, imaginative, ingenious, original, resourceful; constructive, practical; innovative.

invest   vb *lit:* authorize, empower, license; consecrate, dedicate, induct, install, ordain; endow, provide, supply; put (money in), sink (funds in); devote, lay out, spend; beset, besiege, lay siege to, surround.

investigate   vb *lit:* enquire into, examine, explore, go into, look into, probe, study.

invisible   adj *lit:* imperceptible, indiscernible; inconspicuous, unseen; infinitesimal, microscopic; concealed, hidden.

invitation   n *lit:* call, request, suggestion; hospitality, welcome; *fig:* allurement, come-on, inducement, temptation.

invite   vb *lit:* ask, bid, call, request, summon, welcome; *fig:* ask for, court, look for, provoke, tempt; attract, draw.

inviting   adj (pr.pt) *lit:* appealing, attractive, captivating, welcoming, winning; alluring, enticing, seductive, tempting.

invoke   vb *lit:* appeal to, call upon, pray to; beg, petition, supplicate; call up, conjure; apply, implement, put into effect; call in, resort to.

involuntary   adj *lit:* automatic, instinctual, reflex, spontaneous, uncontrolled; accidental, unintended, unintentional; reluctant, unwilling.

involve   vb *lit:* entail, imply, mean, necessitate; contain, cover, include, incorporate, take in; absorb, engross, grip, hold, rivet; affect, concern, touch; connect with, implicate; complicate, embroil, enmesh, entangle.

involved   adj (pa.pt) *lit:* complex, complicated, elaborate, intricate, labyrinthine, tangled; concerned (in), implicated (in), mixed up (in), occupied (in).

irony n *lit:* dissimulation, paradox, sarcasm.

irrational **adj** *lit:* absurd, crazy, illogical, insane, mindless, nonsensical, silly, senseless, unreasonable.

irregular **n** *lit:* reservist, volunteer; part-timer, temporary. **adj** *lit:* amorphous, asymmetrical, crooked, lopsided, lumpy, shapeless, unequal, uneven; fitful, intermittent, odd, patchy, spasmodic, sporadic, unsteady, variable; eccentric, erratic, haphazard; fluctuating, oscillating, varying; abnormal, exceptional, extraordinary, peculiar, queer, unorthodox, unusual; part-time, temporary, unauthorized, unofficial.

irrelevant **adj** *lit:* extraneous, immaterial, inappropriate, not pertinent, unconnected, unrelated; inadmissible, inapplicable.

irrepressible **adj** *lit:* bright, bubbling, buoyant, cheery, ebullient, effervescent; cheeky, impudent, incorrigible; uncontrollable, unstoppable.

irresistible **adj** *lit:* compelling, compulsive, overpowering, overwhelming; inescapable, inexorable; *fig:* enchanting, fascinating, ravishing.

irresponsible **adj** *lit:* ill-advised, ill-judged, reckless, wild; undependable, unreliable, untrustworthy; feckless, flighty, giddy.

irreverent **adj** *lit:* impious, irreligious, sacrilegious; cheeky, disrespectful, impertinent, impudent, saucy.

irritate **vb** *lit:* annoy, be trying, bother, exasperate, get on one's nerves, offend, pester, provoke, rub up the wrong way; inflame; chafe, rub; itch, tickle.

isolate **vb** *lit:* detach, divorce, keep separate, segregate, separate; quarantine.

isolation **n** *lit:* detachment, insularity, seclusion, segregation, separation; loneliness, solitude.

issue **n** *lit:* child, children, offspring, progeny; delivery, dissemination, distribution, publication, supplying; edition, impression, installment; affair, concern, matter, point, question, subject; argument, bone of contention, controversy, problem; conclusion, culmination, finale, outcome, result, upshot. **vb** *lit:* arise, come (forth), emanate, emerge, flow, rise, spring, stem; deliver, disseminate, distribute, emit, publish, put out; announce, broadcast, circulate, release.

itch n *lit:* irritation, tickling, tingling; *fig:* craving, desire, longing, lust, yearning. **vb** *lit:* irritate, tickle, tingle; *fig:* ache, crave, long, lust, pine, yearn.

item n *lit:* article, object, thing; component, detail, particular, unit; entry, matter, point, subject, topic; article, feature, notice, piece, report.

J

jab n *lit:* dig, poke, prod, stab; lunge, nudge, thrust; blow, punch; *fig:* injection, inoculation, vaccination. **vb** *lit:* dig, poke, prod, stab; lunge, nudge, thrust.

jacket n *lit:* blazer, body-warmer, bolero, coat; case, casing, covering, lagging, sheath, wrapper, wrapping; outside, skin, surface; dust cover, envelope, folder. **vb** *lit:* case, cover, lag, sheathe, wrap; enclose, enfold, envelop.

jail n *lit:* lockup, prison; brig, clink, jug, penitentiary, stir; detention center; internment. **vb** *lit:* detain, imprison, lock up, send down; confine, immure, incarcerate, remand.

jam n *lit:* conserve, preserve; crush, press, squeeze, throng; blockage, congestion, obstruction; *fig:* dilemma, predicament, quandary; fix, hole, pickle, scrape, spot. **vb** *lit:* cram, crush, force, pack, press, push, ram, shove, squeeze, stuff, wedge; block, clog, congest, obstruct; bring to a standstill, halt, stick fast, stop; *spec:* improvise.

jar n *lit:* amphora, crock, flagon, jug, pitcher, urn, vase; mug, tankard; container, pot, vessel; bump, jerk, jolt, knock, nudge, percussion, shock, start, vibration, wrench; clash, grating; *fig:* conflict, disagreement, quarrel. **vb** *lit:* bump, jerk, jolt, knock, nudge, rock, shake, vibrate, wrench; clash, grate, rasp; *fig:* agitate, disturb, irritate, rattle; annoy, irk, nettle; bicker, disagree, quarrel, wrangle; clash, jangle, stick out like a sore thumb.

jargon n *lit:* patter, private vocabulary, technical terminology; cant, idiom, usage; *fig:* argot, patois, slang; *spec:* pidgin.

jaunt n *lit:* excursion, tour, trip; expedition, trek; airing, outing, promenade, ramble, stroll; ride, spin. **vb** *lit:* go on an excursion, make a trip, tour; promenade, ramble, saunter, stroll; go for a spin, ride.

jaw n *lit:* mandible, maxilla; pincer; *fig:* chat, gossip; conversation, dialogue, talk; chattiness, talkativeness; scolding. **vb** *lit:* chat, chatter, chew the fat, go on, gossip; censure, criticize, find fault, lecture, scold.

jealous adj *lit:* covetous, envious, green-eyed; grudging, resentful;

possessive, protective, solicitous, vigilant; anxious, mistrustful, suspicious, wary, watchful.

jealousy n *lit:* covetousness, enviousness; resentment; possessiveness, protectiveness, solicitousness, vigilance; anxiety, distrust, mistrust, suspicion, wariness, watchfulness.

jeering n *lit:* boos, catcalls, gibes, heckling, hisses, mockery, obloquy, raillery, ridicule, scoffs, sneers, taunts; abuse, derision. **adj (pr.pt)** *lit:* booing, catcalling, gibing, heckling, hissing, hooting, mocking, ridiculing, scoffing, sneering, taunting; abusive, deriding.

jerk n *lit:* jolt, pull, tug, tweak, twitch, wrench, yank; lurch, twist; spasm, start, tic. *fig:* fool, idiot, stupid person. **vb** *lit:* jar, jolt, pull, tug, tweak, wrench, yank; lurch, twist, veer; go into spasm, start, twitch; bounce, bump, rattle, shake, tremble, vibrate; *fig:* force out, say brokenly, stammer, stutter.

jet n *lit:* gush, spray, stream; fountain, geyser; atomizer, nozzle, spout, sprinkler; airplane, jumbo, plane; *spec:* black lignite (stone). **vb** *lit:* gush, issue, rush, shoot, spew, spout, spray, squirt; fly (by jet aircraft). **adj** *lit:* black, ebony, glossy black.

jewel n *lit:* gemstone, precious stone; brilliant, rock, sparkler; *fig:* gem, paragon, pearl, prize, treasure; find, marvel, rarity, wonder. **vb** *lit:* adorn, beautify, bejewel, deck, decorate, ornament.

jewelry n *lit:* gems, gemstones, precious stones; brilliants, rocks, sparklers; finery, ornaments, regalia, trinkets; bracelets, brooches, pendants, rings, tiaras; diamonds, pearls.

jittery adj *lit:* jumpy, nervous, shaky; anxious, worried; agitated, flustered; fidgety, in a state.

job n *lit:* appointment, assignment, calling, career, charge, duty, employment, function, livelihood, métier, occupation, office, position, post, profession, role, situation, task, vocation, work; affair, business, concern, responsibility; enterprise, piece of work, undertaking, venture; finished product, output, product; act, deed, feat; *fig:* crime, criminal act, felony; embezzlement, fraud. **vb** *lit:* buy and sell, deal in, trade in; hire out, let, rent.

jockey n *lit:* horse rider, rider; presenter, player; operator. **vb** *lit:* jostle, nudge, ride against; *fig:* engineer, manage, manipulate, maneuver; finagle, inveigle, worm.

jocular   adj *lit:* amusing, cheerful, comical, droll, funny, gay, genial, good-humored, humorous, jocose, jocund, joking, jolly, jovial, merry, waggish, witty; facetious, flippant, jokey, mischievous, playful, roguish, teasing, tongue-in-cheek, whimsical.

jog   n *lit:* canter, slow run, trot; excursion, outing, short trip. **vb** *lit:* bounce, jar, jerk, jiggle, joggle, jolt, jostle, jounce, knock, nudge, prod, push, rock, shake, vibrate; canter, lope, trot; *fig:* arouse, prompt, stimulate, stir; urge.

join   n *lit:* junction, seal, seam, suture, union; overlap. **vb** *lit:* cement, combine, connect, couple, fasten together, knit, link, put together, tie together, unite, yoke together; accompany, affiliate with, associate with, converge, get together with, move to be with; adhere, stick together; add, annex, append; enlist, enroll, enter, sign; abut, border on, meet, reach, touch.

joint   n *lit:* articulation, hinge; connection, interface, intersection, junction, node, seam, union; section, segment; cut, roast; *fig:* dive, low dive; marijuana cigarette, reefer. **vb** *lit:* articulate, connect, couple, fasten together, fit together, link, unite; butcher, carve, cleave, cut up, disarticulate, dismember, dissect. **adj** *lit:* collective, combined, communal, concerted, cooperative, shared, united; mutual.

joke   n *lit:* gag, jest, pun, quip, wisecrack; bit of fun, jape, lark, prank; butt, laughingstock, target; absurdity, nonsense. **vb** *lit:* banter, be amusing, be funny, be witty, jest, quip, tell gags, wisecrack; be facetious, chaff, kid, lark about, tease.

joker   n *lit:* buffoon, clown, jester; comedian, comic, humorist, wag, wit; prankster, trickster; wild card; *fig:* contingency, unforeseen factor.

jolly   n *lit:* festivity, jollification, merriment; *fig:* flattery, gratification, humoring. **vb** *lit:* flatter, gratify, humor; coax, wheedle, kid, tease. **adj** *lit:* cheerful, convivial, frolicsome, gay, genial, jocund, jovial, merry, mirthful; carefree, playful; agreeable, delightful, pleasant.

jostle   vb *lit:* bump, collide with, elbow, jar, jiggle, jog, joggle, press against, push against, shove, squeeze; crowd, hustle, throng.

journal n *lit:* magazine, monthly, periodical, weekly; day book, diary, log, record, register; newspaper.

journalist n *lit:* columnist, correspondent, editor, feature writer, hack, newspaperman, reporter, scribe, stringer, subeditor; broadcaster, commentator, newscaster; chronicler, diary writer, record keeper.

journey n *lit:* excursion, expedition, jaunt, odyssey, outing, tour, trek, trip, voyage; pilgrimage; peregrination, ramble, travels, wanderings. **vb** *lit:* drive, go, move, ride, tour, travel, trek, voyage, wend; ramble, roam, rove, wander; make one's way, proceed, progress.

joy n *lit:* delight, elation, exultation, felicity, gladness, happiness, pleasure, satisfaction; bliss, ecstasy, exaltation, rapture. **vb** *lit:* delight, exult, rejoice; enrapture, gladden, please.

joyful adj *lit:* delighted, elated, exultant, happy; blissful, ecstatic, exalted, enraptured, jubilant, rapturous, transported; glad, gratified, pleased, satisfied; delightful, gladdening, gratifying, pleasing, ravishing.

joyous adj *lit:* beatific, ecstatic, exalted, jubilant; cheerful, joyful, rapturous; festive, gladsome, merry; elating, gladdening, heartening, pleasing.

jubilant adj *lit:* elated, euphoric, exultant, joyous, triumphal, triumphant; rejoicing, shouting for joy, thrilled; over the moon.

jubilation n *lit:* celebration, elation, euphoria, exultation, festivity, joy, rejoicing, triumph; applause, cheering, clapping, ovation.

judge n *lit:* bench, justice of the peace, magistrate; appraiser, arbiter, assessor, evaluator; adjudicator, arbitrator, authority, referee, umpire; moderator. **vb** *lit:* dispense justice, hear, sit in judgment on, try; decree, deem, declare, find, pass sentence of, pronounce sentence, rule, sentence; adjudge, appraise, assess, conclude, consider, deduce, determine, discern, estimate, evaluate, rate, suppose, think, value, weigh up; adjudicate, arbitrate, decide, distinguish, differentiate, mediate, referee, settle, umpire.

judgment n *lit:* reason, reasoning; acumen, common sense, discernment, discretion, discrimination, penetration, percipience, prudence, sense, shrewdness, taste, understanding, wisdom; appraisal, assessment, conclusion, consideration, deduction, estimation, evaluation,

valuation; arbitration, decision, decree, finding, opinion, view; ruling, sentence, settlement, verdict; doom, fate; punishment, retribution.

jug n *lit:* crock, ewer, pitcher; carafe, jar, urn; pot; coffeepot; mug, tankard; *fig:* cells, jail, prison. **vb** *lit:* boil, steam, stew; *fig:* imprison, incarcerate, jail.

juice n *lit:* sap; extract, liquor, nectar; enzyme, secretion, serum; fluid, liquid; petrol; current, electricity; *fig:* piquancy; crux, essence, nub. **vb** *fig:* brighten (up), liven (up).

juicy adj *lit:* sappy, succulent, watery, wet; *fig:* colorful, lively, racy, sensational, spicy, vivid; lurid, provocative, risqué, suggestive; lush, richly textured.

jumble n *lit:* clutter, disarray, disorder, hodgepodge, mess, mishmash, muddle; confusion, farrago, mixture. **vb** *lit:* disarrange, disorder, mix, shuffle; confuse, disorganize, muddle; dishevel, entangle, tangle; be mixed, be shuffled.

jumbo adj *lit:* elephantine, mammoth; extra-large, giant, outsized; colossal, enormous, gigantic, huge, immense, massive; *spec:* Boeing 747 aircraft.

jump n *lit:* bound, leap, spring, vault; hop, skip; bounce, jerk, jolt, lurch, start; ditch, fence, hurdle, obstacle; break, gap, hiatus, interval, space; boost, hike, increase, rise, upturn; *fig:* advantage. **vb** *lit:* bound, clear, leap, spring, vault; hop, hurdle, skip; bounce, jerk, jolt, kangaroo, lurch, start; avoid, dodge, evade, get away from, leave, run away from; leave out, miss, omit, pass over; ascend, be boosted, escalate, increase, mount, rise, surge; ambush, pounce on, surprise; *fig:* agree, coincide.

jumpy adj *lit:* jittery, nervous, on edge, tense; anxious, worried; agitated, fidgety, flustered, in a state, nervy; highly strung, restless.

junction n *lit:* joint, seal, seam, suture; connection, coupling, join, linking; crossing, crossroads, intersection; convergence, merging, union; contact, node; border, edge, interface.

junior n *lit:* adolescent, child, juvenile, minor, young person, youth; younger person; assistant, trainee; inferior, subordinate. **adj** *lit:* younger; inferior, lesser, lower, minor, subordinate.

junk n *lit:* bric-a-brac, odds and ends, rummage, scrap, trash; clutter, debris, litter, refuse, rubbish, waste; *fig:* nonsense, old rope; *spec:* Chinese vessel; drugs, narcotics; salt tack. **vb** *lit:* scrap, throw away; abandon, discard, reject.

just   **adj** *lit:* equitable, fair, honest, impartial, right, unbiased, unprejudiced; appropriate, apt, deserved, due, fitting, merited, proper, suitable; accurate, correct, exact, precise, true; decent, good, honorable, righteous, upright; lawful, legal, legitimate. **adv** *lit:* but, merely, only, simply, solely; barely, hardly, scarcely, with difficulty; in the immediate past, lately, recently; absolutely, entirely, exactly, perfectly, precisely, positively, quite, truly; a little, slightly.

justice   **n** *lit:* equity, fairness, honesty, impartiality, rightness; integrity, reason, rectitude, truth; judge, judiciary, law, magistrate; integrity; amends, compensation, correction, recompense, redress, reparation.

justification   **n** *lit:* grounds, rationale, reason, warrant; defense, excuse, explanation, rationalization; vindication; *spec:* alignment, ranging (lines of type); redemption, salvation (in theology).

justify   **vb** *lit:* explain, prove reasonable, validate, warrant; defend, excuse, legitimize, uphold; clear, exculpate, vindicate; *spec:* align, range (lines of type); be the salvation of, redeem (in theology); prove acceptable (in law).

K

keen vb *lit:* bewail, lament, mourn, wail. **adj** *lit:* avid, eager, enthusiastic, fervent, intense, zealous; ardent, devoted, impassioned, passionate; cutting, edged, honed, incisive, penetrating, piercing, pointed, sharp; biting, bitter; acute, astute, canny, clever, discerning, discriminating, perceptive, perspicacious, quick, shrewd; sensitive; *fig:* sardonic, satirical, tart, trenchant.

keep n *lit:* board, livelihood, living, maintenance, subsistence; castle, donjon, fastness, fortress, stronghold, tower. **vb** *lit:* carry, conserve, have, hold, possess, reserve, retain, stock, store, own; accumulate, heap, pile, stack; care for, defend, guard, look after, maintain, mind, preserve, protect, shelter, shield, tend, watch over; conduct, manage, operate, run; board, foster, nurture, support, sustain; arrest, constrain, detain, hold back, impede, prevent, refrain, restrain, stall; block, check, curb, delay, deter, hamper, hinder, inhibit, limit, obstruct, retard; be, carry (on), continue, endure, persevere, persist, remain, stay; last, survive; *fig:* adhere to, celebrate, commemorate, observe, perform; comply with, fulfill, honor, obey, respect.

keeper n *lit:* attendant, caretaker, curator, custodian, guardian; guard, jailer, overseer, superintendent, warden, warder; defender, preserver; owner, possessor, proprietor; *spec:* armature; clasp, catch, socket.

keeping n *lit:* care, charge, custody, guardianship, possession, preservation, protection, reservation, retention; accord, accordance, agreement, conformity, consistency, correspondence, harmony, proportion; adherence, celebration, commemoration, observance, performance.

key n *lit:* latchkey, opener, winder; tuner; ivory, lever, note; bolt, filler, pin, wedge; capstone; character, letter; octave, register, scale, tonal system; caption, explanation, legend, scheme; answer, interpretation, solution, translation; clue, cue, hint, indicator, lead, pointer, sign, signal; focus, hub, pivot. **vb** *lit:* fasten, lock; adjust, loosen, tighten, tune, turn, wind up; differentiate, distinguish, encode, identify, mark, mark out, mark up; align, attune; excite, nerve, stimulate. **adj** *lit:* controlling, crucial, deciding, decisive, essential, pivotal, vital; basic, fundamental, major, principal.

kick   n *lit:* boot, punt; hack, hoof; jerk, jolt, jump; *fig:* drive, force, power, punch, strength, verve, vigor, zest; opposition, resilience, resistance; potency, pungency; boost, buzz, excitement, fillip, stimulation, stimulus, thrill; enjoyment, gratification, pleasure; binge, craze, fad, phase, vogue; *spec:* recoil (of a gun). **vb** *lit:* boot, hack, toe; jerk, jolt, jump, thresh; *fig:* complain, gripe, grumble, protest, rebel; abandon, break, give up, leave off, quit.

kid   n *lit:* child, infant, tot, youngster; teenager; boy, girl; young goat; *spec:* goat leather. **vb** *lit:* bamboozle, deceive, delude, fool, hoax, hoodwink, pretend, trick; banter, joke, rag, tease.

kidnap   vb *lit:* abduct, hijack, hold to ransom, skyjack, take hostage; carry off, seize, steal.

kill   n *lit:* game, prey, quarry; death, destruction, elimination, end. **vb** *lit:* assassinate, butcher, dispatch, do away with, execute, extirpate, massacre, murder, put down, put to death, slaughter, slay; bump off, do in, get rid of, knock off, liquidate, neutralize, rub out, terminate with extreme prejudice, waste; annihilate, destroy, eliminate, eradicate, exterminate, obliterate; *fig:* cancel, quash, scotch, suppress, veto; bring to an end, end, halt, stall, still, stop, terminate; quell, smother, stifle; delete, discard, reject; defeat, overcome, overwhelm, ruin, spoil; fritter away, spend, use up, waste, while away; *spec:* reduce (in metal refining).

killer   n *lit:* assassin, cutthroat, gunman, hit man, murderer, slayer; butcher, slaughterer; executioner; destroyer, exterminator, liquidator, neutralizer.

killing   n *lit:* assassination, carnage, cull, execution, extirpation, fatality, genocide, homicide, massacre, murder, slaughter, slaying; annihilation, destruction, elimination, extermination, obliteration; game prey, quarry; *fig:* cancellation, quashing, scotching, suppression, vetoing ending, halting, stopping, termination; bomb, coup, fortune, gain, profit. **adj** *lit:* deadly, deathly, fatal, lethal, mortal, murderous; destructive; *fig:* arduous, debilitating, exhausting, fatiguing, grueling, punishing, strenuous, tiring; hilarious, uproarious; fascinating, irresistible.

kin   n *lit:* clan, family, folks, kith, relations, relatives, stock, tribe; blood, connections; affinity, consanguinity, relationship. **adj** *lit:* consanguine, related, tied; akin, allied, cognate.

kind n *lit:* brand, category, class, make, sort, style, type, variety; breed, family, genus, ilk, race, species, strain; character, description, fashion, manner, nature, stamp; *spec:* goods, produce (in bartering). **adj** *lit:* beneficent, benevolent, benign, charitable, generous, liberal, munificent, philanthropic; compassionate, considerate, friendly, humane, humanitarian, loving, obliging, sympathetic, tender, thoughtful, understanding; affectionate, amicable, congenial, cordial, courteous, gentle, good, gracious, indulgent.

kindly **adj** *lit:* benevolent, charitable, compassionate, considerate, friendly, helpful, humane, humanitarian, loving, sympathetic, tender, thoughtful, understanding, warm; agreeable, amiable, amicable, congenial, cordial, courteous, genial, gentle, good, indulgent, pleasant. **adv** *lit:* affectionately, benevolently, benignly, compassionately, congenially, considerately, helpfully, humanely, sympathetically, tenderly, thoughtfully, warmly; agreeably, genially.

kindness n *lit:* altruism, beneficence, benevolence, benignity, charity, generosity, goodness, hospitality, liberality, magnanimity, munificence, philanthropy; compassion, consideration, friendliness, friendship, humanitarianism, humanity, love, sympathy, tenderness, thoughtfulness, understanding; affection, indulgence; favor, good deed, good turn, kindly act, service.

king n *lit:* head of state, monarch, ruler, sovereign; emperor, overlord, prince; his majesty; *fig:* best, greatest; magnate, tycoon.

kingdom n *lit:* dominion, nation, realm, state, territory; monarchy, reign, sovereignty; *fig:* area, classification, division, domain, field, province, sphere.

kiosk n *lit:* bookstall, booth, newsstand, stall, stand; telephone booth; ticket office.

kiss n *lit:* osculation; peck, smacker; greeting, salutation; *fig:* caress, contact, glance, graze, touch. **vb** *lit:* osculate; give a peck, peck; greet, salute; neck, smooch; *fig:* alight on, land on; brush, caress, contact, glance off, graze, touch gently.

kit n *lit:* apparatus, gear, impedimenta, outfit, paraphernalia, rig, tackle, trappings; accouterments, effects, equipment, implements, instruments, tools, utensils; materials, parts, pieces, set. **vb** *lit:* accouter, equip, fit, rig, tool, set; furnish, provide, provision, supply.

knack n *lit:* bent, facility, flair, gift, propensity, talent, trick; adeptness, aptitude, art, skill, technique, touch; ability, capacity; adroitness, dexterity.

knife n *lit:* blade, cutter, scalpel, steel; dagger, dirk, poniard, stiletto. **vb** *lit:* cut, lacerate, pierce, slash, stab, wound; *fig:* betray, undermine; impale, penetrate, slice.

knit **vb** *lit:* interlace, intertwine, link up, loop together, tie, weave; affix, bind, cement, connect, join, secure, unite; heal, mend; consolidate, firm up; *fig:* crease, furrow, wrinkle.

knob n *lit:* door handle, handle, projection; boss, button, stud; bump, lump, nodule, protrusion, protuberance, swelling; knot.

knock n *lit:* blow, box, buffet, hit, punch, rap, smack, thump; *fig:* censure, criticism; rebuff, reversal, setback; arrest; *spec:* rattle (of an engine). **vb** *lit:* box, buffet, clap, clip, cuff, drive, hammer, hit, punch, rap, smack, strike, thump, whack; daze, stun; *fig:* belittle, disparage, run down; censure, criticize, condemn; *spec:* rattle (of an engine).

knot n *lit:* bond, bow, joint, ligature; aggregation, assembly, band, bunch, circle, clique, clump, cluster, collection, company, gang, group, squad; mare's nest, mess, tangle; complexity, focus, node; bulge, bump, concretion, knob, lump, swelling; *spec:* nautical mile per hour, type of wading bird. **vb** *lit:* bind, knit, loop, secure, tether, tie, weave; entangle, snarl, tangle, twist; bunch, harden, tighten.

know **vb** *lit:* be acquainted with, be familiar with, recognize; be assured of, be aware of, be certain of, be informed of, be sure of, comprehend, have learned, have memorized, realize, understand; apprehend, grasp, learn, perceive, see; differentiate, discern, distinguish, identify, make out, tell; experience, feel, undergo.

knowing **adj (pr.pt)** *lit:* aware, conscious, deliberate, intended, intentional; competent, enlightened, expert, qualified, skillful, well-informed; acute, astute, clever, cunning, intelligent, perceptive, shrewd; eloquent, expressive, meaningful, significant.

knowledge n *lit:* enlightenment, experience, learning, wisdom;

education, instruction, scholarship, schooling, tuition; erudition, intelligence, science; ability, acquaintance, awareness, certainty, comprehension, consciousness, discernment, familiarity, grasp, intimacy, perception, recognition, understanding; cognizance, information, notice.

knowledgeable adj *lit:* competent, educated, enlightened, experienced, expert, familiar, qualified, skillful, well-informed; astute, clever, intelligent; aware, conversant, erudite, learned, scholarly.

known adj **(pa.pt)** *lit:* acknowledged, admitted, avowed, overt, patent; celebrated, commonplace, famous, noted, popular, recognized, well-known; common, familiar, obvious, plain; certain, distinct, established, factual, sure; called, named.

L

label n *lit:* marker, name tag, tab, tag, ticket, trademark; *fig:* category, classification, description, designation, name, stamp. **vb** *lit:* brand, identify, mark, name, tag; *fig:* characterize, categorize, classify, describe, designate.

lace n *lit:* braid, chiffon, crochet, crochet work, netting, tatting; cord, string, thong, tie. **vb** *lit:* braid, do up, entwine, fasten, interweave, string, thread, tie; *fig:* thrash; *spec:* add in, drug, fortify, mix in, spike (food or drink).

lack n *lit:* absence, dearth, deficiency, deficit, deprivation, famine, need, scarcity, shortage, shortfall, want. **vb** *lit:* be without, do without, fail, miss, need, want.

lacking adj (pr.pt) *lit:* absent, defective, deficient, inadequate, missing, short, wanting.

lad n *lit:* boy, chap, fellow, guy, son, youngster, youth.

laden adj (pa.pt) *lit:* burdened, encumbered, full, loaded, lumbered, oppressed, weighed down.

lag vb *lit:* dawdle, drop back, fall back, fall behind, linger, loiter, straggle, tarry, trail.

lair n *lit:* den, nest, refuge, retreat; *fig:* base, harbor, haven, hideaway, home, sanctuary, shelter, stronghold.

lake n *lit:* dam, loch, mere, pond, pool, tarn; *fig:* reservoir, store.

lame vb *lit:* cripple, disable, injure, maim, wound. **adj** *lit:* crippled, disabled, halt, handicapped, hobbling, injured, limping, maimed, wounded; *fig:* defective, feeble, flimsy, imperfect, inadequate, insufficient, pathetic, poor, unconvincing, weak.

lament n *lit:* complaint, moan; dirge, elegy, threnody, wake. **vb** *lit:* bemoan, bewail, cry about, keen, mourn, sorrow, wail; *fig:* deplore, regret.

lamentable adj *lit:* deplorable, distressing, pathetic, pitiable, pitiful, regrettable, tragic; distressed, miserable, low, meager, poor, unfortunate, wretched.

lamentation n *lit:* complaining, crying, grieving, keening, lament, moan, moaning, mourning, sorrowing, wailing, weeping.

lamp n *lit:* flashlight, headlight, lantern, light, sidelight, torch.

land n *lit:* country, district, nation, realm, region; countryside, ground, soil, terrain, tract; domain, estate, grounds, property, real estate, territory. **vb** *lit:* alight, disembark, dock, touch down; *fig:* arrive, end up; acquire, attain, gain, get, obtain, secure, win; *spec:* get in, plant (a punch).

landlord n *lit:* leaseholder, owner, proprietor; host, hotel keeper, innkeeper.

landmark n *lit:* indicator, marker, milestone, pointer, signpost; feature, monument; *fig:* event, happening, turning point.

landslide n *lit:* avalanche, rockfall. **adj** *fig:* decisive, overwhelming, runaway.

lane n *lit:* alley, passage, path, road, side street, street, track; channel, course.

language n *lit:* argot, dialect, jargon, lingo, patois, tongue; diction, expression, idiom, phraseology, phrasing, speech, terminology, vocabulary, wording, words; oratory, rhetoric, semantics, style; *fig:* alphabet, cipher, code, system.

languid adj *lit:* faint, feeble, flagging, inert, limp, listless, slack, spiritless, torpid, weak, wearied; *fig:* apathetic, lethargic.

lank adj *lit:* drooping, flabby, flaccid, limp, straggling; gaunt, lean, scrawny, skinny, slender, slim, thin.

lanky adj *lit:* gangling, long, tall, ungainly, weedy; lean, scrawny, skinny, thin.

lap n *lit:* circuit, loop, orbit, round, tour; *fig:* part, section, stage. **vb** *lit:* circle, make a circuit, loop, orbit; gently splash, ripple, slap, wash against; lick up, suck up, sip, sup; *fig:* enjoy, love.

lapse n *lit:* error, failure, fault, faux pas, mistake, slip; indiscretion, solecism; duration, interval, period; apostasy. **vb** *lit:* become invalid, become void, expire, pass, run out, stop, terminate; decline, drop, fail, fall away, fall into disuse, stop going, tail off; fall back, sink back; apostatize.

lapsed   adj (pa.pt) *lit:* discontinued, invalid, expired, run out, stopped, terminated; former, past; gone, over, passed.

large   adj *lit:* big, colossal, enormous, extensive, giant, gigantic, great, huge, immense, massive, monumental, substantial, vast; *fig:* expansive, grand.

lark   n *lit:* antic, caper, escapade, frolic, fun, jape, joke, prank, romp; type of bird. **vb** *lit:* antic, be mischievous, cavort, frolic, play, rollick, romp.

lascivious   adj *lit:* concupiscent, lecherous, lewd, libidinous, lustful, wanton; promiscuous; *fig:* erotic.

lash   n *lit:* blow, hit, stroke; stripe, weal; *spec:* ferocity, force, severity (of a person's tongue); sweep, swing, swirl, swish (of an animal's tail). **vb** *lit:* attach together, bind, fasten, join, secure, tie up; beat, birch, flagellate, flog, lay into, scourge, thrash, whip; *fig:* castigate, censure, criticize, lambaste, rebuke, scold, upbraid; *spec:* beat down, cascade, pour (with rain); sweep, swing, swirl, swish (of an animal's tail).

last   n *lit:* concluding one, ending one, final one, terminating one; close, conclusion, end, final time, termination; *spec:* final breath (at death). **vb** *lit:* continue, endure, go on, hold out, keep going, persist, remain, survive; be enough, suffice. **adj** *lit:* closing, concluding, ending, extreme, final, latest, lattermost, rearmost, terminal, ultimate, utmost. **adv** *lit:* afterward, finally, most recently, ultimately.

lasting   adj (pr.pt) *lit:* durable, enduring, indelible, long-standing, perennial, permanent, remanent, undying; abiding, consistent, continual, continuous, ongoing, perpetual, viable.

late   adj *lit:* behindhand, overdue, slow, tardy, unpunctual; dead, deceased, departed, erstwhile, former, last, old, past, preceding, previous; fresh, modern, new, recent. **adv** *lit:* after hours, behindhand, belatedly, dilatorily, over time, tardily, unpunctually.

lately   adv *lit:* freshly, just now, newly, recently.

later   adj *lit:* following, next, subsequent, succeeding, successive. **adv** *lit:* afterward, subsequently, thereafter.

latest **adj** *lit:* contemporary, current, modern, most recent, newest, topical, up-to-date; fashionable, in, modish, trendy.

laudable **adj** *lit:* admirable, commendable, creditable, estimable, meritorious, praiseworthy.

laugh **n** *lit:* cackle, chortle, chuckle, giggle, guffaw, roar, titter; *fig:* hoot, joke, lark, scream; card, clown, comedian, comic, wag, wit. **vb** *lit:* be amused, be convulsed, cackle, chortle, chuckle, crease up, giggle, guffaw, roar, split one's sides.

laughable **adj** *lit:* absurd, ludicrous, nonsensical, preposterous, ridiculous; *fig:* contemptible, derisory.

laughter **n** *lit:* cachinnation, cackling, chortling, chuckling, giggling, guffawing, hilarity, jocularity, laughing, mirth, tittering.

launch **n** *lit:* boat, cutter, dinghy, shallop, sloop, vessel; beginning, commencement, debut, establishing, floating, flotation, inauguration, send-off, setting out, start; discharge, firing off. **vb** *lit:* dispatch, discharge, fire, fling, project, propel, push out, put forth, send off, send out, set going, throw, throw out; begin, commence, embark upon, inaugurate, initiate, open, set off, set out, start, take off; dive, jump, rush at; *spec:* promote, publish (a new book or program).

lavatory **n** *lit:* bathroom, cloakroom, comfort station, convenience, ladies' room, men's room, powder room, public convenience, toilet, washroom, water closet; *spec:* heads (on navy ships).

lavish **vb** *lit:* deluge, heap, pour, shower, spare no expense with, surround with; expend, use to the full; *fig:* squander, waste. **adj** *lit:* abundant, bountiful, copious, effusive, generous, liberal, plentiful, profuse, prolific; *fig:* exaggerated, excessive, extravagant, immoderate, improvident, intemperate, overdone, prodigal, superfluous, unrestrained, wasteful.

law **n** *lit:* act, canon, codex, jurisprudence, ordinance, regulation, rule, statute; axiom, precept; commandment, decree, edict, order; *fig:* legal proceedings, police; *spec:* principle (in science).

law-abiding **adj** *lit:* decent, dutiful, honest, lawful, obedient, orderly, peaceable, upright.

lawful adj *lit:* allowed, authorized, constitutional, legal, legitimate, licit, permissible, permitted, rightful, sanctioned, statutory.

lawless adj *lit:* anarchic, disorderly, insurgent, rebellious, riotous, seditious, ungovernable, unruly, wild; criminal, nefarious, outlawed, shady; uncontrolled, unrestrained.

lawyer n *lit:* advocate, attorney, barrister, counsel, solicitor.

lax adj *lit:* casual, lenient, overindulgent; careless, slipshod; flabby, loose, shapeless, slack, soft; imprecise, indefinite, nonspecific, vague.

lay n *lit:* arrangement, disposition, positioning, site; chant, hymn, lyric, poem, song. vb *lit:* apply, arrange, burden, charge, cover, deposit, dispose, impose, locate, position, put, set down, spread over, station; stake, wager; *fig:* ascribe, assign, attribute, impute; contrive, design, devise, plan, plot; *spec:* bury (one deceased); exorcize; have sex with; produce (an egg). adj *lit:* laic, nonclerical, secular; *fig:* amateur, nonprofessional.

layer n *lit:* bed, ply, stratum, thickness; course, row, seam; coat, coating, covering, film, mantle; *spec:* chicken, hen (of eggs); rooting shoot (of a plant).

layout n *lit:* arrangement, geography, scenario, set; display, presentation; design, draft, outline, plan.

laziness n *lit:* idleness, inactivity, indolence, inertia, slackness, sloth, sluggishness, torpor.

lazy adj *lit:* idle, inactive, indolent, inert, shiftless, slothful, sluggish, torpid, work-shy; *spec:* weak (of heart or eye muscles).

lead n *lit:* advantage, first place, front, precedence, primacy, priority; first player, principal, star, starring role, title part; clue, direction, guidance, guide, hint, suggestion; example, leadership, model, path; *spec:* (electrical) conductor, connection, wire; first play (in cards); leash, rein, string (on a pet); lode (in mining). vb *lit:* be ahead, be first, be in front, excel, outdo, outstrip, pass, precede, surpass; command, direct, govern, head, manage, preside over; conduct, convey, escort, guide, pilot, show, steer, usher; cause, draw, induce, influence, persuade, produce, prompt; begin, commence, initiate, open; *fig:* experience, go forward, go on, live, pass, spend, undergo; *spec:* take the offensive (in a game or sport).

leader n *lit:* captain, chief, commander, conductor, director, guide, head, ruler, superior; first, forerunner, guide, vanguard; principal, star; *spec:* bargain offer; channel (from or in a waterway).

leadership n *lit:* authority, captaincy, chieftaincy, command, control, direction, directorship, guidance, management, organization, regulation, rule, supremacy.

leading **adj (pr.pt)** *lit:* chief, dominant, main, primary, principal, ruling, superior; first, foremost, preeminent; celebrated, important, famous, noted, significant.

leaf n *lit:* blade, bract, frond, petal; *fig:* folio, page, sheet, side; *spec:* board, lath, slat (detachable from window, door, or table); lamina (of gold or silver). vb *lit:* flip, riffle, skim, thumb, turn; *spec:* bud, put out leaves (of trees).

league n *lit:* alliance, association, cartel, compact, confederacy, confederation, federation, partnership, society, union; collaboration; category, class, group; cahoots, conspiracy.

leak n *lit:* discharge, drip, emission, escape, oozing, percolation, seepage, spill, spillage; breach, crack, fissure, hole, opening, puncture; *fig:* informant, informer, mole, sneak, telltale. vb *lit:* discharge, emit, exude, let out; drip out, escape, get out, issue, ooze, percolate, seep, spill, trickle out; get in, infiltrate; *fig:* admit, disclose, divulge, give away, inform, reveal, tell.

lean vb *lit:* heel, incline, list, slant, slope, tilt, tip; be supported, be propped up, rest, weigh; bend down; *fig:* favor, incline, prefer, tend; depend, rely, trust; coerce, intimidate, pressurize. adj *lit:* bony, gaunt, skinny, slender, slim, thin; barren, inadequate, insufficient, meager, mean, poor, scanty, spare, sparse, unproductive, weak; *fig:* unprofitable.

leaning n *lit:* bent, bias, favoritism, inclination, partiality, penchant, predilection, preference, proclivity, taste; aptitude, propensity, tendency.

leap n *lit:* bound, hop, jump, skip, spring, vault; escalation, hike, increase, rise, upsurge; *fig:* distance, journey; enterprise, undertaking; gap, interval; *spec:* jump-off point. vb *lit:* bound, caper, hop, jump, skip, spring, vault; clear, cavort, frisk, gambol; escalate, increase, rise, rocket, soar, surge; *fig:* fly, hasten, hurry, run, rush; *spec:* jump (to a conclusion).

learn vb *lit:* apprehend, be taught, comprehend, grasp, master, memorize, study; ascertain, be informed, be told, come to know, determine, discern, discover, find out, gather, hear, pick up.

learned adj **(pa.pt)** *lit:* cultured, educated, erudite, lettered, literate, scholarly, well-informed, well-read; expert, skillful, skilled, well-versed.

learning n *lit:* education, erudition, knowledge, letters, literacy, scholarship; culture, understanding, wisdom; expertise, lore, skill.

leash n *lit:* chain, lead, line, rein, strap, string, tether, thong; curb; *fig:* control, restraint. vb *lit:* chain, fasten, put on a lead, secure, tether, tie up; *fig:* check, control, curb, restrain.

least n *lit:* fewest, minimum, most minute, slightest, smallest, tiniest; *fig:* lowest, meanest, poorest; most feeble. adj *lit:* fewest, minimal, most minute, slightest, smallest, tiniest; *fig:* lowest, meanest, poorest, most feeble. adv *lit:* by the tiniest amount, minimally, to the slightest degree, to the smallest extent.

leave n *lit:* authorization, consent, dispensation, permission, sanction; freedom, holiday, liberty, time off, vacation; departure, going, parting, withdrawal; farewell, goodbye. vb *lit:* depart, exit, go, move off, pull out, quit, retire from, set out, vacate, withdraw; abandon, cede, desert, evacuate, forget to take, go off without, relinquish, surrender; cease, desist, drop, give up, refrain, stop; assign, commit, give over; *spec:* bequeath to, hand on to, will to.

lecture n *lit:* address, discourse, disquisition, exegesis, lesson, talk; *fig:* admonition, censure, dressing-down, rebuke, scolding, talking-to, telling-off. vb *lit:* address, expound, give a talk, instruct, teach; *fig:* admonish, berate, censure, chide, reprimand, reprove, scold, tell off.

ledge n *lit:* shelf, sill, step; ridge; *spec:* lode, vein (in geology).

leech n *lit:* bloodsucker; *fig:* hanger-on, parasite, sponger.

leer n *lit:* hot glance, smirk, stare. vb *lit:* give the eye, make sheep's eyes, ogle, smirk, stare.

leg n *lit:* limb, member, pin; basis, brace, prop, support, upright; episode, lap, part, section, stage.

legality n *lit:* law, lawfulness, legitimacy; permissibility, validity.

legalize **vb** *lit:* authorize, legitimate, legitimize, license; allow, make official, permit, sanction, validate.

legend **n** *lit:* fable, folklore, myth, saga, story, tale, tradition; caption, device, inscription, key, motto, table of symbols, wording; *fig:* celebrity, hero, prodigy.

legendary **adj** *lit:* apocryphal, fabulous, mythical, traditional; epic, heroic, prodigious; celebrated, famous, illustrious, renowned; fictitious, untrue.

legitimate **adj** *lit:* lawful, legal, licit, statutory; authorized, official, rightful, sanctioned; authentic, correct, fair, genuine, justifiable, logical, normal, proper, real, true, valid, warranted; *spec:* by right of heredity.

leisure **n** *lit:* freedom, holiday, liberty, spare time, time off, vacation; recreation, relaxation, rest, taking it easy. **adj** *lit:* free, holiday, spare, unoccupied.

leisurely **adj** *lit:* comfortable, deliberate, easy, relaxed, restful, slow, unhurried. **adv** *lit:* comfortably, deliberately, easily, relaxedly, restfully, slowly, unhurriedly.

lend **vb** *lit:* advance, give temporarily, loan; *fig:* afford, bestow, confer, give, impart.

length **n** *lit:* distance, extent, measure, reach, span; piece, portion, section, segment; duration, period, stretch, term, time; extensiveness, prolixity, protractedness; *spec:* end-to-end distance (in rowing and horse races); quantity (of a vowel in phonetics).

lengthy **adj** *lit:* drawn-out, extended, long, prolix, protracted; interminable, long-drawn-out, tedious.

less **adj** *lit:* lower, inferior, slighter, smaller; not so much; minor, secondary, subordinate. **adv** *lit:* not so much, not so well, to a lower degree, to a smaller extent. **prp** *lit:* lacking, minus, sans, subtracting, without.

lessen **vb** *lit:* abate, decrease, die away, diminish, dwindle, ease, lighten, moderate, reduce, slow, wind down; become smaller, contract, erode, shrink; *fig:* belittle, disparage, minimize.

lesson **n** *lit:* coaching, instruction, lecture, school period, teaching, tuition; exercise, reading, subject, study; *fig:* example, inspiration, model, moral; admonition, rebuke, reprimand, reproof, scolding, warning.

let   **n** *lit:* hindrance, impediment, interference, obstruction. **vb** *lit:* allow, authorize, enable, give leave, give permission, grant, permit, sanction; assume, suppose; contract out, hire, lease, rent.

lethal   **adj** *lit:* deadly, fatal, mortal, murderous; dangerous, devastating, poisonous, virulent.

let on   **vb** *lit:* dissemble, give the impression, pretend, simulate; disclose, divulge, manifest, reveal, show.

let off   **vb** *lit:* excuse, exempt, release, reprieve, spare; absolve, forgive, pardon; detonate, discharge, explode, fire; emit, exude, give off, release; allow to alight.

let out   **vb** *lit:* discharge, free, liberate, release, set free; augment, enlarge, make larger; emit, sound, voice; betray, disclose, leak, reveal; contract out, hire, lease, rent.

letter   **n** *lit:* character, sign, symbol; communication, dispatch, document, epistle, message, missive, note; *fig:* expression, language, literal meaning, wording.

level   **n** *lit:* altitude, elevation, grade, height, position, rank, standing, status; flat surface, floor, layer, plane, story, stratum; degree, standard. **vb** *lit:* even out, flatten, plane, smooth; bulldoze, pull down, raze, tear down; equalize; *fig:* aim, direct, focus, point, train; be candid, reveal all, tell the truth; *spec:* measure height (in surveying). **adj** *lit:* even, flat, horizontal, plain, plane, smooth, stable, steady, uniform; balanced, commensurate, equable, equal, equivalent, even, flush, parallel; sound.

lever   **n** *lit:* bar, crowbar, handle, jimmy, switch; *fig:* hold, threat. **vb** *lit:* force, jimmy, prize.

leverage   **n** *lit:* power, purchase; *fig:* advantage, ascendancy, clout, influence, pull, weight.

lewd   **adj** *lit:* bawdy, blue, dirty, erotic, indecent, lascivious, libidinous, licentious, obscene, pornographic, salacious, smutty; debauched, lecherous, lustful.

lewdness   **n** *lit:* bawdiness, carnality, debauchery, depravity, indecency, lasciviousness, lechery, licentiousness, lubricity, obscenity, pornography, salaciousness, smut.

liar n *lit:* deceiver, fabricator, falsifier, perjurer, storyteller; fibber, libeler, prevaricator, slanderer; double-crosser, fraud, impostor.

libel n *lit:* calumny, defamation, smear, vilification; slander; *spec:* accusation, charge, complaint (in law); **vb** *lit:* calumniate, defame, malign, smear, traduce, vilify; slander.

liberal adj *lit:* beneficent, bounteous, bountiful, charitable, generous, kind, munificent, philanthropic; abundant, ample, copious, lavish, plentiful, profuse, prolific; broad, easy-going, flexible, free, general, indulgent, lenient, loose, magnanimous, open, tolerant; broad-minded, catholic, disinterested, humanitarian, unbiased, unprejudiced; progressive, radical, reformist; *spec:* cultural, intellectual (as opposed to practical).

liberation n *lit:* deliverance, emancipation, enfranchisement, freedom, freeing, letting go, loosing, release, releasing, rescue, setting free, unbinding, untying; *spec:* disestablishment (of the Church); manumission (of a slave), redemption (of sinners); political reform, social reform (theology).

liberty n *lit:* emancipation, enfranchisement, freedom; autonomy, independence, power, right, self-determination; carte blanche, dispensation, exemption, immunity; authorization, franchise, leave, licence, permission, sanction; leisure, spare time; *fig:* breach of good manners, familiarity, impertinence, impropriety, impudence, insult, presumption.

licence n *lit:* accreditation, certificate, charter, permit, warrant; authority, power, privilege, right; authorization, dispensation, entitlement, leave, permission, sanction; carte blanche, freedom, independence, latitude, liberty; exemption, immunity; excess, immoderation, indulgence, irresponsibility, laxity, profligacy; abandon, anarchy, debauchery, lawlessness, unruliness, wantonness.

license vb *lit:* accredit, certify, warrant; authorize, commission, empower; allow, permit, sanction.

lick n *lit:* lap, slurp; sample, sip, taste; saliva; *fig:* bit, dab, little, speck, spot, touch; clip, pace, rate, speed, velocity; *spec:* anacrusis, intro, riff (in jazz). **vb** *lit:* lap, slurp, taste, tongue; *fig:* ripple against, touch, wash; beat, conquer, defeat, rout, trounce; beat, drub, flog, spank, thrash; beat, excel, outdo, surpass; *spec:* dart, flicker, play over (of flames).

lie **n** *lit:* deception, fabrication, falsehood, falsification, fiction, invention, perjury, story, untruth; fib, libel, prevarication, slander; arrangement, disposition, positioning, site; geography, terrain; aspect. **vb** *lit:* deceive, fabricate, falsify, invent, perjure, tell an untruth; be economical with the truth, equivocate, fib, libel, mislead, misrepresent, prevaricate, slander, tell a story; abide, be, be arranged, be found, be located, be placed, be positioned, be prone, be recumbent, be set, be situated, extend, lean, recline, remain, repose, rest, stretch out; be constituted, consist; be buried, be interred; *spec:* be admissible, be sustainable (in law).

life **n** *lit:* being, being alive, being awake, being conscious, breath, existence, living; biosphere, creatures, human, human being, organisms, person, soul; animation, heart, lifeblood, soul, spirit, vitality; activity, brio, energy, liveliness, verve, vigor, vivacity, zest; duration, lifetime, span, time; autobiography, biography, career, history, memoirs; *fig:* power, validity; period, term.

lift **n** *lit:* elevation, hoisting, raising; rising; advancement, boost, fillip, progress, rise, uplift; drive, ride, transport; *spec:* upward force (in aeronautics). **vb** *lit:* elevate, hoist, hold up, pick up, pull up, raise, support, uplift, upraise; ascend, go up, rise; advance, boost, elate, enhance, exalt, promote, upgrade; cancel, countermand, end, relax, rescind, revoke, terminate; be dispelled, disperse; *fig:* appropriate, purloin, rob, steal, take; arrest, detain; copy, pirate, plagiarize; harvest, reap.

light **n** *lit:* brightness, brilliance, gleam, glint, glow, illumination, incandescence, luminosity, radiance; blaze, effulgence, flash, luminescence, ray, scintillation, sparkle; dawn, daylight, daytime, morning, sun, sunshine; beacon, candle, flame, flare, lighter, match, taper; bulb, lamp, lantern, torch; lighthouse; window; *fig:* aspect, context, interpretation, slant, view; angle, approach, viewpoint; awareness, comprehension, elucidation, enlightenment, explanation, insight, understanding; example, exemplar, model; clue, hint; *spec:* traffic signal. **vb** *lit:* brighten, illuminate, illumine, irradiate; put on, switch on, turn on; fire, ignite, kindle, set ablaze, set on fire, touch a match to; alight, come down, get off, land, perch, settle; chance, come across, encounter, happen,

light   208

stumble; *fig:* clarify, expose; inflame, intoxicate; animate, cheer up. **adj**
lit: bright, brilliant, glowing, illuminated, luminous; sunny; fair, pale,
whitish; blond; clear; delicate, easy, insubstantial, not heavy, portable,
slight, thin, underweight; faint, gentle, indistinct, mild, soft, weak;
unchaste; facile, frivolous, idle, inconsequential, insignificant, paltry,
petty, superficial, trifling, trivial, unimportant; effortless, manageable,
undemanding; amusing, entertaining, funny, pleasing, witty; agile, airy,
athletic, graceful, lithe, nimble; blithe, carefree, cheerful; *fig:* dizzy, giddy,
delirious; less, minus, short; *spec:* bland, digestible, frugal (diet); friable,
loose, sandy (soil).

like   n *lit:* favorite, partiality, predilection, preference; match,
resemblance; counterpart, equal, fellow, parallel. **vb** *lit:* be fond of, care
for, enjoy, love, relish; be partial to, choose to, fancy, prefer, select, take to;
appreciate, approve of, esteem; **adj** *lit:* alike, corresponding, equal,
equivalent, identical, matching, parallel, resembling, similar. **adv** *lit:* in
the same way (as), just (as). **prp** *lit:* similar, similar to, resembling;
befitting, characteristic of; namely, such as; as much as.

likely   adj *lit:* anticipated, expected, probable; believable, credible,
feasible, plausible, reasonable; appropriate, fitting, suitable; fair, favorite,
pleasing, promising. **adv** *lit:* doubtless, in all probability, probably.

likeness   n *lit:* correspondence, resemblance, similarity; appearance,
form, guise, semblance, simulation; copy, facsimile, image, model, replica,
representation; photo, picture, portrait.

liking   n *lit:* bias, inclination, partiality, penchant, predilection,
preference, taste, tendency; affection, fancy, fondness, love; appreciation,
approval, esteem, satisfaction, pleasure.

limit   n *lit:* border, boundary, confines, edge, end, extent, frontier,
perimeter, periphery; ceiling, maximum, termination, ultimate;
restriction, stop, terminus. **vb** *lit:* bound, circumscribe; demarcate, fix,
set, specify; check, confine, hinder, ration, restrict.

limited   adj (pa.pt) *lit:* bounded, circumscribed, defined, fixed;
cramped, confined, hampered, hemmed in, hindered, restricted;
diminished, inadequate, insufficient, minimal, narrow, reduced, short,
unsatisfactory; *fig:* dull, unintelligent; *spec:* assigned (in law).

line   n *lit:* cable, cord, filament, rope, strand, string, thread, wire; bar, dash, rule, streak, stripe, stroke; crease, crow's foot, furrow, groove, score, wrinkle; column, procession, queue, rank, row, sequence, series, succession; border, boundary, edge, limit, mark; configuration, contour, figure, outline; course, direction, path, route, trajectory; transport system; rail, track; hose, tube; *fig:* approach, method, policy, procedure; business, field, forte, interest, job, occupation, profession, specialty, trade; brand, make; card, letter, note, postcard; clue, hint, indication, lead, pointer; plot, story; accordance, correspondence, parallel. **vb** *lit:* draw, inscribe, mark, rule; hatch; crease, furrow, score; align, form a column, range; border, fringe, hem round, skirt, surround; cover, face; fill, reinforce, stuff.

link   n *lit:* connection, contact, coupling, tie; attachment, bond, joint, relationship; *spec:* (electrical) fuse; hoop, loop, ring (of a chain). **vb** *lit:* connect, contact, couple, join, liaise between, make contact between, tie together, unite; attach, bind, bracket, fasten, relate, yoke.

lip   n *lit:* labium; brim, flange, rim; edge, margin, welt; *fig:* cheek, impertinence, impudence, insolence, sauce; *spec:* embouchure (in playing a wind instrument).

liquid   n *lit:* fluid, moisture; liquor.   adj *lit:* flowing, fluid, melted, moist, molten, runny, wet; aqueous, watery; juicy; *fig:* dulcet, mellifluous, smooth, soft, sweet; bright, clear, limpid, translucent; graceful; *spec:* disposable, realizable (assets).

liquor   n *lit:* alcohol, grog, hard stuff, hooch, moonshine, spirits, strong drink; broth, gravy, juice, stock; infusion, solution, suspension.

list   n *lit:* catalog, enumeration, inventory, record, register, roll, tally; file, printout, schedule, tabulation; series; lean, slant, slope, tilt. **vb** *lit:* catalog, enroll, enter, enumerate, inventory, itemize, note down, record, register, write down; file, schedule, tabulate; arrange in order, serialize; cant, heel, incline, lean, slant, slope, tilt, tip.

listen   vb *lit:* attend, be attentive, hear, hearken, pay attention; be advised, heed, mind, take notice.

listless   adj *lit:* apathetic, enervated, impassive, indifferent, languid, spiritless, supine, uninterested, vacant; indolent, lethargic, lifeless, limp, torpid.

literally   adv *lit:* accurately, exactly, faithfully, precisely, strictly, to the letter, verbatim, word for word; actually, in reality, really, truly; *fig:* as it were, in a way, virtually.

litter   n *lit:* debris, garbage, muck, refuse, rubbish, trash; brood, children, cubs, family, kittens, offspring, progeny, pups, young; palanquin, stretcher, travois; bed, couch, pailliasse; mulch; clutter, disorder, jumble, mess. **vb** *lit:* leave lying around, scatter, strew; make a mess; disarrange, disorder, jumble; *spec:* give birth to (a litter of animals).

little   n *lit:* bit, bite, dab, dash, fraction, lick, modicum, morsel, pinch, small amount, spot, taste, touch, trace, trifle; short time. **adj** *lit:* miniature, petite, short, small; diminutive, dwarf, infinitesimal, minute, tiny, wee; meager, scant, skimpy, sparse; insignificant, minor, paltry, trifling, trivial, unimportant; mean, narrow-minded, petty, small-minded.   **adv** *lit:* barely, hardly, scarcely; rarely, seldom; only just, slightly.

live   vb *lit:* be, be alive, breathe, exist, have life, subsist; continue, endure, last, lead, pass, persist, remain, survive; abide, dwell, inhabit, lodge, occupy, reside, stay; be remembered; eat, feed; enjoy life, flourish, revel, thrive; *fig:* accept, put up with, tolerate. **adj** *lit:* alive, animate, breathing, living; active, awake, alert, dynamic, energetic, vigorous; ablaze, alight, burning, connected, glowing, hot, ignited, on, switched on; contemporaneous, current, pertinent, pressing, topical, up-to-date, vital; in play; unexploded; natural, real, unquarried.

lively   adj *lit:* active, brisk, energetic, quick, sprightly, spry, vigorous; agile, alert, animated, chirpy, perky, spirited, vivacious; bright, colorful, exciting, fresh, invigorating, refreshing, stimulating, stirring, vivid; bustling, busy, crowded, eventful.

livid   adj *lit:* anemic, ashen, gray, leaden, pale, pallid, sallow, wan, waxen, white; black-and-blue, bruised, contused, discolored, purple; angry, enraged, fuming, furious, hopping mad, incensed, infuriated, irate.

living   n *lit:* job, livelihood, occupation, work; employment, means, income; support; life-style, way of life; being, existence, life, subsistence. **adj** *lit:* alive, being, existing, live, organic, subsisting; active, contemporary, current, extant, ongoing, operative; continuing, persisting, remaining; strong, vigorous; lifelike, vivid; dwelling, lodging, occupying, residential, residing, staying.

load   n *lit:* burden, cargo, charge, weight; consignment, freight, shipment; *fig:* encumbrance, millstone, onus, pressure; affliction, busyness, trouble, worry; amount, host, lot, mass, multitude, quantity; *spec:* output (in power, of an engine); force, power, work (in physics). **vb** *lit:* burden, charge, put in, put on, weigh down; cram, fill, heap, pack, pile on, stack, stuff; encumber; *fig:* oppress, trouble, worry; bias, prejudice, slant, weight; *spec:* charge, prime (a firearm); fix, rig (dice).

loaded   adj (pa.pt) *lit:* burdened, charged; crammed, filled, heaped, packed, piled, stacked, stuffed; encumbered, laden; *fig:* anxious, oppressed, troubled, worried; biased, leading, slanted, weighted; affluent, moneyed, rich, wealthy, well-heeled, well off, well-to-do; drunk, inebriated, intoxicated, stoned; *spec:* adulterated, drugged, fortified; charged, primed; fixed, rigged.

loan   n *lit:* advance, credit; mortgage, overdraft; accommodation, use. **vb** *lit:* advance, give temporarily, let someone have for a time, lend.

local   n *lit:* inhabitant, native, resident. **adj** *lit:* community, district, neighborhood, parish, parochial, provincial, regional, suburban; confined, limited, restricted; *spec:* topical (in medicine); slow (train).

locate   vb *lit:* establish, fix, found, place, put, seat, set, site, situate; detect, discover, find, pin down, pinpoint, trace, track down.

lock   n *lit:* bolt, clasp, fastening, latch, padlock; clutch, embrace, grapple, grasp, hold, hug; linkage, mesh; curl, ringlet, strand, tress; *spec:* (airtight) chamber (on a space-ship); firing mechanism (on a gun); turning-circle (on a car). **vb** *lit:* bar, bolt, close, fasten, latch, seal, secure, shut; engage, entwine, link, mesh, unite; clasp, clutch, embrace, enclose, grapple, grasp, hold, hold fast, hug, jam together, press.

lodge   n *lit:* cabin, chalet, cottage, house, hut, log cabin, shelter, villa; den, haunt, lair, retreat; gate house, porter's room, reception; meeting place; *fig:* assembly, branch, chapter, club, society. **vb** *lit:* accommodate, billet, board, harbor, put up, quarter, shelter; dwell, room, spend the night, stay, stop, temporarily reside; adhere, catch, embed, get stuck, implant, stick; deposit, file, lay, make, place, put, record, register, submit; be vested (in).

lodger   n *lit:* boarder, paying guest, roomer, tenant; guest, inhabitant, occupant, resident.

lodgings n *lit:* accommodation, board, boarding, place to stay, quarters, room, rooms, shelter; abode, dwelling, residence; harbor.

lofty adj *lit:* high, soaring, tall, towering; *fig:* dignified, elevated, exalted, lordly, majestic, noble, stately, superior; grand, illustrious, sublime; arrogant, disdainful, haughty, overweening, patronizing, proud, snooty, supercilious.

loiter vb *lit:* amble, dawdle, idle, loaf, stroll; hang about, skulk; delay, linger.

loneliness n *lit:* desolation, solitude; aloneness, isolation, seclusion, solitariness.

lonely adj *lit:* abandoned, alone, deserted, desolate, forsaken, friendless, solitary, unaccompanied; apart, isolated, remote, secluded, single, unfrequented, uninhabited, withdrawn.

long vb *lit:* crave, hunger, lust, pine, wish, yearn. **adj** *lit:* elongated, extended, extensive, far-reaching, lengthy, stretched; interminable, prolonged, protracted, slow, sustained; distant, remote; *spec:* accented, stressed (syllable). **adv** *lit:* continually, through; extendedly, extensively, for years; distantly, remotely.

longing n *lit:* covetousness, craving, desire, hunger, itch, lust, thirst, yearning; ambition, aspiration, urge, wish, yen. **adj** *lit:* covetous, desirous, hungry, lustful, wishful, wistful, yearning; avid, eager.

look n *lit:* air, appearance, aspect, bearing, cast, complexion, demeanor, expression, manner, mien, semblance; examination, inspection, review, search, survey, view; gaze, observation, stare; eyeful, gander, glance, glimpse, once-over, peek, sight, squint. **vb** *lit:* behold, contemplate, examine, gaze, inspect, observe, regard, scan, scrutinize, see, stare, study, survey, view, watch; gawp, glance, goggle; appear, seem; display, evince, exhibit, manifest, show; face, give (on to); hope.

look after vb *lit:* attend, care for, mind, nurse, tend; guard, protect, supervise, watch over; attend to, take care of.

look forward to vb *lit:* anticipate, await, be eager for, expect, wait for; hope for, long for, wish for, yearn for.

look into vb *lit:* check, examine, go into, inspect, scrutinize, study; check out, explore, follow up, investigate, probe, research.

lookout n *lit:* guard, sentinel, sentry, watchman; alert, guard, vigil, watch; crow's nest, observation post, tower, watch tower; *fig:* affair, business, concern, department, worry; outlook, prospect.

loop n *lit:* doubling, coil, convolution, curl, eyelet, hoop, noose, ring, whorl; bend, curve, spiral, twist; *spec:* closed (electrical) circuit. vb *lit:* circle, coil, curl, encircle; bend, curve, spiral, turn; braid, connect, double over, fold, join, knot, twist, wind round.

loose vb *lit:* detach, disconnect, disengage, free, let go, liberate, release, set free, unbind, undo, unfasten, unleash, untie; hurl, shoot, throw; relax, slacken. adj *lit:* detached, disconnected, free, mobile, open, unattached, unconfined, unrestricted, unsecured, untied; flexible, free-moving, lithe, relaxed, slackened, wobbly; baggy, hanging, slack, sloppy; diffuse, ill-defined, imprecise, indefinite, inexact, vague; careless, inattentive, lax, negligent, thoughtless; *fig:* disreputable, dissolute, fast, immoral, lewd, promiscuous, wanton.

loosen vb *lit:* let out, open, relax, slacken, untie, unzip; *fig:* ease up, let up, moderate, soften, weaken.

lord n *lit:* liege, master, owner, ruler; king, monarch, prince, sovereign; noble, nobleman, peer; commander, governor, leader, superior; *spec:* dominant planet (in astrology).

lose vb *lit:* forget, mislay, misplace, miss; be defeated, capitulate, fail, give up, surrender, yield; default on, forfeit, pass up; be depleted by, be deprived of, be drained of, exhaust, expend, use up; be bereaved of; squander, waste; stray from, wander from; dodge, elude, escape, evade, give the slip, shake off.

loser n *lit:* capitulator, defeated party, yielder; defaulter, sufferer; also-ran, dud, failure, flop, has-been, lame duck, no-hoper, second-rater.

lost adj *lit:* mislaid, misplaced, missing; disappeared, vanished; adrift, astray, baffled, bewildered, disoriented, perplexed, puzzled; destroyed, ruined, wrecked; conceded, forfeited; abstracted, engrossed, entranced, preoccupied, rapt; dissipated, misapplied, misspent, misused, squandered, wasted; *fig:* dead, gone, lapsed, over, past; abandoned, depraved, dissolute, fallen, promiscuous, wanton.

lot n *lit:* abundance, amount, deal, heap, host, mass, multitude, plenitude, plethora, quantity, stack; batch, bunch, collection, crowd, group, set; chance, destiny, doom, fate, kismet, hazard, portion; choice, lucky dip, random selection, selection; allocation, cut, part, piece, quota, ration, share; plot, property, site; *fig:* character.

loud **adj** *lit:* blaring, clamorous, deafening, ear-splitting, forte, fortissimo, noisy, piercing, resounding, sonorous, stentorian, thunderous; brash, raucous, rowdy, strident; *fig:* blatant, brassy, coarse, crass, flashy, garish, gaudy, lurid, obtrusive, ostentatious, showy, tasteless, vulgar.

love **n** *lit:* adoration, affection, attachment, devotion; adulation, infatuation; ardor, passion; amity, fancy, fondness, friendship, liking, regard, soft spot, tenderness, warmth, weakness; *fig:* nil, nought, zero; free, nothing; *spec:* beloved, darling, dear, dearest, sweetheart. **vb** *lit:* adore, be affectionate toward, be attached to, be devoted to, be very fond of, cherish, dote on, hold dear; adulate, idolize, worship; appreciate, enjoy, fancy, have a soft spot for, have a weakness for, like very much, prize, relish, savor, take great pleasure in, treasure.

lovely **adj** *lit:* beautiful, exquisite, gorgeous, ravishing; captivating, delightful, enchanting, eye-catching, fascinating, stunning; alluring, bewitching, desirable; appealing, attractive, charming, engaging, fair, handsome, lovable, pleasing, pretty, sweet, winning.

lover **n** *lit:* friend, mistress, paramour; admirer, beau, boyfriend, fiancé, fiancée, girlfriend, suitor, sweetheart; aficionado, connoisseur, devotee, fan; adulator, idolizer, worshiper.

low **n** *lit:* depression, hollow; bottom level, minimum; *spec:* depression, cyclone (in meteorology). **vb** *lit:* moo, ululate. **adj** *lit:* deep, depressed, ground-level, prone, prostrate, sunken; little, shallow, short, small, squat, stunted; deficient, depleted, inadequate, meager, primitive, reduced, scant, sparse; inferior, insignificant, mediocre, paltry, poor, shoddy, trifling; coarse, common, disreputable, rough, rude, vulgar; base, contemptible, degraded, depraved, gross, ignoble, ill-bred, servile, sordid, undignified; humble, mean, obscure, plebeian; cheap, economical, inexpensive, modest; debilitated, feeble, frail, ill, weak; gentle, hushed, muted, quiet, soft, subdued; blue, dejected, depressed, despondent, disheartened, down, forlorn, glum, miserable, morose, sad, unhappy; *spec:* less ornate, less rigorous, simplified (Church, or mass). **adv** *lit:* down, short, to a depressed level, under; to the horizon; humbly, meanly; gently, mutedly, quietly, softly.

lower   vb *lit:* drop, haul down, let down, pull down; fall, sink, submerge; depress; abate, curtail, cut, decrease, diminish, lessen, moderate, reduce, slash; belittle, bring down, debase, degrade, demean, devalue, disgrace, dishonor, humble, humiliate; condescend, deign, stoop; dilute, mute, soften, subdue, tone down. **adj** *lit:* closer to the ground; nearer to the horizon; cut, decreased, diminished, lessened, reduced, slashed; inferior, lesser, minor, smaller, subordinate. **adv** *lit:* below, beneath, closer to the ground, farther down, farther below, farther under, under, underneath; nearer to the horizon.

loyal   adj *lit:* devoted, faithful, staunch, steadfast, true, trusty; attached, constant, dependable, trustworthy, unswerving; dutiful, patriotic.

loyalty   n *lit:* allegiance, devotion, faithfulness, fealty, fidelity, staunchness, steadfastness, trustiness; attachment, constancy, dependability, trustworthiness; patriotism, sense of duty.

lubricate   vb *lit:* grease, make smooth, oil; make slippery, wet; *fig:* aid, assist, expedite, smooth; bribe.

luck   n *lit:* chance, fortuitousness, happenstance, hazard; good fortune, serendipity; accident; destiny, fate, lot.

luckless   adj *lit:* ill-fated, ill-starred, unfortunate, unlucky, unpropitious; doomed, jinxed, star-crossed; hapless, unhappy, wretched.

lucky   adj *lit:* fortuitous, fortunate, serendipitous; blessed, charmed; auspicious, propitious.

lull   n *lit:* calming, let-up, interval, pause, respite, subsiding; calm, quiet, silence, stillness. **vb** *lit:* allay, calm, pacify, soothe, still, subdue, tranquilize; hush; abate, decrease, diminish, ease off, let up, moderate, slacken, subside, wane.

lump   n *lit:* bulge, bump, growth, protrusion, protuberance, swelling, tumor; bit, chunk, clod, gobbet, hunk, mass, piece; gross, whole; deadweight, lot, mass. **vb** *lit:* aggregate, batch, bunch, combine, conglomerate, group, mass, pool, put together; endure, put up with, stand.

lunatic   n *lit:* madman, madwoman, maniac, psychopath; psycho. **adj** *lit:* crazy, demented, deranged, insane, mad, maniac, psychotic, raving, unbalanced; barmy, bananas, bats, cuckoo, gaga, loony, nuts, nutty, unhinged; asinine, crackbrained, daft, foolish, idiotic, imbecilic, inane, moronic; cranky, dotty, eccentric, weird; berserk; reckless, wild.

lunge n *lit:* jab, pass, stab, swing, swipe, thrust; charge, pounce; lurch, plunge. **vb** *lit:* hit out, jab, poke, stab, strike out, swing out, swipe, thrust; bound, charge, jump, leap, pounce; drop, fall, lurch, plunge.

lurch n *lit:* dip, drop, fall, plunge, slump; roll, stagger. **vb** *lit:* dip, drop, fall, plummet, plunge, sink, slump, tumble; pitch, reel, roll, stagger, stumble, totter, veer.

lure n *lit:* bait, carrot, decoy; attraction, enticement, inducement, temptation; allure, charm. **vb** *lit:* decoy, ensnare, inveigle, seduce; attract, draw, entice, invite, lead on, tempt; allure, charm.

lurk **vb** *lit:* be furtive, be stealthy, creep, hide, lie in wait, loiter with intent, prowl, skulk, slink, steal; be hidden, lie low.

lush adj *lit:* dense-growing, flourishing, green, juicy, luxuriant, succulent, tender, verdant; *fig:* lavish, luxurious, opulent, rich, sumptuous; abundant, prolific, teeming; extravagant, flowery, ornate.

lust n *lit:* desire, libido, passion; carnality, concupiscence, lasciviousness, lewdness, sensuality, wantonness; appetite, craving, cupidity, greed, longing, thirst; relish. **vb** *lit:* be aroused, feel desire; crave, hunger, long, thirst, yearn.

luster n *lit:* gleam, glistening, glitter, gloss, sheen, shimmer, shine, sparkle; brilliance, dazzle, radiance, resplendence; *fig:* fame, glory, honor, illustriousness, renown, splendor; *spec:* glass pendant (of a chandelier); glaze (on ceramics).

lusty adj *lit:* brawny, healthy, powerful, robust, stalwart, stout, strapping, strong, sturdy, vigorous; red-blooded, virile; energetic, hearty.

luxuriant adj *lit:* dense-growing, flourishing, lush, prolific, rich, teeming, thriving, verdant; fecund, fertile, fruitful; abundant, copious, lavish, plentiful, profuse; elaborate, excessive, extravagant, florid, flowery, ornate, superabundant.

luxurious adj *lit:* costly, expensive, grand, lavish, magnificent, opulent, rich, sumptuous; cushy, epicurean, pampered, self-indulgent, sybaritic; comfortable, palatial, plush, richly furnished, well-appointed.

luxury   n *lit:* grandeur, magnificence, richness, sumptuousness; affluence, expense, opulence; comfort, gratification, indulgence, pleasure, satisfaction; extra, extravagance, self-indulgence, treat.

lying   n *lit:* deceit, deception, dissimulation, fabrication, falsehoods, falsification, mendacity, perjury, storytelling, untruthfulness; fibbing, libel, prevarication, slander; fraud, imposture, misrepresentation. **adj (pr.pt)** *lit:* deceitful, dishonest, dissembling, double-crossing, false, mendacious, perjuring, two-faced, untruthful; devious, perfidious, treacherous; fibbing, prevaricating; fraudulent.

M

machine n *lit:* apparatus, appliance, device, gadget, mechanism, tool; engine, generator, motor; airplane, aircraft, car, motorbike, vehicle; *fig:* infrastructure, organization, setup, system; android, automaton, robot, workaholic. **vb** *lit:* finish, make, manufacture, saw, turn.

macho adj *lit:* aggressive, dominant, domineering, he-man, male, muscular, powerful, strong, strong-willed, tough, virile.

mad adj *lit:* certifiable, insane, psychopathic, psychotic; crazy, deranged, demented, lunatic, unbalanced, unhinged; *fig:* asinine, half-baked, daft, idiotic, irrational, irresponsible, ludicrous, nonsensical, preposterous, senseless, unworkable; fanatical (about), wild (about); agitated, excited, frantic, hectic, hysterical, riotous; berserk, furious, hysterical, incensed, spare.

made vb (pa.pt) *lit:* built, composed, constituted, constructed, fashioned, formed, generated, invented, manufactured, originated, produced, shaped; designed, devised, drafted, drawn up, framed; enacted, passed; appointed, elected, installed, ordained; had (one do something); added up to, amounted to, came to, totaled; earned, gained, netted, received; reckoned to be; arrived in time for, caught, got, reached; knew, recognized.

madly adv *lit:* crazily, dementedly; idiotically, irrationally, irresponsibly, nonsensically, senselessly; agitatedly, excitedly, frantically, hectically, hysterically, recklessly, riotously, wildly; desperately, devotedly, intensely, passionately.

madness n *lit:* derangement, insanity, lunacy, psychopathy, psychosis; dementia, irrationality; aberration, craziness, daftness, folly, recklessness, wildness; passion; rage; excitement, fever, frenzy, intoxication.

magazine n *lit:* journal, monthly, paper, periodical, weekly; ammunition dump, arsenal, powder store.

magic n *lit:* black arts, necromancy, sorcery, spells, witchcraft, wizardry; paranormal, supernatural; conjuring, hocus-pocus, legerdemain, sleight of hand, trickery; *fig:* charisma, enchantment, fascination, magnetism, power; fire, life, spark.

magician **n** *lit:* enchanter, enchantress, sorcerer, warlock, witch, wizard; conjuror, illusionist, prestidigitator; *fig:* miracle-worker, wonder-worker; genius, expert, virtuoso.

magnetic **adj** *lit:* attractive; *fig:* captivating, charming, enchanting; fascinating, hypnotic, mesmerizing.

magnificence **n** *lit:* glory, grandeur, lavishness, luxury, opulence, pomp, resplendence, splendor, sumptuousness.

magnificent **adj** *lit:* exalted, fine, glorious, grand, grandiose, imposing, lavish, luxurious, majestic, opulent, princely, resplendent, splendid, sumptuous, superb.

magnify **vb** *lit:* amplify, blow up, enlarge, expand; heighten, increase, intensify; laud, praise, worship; *fig:* exaggerate, inflate, overdo, overstate.

magnitude **n** *lit:* amplitude, capacity, dimensions, extent, immensity, measure, proportions, quantity, scale, size, volume; *fig:* consequence, eminence, importance, note, significance, weight; *spec:* brightness, brilliance (of a star).

mail **n** *lit:* correspondence, letters, post; amour, chain link. **vb** *lit:* dispatch, post, send.

main **n** *lit:* might, power, strength, weight; cable, channel, duct, pipe; high sea, ocean. **adj** *lit:* cardinal, chief, critical, essential, important, leading, preeminent, primary, principal, vital; extensive, great, large, strong; mere, pure, sheer.

mainly **adv** *lit:* chiefly, for the most part, largely, mostly, predominantly, primarily, principally, substantially; generally, on the whole, usually.

maintain **vb** *lit:* care for, foster, keep up, look after, nurture, preserve, provide for, take care of; carry on, conserve, continue, keep, retain, sustain; allege, assert, aver, claim, contend, declare, hold, insist, state; defend, stand by, uphold.

maintenance **n** *lit:* care, fostering, looking after, nurturing, preservation, provision, upkeep; conservation, continuance, retention, sustaining; defense, protection; allowance, grant, keep, living, support; alimony, award.

majestic adj *lit:* august, dignified, exalted, grand, imperial, imposing, lofty, magnificent, princely, regal, royal, stately.

majesty n *lit:* dignity, glory, grandeur, greatness, loftiness, magnificence, pomp, splendor, state, stateliness.

major adj *lit:* great, important, leading, main, notable, outstanding, preeminent, significant, weighty; elder, senior.

majority n *lit:* best part, bulk, preponderance; adulthood, maturity, seniority.

make n *lit:* brand, design, form, kind, mark, model, shape, sort, style, type, variety; constitution, manufacture; build, composition. **vb** *lit:* build, construct, create, fabricate, fashion, form, generate, invent, manufacture, originate, produce, put together, shape; design, devise, draft, draw up, frame; conclude, contract; enact, pass; convert, turn; appoint, elect, install as, ordain; have (one do something); add up to, amount to, come to, total; score; contribute, put forward; earn, gain, net, realize, receive; reckon to be; arrive in time for, catch, get, reach; know, recognize.

make do vb *lit:* cope, get by, manage (with), scrape by; be content (with).

make out vb *lit:* detect, discern, distinguish, perceive, see; decipher, read; comprehend, grasp, understand; allege, assert, claim, maintain, suggest; feign, pretend; complete, draft, draw up, fill out, write out; cope, fare, get by, get on, manage; prosper, succeed.

make-up n *lit:* cosmetics, face; greasepaint; composition, constitution, construction, formation, structure; layout; *fig:* character, disposition, nature, temperament.

make up vb *lit:* compose, comprise, constitute, form; compensate for, complete, fill, supply; come up with, concoct, create, devise, dream up, fabricate, hatch, invent, write; atone (for), make amends (for); mend, repair; become friends again, be reconciled, make peace; make overtures (to); settle in (one's mind).

male n *lit:* boy, man; lad; boar, buck, bull, cock, dog, jack, ram, tom. **adj** *lit:* manly, masculine, virile; butch, macho.

maltreat   vb *lit:* abuse, be cruel to, be rough with, bully, ill-treat; damage, hurt, injure.

man   n *lit:* male; person; individual; Homo sapiens, humanity, humankind, human race, people; gentleman; chap, guy; boyfriend, husband, lover, spouse; attendant, employee, hand, male servant, retainer, valet, worker; soldier; follower; team member; *spec:* piece (chess, checkers). **vb** *lit:* crew, garrison, people, staff.

manage   vb *lit:* administer, be in charge of, control, direct, oversee, run, superintend, supervise; manipulate, operate, use, wield; carry out, cope with, do, execute, handle, perform; accomplish, bring off, effect; contrive, engineer, orchestrate; cope, fare, get by, get on, make out, survive; have time for.

manageable   adj *lit:* amenable, compliant, controllable, docile, submissive, tractable; achievable, attainable, possible; easy; convenient.

management   n *lit:* administration, board, directors; charge, control, government, handling, running, supervision; manipulation, use, wielding.

mangled   adj (pa.pt) *lit:* pressed, wrung; bent, broken, crooked, crushed, deformed, disfigured, distorted, lamed, maimed, mutilated, ripped, torn; *fig:* garbled, misrepresented, travestied.

manhandle   vb *lit:* haul, heave, lug, maneuver, pull, push, roll, shove; fondle, grope, maul, paw; abuse, knock about, rough up.

manifest   n *lit:* bill of lading, cargo checklist; passenger list. **vb** *lit:* demonstrate, display, evince, exhibit, make evident, make visible, reveal, show; announce, declare. **adj** *lit:* apparent, clear, evident, obvious, patent, plain, visible.

manifestation   n *lit:* appearance, demonstration, display, exhibition, revelation, show; evidence, indication, sign, symptom; example, instance; apparition, materialization.

manipulation   n *lit:* command, control, direction, driving, guidance, handling, management, maneuvering, piloting, steering, use, wielding; arrangement, contrivance, engineering, orchestration, organization.

manliness   n *lit:* machismo, maleness, masculinity, muscularity, virility; bravery, courage, hardihood, intrepidity, valor; chivalry, gallantry, gentlemanliness.

manner   n *lit:* approach, means, measures, method, mode, procedure, process, steps, way; custom, fashion, habit, practice, routine, style, usage; air, appearance, comportment, demeanor, mien, tone; attitude, behavior; category, form, kind, nature, sort, strain, type, vein.

mannerism   n *lit:* characteristic, foible, habit, idiosyncrasy, quirk, trait; affectation, distortion.

manners   n *lit:* courtesy, decorum, etiquette, good form, proprieties, protocol, refinement, social graces; behavior, conduct, mores.

mantle   n *lit:* cape, hood; cloak, redingote; *fig:* covering, curtain, screen, shroud, veil; *spec:* feathers; stratum (of rock between the earth's core and crust). vb *lit:* blanket, cloak, cover, envelop, mask, screen, shroud, veil.

manual   n *lit:* bible, compendium, guidebook, handbook, instruction book, textbook, vade mecum, workshop reference; keyboard. **adj** *lit:* hand-cranked, hand-operated.

manufacture   n *lit:* assembly, construction, mass production, production; end product, product. vb *lit:* assemble, build, construct, make, mass-produce, process, produce, put together, turn out; *fig:* come up with, concoct, devise, fabricate, make up, think up.

manure   n *lit:* droppings, dung, muck; fertilizer, mulch.

march   n *lit:* haul, hike, tramp, trek, walk; advance, development, progress; (on the) way; demo, demonstration, parade, procession; military tune; border, boundary; borderland, edge, frontier, margin. vb *lit:* hike, step out, stride out, traipse, tramp, tread, trek, walk; abut, adjoin, border, bound.

margin   n *lit:* border, boundary, edge, limit, perimeter, periphery, verge; allowance, elbow room, latitude, leeway, play, room, surplus.

marginal   adj *lit:* bordering, peripheral; insignificant, minimal, negligible, outside, slight, tiny.

marijuana   n *lit:* cannabis, ganja, grass, hash, hashish, hemp, pot, smoke, weed.

mark   n *lit:* blot, splotch, spot, stain; badge, brand, device, emblem, logo, signature, symbol, token; label, tag; blemish, dent, nick, scar, scratch; footprint, sign, trace, vestige; criterion, level, line, norm, yardstick; aim, goal, jack, objective, target; dupe, greenhorn, innocent, patsy, sucker; model, type; consequence, distinction, eminence, note, standing; point, unit. **vb** *lit:* blot, splotch, spot, stain; sign, write on; brand, label, tag; blemish, dent, nick, scar, scratch; exemplify, illustrate, register, show; attend to, mind, note, pay heed to, watch; assess, evaluate, grade.

marked **adj (pa.pt)** *lit:* splotched, spotted, stained; branded, identified, indicated, labeled, tagged; blemished, dented, imperfect, nicked, scarred, scratched; clear, conspicuous, distinct, manifest, obvious, patent, pronounced, striking; emphatic, extreme, great, surprising, unexpected; suspected, threatened, watched; dead, doomed, ill-fated.

market **n** *lit:* bazaar, mart; souk, town square; stock exchange; buying public, consumers, purchasers; demand. **vb** *lit:* hawk, peddle, sell, vend; advertise, hype, plug, promote, push.

maroon **vb** *lit:* abandon, cast away, desert, isolate, leave high and dry, rat on, run out on, strand. **adj** *lit:* chestnut, red-brown; mauve, violet.

married **adj (pa.pt)** *lit:* hitched, spliced, wed, wedded; conjugal, connubial, marital.

marrow **n** *lit:* core, pith, substance; *fig:* crux, heart, kernel, nub; essence, gist, spirit; best part, juice.

marry **vb** *lit:* be wed, get hitched, get spliced, take the plunge, tie the knot, wed; ally, join, link, match, put together, unite.

marvel **n** *lit:* phenomenon, prodigy, wonder; expert, genius, virtuoso. **vb** *lit:* be awed, gape, wonder; be astonished, be overwhelmed.

marvelous **adj** *lit:* amazing, astonishing, astounding, phenomenal, prodigious, wonderful; fabulous, fantastic, incredible, unbelievable.

mask **n** *lit:* domino; visor; *fig:* camouflage, cloak, cover, disguise, front, veil. **vb** *lit:* camouflage, cloak, conceal, cover, disguise, screen, veil.

mass **n** *lit:* entirety, sum, totality, whole; body, bulk, matter, substance; dimensions, magnitude, scale, size; block, chunk, lump, piece; accumulation, amount, collection, heap, load, lot, pile, quantity; crowd, horde, host, mob, multitude, throng; majority; lower class(es); *spec:* communion service, Eucharist, holy communion, the Lord's supper. **vb** *lit:*

accumulate, assemble, collect, congregate, muster, rally; concentrate (together), flock, swarm.

master n *lit:* captain, chief, commander, head, lord, principal, skipper; overseer, owner; boss, director, employer; guide, instructor, teacher, tutor; guru, swami; ace, adept, expert, virtuoso; *fig:* model, mold, original, pattern. **vb** *lit:* command, control, dominate, rule; become good at, grasp, learn; break, bridle, curb, domesticate, overpower, subdue, subjugate, tame. **adj** *lit:* chief, foremost, grand, main, prime, principal; adept, expert, skilled, virtuoso; *fig:* model, original; *spec:* skeleton (key).

mastermind n *lit:* brains, engineer, genius, organizer, planner. **vb** *lit:* arrange, be the brains behind, engineer, orchestrate, organize, plan.

mastery n *lit:* authority, control, domination, dominion, rule, supremacy, whip hand; triumph, victory; command, grasp, knowledge, understanding; ability, dexterity, expertise, skill, virtuosity.

match n *lit:* complement, counterpart, equal, equivalent; copy, duplicate, look-alike, replica, ringer, twin; competitor, rival; bout, competition, contest, game; alliance, marriage, pairing, partnership; light, lucifer; fuse. **vb** *lit:* compare, equal, parallel, rival; oppose (against), pit (against); agree with, blend with, go with, harmonize with, suit; ally, couple, marry, pair, partner, put together.

matchless adj *lit:* incomparable, inimitable, peerless, perfect, superior, unequaled, unique, unrivaled.

mate n *lit:* partner, spouse; husband, lover, wife; buddy, chum, pal; associate, companion, comrade, crony; colleague, coworker, partner; aide, assistant, henchman, second-in-command; complement, counterpart, fellow, match, twin. **vb** *lit:* match, pair; marry, wed; breed, copulate, couple.

material n *lit:* matter, substance; constituents, element(s); cloth, fabric; data, evidence, information, schema; apparatus, implement(s), instrument(s), tool(s). **adj** *lit:* concrete, corporeal, palpable, physical, tangible; essential, important, key, significant, vital; applicable (to), germane (to), pertinent (to), relevant (to).

matter n *lit:* material, substance; affair, case, circumstance, concern, event, incident, occurrence, question, situation, subject, thing; argument, gist, point, purport, sense; contents, copy, text; consequence, importance, moment, significance; amount, quantity; difficulty, problem, trouble. **vb** *lit:* be important, count, make a difference, signify.

mature **vb** *lit:* be fully developed, come of age, grow up, reach adulthood; bloom, blossom, mellow, ripen, season; *fig:* become payable, fall due. **adj** *lit:* adult, full-grown, grown-up, of age; fully fledged, mellow, ready, ripe, seasoned; *fig:* due, payable; practical, prudent, wise.

maturity **n** *lit:* adulthood, age of reason, majority, manhood, womanhood, years of discretion; bloom, blossoming, mellowness, ripeness; *fig:* common sense, poise, practicality, prudence, wisdom.

maul **vb** *lit:* claw, lacerate, mangle; batter, beat, knock (about), thrash; manhandle, treat roughly; abuse, fumble, grope, molest, paw.

maximum **n** *lit:* best, chief, greatest, highest, largest, most; apogee, ceiling, crest, height, peak, pinnacle, summit, top, zenith.

maze **n** *lit:* labyrinth; *fig:* complex, mesh, system, tangle, web; puzzle, state of bewilderment.

mean **n** *lit:* average, intermediate, median, medium, middle; norm, par, standard. **vb** *lit:* betoken, connote, denote, express, indicate, signify, stand for; drive at, imply, insinuate, refer to, say, suggest; entail, involve, lead to, result in; aim (to), be resolved (to), intend (to), plan (to), propose (to), purpose (to); design (to), destine (to), fate (to), foreordain (to), make (to), predestine (to). **adj** *lit:* average, intermediate, median, medium, middle; normal, standard; close-fisted, miserly, near, parsimonious, penny-pinching, stingy, tight; beggarly, contemptible, low, seedy, shabby, sordid, squalid, wretched; base, degenerate, degraded, dishonorable, shameful; common, humble, inferior, low-born, menial, ordinary, plebeian; *fig:* bad-tempered, cantankerous, disagreeable, ornery, rude, sour; dangerous; clever, shrewd, tricky.

meaning **n** *lit:* connotation, import, interpretation, purport, significance; drift, gist, implication, insinuation, point, sense, substance, suggestion; force, thrust, validity, value; aim, design, intention, object, purpose. **adj** *lit:* eloquent, expressive, pregnant, significant, speaking.

meaningless **adj** *lit:* aimless, empty, hollow, pointless, purposeless, useless, worthless; garbled, incomprehensible, unintelligible.

means **n** *lit:* agent, instrument, medium, method, mode, process, way;

agency, instrumentality, methodology, procedure; capital, funds, income, property, resources, substance, wealth, wherewithal; (by) dint (of).

meanwhile adv *lit:* at the same time, concurrently, contemporaneously, simultaneously; for the duration, for the moment, in the interim, in the meantime.

measure n *lit:* gauge, meter, rule, ruler, scale, scoop, tape; optic; benchmark, criterion, line, norm, standard, touchstone, unit, yardstick; allocation, proportion, quota, ration, share; amount, quantity; degree, extent, range, scope; dimensions, magnitude, size; column width, page width; action, course, maneuver, ploy, step; act, bill, law, resolution, statute; beat, cadence, rhythm; dance; foot, meter; *fig:* moderation, restraint. **vb** *lit:* calibrate, determine, gauge, mark (off/out), quantify, value; deal (out), dole (out), mete (out).

measurement n *lit:* calibration, gauging, quantifying, valuation; amplitude, dimensions, extent, magnitude, proportions, size.

meat n *lit:* flesh, viands; brawn, muscle; chow, food, grub, nourishment, provisions, rations, subsistence, victuals; *fig:* essence, heart, marrow, nub, pith, substance.

meaty adj *lit:* beefy, brawny, burly, hulking, muscular, strapping; nourishing, rich; *fig:* concentrated, meaningful, pithy.

mechanical adj *lit:* automated, automatic, machine-operated; emotionless, impersonal, machinelike, unfeeling; constant, habitual, mindless, monotonous, perfunctory, reflex, routine, unchanging, unthinking.

mechanism n *lit:* apparatus, appliance, device, gadget, machine; action, cogs, machinery, works; functioning, operation, performance, working; means, method, procedure, system, technique.

medicine n *lit:* medicament, medication, therapy, treatment; drug; capsule, pill, tablet; pathology; *fig:* punishment; charm, magic, spell.

mediocre adj *lit:* average, commonplace, medium, ordinary, undistinguished; indifferent, less than ordinary, pedestrian, second-rate, uninspired.

mediocrity n *lit:* ordinariness, undistinguished nature; lack of inspiration, pedestrianism; lightweight, nonentity.

medium   **n** *lit:* average, middle; compromise, midpoint; agency, channel, instrument, means, organ, vehicle; method, mode, process, way; mouthpiece, spiritist, spiritualist, transmitter; atmosphere, conditions, environment, milieu, setting. **adj** *lit:* average, intermediate, median, middle, middling.

meek   **adj** *lit:* docile, gentle, humble, mild, submissive, unassuming; deferential, modest, peaceable; spineless, tame, weak.

meet   **vb** *lit:* come across, encounter, find, happen on, run into; greet, welcome; assemble, congregate, convene, gather, muster, rally; compete with, confront, contend against, do battle with, face, line up against; adjoin, connect, converge, join, merge, touch; *fig:* come up to, comply with, fulfill, match, measure up to, satisfy; bear, endure, experience, undergo. **adj** *lit:* appropriate, correct, fitting, proper, right, seemly, suitable.

meeting   **n** *lit:* encounter; assignation, rendezvous, tryst; conclave, conference, convention, convocation, gathering, get-together, rally; service; concourse, confluence, conjunction, convergence, junction, merging; crossing.

mellow   **vb** *lit:* age, mature, ripen, soften, sweeten. **adj** *lit:* full, juicy, mature, rich, ripe, soft, sweet; *fig:* mellifluous, rounded, smooth, tuneful; elevated, expansive, happy, jolly, merry.

melodramatic   **adj** *lit:* exaggerated, histrionic, overdone, sensational, stagy, theatrical.

melody   **n** *lit:* air, theme, tune; lay, song, strain; tunefulness.

melt   **vb** *lit:* deliquesce, dissolve, fuse, liquefy, thaw; fade (away), vanish (away); *fig:* disarm, charm, soften.

member   **n** *lit:* associate; representative; appendage, component, constituent, element, limb, organ, part; *fig:* clause.

memoirs   **n** *lit:* autobiography, diaries, history, life, life story; experiences, reminiscences; documents, journals, papers, records, transactions.

memorable   **adj** *lit:* emotive, impressive, indelible, moving, notable, remarkable, striking, unforgettable; extraordinary, odd, strange; historic, important; catchy, haunting.

memory n *lit:* recall, recollection; powers of retention; remembrance, reminiscence; commemoration, memorial; fame, renown, reputation; data bank, data base.

menace n *lit:* threat; danger, hazard; *fig:* nuisance, pain, pest. **vb** *lit:* bully, frighten, intimidate, terrorize; threaten; loom over, overshadow.

mend **vb** *lit:* fix, patch up, repair, replace; renovate, restore; better, correct, rectify; heal, improve, knit, recover.

mental **adj** *lit:* intellectual; psychological; internal, notional; *fig:* deranged, insane, psychotic, unbalanced.

mention n *lit:* acknowledgment (of), allusion, citation, plug, reference, tribute. **vb** *lit:* acknowledge, allude to, bring up, cite, make known, name, refer to, touch upon.

mercenary n *lit:* dog of war, free lance, hired soldier, soldier of fortune. **adj** *lit:* hired, paid; avaricious, greedy, money-grubbing, venal.

merchant n *lit:* dealer, retailer, seller, shopkeeper, trader, tradesman, wholesaler.

merciful **adj** *lit:* clement, compassionate, humane, lenient, magnanimous; forgiving.

merciless **adj** *lit:* callous, cruel, hard-hearted, harsh, heartless, implacable, inhumane, pitiless, ruthless; strict, unforgiving.

mercy n *lit:* clemency, compassion, grace, humanity, leniency, magnanimity, pity, quarter; forgiveness; *fig:* blessing, godsend, relief; (at the) disposition (of).

mere **adj** *lit:* plain, pure, sheer, simple, stark, unadulterated, unmitigated; callow, green, young; insignificant, trifling, trivial, unimportant.

merit n *lit:* credit; excellence, meed, quality, value, virtue, worth; advantage, strong point. **vb** *lit:* be worthy of, deserve, rate, warrant; earn.

merry **adj** *lit:* blithe, carefree, convivial, droll, fun, happy, jolly, waggish; *fig:* fuddled, high, mellow, sozzled, tipsy, woozy.

mesh n *lit:* net, network, plexus, reticulation; lattice, web, webbing;

tangle, toils. **vb** *lit:* ensnare, entangle, net, snare, tangle; connect, coordinate, dovetail, engage, interlock; heal, knit.

mess n *lit:* clutter, confusion, jumble, mishmash, shambles; chaos, disarray, untidiness; blot, blotch, smear, smudge, splotch; bungle, hash; *fig:* fix, jam, muddle, pickle, predicament, spot; *spec:* dining room, refectory, sitting (in the armed forces). **vb** *lit:* clutter (up), disorganize, jumble (up); blot, smear, smudge; foul (up), hash (up), muck (up), muddle; dirty, foul, pollute, soil; fiddle (with), interfere (with), meddle (with), tinker (with); fiddle (with), play (with).

message n *lit:* communiqué, dispatch, memo, news, word; import, meaning, moral, point, sense, theme.

messenger n *lit:* bearer, carrier, courier, emissary, envoy, go-between.

messy adj *lit:* cluttered, disorganized, jumbled, muddled; blotchy, smeared, smudged; dirty, muddied, muddy, polluted, soiled; disheveled, matted, slovenly, tangled, unkempt.

method n *lit:* approach, fashion, manner, mode, practice, procedure, process, routine, system, technique, way; form, order, planning, structure; classification.

methodical adj *lit:* businesslike, disciplined, efficient, orderly, planned, regular, systematic, tidy.

microscopic adj *lit:* minuscule, minute, tiny; infinitesimal.

middle n *lit:* center, midpoint; mean, medium; midriff, stomach, waist; (in the) midst (of). **adj** *lit:* central; mean, median, medium; intermediate.

midget n *lit:* person of restricted growth; dwarf; homunculus, pygmy; manikin; half-pint, shrimp. **adj** *lit:* dwarf, miniature, pocket, pygmy, tiny.

mighty adj *lit:* forceful, powerful, strong, vigorous; brawny, muscular, stalwart, strapping; colossal, enormous, gigantic, huge, immense, massive, vast.

migrate vb *lit:* journey, move on, shift camp, travel, trek, voyage; move elsewhere, pass (through).

mild adj *lit:* easygoing, gentle, meek, peaceable, placid, serene, temperate, tender, tranquil; moderate, pleasant, warm; bland, soothing.

military n *lit:* armed forces, army, services, war office. **adj** *lit:* army, service.

milk n *lit:* lactation; juice, sap. **vb** *lit:* cream, draw off, express, extract, tap; *fig:* bleed, drain, wring; exploit, impose upon, take advantage of.

mill n *lit:* crusher, grinder; factory, plant, processing plant, works. **vb** *lit:* crush, granulate, grind, powder, press, pulverize, punch, stamp; crowd (around), swarm (about), throng (around).

mind n *lit:* brain, gray matter, intellect, intelligence, reason; consciousness, psyche, subconscious; marbles, rationality, sanity, wits; memory, recollection; thoughts; *fig:* genius, thinker; attitude, judgment, opinion, thoughts, way of thinking; imagination; attention, concentration; fancy (to), urge (to), wish (to). **vb** *lit:* care, disapprove, feel strongly about, object, take offense; attend to, heed, listen to, mark, note; comply with, follow, obey; ensure that, make certain that, take care that; keep an eye on, look after, take care of, watch over; beware of, look out for; *fig:* recall, remember.

mindless adj *lit:* automatic, mechanical; casual, gratuitous, incidental, indifferent, unreasoning; careless, forgetful, negligent, unmindful; asinine, idiotic, moronic, obtuse.

mine n *lit:* bomb, explosive device, shell; excavation, gallery, pit, quarry, shaft, tunnel; *fig:* fund, hoard, stock, store, wealth. **vb** *lit:* lay a bomb, sink a bomb; dig (for), excavate (for), quarry (for); subvert, tunnel under.

minimal adj *lit:* infinitesimal, minuscule, minute, tiny; invisible, virtually nonexistent; nominal, token.

minimize vb *lit:* deprecate, make light of, play down, tone down; keep as small as possible, reduce as much as possible; *fig:* decrease, diminish, shrink.

minimum n *lit:* least, lowest, slightest, smallest; bottom, nadir.

minister n *lit:* clergyman, cleric, padre, parson, preacher, priest, vicar; cabinet/government member, consul, diplomat, envoy; agent, lieutenant, official, subordinate. **vb** *lit:* attend to, serve, take care of.

minor adj *lit:* immature, juvenile, underage; inconsequential, insignificant, negligible, petty, slight, trifling, trivial, unimportant; junior, subordinate; younger.

minority   n *lit:* lesser number, smaller group; losing voters; childhood years.

mint   n *lit:* coin factory, herb; *fig:* origin, source; bomb, fortune, king's ransom, packet, tidy sum. **vb** *lit:* cast, coin, punch, stamp, strike; *fig:* come up with, create, devise, invent, make up, produce, think up. **adj** *lit:* brand-new, fresh, perfect, undamaged, unused.

minute   n *lit:* agenda, memorandum, note(s), record(s); *fig:* flash, instant, jiffy, moment, second, tick. **vb** *lit:* log, make a transcript of, record, register, take notes of. **adj** *lit:* diminutive, fine, microscopic, minuscule, tiny; insignificant, negligible, trifling, trivial, unimportant; detailed, exhaustive, meticulous, precise, punctilious, scrupulous.

miraculous   adj *lit:* divine, providential; supernatural; extraordinary, incredible, inexplicable; phenomenal, unaccountable, unbelievable; magic, magical, wondrous.

mirror   n *lit:* glass, looking glass; double, image, likeness, reflection, twin. **vb** *lit:* depict, display, reflect, show; echo, emulate; copy, simulate.

misapprehension   n *lit:* error, false impression, misconception, misconstruction, misunderstanding.

misbehave   vb *lit:* act up, be disobedient, be naughty, be mischievous, be rude, get into trouble, muck about.

mischief   n *lit:* disobedience, misbehavior, naughtiness; boisterousness, devilment, horseplay, shenanigans; damage, harm, hurt, injury, trouble; *fig:* devil, nuisance, pest, rogue, scamp.

mischievous   adj *lit:* badly behaved, disobedient, impish, misbehaving, naughty, troublesome, vexatious; boisterous, careless, riotous, rough; deleterious, detrimental, malign, spiteful; destructive, evil, harmful, injurious, pernicious, wicked.

miser   n *lit:* hoarder, penny-pincher, Scrooge, skinflint.

miserable   adj *lit:* blue, brokenhearted, dejected, depressed, desolate, despondent, dismal, doleful, down, gloomy, grief-stricken, heartbroken, melancholy, sorrowful, suffering, unhappy, wretched; bankrupt, destitute, impoverished, penniless, poor; base, deplorable, low, mean, pitiable, shabby, shameful, sordid, sorry, squalid.

miserly adj *lit:* avaricious, close-fisted, grasping, mean, parsimonious, penny-pinching, stingy, tight.

misery n *lit:* dejection, depression, despair, distress, grief, melancholy, sadness, sorrow, suffering, unhappiness, wretchedness; destitution, pennilessness, penury, poverty; meanness, shabbiness, sordidness, squalor; burden, hardship, misfortune, trial, tribulation, woe.

misgiving n *lit:* anxiety, apprehension, fear, qualm, reservation, scruple, suspicion, worry.

misguided adj *lit:* deluded, ill-advised, led astray, misled; imprudent, injudicious, indiscreet, misplaced, unwise; mistaken.

misinterpret vb *lit:* misapprehend, misconstrue, misread, misunderstand; distort, falsify, garble, misrepresent, pervert, travesty.

misleading adj (pr.pt) *lit:* ambiguous, confusing, deceptive, fallacious, false, inaccurate, specious, unrepresentative.

miss vb *lit:* be late for, forgo, lose; fail to grasp, let slip; fail to notice, pass over, overlook; jump, leave out, neglect, omit, skip; long for, pine for, yearn for.

missing adj *lit:* absent, gone astray, lacking, lost, mislaid, misplaced, not there, unaccounted for.

mist n *lit:* fog, smog, vapor; condensation, drizzle, spray.

mistake n *lit:* blunder, error, fault, gaffe, howler, inaccuracy, miscalculation, misconception, misunderstanding, oversight, slip. vb *lit:* get wrong, misinterpret, misunderstand; miscalculate, misjudge.

mistaken adj (pa.pt) *lit:* misguided, misinformed, wide of the mark; inaccurate, incorrect, wrong; ill-advised, ill-judged, imprudent, unwise.

mix n *lit:* assortment, blend, compound, medley, mixture, variety; combination, proportions, ratio; ingredients, mixture, paste. vb *lit:* blend, combine, compound, diffuse, fuse, intermingle, merge, stir together; shuffle; associate (with), get on (with), hang out (with), mingle (with), socialize (with).

moan n *lit:* groan, lament, sob, wail; *fig:* beef, complaint, gripe, grouse. vb *lit:* groan, keen, lament, sob, whine; beef, carp, complain, gripe, grouse, grumble.

mob n *lit:* crew, crowd, flock, herd, gang, group, horde, host, mass, multitude, press, set, throng; hoi polloi, masses, proles, rabble, riffraff, scum. vb *lit:* crowd, jostle, surround.

mock vb *lit:* deride, insult, jeer at, laugh at, ridicule, scoff at, sneer at, taunt; ape, burlesque, caricature, lampoon, send up, take off. adj *lit:* artificial, bogus, counterfeit, ersatz, fake, false, imitation, phony, sham, spurious.

mockery n *lit:* contumely, derision, gibes, insults, ridicule, scorn; farce, travesty.

model vb *lit:* archetype, example, exemplar, mold, original, pattern, prototype; copy, dummy, mock-up, replica, reproduction; design, plan, representation; kind, make, mark, sort, style, type, version; poser, sitter, subject; mannequin. vb *lit:* construct, design, devise, fashion, form, mold, pattern, shape, style; display, exhibit, show off. adj *lit:* facsimile, imitation; miniature, scaled-down; exemplary, ideal, perfect.

moderate vb *lit:* calm, control, curb, mitigate, repress, restrain, soften, tame, tone down; chair, preside over; arbitrate (between), mediate (between). adj *lit:* average, fair, medium, middling, passable, reasonable, tolerable; indifferent, mediocre, ordinary; medium-sized; equable, mild, peaceable, restrained, temperate.

modern adj *lit:* contemporary, current, latest, new, novel, present-day, recent, state-of-the-art, twentieth-century, up-to-date.

modernize vb *lit:* bring up to date, renovate, revamp, update.

modest adj *lit:* bashful, diffident, humble, meek, reserved, retiring, self-effacing, shy; chaste, decent, demure; fair, moderate, reasonable, unpretentious.

modesty n *lit:* bashfulness, diffidence, humility, meekness, reserve, reticence, self-effacement; chastity, decency, demureness; moderation, unpretentiousness.

modification n *lit:* adjustment, alteration, change, refinement; modulation; lessening, lowering, moderation, reduction.

modify vb *lit:* adjust, alter, change, convert, refine, revise; modulate; lessen, lower, moderate, reduce, tone down.

moist adj *lit:* clammy, damp, dank, humid, sodden, soggy, sweaty, wet; rainy, watery.

moisture n *lit:* damp, dampness, dankness, humidity; fluid, liquid.

mold n *lit:* fungus, mildew, saprophyte; dust, earth, loam, soil; die, matrix, pattern, stencil, template; cast; *fig:* build, configuration, fashion, form, kind, shape, style, type; caliber, character, quality, stamp. vb *lit:* cast, model, sculpt; create, fashion, form, shape; *fig:* control, direct, guide, influence, inform.

molest vb *lit:* abuse, fondle, grope, interfere with, maltreat, manhandle; badger, bother, harass, harry, hound, importune, pester, plague, worry; annoy, irritate, vex.

moment n *lit:* instant, second, split second, twinkling of an eye; juncture, point, time; concern, consequence, historicity, importance, significance, weight.

momentous adj *lit:* consequential, crucial, decisive, fateful, historic, important, significant, weighty.

momentum n *lit:* drive, energy, force, impetus, motion, thrust.

money n *lit:* assets, capital, cash, currency, finances, funds, legal tender, liquidity, riches, sterling, wealth.

monitor n *lit:* overseer, supervisor, warden; prefect; alarm, detector, gauge, meter, scanner, tester; screen. vb *lit:* observe, oversee, supervise, watch over; keep track of, record, scan, screen.

monkey n *lit:* primate, simian; ape; *fig:* imp, jackanapes, rascal, rogue, scamp, scapegrace; (make a) fool (of); ass, laughing-stock; *fig:* hammer, pile driver. vb *lit:* fiddle (with), meddle (with), tamper (with); fool (about), mess (about), play (about).

monotonous adj *lit:* constant, continual, mindless, relentless, repetitious, repetitive, uniform, unvarying; boring, humdrum, soporific, tedious, wearisome.

monster n *lit:* freak, mutant, obscenity; animal, beast, brute, savage; demon, devil, fiend; colossus, giant, jumbo, mammoth, whopper. adj *lit:* colossal, enormous, giant, huge, immense, jumbo, mammoth, massive, vast, whopping.

monstrous **adj** *lit:* abnormal, deformed, freakish, grotesque, malformed, mutant, obscene, teratological, unnatural; bestial, brutal, brutish, savage; cruel, demonic, diabolical, evil, fiendish, inhuman, loathsome, satanic, vicious; frightful, gruesome, hideous, horrible; colossal, enormous, giant, huge, immense, jumbo, mammoth, massive, vast, whopping.

monumental **adj** *lit:* commemorative, memorial; columnar, monolithic, statuary; awesome, classic, epoch-making, historic, lasting, outstanding, significant; *fig:* colossal, enormous, giant, huge, immense, jumbo, mammoth, massive, vast, whopping.

mood **n** *lit:* disposition, humor, state of mind, temper; bad temper, melancholy, moroseness, sulkiness.

moody **adj** *lit:* capricious, changeable, erratic, fitful, mercurial, temperamental, unpredictable, volatile; bad-tempered, broody, crotchety, gloomy, ill-humored, melancholy, morose, petulant, sulky, sullen, touchy.

mop **n** *lit:* sponge, squeegee, swab; cloth, rag; brush, shock, tangle, thatch; face, grimace. **vb** *lit:* absorb, soak (up), stem; sponge, swab, wipe (up).

moral **n** *lit:* lesson, message, point; envoy, ethic(s), ideal(s), principle(s), scruple(s). **adj** *lit:* ethical, principled; decent, good, honest, honorable, proper, upstanding, virtuous; intellectual, mental; likely, probable.

morality **n** *lit:* ethics, ideals, integrity, principles, standards; decency, goodness, honesty, honor, propriety, virtue.

morbid **adj** *lit:* downcast, melancholy, pessimistic; brooding, gloomy, grim, somber; ghastly, ghoulish, gruesome, macabre, sick, unhealthy; diseased, ill, infected, sickly; fatal, malignant, necrotic, terminal.

more **adj** *lit:* additional, extra, further, supplementary; different, fresh, new, other; of greater size; of greater quantity. **adv** *lit:* to a greater degree, to a greater extent; further; longer; additionally, again.

moreover **adv** *lit:* additionally, also, besides, further, furthermore, in addition, likewise, too.

mortal **n** *lit:* human being, individual, person. **adj** *lit:* human; corporeal, temporal; impermanent, transient, waxing and waning; deadly, fatal, lethal, terminal; deathly; to the death.

most adj *lit:* (the) greatest amount of, (the) greatest degree of, (the) greatest measure of, (the) greatest number of; nearly all, the great majority of. **adv** *lit:* extremely; principally; to the greatest degree, to the greatest extent.

mother n *lit:* ma, mama, old lady; matron, parent; abbess, prioress, superior. **vb** *lit:* bear, engender, give birth to, produce; care for, cherish, foster, nurture, raise, rear, tend; *fig:* baby, fuss over, make a fuss of, mollycoddle, pamper.

motion n *lit:* advance, movement, passage, progress, travel, way; proposal, proposition, subject, submission, theme, topic; gesticulation, gesture, signal, wave; bowel movement, defecation, evacuation.

motionless adj *lit:* at rest, immobile, inert, static, stationary, still, unmoving; fixed, frozen, paralyzed, stopped, transfixed; crouched, in wait, tensed.

motivate vb *lit:* act as an incentive, bring (to), cause (to), drive (to), induce (to), inspire (to), instigate, prompt (to), stimulate (to), stir (to).

motive n *lit:* aim, design, intention, object, purpose, rationale, reason, reasoning, thinking; incentive, inducement, stimulus. **adj** *lit:* activating, driving, impulsive, operative, propelling.

motto n *lit:* catchphrase, inscription, logo, slogan; maxim, precept, watchword; caption, headline, legend.

mount n *lit:* backing, frame, setting; slide; base, plinth, podium, stand; gun carriage; horse, nag, ride, steed. **vb** *lit:* frame, put in a frame; put on a slide; fix on a base, set; ascend, climb, go up, scale; climb on to, climb up on, get on to, get up on; accumulate, build (up), escalate, grow, increase, intensify, pile (up); organize, produce, put on, stage; deliver, launch, make, put into effect; install, place, position; *spec:* keep, stand (guard).

mountain n *lit:* crag, fell, height, peak, summit; *fig:* heap, mass, pile, stack.

mountainous adj *lit:* alpine, highland, upland; craggy, precipitous, rocky, serrated, sheer, soaring, towering; *fig:* enormous, giant, huge, immense, mammoth, massive, vast.

mourn vb *lit:* bewail, grieve (for), lament, sorrow (for), weep for; miss; deplore, regret.

mournful adj *lit:* disconsolate, grief-stricken, heartbroken, heavyhearted, inconsolable, melancholy, miserable, sad, sorrowful, unhappy, wretched; affecting, elegiac, piteous, plaintive, tragic.

mourning n *lit:* bereavement, grief; grieving, lamentation, sorrowing, weeping; black, widow's weeds.

mouth n *lit:* jaws, lips; aperture, entrance, inlet, opening, stoma; estuary; *fig:* cheek, insolence, lip, sauce; chatter, gab, talk; boasting, bragging, hot air; spokesperson. vb *lit:* mime; declaim, orate, spout; *spec:* train (a horse) to the bit.

move n *lit:* go, play, turn; action, maneuver, motion, shift, stroke; gambit, initiative, ploy, strategy; change of address, relocation, transfer; campaign, plan, proposal, suggestion. vb *lit:* advance, budge, go, pass, proceed, progress, shift, travel; change address, relocate, transfer; depart (from), go away, leave, migrate (from); bring, carry, convey, fetch, take, transport, transpose; activate, drive, propel, power, push; affect, agitate, excite, stir, touch; *fig:* cause (to), induce (to), influence (to), inspire (to), lead (to), prompt (to), stimulate (to); advocate, propose, recommend, suggest.

movement n *lit:* activity, agitation, development, progress, shift, stirring; maneuver, operation, progression; action, mechanism, works; exercise, gesture, motion; current, drift, flow, tendency, trend; campaign, caucus, drive, organization, party; beat, meter, pace, rhythm, tempo; *spec:* division, section (of a musical work).

moving adj (pr.pt) *lit:* mobile; portable; powering, propelling; *fig:* affecting, emotive, pathetic, piteous, poignant, touching; dynamic, exciting, inspiring, motivating, stimulating.

much n *lit:* a good deal, a great deal, a lot, lots, the majority. adj *lit:* abundant, copious, plenteous; considerable, great, substantial. adv *lit:* considerably, exceedingly, greatly; approximately, nearly; indeed, to a great degree, to a great extent.

muddled adj (pa.pt) *lit:* chaotic, confused, disordered, disorganized, jumbled, mixed, scrambled, tangled; bewildered, disoriented, perplexed, vague.

muddy vb *lit:* bespatter, dirty, get mud on, smear, soil; *fig:* blur, cloud, confuse, obscure. adj *lit:* bespattered, dirty, miry, slimy, slushy, wet;

boggy, marshy, swampy; foul, impure, turbid; *fig:* dingy, dull, flat; blurred, cloudy, confused, obscure, vague, woolly.

muffle *vb lit:* cloak, conceal, cover, envelop, hood, mask, swathe; deaden, dull, mute, silence, stifle, suppress.

muggy *adj lit:* close, humid, oppressive, sticky, stifling, sultry.

multiple *adj lit:* manifold, numerous, sundry, various; collective, compound; repeated.

multiply *vb lit:* accumulate, expand, increase, spread; repeat; breed, proliferate, propagate, reproduce.

multitude *n lit:* army, crowd, horde, host, legion, mass, sea, swarm, throng; herd, mob, proletariat, rabble.

mundane *adj lit:* banal, boring, commonplace, everyday, humdrum, ordinary, platitudinous, prosaic, trite; earthly, human, mortal, secular, temporal, worldly.

murder *n lit:* assassination, homicide, killing; carnage, massacre, slaughter; *fig:* agony, hell, torture. **vb** *lit:* assassinate, do to death, kill; bump off, do in, hit, rub out, waste; massacre, slaughter, slay; *fig:* abuse, mangle, ruin, spoil; drub, hammer, thrash out of sight, trounce.

murky *adj lit:* black, dark, dim, dusky, gloomy; gray, hazy, misty; *fig:* obscure, shady.

murmuring *adj (pr.pt) lit:* babbling, droning, humming, purring, rippling, rumbling, rustling, trickling, whispering; listless, muttering, restive, restless, unquiet, unsatisfied.

muscle *n lit:* ligament, sinew, tendon; extensor, flexor; *fig:* brawn, power, stamina, strength; clout, force, weight. **vb** *lit:* butt (in), elbow (in), force a way (in), thrust one's way (in).

muscular *adj lit:* brawny, lusty, powerful, robust, stalwart, strapping, strong; athletic, vigorous.

musical *adj lit:* euphonious, harmonious, melodic, melodious, orchestral, symphonic, tuneful.

musician *n lit:* bandsman, group member, orchestra member, performer, player, singer; arranger, composer; conductor.

must   n *lit:* essential, imperative, necessity, prerequisite, requirement, sine qua non; semifermented juice. **vb** *lit:* be obliged to, have to; ought to, should.

musty   adj *lit:* damp, dampish, mildewed, moth-eaten, moldy, stale.

mute   vb *lit:* dampen, deaden, hush, muffle, silence, soften, tone down, turn down. **adj** *lit:* aphonic, dumb, silent, speechless, voiceless; mum, unspoken, wordless.

mutilate   vb *lit:* cripple, damage, deform, disfigure, lame, maim, mangle; *fig:* abbreviate, abridge, butcher, censor, cut, distort, spoil.

mutiny   n *lit:* defiance, disobedience, insurrection, rebellion, revolt, riot, rising, uprising. **vb** *lit:* rebel, revolt, rise up.

muzzle   n *lit:* mouth, snout; cage, clamp, guard; mouthpiece, respirator; barrel. **vb** *lit:* curb, gag, silence; *fig:* censor, restrict, suppress.

mysterious   adj *lit:* cryptic, enigmatic, incomprehensible, inexplicable, insoluble, obscure, perplexing, puzzling, strange, uncanny, weird; furtive, secretive; concealed, covert, hidden, secret.

mystery   n *lit:* enigma, puzzle, riddle, secret; obscurity, secrecy; rite, ritual, sacrament.

mystical   adj *lit:* cabalistic, esoteric, metaphysical, occult, paranormal, preternatural, supernatural, transcendental; ritual, symbolic.

N

nab vb *lit:* catch, grab, grasp, seize suddenly; snatch away, steal; *fig:* apprehend, arrest.

nag n *lit:* hack, horse, jade; scold, shrew, termagant. vb *lit:* goad, henpeck, scold, upbraid; annoy, badger, chivvy, harass, pester; irritate, plague, provoke, vex.

nagging adj (pr.pt) *lit:* bothersome, distressing, irritating, painful, vexatious, worrisome; continuous, persistent; scolding, shrewish.

nail n *lit:* peg, pin, tack; horn, keratin. vb *lit:* pin, tack; attach, fasten, fix, join, secure; hammer; *fig:* catch, seize.

naive adj *lit:* artless, frank, guileless, ingenuous, innocent, jejune, unsophisticated, unworldly; childlike, natural, open, simple, trusting; unaffected, unpretentious; callow, credulous, green, gullible.

name n *lit:* agnomen, appellation, cognomen, handle, moniker, sobriquet; denomination, designation, title; celebrity, personality; reputation; epithet, nickname. vb *lit:* call, designate, dub, entitle, style, term; baptize, christen, denominate, label; identify, specify; cite, mention, nominate.

nap n *lit:* doze, siesta, sleep, snooze; rest; pile, shag; down, fiber; cert, dead cert, hot tip, winner. vb *lit:* doze, drop off, drowse, sleep, snooze; tip a winner.

narrate vb *lit:* recite, recount, relate, set forth, tell; describe, detail, report; chronicle.

narrator n *lit:* commentator, reporter, storyteller, voice over; raconteur, speaker; author, chronicler, novelist, writer.

narrow vb *lit:* constrict, reduce, tighten; decrease, diminish; *fig:* limit, simplify. adj *lit:* attenuated, fine, slim, thin; close, confined, constricted, tight; meager, restricted, scanty; *fig:* biased, dogmatic, partial, prejudiced; exclusive, select; avaricious, mean, niggardly.

narrowly adv *lit:* barely, by a whisker, just, only just; carefully, closely, painstakingly.

narrow-minded   adj *lit:* petty, illiberal, insular, shortsighted, straitlaced; biased, intolerant, prejudiced; bigoted, opinionated.

nastiness   n *lit:* malevolence, malice, malignity, meanness, offensiveness, spitefulness, viciousness; defilement, filth, foulness, squalor, uncleanliness, vileness; indecency, licentiousness, obscenity, pornography.

nasty   adj *lit:* dirty, disgusting, filthy, foul, loathsome, nauseating, objectionable, obnoxious, odious, offensive, repellent, repugnant, sickening, vile; bad, dangerous, serious, severe; abusive, despicable, disagreeable, mean, spiteful, unpleasant, vicious.

national   n *lit:* citizen, compatriot, native; inhabitant, resident, subject. **adj** *lit:* civil, governmental, public, state; nationwide; patriotic; domestic, internal.

nationwide   adj *lit:* country-wide, national; general, overall, universal.

native   n *lit:* aborigine, inhabitant; citizen, dweller, national, resident. **adj** *lit:* domestic, indigenous, local, born (to); inborn, inbred, innate, intrinsic; mother, vernacular.

natty   adj *lit:* snappy, snazzy; chic, elegant, fashionable, stylish, well-dressed; dapper, neat, smart, spruce, trim.

natural   n *lit:* genius; *fig:* certainty; *spec:* white note (on a piano). **adj** *lit:* common, logical, normal, ordinary, typical, usual; characteristic, inborn, inherent, instinctive, native; artless, genuine, ingenuous, simple, spontaneous, unpretentious, unsophisticated; organic, plain, pure, unrefined, whole.

naturally   adv *lit:* congenitally, essentially, inherently, innately, instinctively; artlessly, genuinely, ingenuously, simply, spontaneously, unpretentiously; organically; normally, typically; *fig:* certainly, of course; absolutely.

nature   n *lit:* character, constitution, essence, make-up, quality; category, kind, sort, style, type, variety; cosmos, earth, environment, universe; disposition, outlook, temper, temperament; country, countryside, scenery.

naughty   adj *lit:* bad, disobedient, misbehaving, mischievous, refractory, roguish, wayward, wicked; ribald, vulgar.

navigate vb *lit:* plot a course, steer; maneuver, pilot, sail; *fig:* direct, guide, skipper; find one's way (through), make one's way (to).

navigator n *lit:* helmsman, mariner, pilot, steersman; codriver, map reader.

near vb *lit:* approach, close on, draw up toward, get closer to. adj *lit:* close, close by; adjacent, adjoining, at close quarters, nigh; approaching, imminent, impending, looming, threatening; *fig:* closely related, dear, familiar, intimate; close-fisted, mean, miserly, parsimonious, stingy, tight. adv *lit:* close, nigh; into proximity, within reach; almost, close on. prp *lit:* close to, nigh unto; adjacent to, alongside, not far from.

nearby adj *lit:* adjacent, adjoining, neighboring; *fig:* convenient, handy.

near by adv *lit:* close by, close at hand, not far away.

neat adj *lit:* accurate, fastidious, methodical, nice, orderly, precise, shipshape, smart, straight, systematic, tidy, trim; adroit, deft, dexterous, handy, nimble, skillful, stylish; pure, straight, unadulterated, undiluted.

neatness n *lit:* accuracy, fastidiousness, orderliness, smartness, tidiness, trimness; adroitness, deftness, dexterity, handiness, nimbleness, preciseness, skillfulness, stylishness.

necessarily adv *lit:* by definition, inescapably, inevitably, inexorably, of necessity, perforce, unavoidably, willy-nilly; certainly, without question.

necessary adj *lit:* essential, imperative, indispensable, mandatory, obligatory, vital; compulsory, de rigueur, required; inevitable, unavoidable.

necessitate vb *lit:* call for, demand, dictate, leave no choice but, make necessary, render indispensable, require; entail.

necessity n *lit:* essential, indispensability, prerequisite, requirement, want; demand, need; compulsion, obligation; extremity, penury, privation.

need n *lit:* deprivation, lack, inadequacy, insufficiency, paucity, privation, shortage, want; penury, poverty; demand, exigency, requirement, urgency. vb *lit:* call for, demand, necessitate; lack, miss, require, want.

needle n *lit:* point, prong, spicule, spike, tine; stylus; hypodermic syringe; gnomon, pointer; obelisk. **vb** *lit:* aggravate, bait, goal, provoke, spur; annoy, harass, irk, nag, nettle, pester, prick, prod, ruffle, sting.

needless adj *lit:* causeless, gratuitous, groundless, pointless, superfluous, uncalled-for, unnecessary, unwanted, useless.

needy adj *lit:* deprived, impecunious, indigent, poor, poverty-stricken; friendless, homeless.

negative n *lit:* no; contradiction, denial, refusal, veto; *spec:* reversed-out image (on film). **adj** *lit:* contradictory, contrary, dissenting, opposing, rejecting, resisting; antagonistic, counteractive; gloomy, pessimistic, unenthusiastic, unwilling; colorless, insipid.

neglect n *lit:* disregard, inattention, indifference, unconcern; default, dereliction, forgetfulness, laxity, oversight, remissness, slackness. **vb** *lit:* disregard, ignore, overlook, pass over; evade, forget, omit, shirk, skimp.

negotiate vb *lit:* bargain, deal, haggle; debate, discuss, parley, work out; get over, get past, get round, pass through.

nerve n *lit:* neural tract; sinew, tendon; *fig:* bravery, courage, determination, firmness, grit, guts, intrepidity, mettle, pluck, resolution, will; audacity, brazenness, cheek, effrontery, impudence, temerity. **vb** *lit:* brace, encourage, fortify, steel.

nerve-racking adj *lit:* frightening, ghastly, grim, gripping, harrowing, heart-stopping, horrific, sickening, terrifying; formidable, stressful.

nervous adj *lit:* agitated, anxious, edgy, fidgety, flustered, highly strung, jittery, jumpy, on edge, shaky, tense, uneasy, uptight.

nervousness n *lit:* agitation, anxiety, edginess, jumpiness, tension, uneasiness.

nest n *lit:* hatchery, home; *fig:* den, hideaway, lair; haunt, refuge, retreat; hotbed; *spec:* set (of tables).

net n *lit:* mesh, trawl; lacework, lattice, reticulum; web. **vb** *lit:* capture, catch, enmesh, ensnare, nab, trap; *fig:* bring in, gain, earn, make, realize. **adj** *lit:* after taxes, clear, take-home; closing, final.

network n *lit:* grid, grille, mesh; organization, structure, system; circuitry, complex, labyrinth, maze, plexus, web.

neutral adj *lit:* disinterested, even-handed, impartial, nonaligned, noncommittal, unbiased, uncommitted, uninvolved; achromatic, colorless, dull, expressionless, indistinct, toneless, undefined.

new adj *lit:* fresh, latest, novel, original, pristine, unused, virgin; advanced, contemporary, current, modern, modish, recent, topical, ultramodern, up-to-date; added, additional, extra, supplementary; altered, different, improved, redesigned, reissued, restored; unexperienced, unexpected, unfamiliar, untried.

news n *lit:* information, intelligence, tidings, word; latest; account, bulletin, communiqué, dispatch, report, statement, story; advice, disclosure, release; gossip, hearsay, rumor.

next adj *lit:* ensuing, later, subsequent, succeeding; consequent, resulting; adjacent, closest, nearest. **adv** *lit:* afterward, later, subsequently, thereafter, thereupon; in turn.

nice adj *lit:* agreeable, amiable, charming, courteous, delightful, friendly, likable, pleasant, well-mannered; dainty, neat, tidy, trim; accurate, careful, delicate, exacting, fastidious, meticulous, precise, scrupulous, subtle; cultured, respectable, well-bred.

niche n *lit:* alcove, hollow, nook, recess; *fig:* calling, position, slot, vocation.

nickname n *lit:* agnomen, familiar name, moniker, pet name, sobriquet; diminutive; epithet.

night n *lit:* dark, darkness, early hours, evening, hours of darkness, moonlight hours, nighttime, small hours. **adj** *lit:* nocturnal; after dark, late; *spec:* sleeper (train).

nil n *lit:* love, nought, none, no score, nothing, zero, zilch.

nimble adj *lit:* agile, limber, lithe; active, brisk, lively, quick, sprightly; dexterous, proficient.

nip n *lit:* dram, draught, drop, finger, mouthful, sip, taste, tot; bite, chill, frost. **vb** *lit:* bite, nibble, snap; clip, pinch, squeeze, tweak; *fig:* check, thwart.

nippy adj *lit:* biting, chilly, sharp; agile, fast, lively, nimble, quick, spry.

nit-picking **adj (pr.pt)** *lit:* carping, fault-finding, finicky, hairsplitting, pedantic, quibbling.

nobility **n** *lit:* aristocracy, high society, nobles, society, upper class; dignity, excellence, greatness, illustriousness; honor, integrity, uprightness.

noble **n** *lit:* aristocrat, patrician, peer. **adj** *lit:* aristocratic, blue-blooded, high-born, titled; dignified, eminent, excellent, impressive, splendid; honorable, magnanimous, upright.

nobody **n** *lit:* lightweight, nonentity. **prn** *lit:* none, no one.

nod **n** *lit:* bob, bow, duck; acknowledgment, indication, sign. **vb** *lit:* bob, bow, duck one's head; acknowledge, indicate, signal; agree, assent, concur; doze, droop, drop off.

noise **n** *lit:* sound; clamor, clatter, commotion, din, pandemonium, racket, tumult; babble, hubbub, outcry, uproar.

noiseless **n** *lit:* inaudible, silent, soundless; hushed, muted, quiet.

noisy **adj** *lit:* clamorous, deafening, ear-splitting, loud, piercing, tumultuous, uproarious, vociferous; cacophonous, strident.

nominate **vb** *lit:* appoint, assign, choose, designate, name, propose, recommend, select.

nominee **n** *lit:* choice, proposal, suggestion; aspirant, candidate, contestant, entrant, runner.

nondescript **adj** *lit:* commonplace, dull, mousy, ordinary, undistinguished, uninteresting, unremarkable, vague.

none **adv** *lit:* in no way, not at all, to no extent. **prn** *lit:* nobody, no one; not any, not one; not a bit, no part, nothing.

nonplus **vb** *lit:* baffle, bewilder, confound, discomfit, disconcert, discountenance, dumbfound, mystify, perplex, puzzle, take aback.

nonsense **n** *lit:* absurdity, blather, bunk, claptrap, drivel, fatuity, folly, gibberish, inanity, rot, rubbish, trash, twaddle.

nonstop **adj** *lit:* direct; ceaseless, constant, continuous, endless, incessant, relentless, uninterrupted, unremitting. **adv** *lit:* ceaselessly, constantly, continuously, endlessly, incessantly, relentlessly, steadily, uninterruptedly, unremittingly.

nook   n *lit:* alcove, corner, cranny, crevice, niche, recess.

normal   adj *lit:* average, common, natural, ordinary, regular, run-of-the-mill, standard, usual; rational, reasonable, well-adjusted.

nose   n *lit:* proboscis; hooter, snout, trunk; front; *fig:* smell, sensitivity; aroma, bouquet, fragrance. **vb** *lit:* smell, sniff (out); nudge, push, shove; *fig:* meddle, pry, snoop.

notable   adj *lit:* distinguished, eminent, famous, outstanding, remarkable; conspicuous, evident, marked, striking, unusual; manifest, noticeable.

notably   adv *lit:* especially, particularly; conspicuously, distinctly, manifestly, markedly, outstandingly, strikingly; remarkably, uncommonly.

note   n *lit:* jotting, memo, memorandum, minute; communication, letter, message, reminder; aside, comment, observation, remark; mark, sign, symbol, token; heed, notice; distinction, prestige, renown. **vb** *lit:* notice, perceive, see; mention, observe, remark; jot down, record.

noted   adj (pa.pt) *lit:* acclaimed, celebrated, distinguished, eminent, illustrious, prominent, renowned, well-known; logged, minuted, recorded, registered.

notice   n *lit:* attention, consideration, heed, note, regard; announcement, intelligence, news, notification; advertisement, poster; critique, review; advice, forewarning, warning; dismissal, eviction order. **vb** *lit:* detect, discern, note, observe, perceive, see, spot; heed, mind.

noticeable   adj *lit:* discernible, perceptible; clear, conspicuous, evident, manifest, obvious, plain, striking.

notification   n *lit:* advice, information, intelligence, message, notice, warning; announcement, declaration, statement.

notify   vb *lit:* advise, inform, send word to, tell, warn; announce to, declare to, proclaim to.

notion   n *lit:* brain wave, idea, thought; belief, concept, impression, opinion, understanding; inkling, knowledge; desire, fancy, inclination, sentiment, wish.

notwithstanding   **adv** *lit:* however, nevertheless, nonetheless, still, yet. **prp** *lit:* despite, in spite of. **cnj** *lit:* although, though.

nourish   **vb** *lit:* feed, nurture, sustain, tend; comfort, cultivate, encourage, foster, promote, supply.

nourishing   **adj (pr.pt)** *lit:* healthful, nutritious, nutritive, sustaining; beneficial, wholesome.

novel   **n** *lit:* story, tale; book, volume, work; romance; narrative. **adj** *lit:* fresh, innovative, new, original; different, rare, singular, strange, unusual.

novelty   **n** *lit:* freshness, innovation, newness, originality; oddity, strangeness, unfamiliarity; curiosity, gimmick; knickknack, trifle, trinket; memento, souvenir.

now   **adv** *lit:* at once, immediately, instantly, promptly, straight away; any more, nowadays, these days; once. **cnj** *lit:* in that, since; for, the fact is, well.

nude   **n** *lit:* naked figure; altogether, birthday suit. **adj** *lit:* au naturel, bare, in the altogether, in the buff, naked, stark naked, stripped, uncovered, undressed.

nuisance   **n** *lit:* annoyance, bore, bother, inconvenience, irritation, pest, plague, trouble, vexation.

numb   **adj** *lit:* dead, frozen, immobilized, insensible, insensitive, paralyzed, unfeeling; *fig:* dazed, overwhelmed, shocked, stunned.

number   **n** *lit:* digit, figure, integer, numeral, unit; amount, quantity, sum, total; company, multitude, throng; copy, edition, issue; *fig:* aria, song, tune; item, product. **vb** *lit:* count, include in, total; classify, designate, label, rank.

numbered   **adj (pa.pt)** *lit:* categorized, classified, designated; limited, totaled.

numbness   **n** *lit:* deadness, dullness, immobilization, insensibility, insensitivity, paralysis, unfeeling; *fig:* daze, shock, torpor.

numerous   adj *lit:* many, plentiful; abundant, copious, profuse; myriad, countless, host of, multitude of.

nurse   vb *lit:* care for, look after, nurture, tend, treat; cultivate, foster, garden, nourish; breast-feed, suckle.

nursery   n *lit:* créche, playroom; allotment, garden, garden center, kitchen garden, orchard, plantation.

nut   n *lit:* seed; drupe, kernel, stone; *fig:* head; brain, intelligence, mind; problem; buff, enthusiast, fanatic; *spec:* screw. **vb** *lit:* gather nuts.

O

oaf n *lit:* blockhead, clod, dolt, dunce, fool, imbecile, lout, lummox, nincompoop, simpleton.

oafish adj *lit:* bovine, dim, dull, dumb, loutish, obtuse, stupid, thick; clumsy.

oar n *lit:* pole, scull; blade; paddle. **vb** *lit:* paddle, row, scull.

oath n *lit:* promise, vow, word; bond, pledge; curse, expletive, imprecation, profanity, swearword.

obedience n *lit:* compliance, conformability, docility, dutifulness, submission, submissiveness, subservience, tractability; acquiescence, demureness, readiness, willingness; accordance.

obedient adj *lit:* compliant, conformable, docile, dutiful, submissive, subservient, tractable; acquiescent, amenable, biddable, demure, ready, willing; law-abiding.

obese adj *lit:* chubby, corpulent, fat, gross, overweight, paunchy, plump, podgy, portly, roly-poly, rotund, stout, tubby.

obey vb *lit:* be ruled by, bow to, serve, take orders from; comply, do what one is told, submit; act upon, carry out, discharge, execute, fulfill, perform; abide by, follow, heed, keep, mind, observe.

object n *lit:* article, body, item, thing; phenomenon; fact, reality; design, intention, point, purpose; aim, end, goal, target; butt, focus. **vb** *lit:* demur, protest; be opposed (to), take exception (to).

objection n *lit:* demur, exception, opposition, protest, remonstration; counterargument.

objectionable adj *lit:* disagreeable, displeasing, distasteful, obnoxious, offensive, repugnant, unpleasant, unseemly.

objective n *lit:* aim, end, goal, target; aspiration, intention; design, purpose. adj *lit:* detached, disinterested, dispassionate, equitable, fair, impartial, impersonal, just, unbiased, uninvolved, unprejudiced.

obligation n *lit:* duty, liability, responsibility; burden, charge, commitment, requirement; must; debt, promise, trust, understanding.

oblige vb *lit:* do a favor, gratify, indulge, please; favor, serve; compel, constrain, force, impel, require.

obliged adj (pa.pt) *lit:* beholden, grateful, indebted, thankful; appreciative, gratified, pleased; bound, compelled, forced, required.

obliging adj (pr.pt) *lit:* accommodating, good-natured, helpful, willing; considerate, eager to please, generous, kind, openhearted; agreeable, amiable, civil, courteous, friendly.

oblivion n *lit:* insensibility, unawareness, unconsciousness; blackness, darkness, nothingness, vacuum, void; extinction; abstraction, forgetfulness, negligence; abeyance, limbo.

oblivious adj *lit:* blithe, heedless, uncaring, unconcerned; forgetful, inattentive, negligent, unmindful, unobservant.

obscene adj *lit:* bawdy, blue, filthy, perverted, pornographic, smutty; coarse, dirty, gross, immoral, improper, indecent, lewd, licentious, ribald, salacious, suggestive; *fig:* disgusting, horrible, sickening, vile.

obscenity n *lit:* bawdiness, filthiness, perversion, pornography, smut; coarseness, dirtiness, grossness, immorality, lewdness, licentiousness, suggestiveness, vileness; expletive, four-letter word, profanity, swearword; *fig:* atrocity, offense, outrage, vileness.

obscure vb *lit:* adumbrate, blur, cloud, dim, dull, obfuscate; conceal, cover, disguise, eclipse, hide, mask, screen, shade, shroud, veil. adj *lit:* abstruse, ambiguous, cryptic, enigmatic, esoteric, mysterious, opaque, recondite, vague; concealed, hidden, veiled; blurred, clouded, dim, faint, hazy, murky, shady, somber; humble, lowly, minor, nameless, remote, undistinguished, unheard-of, unimportant, unknown.

obscurity n *lit:* abstruseness, ambiguity, complexity, incomprehensibility, mysteriousness, opacity, vagueness; dimness, gloom, haziness, murkiness, shadows; insignificance, lowliness, unimportance.

observant adj *lit:* alert, eagle-eyed, vigilant, wary, watchful, wide awake; attentive, insightful, penetrative, perceptive, percipient, quick on the uptake; heedful, mindful.

observation n *lit:* inspection, monitoring, scrutiny, study, surveillance, watch; comment, finding, note, opinion, reflection, thought; *spec:* reading (on an instrument, dial).

observe vb *lit:* espy, notice, perceive, see, spot; keep an eye on, keep under observation, look at, monitor, regard, study, view, watch, witness; comment, mention, note, remark, state; abide by, adhere to, comply with, follow, heed, obey; celebrate, commemorate, keep.

obsessed adj (pa.pt) *lit:* consumed, dominated, fixated, gripped, haunted, infatuated, manic, monopolized, one-track-minded, possessed.

obsession n *lit:* bee in one's bonnet, fixation, hang-up, infatuation, mania, phobia, thing; fanaticism; preoccupation, ruling passion.

obsessive adj *lit:* compulsive, fixated, manic, paranoid, phobic; consuming, dominating, fanatical, haunting, passionate, overwhelming; constant, persistent.

obstacle n *lit:* barrier, blockage, impediment, obstruction; check, hindrance, hitch, hurdle, pitfall, stumbling block; difficulty, snag.

obstinate adj *lit:* dogged, immovable, persistent, pertinacious, steadfast, tenacious; headstrong, inflexible, intractable, mulish, pigheaded, recalcitrant, stubborn, willful; firm, strong-minded.

obstruct vb *lit:* bar, barricade, block, prevent; check, curb, delay, hinder, hold up, impede, interfere with, interrupt, slow down, stall; hamstring, inhibit, restrict; foil, frustrate, parry, thwart; get in the way of, obscure.

obstruction n *lit:* bar, barricade, barrier, blockage; check, hindrance, hold-up, impediment, stop; difficulty, snag.

obtain vb *lit:* acquire, come into possession of, get, get hold of, procure; attain, gain, secure, win; catch, hold on to, possess oneself of, take; be, exist, prevail, remain, stand.

obvious adj *lit:* clear, conspicuous, distinct, evident, indisputable, manifest, marked, palpable, patent, plain, pronounced, self-evident, straightforward, undeniable, unmistakable; apparent, noticeable, overt, perceptible, recognizable, visible.

occasional adj *lit:* desultory, infrequent, intermittent, irregular, odd, rare, sporadic; ceremonial, formal.

occasionally adv *lit:* at times, every now and then, from time to time, infrequently, intermittently, irregularly, on and off, once in a while, periodically, sometimes, sporadically.

occupation n *lit:* craft, employment, job, line of work, profession, trade, work; activity, pursuit; métier, vocation; incumbency, habitation, possession, residence, tenancy, tenure; conquest, domination, invasion, subjugation; sit-in, squat, takeover.

occupied adj (pa.pt) *lit:* busy, hard at it, tied up, working; inhabited, lived-in; engaged, full, taken, unavailable.

occur vb *lit:* befall, come to pass, eventuate, happen, pass, take place, transpire; fall out, turn out; appear, arise, be, crop up, exist, materialize, turn up; be suggested (to one), come (to one).

odd adj *lit:* abnormal, bizarre, extraordinary, freakish, outlandish, peculiar, strange, unusual, weird; curious, funny, quaint, singular; exceptional, rare; mysterious, uncanny; casual, incidental, occasional, random; miscellaneous, sundry, various; alternate, uneven; leftover, remaining, single, solitary, spare, surplus.

odds n *lit:* chances, likelihood, probability; difference, disparity, distinction; *fig:* (at) loggerheads, (at) variance.

odor n *lit:* aroma, bouquet, fragrance, perfume, scent; redolence, smell, stench, stink; air, atmosphere, aura, quality, spirit.

off adj *lit:* finished, unavailable; absent, on leave, on vacation; deferred, postponed; free, quiet, slack; bad, below par, poor, substandard; decomposed, moldy, rancid, rotten. adv *lit:* apart, aside, away, elsewhere, out.

offend vb *lit:* affront, insult, outrage, slight, snub; anger, annoy, disgruntle, irritate, miff, provoke, rile, upset, vex; disgust, nauseate, repel, sicken; be repugnant to, to be unacceptable to; commit a crime (against), transgress (against), trespass (against).

offender n *lit:* criminal, lawbreaker, transgressor; sinner, wrongdoer; culprit, guilty party, malefactor, miscreant.

offense   n *lit:* crime, misdemeanor, transgression, trespass; affront, insult, slight, snub; harm, hurt, wrong; hard feelings; anger, annoyance, displeasure, indignation, pique, resentment, umbrage.

offensive   n *lit:* attack, onslaught, push; invasion; warpath. **adj** *lit:* affronting, insulting, insolent, rude; abusive, discourteous, objectionable, unacceptable; aggressive, attacking, belligerent, intrusive, provocative; angering, enraging, infuriating, outrageous; disgusting, nauseating, obnoxious, revolting, vile.

offer   n *lit:* bid, proposition, tender; proposal, suggestion; suit. **vb** *lit:* display to, hold out to, make available to, present to, proffer, put to, show to; bid, tender; propose, put forward, submit, suggest; put on the market, put up for sale; come forward, volunteer (to).

office   n *lit:* capacity, function, role; appointment, employment, occupation, post, situation, station; bureau, department, section; business premises, company address, working environment; employees, staff, workers; act of worship, service.

officer   n *lit:* person of rank, person of authority; executive, official; agent, functionary, representative; dignitary.

official   n *lit:* person of authority, officer; executive; agent, functionary, representative; dignitary. **adj** *lit:* authoritative, authorized, sanctioned; certified, endorsed, legitimate; accredited, authentic, bona fide, formal, proper.

offset   vb *lit:* cancel out, counteract, counterbalance, make up for. **adj** *lit:* contrasted, highlighted; balanced, equipoised.

offspring   n *lit:* child, descendant, heir; children, descendants, heirs, progeny, issue, seed; successors.

often   adv *lit:* frequently, repeatedly, time after time; commonly, generally.

oily   adj *lit:* greasy, well-lubricated; sebaceous; black, inky, sticky, tarry; *fig:* fawning, smooth, slippery, unctuous.

okay   n *lit:* approval, assent, consent; authorization, go-ahead, green light, permission. **vb** *lit:* agree to, approve, authorize, pass, permit, sanction. **adj** *lit:* acceptable, adequate, all right, good enough, in order, not bad, passable, satisfactory, tolerable; correct; fine, good. **adv** *lit:* adequately, passably, satisfactorily, well enough; correctly.

old n *lit:* aged, elderly, senior citizens. **adj** *lit:* of age; advanced in years, elderly, getting on, past one's prime; in one's dotage; aboriginal, age-old, ancient, antediluvian, primeval, primordial; experienced, practiced, veteran; customary, familiar, habitual, long-established, time-honored, traditional; clichéd, hackneyed; antique, archaic, obsolete, out-of-date, unfashionable; earlier, erstwhile, ex-, former, last, original, previous; dead, empty, rejected, worn-out.

old-fashioned adj *lit:* antiquated, archaic, dated, obsolescent, obsolete, outmoded, out of date, passé, unfashionable; fuddy-duddy, fusty, musty, stick-in-the-mud.

omission n *lit:* exclusion, leaving out; jump, skip; gap, hiatus, interval; negligence, oversight; avoidance, inaction.

omit vb *lit:* drop, exclude, leave out; delete, eliminate, erase; jump, pass over, skip; neglect, miss, overlook.

on adj *lit:* active, functioning, operative, performing, working; available; happening, occurring, taking place; allowable, permissible. **adv** *lit:* ahead, forward, further, more; during, in, when, while; into activity, into functioning, into operation. **prp** *lit:* atop; adhering to, stuck to; in regard to, with reference to; by means of, through, with.

once adj *lit:* erstwhile, former, prior, sometime. **adv** *lit:* at one time, formerly, in the past, long ago, previously; on a single occasion, just one time. **cnj** *lit:* any time, when, whenever; if, if ever.

one adj *lit:* a, a certain, an, a single, a sole; joined, united. **prn** *lit:* anybody, somebody; an example, a sample.

only adj *lit:* lone, single, sole, unique. **adv** *lit:* just, merely; purely; at most.

ooze n *lit:* ebb, gentle flow; dregs, grounds, lees; alluvium, mud, silt, slime; discharge, dribble, drip, exudation, seepage, weeping. **vb** *lit:* dribble, drip, exude, leak, seep, weep; discharge, drain, emit.

open vb *lit:* throw wide, uncover, unlock, unseal; uncork, unwrap; expand, spread out, unfold; disclose, divulge, reveal; begin, commence, inaugurate, kick off, launch, set in motion, start; come apart, separate, split. **adj** *lit:* ajar, gaping, revealed, spread out, unclosed, unfolded, unlocked; bare, exposed, undefended, unfortified, unprotected; accessible, public, spacious, sweeping, unenclosed, unfenced, wide-open; unengaged, unoccupied, vacant; blatant, clear, flagrant, overt, plain, unconcealed; arguable, debatable, undecided, unsettled; impartial, objective, uncommitted; liable (to), susceptible (to), vulnerable (to); candid, frank, guileless, honest, sincere; generous, liberal, munificent.

opening **n** *lit:* aperture, fissure, fistula, gap, hole, orifice, perforation, rupture, slot, vent; break, chance, opportunity, vacancy; beginning, commencement, inauguration, kickoff, launch, onset, start. **adj (pr.pt)** *lit:* commencing, first, inaugural, initial, introductory.

openly **adv** *lit:* candidly, forthrightly, frankly, plainly, unreservedly; blatantly, flagrantly, overtly, publicly.

operate **vb** *lit:* act, function, go, perform, run, work; be in charge of, handle, manage, maneuver, use, wield; perform surgery.

operation **n** *lit:* action, functioning, performance, running, working; activity, movement; handling, management, manipulation, maneuvering, use, wielding; affair, campaign, exercise, procedure; deal, proceeding, undertaking; surgical procedure.

operative **n** *lit:* employee, hand, worker; executive. **adj** *lit:* active, functioning, on, performing, running, working; effective, efficient, functional, usable, serviceable, workable; crucial, influential, key, relevant, significant.

operator **n** *lit:* button-pusher, driver, handler, user, wielder, worker; administrator, agent, contractor, franchise holder, representative, trader; chief, manipulator, wheeler-dealer.

opinion **n** *lit:* assessment, estimation, impression, judgment, point of view, view; belief, conception; ideas, sentiments, thoughts; supposition, theory.

opponent **n** *lit:* adversary, antagonist, challenger, co-contestant, disputant; enemy, foe, rival.

opportunity **n** *lit:* break, chance, opening; convenient moment, occasion, time.

oppose **vb** *lit:* act against, be against, counter, dispute, fight, resist, speak against, take issue with; contradict, defy, stand up to; confront, face; bar, hinder, obstruct; contrast, counterbalance.

opposing **adj (pr.pt)** *lit:* alternative, contesting, other, rival; confronting, facing; antipathetic, conflicting, contrary, hostile, incompatible, irreconcilable.

opposite **n** *lit:* antithesis, contrary, converse, reverse. **adj** *lit:* alternate, facing, other; contradictory, contrary, different, reverse; adverse, antagonistic, irreconcilable.

opposition **n** *lit:* counteraction, defense, resistance; blocking, obstruction; antagonism, hostility; antagonist, rival; competition, opponent, other side.

oppressive **adj** *lit:* burdensome, grinding, onerous, severe; despotic, overbearing, repressive, tyrannical; close, heavy, overpowering, stifling, suffocating.

oppressor **n** *lit:* despot, dictator, persecutor, subjugator, tyrant; bully, martinet, ogre, slave driver.

optimistic **adj** *lit:* hopeful, inclined to look on the bright side, Micawberish; confident, positive; buoyant, cheerful.

option **n** *lit:* alternative, choice; decision, preference, selection.

optional **adj** *lit:* discretionary, noncompulsory, voluntary; additional, extra, supplementary.

orb **n** *lit:* ball, globe, sphere; *fig:* celestial body, celestial sphere; world; eyeball; time cycle.

orbit **n** *lit:* circumnavigation, encircling motion, revolution, rotation; circle, cycle; course, path; *fig:* ambit, compass, range, scope, sphere; *spec:* eyeball socket. **vb** *lit:* circle, circumnavigate, encircle, revolve around.

ordeal **n** *lit:* labor, nightmare, torment, tribulation, uphill struggle; test, trial.

order **n** *lit:* command, decree, directive, injunction, mandate, ordinance, rule; application, booking, request, reservation; alignment, arrangement, line, organization, regularity, symmetry, tidiness; calm, control, discipline, peace, propriety, quiet; categorization, classification, codification, grouping, progression; breed, family, genre, ilk, kind, sort, type; caste, class, grade, hierarchy, position, rank; association, brotherhood, company, fraternity, guild, league, lodge, society; (in) place, (in) sequence, (in) turn; (in) commission, (in) service; (out of) operation, (out of) repair. **vb** *lit:* command, decree, direct, instruct, ordain, prescribe, require; apply for, book, contract for, request, reserve; adjust, align, arrange, marshal, regulate; catalog, classify, sort out.

orderly **adj** *lit:* methodical, neat, regular, shipshape, systematic, tidy, trim; businesslike, controlled, formal, restrained; calm, disciplined, law-abiding, quiet, well-behaved.

ordinarily **adv** *lit:* as a rule, commonly, generally, habitually, in general, normally, usually.

ordinary **adj** *lit:* common, everyday, habitual, humdrum, normal, regular, standard, typical, usual; common or garden, customary, familiar, household, humble, plain, prosaic, simple, unpretentious, unremarkable; average, clichéd, commonplace, hackneyed, indifferent, mediocre, pedestrian, unexceptional.

organic **adj** *lit:* biological, biotic, living, natural; anatomical, constitutional, inherent, integral, structural; integrated, ordered, structured, systematic.

organism **n** *lit:* animal, being, creature, living thing; integrated structure.

organization **n** *lit:* assembly, composition, construction, coordination, design, formation, framework, plan, planning, structure, structuring; alignment, arrangement, conformation, grouping, make-up; association, body, company, concern, consortium, corporation, group, institution, syndicate.

organize **vb** *lit:* assemble, compose, construct, coordinate, design, form, frame, plan, structure; combine, join together, unite; align, arrange, group, line up, marshal, put in order, set up; classify, codify; be responsible for, manage, orchestrate, run, see to, take care of.

orgy **n** *lit:* bacchanal, carousel, debauch, revelry; binge, splurge, spree; *fig:* fit, frenzy, storm.

origin **n** *lit:* roots, source; beginning, commencement, outset, start;

basis, creation, derivation, emergence, foundation, fount, genesis; ancestry, extraction, lineage, pedigree, provenance, stock.

original n *lit:* first, master, true one; archetype, model, paradigm, pattern, prototype; *fig:* anomaly, character, eccentric, oddity, weirdo. **adj** *lit:* early, first, initial, starting; authentic, first-hand, genuine, master, true; creative, fresh, imaginative, ingenious, innovative, innovatory, inventive, new, novel, unprecedented, unusual.

originally adv *lit:* at first, first, initially, in the first place, to begin with; prehistorically; imaginatively, ingeniously, innovatively, inventively.

originate vb *lit:* arise, begin, come, derive, emanate, emerge, spring, start; bring about, create, evolve, initiate, pioneer, set up.

originator n *lit:* architect, author, creator, designer, deviser, founder, inventor, pioneer.

ornament n *lit:* decoration, jewel, trinket; adornment, embellishment, frill, garnish, trimming; *fig:* flower, glory, pride, treasure. **vb** *lit:* adorn, decorate, embellish, festoon, garnish, trim; *fig:* grace, honor.

ornamental adj *lit:* decorative, embellishing; artistic, picturesque, scenic; extra, inessential, supplementary.

ornate adj *lit:* bedecked, elaborate, florid, ornamented, showy; lavish, rich, sumptuous.

other adj *lit:* additional, ancillary, auxiliary, extra, further, more, remaining, spare, supplementary; alternative, contrasting, different, dissimilar, diverse, separate, variant.

otherwise adj *lit:* different. **adv** *lit:* alternatively, differently; apart from this, except for this. **cnj** *lit:* if not, or else.

out adj *lit:* absent; dismissed, disqualified, eliminated; at fault, incorrect, in error, wrong; striking, on strike; exposed, in the open, public; blooming, in bloom. **adv** *lit:* away, elsewhere, outside; not allowed, not on, unacceptable; antiquated, behind the times, dated, old-fashioned; at an end, dead, exhausted, expired, finished; completely, thoroughly, unreservedly; in society; lengthwise; from a total (of), from the midst (of). **prp** *lit:* outside.

outbreak n *lit;* epidemic, upsurge; burst, eruption, explosion, flare-up, rash.

outburst n *lit;* discharge, eruption, outpouring, surge; explosion, fit of temper, storm, tantrum; interpolation, interruption, intrusion.

outcome n *lit;* conclusion, consequence, end result, result, upshot; aftermath.

outcry n *lit;* complaint, howl, hullabaloo, protest, screech; commotion, uproar, yell.

outdated adj *lit;* antiquated, archaic, behind the times, out of date, passé, unfashionable.

outdo vb *lit;* beat, excel, surpass, transcend, outstrip; get the better of, outmaneuver, overcome.

outer adj *lit;* cortical, exterior, external, outlying, outside, peripheral, superficial.

outfit n *lit;* clothes, costume, dress, get-up, suit; accouterments, gear, trappings; clique, company, crew, group, organization, set, squad, team, unit. vb *lit;* equip, fit out, kit out, stock, supply.

outgoing adj *lit;* approachable, easy, extrovert, friendly, gregarious, open, sociable; departing, ex-, former, past, retiring.

outing n *lit;* airing, excursion, expedition, jaunt, spin, trip.

outlaw n *lit;* criminal, malefactor, miscreant; bandit, brigand, desperado, marauder; fugitive, outcast. vb *lit;* ban, banish, bar, exclude, make illegal, proscribe.

outline n *lit;* contour, delineation, form, profile, shape, silhouette; draft, framework, layout, plan, sketch; bare facts, rough idea, summary, synopsis silhouette. vb *lit;* delineate; draft, plan, sketch, summarize.

outlook n *lit;* attitude, frame of mind, standpoint, view; expectations, forecast, prospect; aspect, panorama, scene, vista.

outrage n *lit;* atrocity, barbarism, enormity, inhumanity; affront, insult, profanation; injury, offense, rape, violation; anger, fury, indignation, resentment. vb *lit;* affront, incense, infuriate, madden, offend, shock; injure, insult.

outrageous adj *lit;* atrocious, barbaric, infamous, monstrous, unspeakable; disgraceful, iniquitous, scandalous; exorbitant, immoderate, preposterous, shocking.

outright adj *lit;* definite, direct, straightforward; absolute, arrant, complete, downright, out-and-out, thorough, total, unqualified, utter. adv *lit;* absolutely, completely, explicitly, overtly, thoroughly, without hesitation; at once, immediately, instantaneously, instantly, straight away, there and then.

outside n *lit;* cortex, exterior, facade, front, surface; topside; hide, peel, skin; extreme, most. adj *lit;* exterior, external, outdoor, outer, outermost, outward, surface; extramural; extraneous; distant, marginal, negligible, slight, slim, small, unlikely. adv *lit;* on the exterior, to the exterior. prp *lit;* beyond, excluded from, the far side of; excepted from, exempt from; apart from.

outspoken adj *lit;* blunt, candid, direct, forthright, frank, free; explicit.

outstanding adj *lit;* arresting, conspicuous, eye-catching, noteworthy, prominent, striking; eminent, excellent, exceptional, great, preeminent, superlative; due, owing, payable, remaining, unpaid, unsettled.

outward adj *lit;* exterior, external, outer, outside, surface; apparent, evident, ostensible, overt, superficial, visible.

outwardly adv *lit;* apparently, as far as one can see, externally, on the face of it, ostensibly, overtly, seemingly, superficially, to all intents and purposes, visibly.

outweigh vb *lit;* be more important than, be preponderant over, eclipse, have more clout than, predominate over, prevail over, take precedence over.

over adj *lit;* accomplished, ancient history, completed, concluded, finished, past, settled; closed; done; left, remaining, spare, surplus. adv *lit;* above one, overhead; across. prp *lit;* above, atop, on, on top of, superior to; exceeding, in excess of, more than.

overall adj *lit;* all-embracing, complete, comprehensive, general, inclusive, long-term, total. adv *lit;* generally speaking, in general, in the long term, on the whole.

overbearing adj *lit;* arrogant, autocratic, bossy, dictatorial, domineering, haughty, high-handed, officious, peremptory, supercilious, superior.

overcast **adj** *lit:* clouded, cloudy, dismal, dull, gray, leaden, lowering, threatening.

overcome **vb** *lit:* beat, conquer, crush, defeat, get the better of, overpower, prevail over, subdue, vanquish; be victorious over, rise above, surmount; come through, survive, weather. **adj** *lit:* affected, bowled over, overwhelmed, speechless, ecstatic, elated; horrified, terrified; awestruck; dumbstruck, flabbergasted.

overcrowded **adj (pa.pt)** *lit:* choked, congested, crammed, full, overpopulated, packed.

overdo **vb** *lit:* overwork at; exaggerate, overact; belabor, take to extremes, overstate; overuse.

overdue **adj** *lit:* behind schedule, behind time, late, unpunctual; outstanding, owing.

overeat **vb** *lit:* binge, eat like a horse, gorge, guzzle, make a pig of oneself, pack it away, pig out, stuff oneself.

overflow **n** *lit:* discharge, flood, inundation; surplus. **vb** *lit:* flood, pour over, run over, spill over; drown, immerse, inundate, submerge, swamp.

overhang **n** *lit:* projection, protrusion. **vb** *lit:* bulge over, jut over, loom over, project over, protrude over, stick out over; *fig:* be imminent over, loom over, threaten.

overindulgence **n** *lit:* excess, immoderation, intemperance, surfeit.

overlook **vb** *lit:* command a view of, front on, look over; fail to notice, forget, miss, pass over; disregard, ignore, let one off with, let pass, omit, skip, turn a blind eye to.

overtake **vb** *lit:* get past, outdistance, outdo, pass; catch unprepared, engulf, overwhelm, strike, take by surprise.

overthrow **n** *lit:* deposing, dethronement, downfall, ejection, expulsion, ouster, removal, undoing; defeat, destruction, rout, ruin, subjugation, suppression. **vb** *lit:* bring down, depose, dethrone, eject, expel, oust, remove, undo; defeat, destroy, rout, ruin, subdue, subjugate, suppress; abolish, do away with, demolish, overturn, put an end to, topple, raze.

overturn vb *lit:* capsize, keel over, knock over, tip over, topple, tumble, upend; annul, countermand, invalidate, repeal, reverse; depose.

overweight adj *lit:* bulky, chubby, corpulent, fat, gross, heavy, hefty, massive, obese, plump, podgy, portly, stout, tubby.

owe vb *lit:* be in arrears; be under an obligation to pay, have to give, should give.

owing adj *lit:* due, outstanding, unpaid, unsettled.

owing to adv *lit:* as a result of, because of, due to, in consequence of, on account of.

own vb *lit:* have, hold, possess, retain; acknowledge, admit (to), avow, concede (to), confess (to), go along with, grant. adj *lit:* individual, personal, private.

owner n *lit:* landlord, proprietor; possessor, retainer; master.

P

pace n *lit:* step, stride; gait, tread, walk; momentum, motion, rate, speed, tempo, velocity. **vb** *lit:* march, pound, stride; patrol; count (out), mark (out), measure (out).

pack n *lit:* bale, bundle; burden, load; haversack, knapsack, rucksack; band, bunch, crowd, gang, group, herd, troop; collection, deck, kit, set; application; carton, packet. **vb** *lit:* batch, bundle, parcel up; burden, load, store, stow; cram, fill, jam, press, ram, stuff; crowd, mob, throng; compact, compress.

package n *lit:* box, carton, packet, parcel; amalgamation, combination; unit, whole; deal, enterprise, transaction; product. **vb** *lit:* batch, box, pack, parcel up, wrap up; assemble, make, manufacture, put it all together.

packed adj (pa.pt) *lit:* congested, crammed, crowded, full, jammed, overloaded, seething, swarming.

pad n *lit:* buffer, cushion, guard, protection, shield, wad; block, jotter, notebook, notepad; paw, sole; apartment, flat, room; heliport, launching platform. **vb** *lit:* cushion, fill, line, stuff; *fig:* digress, draw (out), fill (out), prevaricate.

pagan n *lit:* heathen, unbeliever; infidel; atheist. **adj** *lit:* godless, heathen, unbelieving; irreligious, ungodly.

page n *lit:* folio, leaf, sheet, side; attendant, servant, squire. **vb** *lit:* call for, have called for, send to find.

pain n *lit:* ache, agony, discomfort, pang, smarting, soreness, throb; anguish, distress, suffering, woe; grief, sadness; *fig:* bore, bother, nuisance, pest. **vb** *lit:* hurt, smart, wound; chafe, discomfort, torment; *fig:* afflict, aggrieve, agonize, distress; annoy, gall, harass, irritate, vex, worry.

painful adj *lit:* aching, agonizing, excruciating, hurting, raw, smarting, sore, throbbing; abhorrent, awful, distressing, dreadful, nasty, terrible, unpleasant; arduous, difficult, hard, tedious, trying.

painkiller n *lit:* analgesic, anodyne, palliative, sedative; drug, pill, tablet.

painstaking adj *lit:* assiduous, careful, conscientious, meticulous, punctilious, scrupulous, thorough.

paint n *lit:* color, dye, pigment, tint, wash; emulsion, enamel; cosmetics, make-up. **vb** *lit:* color, dye, enamel, tint; depict, draw, picture, portray, represent, sketch; brush (on), coat, daub, decorate, put (on), slap (on); *fig:* describe, evoke, picture.

pair n *lit:* brace, couple, doublet, duo, twosome. **vb** *lit:* bracket, couple, match, put together, yoke; marry, mate, wed.

pale **vb** *lit:* blanch, blench, go white, whiten; dim, dull, fade; *fig:* decrease, diminish, lessen. **adj** *lit:* anemic, ashen, bleached, faded, pallid, sallow, wan, washed-out, whitish; dim, faint, feeble, thin, weak.

palm n *lit:* hand, paw; coconut tree, date tree; *fig:* glory, laurels, success, triumph, trophy, victory. **vb** *lit:* conceal in one's hand; steal, thieve, walk off with; *fig:* fob (off with); pass (off as).

pampered adj (pa.pt) *lit:* babied, coddled, cosseted, indulged, mollycoddled, spoilt.

pan n *lit:* cooking tray, pot, saucepan, vessel; basin, concavity, depression, hollow; *fig:* face, features; *spec:* drum (in a steel band); floe (of ice); priming area (on a flintlock). **vb** *lit:* search (for), sift, wash; *fig:* scan, sweep, track; censure, criticize, flay, knock; come (out), turn (out).

panel n *lit:* oblong, rectangle; board, lath, plank, strip; fencing, hurdle, paling; dashboard, instrument board, switchboard; painting, picture; *fig:* discussion group, jury; *spec:* box, frame, inset, key (on a page); division, section (of a coal mine, of a hull); list (of clients, of consultants, of doctors, of jurors, of patients).

pang n *lit:* gripe, pain, prick, stab, twinge; stitch; ache; *fig:* qualm, scruple.

panic n *lit:* alarm, consternation, fear, fright, hysteria; red alert, scare. **vb** *lit:* become hysterical, go to pieces, lose one's nerve, overreact; alarm, frighten, put the wind up, scare; unnerve.

pant **vb** *lit:* blow, gasp, heave, puff, wheeze; *fig:* hunger (for), long (for), pine (for), yearn (for).

pants n *lit:* bloomers, briefs, drawers, panties, shorts, slacks, trousers, underpants.

paper n *lit:* document(s); certificate, deed, instrument; dossier(s), file(s); account(s), receipt(s); daily, journal, newspaper, organ, periodical, tabloid; article, dissertation, essay, monograph, study, thesis, treatise; examination; wrapping.

par n *lit:* average, norm, standard, usual; balance, equality, equilibrium, level, parallel.

parade n *lit:* array, cavalcade, pageant, procession; military display, trooping; display, exhibition, flaunting, ostentation, show; esplanade, promenade; *spec:* defense, parry (in fencing). **vb** *lit:* march past, process; brandish, display, flaunt, show off, vaunt; troop.

paradise n *lit:* garden of Eden, heaven; life to come, next world; Elysian fields, happy hunting ground, Promised Land, Utopia; *fig:* bliss, ecstasy, joy, rapture.

parallel n *lit:* analogy, comparison, correlation, likeness, resemblance, similarity; analog, counterpart, duplicate, equal, equivalent, match. **vb** *lit:* agree with, be alike with, correlate to, correspond with, equal, match; balance, complement. **adj** *lit:* aligned, alongside, side by side; analogous, compatible, complementary, uniform.

paralysis n *lit:* ataxia, paresis; immobility, numbness, palsy; *fig:* disruption, shutdown, stasis, stillness, stoppage.

paralyze vb *lit:* anesthetize, benumb, immobilize, numb; cripple, debilitate, disable, lame; *fig:* arrest, halt, stop, transfix.

parasite n *lit:* bloodsucker; *fig:* hanger-on, leech, scrounger, sponger; drone.

parcel n *lit:* carton, package, packet; batch, bunch, bundle; bit, portion, part; area, lot, plot, site. **vb** *lit:* do (up), pack (up), wrap (up); apportion (out), deal (out), mete (out), share (out).

parched adj *lit:* arid, dehydrated, desiccated, dry; thirsty; scorched, shriveled, withered.

pardon n *lit:* forgiveness; absolution, mercy, remission, reprieve; amnesty, grace; acquittal, discharge, exoneration; *spec:* (papal) indulgence. **vb** *lit:* forgive; absolve, free, let off, release from, remit, reprieve; acquit, exculpate, excuse, overlook.

parent n *lit:* father, mother, procreator, progenitor, sire; guardian; author, creator, generator, originator, source; derivation, prototype.

park n *lit:* estate, garden, grounds, nature reserve, reservation, woodland; playground, playing field, recreation ground. **vb** *lit:* dump, leave, put down; pull up, station, stop.

part n *lit:* bit, fraction, fragment, piece, portion, scrap, section, sector, segment, share; component, constituent, element, ingredient, module, unit; limb, member, organ; area, district, region, territory, vicinity; behalf, cause, concern, interest; duty, function, involvement, say, task; character, role, voice; conduct, disposition, temperament. **vb** *lit:* detach, disconnect, disjoin, divide, put asunder, rend, separate, sever, split, tear; break up, go separate ways, leave, quit, split up, withdraw.

partial adj *lit:* biased, discriminatory, one-sided, partisan, prejudiced, unfair; incomplete, part, unfinished.

participant n *lit:* competitor, contestant, contributor, member, partaker; partner, shareholder.

particle n *lit:* atom, bit, grain, ion, iota, jot, mite, molecule, scrap, shred, speck; crumb; prefix, suffix.

particular n *lit:* circumstance(s), detail(s), fact(s), specification(s). **adj** *lit:* choosy, fastidious, finicky, fussy, meticulous, painstaking, thorough; detailed, itemized, minute; distinct, exact, special, specific; distinctive, remarkable, singular, unusual.

particularly adv *lit:* decidedly, distinctly, especially, explicitly, expressly, intimately, markedly, notably, outstandingly, specifically; individually, peculiarly, singularly, uncommonly, unusually.

partition n *lit:* barrier, divider, fence, screen, septum, wall; division, segregation, separation; apportioning, distribution, rationing out; allocation, portion, ration, share. **vb** *lit:* divide, fence (off), screen, wall (off); cut up, segment, separate, split up, subdivide; allocate, apportion.

partner n *lit:* ally, associate, collaborator, colleague, cofounder, confederate; abetter, accomplice; companion, comrade, mate; bedfellow, boyfriend, consort, girlfriend, husband, spouse, wife.

party   n *lit:* celebration, do, festivity, gala, get-together, reception, social gathering, soiree, thrash; band, body, bunch, company, detachment, group, squad, team, unit; alliance, association, clique, coalition, confederacy, faction, grouping, set, side; individual, person; contractor, defendant, litigant, plaintiff.

pass   n *lit:* canyon, col, defile, gap; authorization, identification, permit, safe-conduct, warrant; free ticket, season ticket, voucher; advances, approach, overture, sexual advance; plight, predicament, situation, state of affairs; lunge, push, thrust; brandishing, gesticulation, wave; *spec:* success (in an examination). **vb** *lit:* depart, elapse, go by, leave, move, proceed; beat, exceed, excel, outdo, surmount, surpass, transcend; get through, graduate, qualify; do, suffice; fill, occupy, spend, while away; befall, happen, occur, take place; convey, give, hand, kick, throw, transfer, transmit; accept, approve, authorize, enact, legislate, ratify, sanction, validate; declare, pronounce; disregard, ignore, miss, omit, overlook, skip; defecate, discharge, evacuate, excrete, micturate, urinate; blow over, cease, die, dwindle, ebb, expire, fade, vanish, wane; be seen (as), be taken (for).

passage   n *lit:* corridor, doorway, entrance, exit, hall, lobby, vestibule; crossing, journey, tour, trek, trip, voyage; avenue, course, lane, path, road, route, thoroughfare, way; advance, flow, passing, progress, transition; clause, excerpt, extract, piece, quotation, reading, section, text; acceptance, enactment, legislation, ratification.

passing   n *lit:* death, decease, demise, end; overhauling, overtaking. **adj** *lit:* incidental, fortuitous; casual, cursory, hasty, shallow, superficial; brief, ephemeral, fleeting, momentary, transitory.

passion   n *lit:* ardor, eagerness, emotion, ferocity, fervor, fire, intensity, spirit, vehemence, voracity, zeal; craving, desire, lust; enthusiasm, fondness, infatuation, love; craze, mania, obsession; anger, ire, rage, resentment, wrath; frenzy, storm.

passionate   adj *lit:* amorous, ardent, erotic, hot, loving, lustful, sensual, sexy; aflame, eager, enthusiastic, excited, fervent, fiery, heartfelt, intense, spirited, vehement, zealous; emotional, wild; hot-headed, irascible, irritable, quick-tempered, stormy, tempestuous, violent.

passive   adj *lit:* inactive, inert; long-suffering, patient, resigned, submissive, unresisting; acquiescent, compliant, docile.

past n *lit:* days gone by, former times, good old days, times past; background, experience, history, life, particulars, previous life, record. **adj** *lit:* completed, done, extinct, finished, gone, over; ancient, bygone, old, previous; earlier, erstwhile, former, preceding, quondam. **adv** *lit:* by, on; beyond, to the far side of; over. **prp** *lit:* beyond, farther than, outside, over; after, subsequent to.

patch n *lit:* darn, reinforcement, replacement; bit, fragment, scrap, shred; area, ground, land, manor, stretch, vicinity; period, time; *spec:* cover, pad (over an eye); overlay (in printing). **vb** *lit:* cover over, darn, fix (up), mend, repair; treat; put (together), reconnect (together); *fig:* make (up).

paternal adj *lit:* fatherly, parental; avuncular, benevolent, protective, solicitous; family, hereditary, patrimonial.

path n *lit:* alley, footway, gangway, passage, pavement, sidewalk, track, trail, walk, walkway; course, direction, line, route, way.

pathetic adj *lit:* affecting, distressing, heartrending, moving, pitiable, sad, touching; *fig:* abysmal, feeble, lamentable, petty, weak, wet; hopeless, useless, worthless.

patience n *lit:* endurance, forbearance, perseverance, sufferance, tolerance; calmness, composure; diligence, fortitude, persistence.

patient n *lit:* invalid, sufferer; victim; case, client. **adj** *lit:* enduring, forbearing, long-suffering, persevering, resigned, stoic, suffering, tolerant; calm, composed, cool; diligent, persistent; lenient, magnanimous, understanding.

patrol n *lit:* policing, rounds, safeguarding, reconnaissance, watch; guard, sentinel, watchman. **vb** *lit:* guard, inspect, keep watch over, make the rounds, police, reconnoiter.

patron n *lit:* benefactor, sponsor; angel, backer; champion, defender, guardian, protector; client, customer, shopper.

patronize vb *lit:* be condescending to, be lofty with, look down on, talk down to; fund, sponsor; back, support; be a client of, buy from, do business with, frequent, trade with.

pause n *lit:* break, breather, delay, gap, halt, interlude, intermission, interval, lull, respite, stoppage; hesitation; interruption, suspension. **vb**

lit: break off, delay, halt, have a breather, rest, stop briefly; falter, hesitate, waver.

paw **n** *lit:* foot, hand; pad; claws; mitt. **vb** *lit:* finger, fondle, grope, maul, molest; feel, grab, handle roughly, manhandle; *spec:* kick, strike (the ground restlessly).

pawn **n** *lit:* collateral, deposit, pledge, security; bond, hock; cat's-paw, dupe, instrument, puppet, stooge, tool. **vb** *lit:* deposit, hock, pledge, stake.

pay **n** *lit:* earnings, fee, hire, remuneration, salary, stipend, wages; emolument, income, takings; reimbursement. **vb** *lit:* cough up, foot, settle; clear, honor; recompense, reimburse, remunerate; be advantageous, benefit, be worthwhile, repay; bring in, return, yield; be profitable, make a return, provide a living; bestow, extend, give, present, proffer, render; *fig:* answer (for), make amends (for), suffer (for).

payment **n** *lit:* emolument, fee, hire, remuneration, salary, stipend, wages; advance, deposit, outlay, premium; remittance, settlement.

peace **n** *lit:* calm, hush, quiet, repose, restfulness, serenity, silence, stillness, tranquility; amity, concord, friendliness, harmony; armistice, cessation of hostilities, treaty, truce; *spec:* ease (of mind).

peaceful **adj** *lit:* calm, hushed, placid, quiet, restful, serene, silent, still, tranquil, undisturbed, unruffled; amicable, friendly, harmonious, on good terms; nonmilitary.

peak **n** *lit:* apex, crest, pinnacle, point, summit, tip, top; *fig:* climax, culmination, high point, maximum, zenith. **vb** *lit:* climax, come to a head, reach a maximum.

peal **n** *lit:* chime, chiming, clangor, resonance, reverberation, ringing, sounding, tolling; *spec:* carillon, set (of bells). **vb** *lit:* chime, clang, resonate, resound, reverberate, ring, sound, toll.

peculiar **adj** *lit:* abnormal, bizarre, freakish, funny, odd, outlandish, strange, weird; curious, extraordinary, quaint, singular, unusual; characteristic, distinctive, idiosyncratic, individual, own, particular, private, specific, unique.

pedestrian **n** *lit:* walker; footslogger, hiker; passerby. **adj** *lit:* on foot, walking; *fig:* boring, dull, long-winded, prosaic, slow, tedious, trite, unimaginative.

peel n *lit:* rind, skin; bark; outer layer. **vb** *lit:* pare, skin, strip (off); flake off.

peep n *lit:* glance, glimpse, look, peek; cheep, chirp, chirrup, squeak, twitter. **vb** *lit:* glance, peek, sneak a look; appear briefly, be partly visible; cheep, chirp, chirrup, squeak, twitter.

peer n *lit:* aristocrat, lord, noble, nobleman; equal. **vb** *lit:* gaze, look (at), take a close look (at); look (out), peep (out).

peerage n *lit:* aristocracy, lords, nobility, peers.

peevish adj *lit:* cantankerous, cross, crusty, fretful, grumpy, ill-tempered, irascible, petulant, short-tempered, snappy, sulky, surly, testy, touchy, waspish.

peg n *lit:* bolt, pin, stake; hook, key; dram, drink, tot; *fig:* degree, step; leg; *spec:* wooden leg. **vb** *lit:* attach, fasten, fix, join, secure; freeze, hold, limit, set; *fig:* plug (away at), work (away at).

pelt n *lit:* fell, fur, hide, skin; (at full) speed. **vb** *lit:* assail (with), bombard (with), pepper (with), shower (with); bucket down, pour, rain; career, dash, race, rush, speed, tear.

pen n *lit:* ballpoint, felt-tip, marker, nib, quill; cage, coop, enclosure, hutch, sty; *fig:* prison; *spec:* female swan. **vb** *lit:* be the author of, jot down, write; cage, confine (in), coop up, enclose (in), fence (in), hedge (in), shut (in).

penalize vb *lit:* discipline, fine, imprison, punish; handicap, put at a disadvantage.

penalty n *lit:* punishment; fine, forfeit, imprisonment; disadvantage, handicap; free kick, spot kick.

pending adj *lit:* hanging fire, remaining undecided, unsettled, up in the air. **prp** *lit:* awaiting, until; during.

penetrate vb *lit:* enter, go through, perforate, pierce; get (into), infiltrate, permeate, seep, suffuse; *fig:* get through to, impress, reach, touch; comprehend, fathom, figure out, unravel, work out.

penetrating adj *lit:* biting, pervasive, piercing, pungent, sharp, shrill; *fig:* acute, astute, discerning, incisive, keen, perceptive, quick, searching, sharp, shrewd.

pension n *lit:* allowance, benefit; annuity, superannuation; *spec:* boarding house, guest house.

people n *lit:* human beings, humankind, persons; citizens, community, inhabitants, nation, population, tribe; general public, laity, masses, mob, populace, voters; family, folks, household, kinfolk, parents; party, side, team; employees, staff. **vb** *lit:* inhabit, occupy, settle; populate.

peppery adj *lit:* fiery, hot, piquant, pungent, spicy; *fig:* hot-tempered, irascible, irritable, snappy, touchy, waspish; biting, caustic, sarcastic, sharp, stinging.

perceive vb *lit:* become aware of, discern, notice, recognize, spot; be aware of, behold, distinguish, observe, see; apprehend, comprehend, conclude, deduce, gather, get, grasp, realize, understand.

perception n *lit:* apprehension, discernment, grasp, recognition; awareness, observation, sense; impression, notion, understanding; consciousness, sensation.

perceptive adj *lit:* acute, alert, astute, discerning, observant, percipient, quick, sharp, shrewd.

perch n *lit:* branch, pole, resting place, roost; seat; bar, peg. **vb** *lit:* alight (on), land (on), rest, settle; sit (on); balance (on).

perfect vb *lit:* complete, consummate, effect, finish, fulfill; accomplish, carry out, perform; cultivate, develop, improve, polish up. **adj** *lit:* absolute, complete, consummate, entire, finished, unadulterated, utter, whole; excellent, faultless, flawless, ideal, impeccable, sublime, superb, unblemished, untarnished; accurate, correct, exact, precise, unerring; accomplished, adept, expert, masterly, polished, skillful.

performance n *lit:* accomplishment, achievement, carrying out, completion, discharge, execution, exploit, feat; action, behavior, conduct, efficiency, functioning, operation, practice, working; acting, appearance, exhibition, interpretation, portrayal, presentation, production, representation; act, fuss, palaver, to-do.

period n *lit:* span, spell, time, while; interval, season, stage, stretch, term; cycle, revolution; age, epoch, era; dot, full stop, point.

perish vb *lit:* be killed, die, expire, lose one's life, pass away; be destroyed, go under, vanish; decay, decompose, rot, waste, wither.

perky adj *lit:* brisk, jaunty, pert, saucy, self-assertive.

permanent adj *lit:* fixed, immutable, imperishable, indelible, indestructible, invariable, lasting, perpetual, persistent, steadfast, unchanging.

permit n *lit:* authorization, documentation, licence, papers, pass, ticket, visa, warrant. vb *lit:* allow, authorize, consent to, endorse, give leave to, grant, licence, sanction; acquiesce in, submit to, tolerate.

perpetual adj *lit:* eternal, everlasting, never-ending, undying, unending; constant, continual, endless, incessant, interminable, persistent, recurrent, unceasing, uninterrupted, unremitting.

perplex vb *lit:* baffle, bewilder, confound, confuse, dumbfound, puzzle, stump; complicate, entangle, jumble, mix up, tangle.

persecute vb *lit:* ill-treat, maltreat, oppress, torment, victimize; afflict, molest; harass, hound, hunt, pursue; *fig:* annoy, badger, bother, pester, worry.

persevering adj (pr.pt) *lit:* diligent, dogged, indefatigable, lasting, persistent, pertinacious, tenacious; resolute, steadfast; long-suffering, patient.

persist vb *lit:* be dogged (in), be tenacious (in), persevere (in), stand firm (in); carry on, continue, keep going, keep up, last, remain.

persistent adj *lit:* assiduous, dogged, indefatigable, pertinacious, resolute, steadfast, tenacious, tireless; immovable, obdurate, obstinate, stubborn; constant, continual, continuous, incessant, lasting, perpetual, relentless, remaining, unrelenting, unremitting.

personality n *lit:* appearance, character, disposition, make-up, nature, temper, temperament; identity; attractiveness, charisma, charm, magnetism; dynamism; *fig:* celebrity, household name, personage, star.

personnel n *lit:* employees, hands, members, people, staff, workers, work force.

perspire vb *lit:* sweat, swelter; drip, exude, secrete.

persuade vb *lit:* coax, entice, induce, influence, prevail upon; egg on, incite; convince (that), satisfy (that).

persuasion n *lit:* cajolery, enticement, exhortation, inducement, wheedling; belief, conviction, creed, faith, opinion, tenet, view; cult, denomination, faction, party, school of thought, sect, side.

pert adj *lit:* bold, forward, free-speaking, impudent, provocative, saucy; jaunty, stylish; in good spirits, lively.

perturb vb *lit:* agitate, alarm, bother, disconcert, disquiet, disturb, fluster, ruffle, upset, worry; confuse, disarrange, muddle, unsettle.

perverse adj *lit:* abnormal, depraved, deviant, immoral, unnatural; awkward, argumentative, intractable, mulish, obdurate, obstinate, pigheaded, stubborn, wayward, willful; cantankerous, fractious, ill-tempered, peevish, refractory, sullen, surly.

pervert n *lit:* debauchee; deviant. vb *lit:* distort, falsify, misinterpret, misrepresent, misuse, twist, warp; corrupt, debase, debauch, deprave, lead astray, subvert.

pest n *lit:* annoyance, bore, bother, irritation, nuisance, pain, trial; blight, curse, infection, infestation, parasite, pestilence, plague.

pet n *lit:* darling, favorite, jewel, treasure; animal; huff, rage, tantrum. vb *lit:* baby, coddle, cosset, pamper, spoil; caress, fondle, pat, stroke; cuddle, kiss, neck, smooch. adj *lit:* cherished, dearest, favored, particular, preferred, special; caged, domesticated, family, tame, trained.

petition n *lit:* appeal, application, entreaty, plea, request, suit, supplication. vb *lit:* appeal to, ask, beg, beseech, call upon, entreat, plead with, solicit, supplicate; urge.

petty adj *lit:* contemptible, insignificant, little, measly, minor, negligible, paltry, slight, trivial, unimportant; cheap, grudging, mean, shabby, stingy; inferior, lower, subordinate.

phase n *lit:* juncture, period, stage, time; condition, development, state; chapter. vb *lit:* carry out by stages; make regular; synchronize; get (in), move (in); get (out), move (out).

phenomenal adj *lit:* extraordinary, fantastic, miraculous, outstanding, prodigious, remarkable, sensational, singular, unique, unparalleled.

phenomenon n *lit:* circumstance, event, fact, happening, incident, occurrence; exception, marvel, miracle, prodigy, rarity, sensation, wonder.

philosophy   n *lit:* logic, metaphysics, rationalism, reasoning, thinking, thought; attitude to life, beliefs, convictions, ideology, principles, tenets, values, viewpoint; composure, coolness, equanimity, resignation, self-possession, stoicism.

phlegmatic   adj *lit:* apathetic, cold, dull, frigid, heavy, impassive, lethargic, placid, sluggish, stoic, stolid, undemonstrative, unemotional, unimpressed.

phony   n *lit:* counterfeit, fake, forgery, fraud, impostor, pretender, sham. adj *lit:* affected, assumed, bogus, counterfeit, ersatz, fake, forged, imitation, sham, trick.

photograph   n *lit:* halftone, likeness, picture, print, shot, slide, snap, snapshot, transparency. vb *lit:* film, shoot, snap, take a picture of.

phrase   n *lit:* clause, expression, motto, proverb, remark, saying, slogan, tag, term. vb *lit:* articulate, couch, express, formulate, frame, put, say, word.

physical   adj *lit:* bodily, carnal, corporeal; fleshly, profane, secular, temporal, unspiritual; actual, material, natural, palpable, real, solid, tangible, visible.

pick   n *lit:* choice, decision, option, preference, selection; choicest, elite, flower, pride; adze, ax, hammer; hook, spike. vb *lit:* choose, decide upon, elect, opt for, select, settle upon, single out; instigate, provoke, start; nibble (at), peck (at); break open, crack, force, jimmy, open, prize open.

picture   n *lit:* depiction, description, image, impression, re-creation, replica, representation, reproduction; artwork, drawing, engraving, illustration, likeness, painting, photograph, portrait, print, sketch; film, motion picture, movie; *fig:* carbon copy, double, duplicate, living image, portrait, twin; archetype, embodiment, epitome, essence, personification. vb *lit:* conceive of, see, visualize; depict, describe, draw, illustrate, map, paint, photograph, plan, portray, render, represent, sketch.

piece   n *lit:* bit, chunk, division, fraction, iota, morsel, mouthful, portion, section, segment, slice; fragment, scrap, sherd, smithereens; article, composition, creation, item, production, work of art; example, sample, specimen; firearm, gun, pistol, revolver; coin; *fig:* entity, unity, whole; instance, occurrence, stroke; *spec:* playing token (in checkers, chess). **vb** *lit:* connect (together), fit (together), fix (together), patch (together).

pier n *lit:* breakwater, jetty, mole, quay, wharf; buttress, column, pile, pillar, upright; stand, support.

pierce vb *lit:* drill, penetrate, prick, puncture, run through, spike, stab, transfix; *fig:* cut to the quick, move, pain, sting, strike, thrill, wound.

piercing adj *lit:* earsplitting, high-pitched, shattering, shrill; arctic, biting, bitter, freezing, numbing, raw; acute, agonizing, excruciating, exquisite, intense, racking, sharp, stabbing; *fig:* alert, keen, penetrating, perceptive, probing, searching, shrewd.

pig n *lit:* boar, hog, piglet, porker, sow, swine; *fig:* glutton, guzzler; animal, beast, brute, slob; burden, chore, hardship, problem; *spec:* ingot, mold (in an iron foundry).

pile n *lit:* accumulation, heap, hoard, mound, stack; building, edifice, structure; beam, column, pier, pillar, support, upright; fiber, hair, nap, shag; battery, generator, reactor; *fig:* large amount, lot, quantity; fortune, mint, packet. **vb** *lit:* accumulate, amass, gather, heap, hoard, stack, store; crowd, crush, flood, jam, pack, rush.

pillage n *lit:* despoliation, looting, plundering, rapine, robbery, sack; booty, loot, plunder, spoils. **vb** *lit:* despoil, loot, maraud, plunder, raid, ransack, ravage, rob, sack, strip.

pilot n *lit:* airman, aviator; guide, helmsman, steersman; captain, coxswain, navigator. **vb** *lit:* control, direct, drive, fly, guide, handle, navigate, operate, steer. **adj** *lit:* experimental, initial, introductory, preliminary trial.

pin n *lit:* nail, tack; needle, spike; key, peg, rod; axle, bar, crosspiece, lever, spindle, toggle; skittle. **vb** *lit:* affix, attach, fasten, fix, nail, secure, tack; *fig:* hold down, immobilize, pinion, restrain.

pinch n *lit:* nip, squeeze, tweak; bit, dash, soup, speck, taste; *fig:* crisis, emergency, hardship, plight, predicament. **vb** *lit:* nip, squeeze, tweak; chafe, confine, cramp, crush; afflict, oppress; economize, scrimp; *fig:* filch, pilfer, purloin, snatch, steal; apprehend, arrest, pull in, take into custody.

pine vb *lit:* ache, hanker, hunger (for), long, lust, wish, yearn; grieve (for); decline, droop, dwindle, fade, languish, sicken, waste, wilt, wither.

pinnacle n *lit:* acme, apex, crest, height, peak, summit, vertex, zenith; obelisk, spire, steeple.

pioneer n *lit:* colonizer, frontiersman, settler; explorer, leader; deviser, discoverer, founder, innovator, inventor. **vb** *lit:* devise, develop, discover, initiate, instigate, invent, launch, open up.

pipe n *lit:* channel, conduit, cylinder, duct, flue, hose, tube, vessel; briar; fife, flute, penny whistle, whistle; *spec:* mass, vein (of ore); vent (of a volcano). **vb** *lit:* channel, duct, convey, lead, siphon; play, whistle; *fig:* speak shrilly, trill, tweet, twitter, warble.

pirate n *lit:* brigand, buccaneer, corsair, freebooter, raider; copyright breaker, plagiarist. **vb** *lit:* copy, lift, plagiarize, poach; appropriate, take over.

pit n *lit:* hole, mine, shaft; abyss, chasm; crater, dent, indentation, trench. **vb** *lit:* dent, gouge, indent, nick, notch, scar; *fig:* match, oppose, set (against).

pitch n *lit:* arena, ground, playing field, sports field; gradient, incline, slant, slope, tilt; degree, height, level, point; modulation, sound frequency, tone; *fig:* line, patter, sales talk, spiel. **vb** *lit:* cast, chuck, fling, heave, launch, sling, throw, toss; erect, plant, put up, set up, station; flounder, lurch, plunge, wallow; dive, drop, topple, tumble.

pitiful adj *lit:* distressing, heartrending, pathetic, piteous, sad, wretched; abject, contemptible, despicable, miserable, shabby, sorry, worthless.

pity n *lit:* compassion, empathy, feeling, sympathy; clemency, mercy; commiseration; sad thing, shame. **vb** *lit:* be compassionate toward, bleed for, commiserate with, empathize with, feel for, sympathize with.

place n *lit:* location, position, site, spot, venue; area, district, locality, manor, neighborhood, region, vicinity; town, village; accommodation, dwelling, home, house, property, residence; chair, reservation, seat; stead; *fig:* room, space; affair, concern, function, prerogative, responsibility; precedence; office, rank, station, status; appointment, employment, job, post. **vb** *lit:* deposit, lay, put, rest, set, stand; arrange, dispose, locate, position, situate, station; allocate, appoint, assign, commission, put out; invest; establish, fix; classify, grade, group, order, sort; identify, know, recognize, remember.

plague   n *lit:* epidemic, pandemic, pestilence; affliction, blight, contagion, disease, infection, infestation; *fig:* curse, scourge, trial; aggravation, annoyance, bother, nuisance, pain, pest. **vb** *lit:* afflict, annoy, badger, bother, fret, harass, hassle, persecute, pester, tease, trouble, worry.

plain   n *lit:* plateau, prairie, steppe, tablelands; heath, moor, open country. **adj** *lit:* even, flat, level, smooth; clear, conspicuous, distinct, evident, obvious; comprehensible, legible, unambiguous; blunt, candid, forthright, frank, outspoken, straightforward; common, everyday, homely, ordinary; discreet, modest, restrained, simple, unadorned, unaffected, unpretentious; austere, bare, Spartan, stark; ill-favored, unalluring, unattractive, unprepossessing.

plaintive   adj *lit:* heartrending, melancholy, mournful, pathetic, piteous, sad, wistful, woeful.

plan   n *lit:* design, draft, idea, plot, project, proposal, proposition, scheme, strategy; method, program, scenario, schema, script; blueprint, chart, diagram, drawing, elevation, layout, map, sketch. **vb** *lit:* design, devise, draft, formulate, plot, scheme, think up; arrange, contrive, lay out, map out, organize, outline, project, propose; aim (to), intend (to), mean (to), propose (to).

plane   n *lit:* flat, level, surface; degree, layer, stratum; airplane, aircraft, jet; file, rasp, scraper, shaver, smoother. **vb** *lit:* glide, skate, skim; carom. **adj** *lit:* even, flat, flush, level, smooth, uniform.

plant   n *lit:* flower, vegetable, vegetation; cutting, offshoot; *fig:* factory, foundry, mill, works; apparatus, equipment, gear, machinery; agent, informer, inside man, mole, spy, undercover agent. **vb** *lit:* disseminate, embed, put in, scatter, seed, sow; *fig:* establish, found, institute; place, post, station, settle; convey, deliver, strike.

plate   n *lit:* dish, platter; lamina, layer, panel, sheet; badge, panel; block, mold, stencil; brace, denture; *fig:* illustration, print; cup, trophy; foot; *spec:* base (in baseball); precious metal, silver; racing horseshoe. **vb** *lit:* coat, cover, electroplate, gild, laminate, overlay.

platform   n *lit:* dais, podium, rostrum, stage; basis, raised surface; railway station; gun mounting; oil rig; *fig:* manifesto, policy; party program.

play   n *lit:* comedy, drama, performance, piece, stage show, tragedy;

diversion, entertainment, fun; leisure activity, pastime, recreation, sport; gambling, gaming; exercise; *fig:* leeway, margin, movement, range, room, scope, slack, space; (in) action, (in) function, (in) operation. **vb** *lit:* amuse oneself, entertain oneself, have fun; frolic, gambol, revel, romp; toy (with), trifle (with); compete, contend against, participate, take on, take part in, vie with; act, impersonate, portray, take the part of; bet on, gamble on, speculate on, wager on; discharge (over), shower (over), spray (over); make music with, perform with; allow leeway, give room.

playful   **adj** *lit:* coy, flirtatious, frisky, frolicsome, humorous, impish, kittenish, lively, merry, mischievous, roguish, sportive, sprightly, vivacious, waggish.

plea   **n** *lit:* appeal, entreaty, intercession, petition, request, supplication; argument, claim, defense, excuse, explanation, vindication.

plead   **vb** *lit:* appeal, ask, beg, beseech, entreat, implore, petition, request; argue, assert, claim, give as an excuse, maintain.

pleasant   **adj** *lit:* agreeable, delectable, delightful, enjoyable, gratifying, pleasurable, refreshing, satisfying, welcome; affable, amiable, charming, cheerful, congenial, engaging, friendly, good-humored, likable, nice.

please   **vb** *lit:* delight, gladden, gratify; amuse, charm, cheer; humor, indulge, serve; content, satisfy, suit; be inclined, choose, like, see fit, want, wish.

pleasure   **n** *lit:* delectation, delight, gratification; amusement, contentment, enjoyment, happiness, satisfaction; choice, desire, inclination, preference, will, wish.

pledge   **n** *lit:* assurance, oath, undertaking, vow, word of honor; bail, bond, deposit, guarantee, pawn, security; *fig:* health, toast. **vb** *lit:* contract, give one's word, promise, undertake, vouch, vow; guarantee, mortgage; *fig:* drink the health of, drink to, toast.

plenty   **n** *lit:* ample, heaps, lots, masses, much, oodles, piles, quantities, stacks, superabundance; abundance, copiousness, fruitfulness, profusion; affluence, luxury, opulence, prosperity, wealth.

plot   **n** *lit:* conspiracy, intrigue, machination, plan, scheme; allotment, area, lot, patch, site, stretch, tract; action, gist, scenario, schema, story, story line, thread. **vb** *lit:* collude, conspire, intrigue, machinate, plan,

scheme; calculate, chart, compute, draft, draw, map, outline; concoct, cook
up, design, devise, frame; arrange for, organize, set up.

pluck n *lit:* backbone, bravery, courage, grit, guts, mettle, nerve,
resolution, spirit. **vb** *lit:* cull, gather, pick, pull out; jerk, pull, snatch, tug,
yank; pick, strum, thrum, twang; *fig:* fleece, rob; *spec:* defeather (a bird).

plug n *lit:* bung, cork, spigot, stopper; cake, quid, wad; *fig:*
advertisement, mention, push. **vb** *lit:* block, bung, cork, cover, pack, stop,
stuff; *fig:* advertise, build up, hype, promote, publicize, push; gun down,
put a bullet in, shoot; drudge (away at), grind (away at), peg (away at), slog
(away at).

plunge n *lit:* dive, drop, fall, immersion, swoop. **vb** *lit:* dive, drop, fall,
lurch, nosedive, pitch, plummet, swoop, tumble; dip, douse, dunk,
immerse, sink, submerge; *fig:* career, dash, fling oneself, hurtle.

ply **vb** *lit:* carry on, exercise, practice, pursue, work at; employ, use,
utilize; handle, manipulate, wield; assail, beset, bombard, deluge,
importune; cruise, prowl, sail, travel.

poet n *lit:* lyricist, rhymer, versifier; bard, troubadour, skald; *fig:*
aesthete.

poetic adj *lit:* aesthetic, descriptive, sensitive, sensual, sublime, vivid;
affecting, ecstatic, moving; elegiac, in verse, lyrical, metrical, rhyming,
rhythmical.

point n *lit:* dot, full stop, period, speck; location, place, position, site,
spot; apex, end, spike, summit, tine; cape, headland, promontory; mark,
score, unit; *fig:* degree, extent, stage; instant, juncture, moment, time;
aim, end, goal, intention, motive, object, purpose, reason; core, crux,
essence, gist, idea, meaning, theme; aspect, detail, feature, instance, item,
particular; attribute, characteristic, peculiarity, trait; *spec:* bearing (of a
compass); nib (of a pen). **vb** *lit:* call attention (to), direct (to); pick (out),
single (out); aim (at), direct (at), level (at), train (at); sharpen, taper, whet.

pointless adj *lit:* aimless, futile, inane, irrelevant, meaningless,
nonsensical, unproductive, useless, vain, worthless.

poison n *lit:* toxin, venom; *fig:* contamination, corruption, malignancy.
vb *lit:* administer a lethal dose to; contaminate, kill, pollute; *fig:*

embitter, sour; corrupt, defile, mar, taint, undermine; deprave, pervert, warp.

poisonous adj *lit:* toxic, venomous; corrosive; deadly, fatal, lethal, virulent; *fig:* malicious, pernicious, scathing, vicious.

pole n *lit:* boom, handle, mast, paling, post, rod, shaft, stick; electrode, terminal; *fig:* antipode, extremity.

police n *lit:* constabulary, force, law. **vb** *lit:* control, guard, monitor, patrol, regulate, supervise, watch.

policy n *lit:* code, line, method, practice, procedure, protocol, rule, strategy; approach, custom; *fig:* discretion, prudence, shrewdness; cunning.

polish n *lit:* varnish, wax; brightness, finish, gloss, luster, sheen, sparkle; *fig:* class, finesse, panache, refinement, style. **vb** *lit:* buff, burnish, clean, shine, wax; *fig:* brush (up), touch (up).

polish off vb *fig:* consume, down, eat up, finish up, wolf down; bump off, dispose of, do away with, eliminate, finish off, get rid of, kill, liquidate, murder.

polite adj *lit:* civil, courteous, mannerly, well-mannered; civilized, cultured, elegant, genteel, polished, well-bred.

poll n *lit:* ballot, election, plebiscite, referendum, vote; census, survey; count, figures, returns, tally. **vb** *lit:* ballot, hold a referendum, take it to a vote; canvass, register, notch up, tally; interview, question, survey.

pollute vb *lit:* contaminate, dirty, foul, infect, soil, taint; *fig:* corrupt, defile, deprave, desecrate, mar, profane, sully.

pompous adj *lit:* bloated, grandiose, ostentatious, portentous, pretentious, priggish, self-important, snobbish, vainglorious; boastful, bombastic, inflated, orotund, overblown, turgid.

ponder vb *lit:* brood, cerebrate, cogitate, contemplate, deliberate, give thought to, mull (over), muse, puzzle (over), ruminate, think about.

pool n *lit:* lake, mere, pond, puddle, reservoir, tarn; swimming bath; *fig:* collective, consortium, group, syndicate, team; funds, jackpot, kitty, stakes. **vb** *lit:* amalgamate, combine, group, merge, share.

poor adj *lit:* badly off, destitute, hard up, impoverished, needy, penurious, poverty-stricken; deficient, inadequate, insufficient, meager, niggardly, reduced, scanty, skimpy, sparse; faulty, inferior, mediocre, rotten, rubbishy, shabby, shoddy, sorry, worthless; bad, bare, barren, depleted, infertile, exhausted, infertile, unproductive; hapless, ill-fated, miserable, pathetic, unfortunate, wretched; humble, insignificant, mean, modest, paltry, trivial.

popular adj *lit:* common, conventional, general, prevailing, public, standard, stock, ubiquitous, widespread; approved, famous, fashionable, favorite, in, in demand, sought-after, well-liked.

population n *lit:* community, denizens, inhabitants, natives, people, residents, society.

port n *lit:* anchorage, harbor, haven, marina, mooring, roads; door, doorway, embrasure, gate, outlet, shutter, window; larboard, left-hand side; fortified red wine.

portion n *lit:* bit, morsel, part, piece, segment; allocation, allotment, allowance, lot, quota, ration, share; helping, serving; *fig:* destiny, fate, fortune, luck. **vb** *lit:* dole (out), parcel (out), share (out).

pose n *lit:* attitude, bearing, demeanor, posture, stance; affectation, facade, front, masquerade, pretense, role. **vb** *lit:* model, sit (for); masquerade (as), pass oneself off (as); posture, put on airs, show off, strike an attitude; arrange, position; advance, present, propound, put forward, set.

position n *lit:* bearings, locale, location, place, site, situation, whereabouts; attitude, pose, stance; job, office, post; *fig:* angle, outlook, point of view, standpoint; circumstances, pass, plight, predicament, state, strait(s); caste, class, importance, prestige, rank, standing, status; capacity, function, role. **vb** *lit:* arrange, array, lay out, place, put, set.

positive adj *lit:* categorical, certain, conclusive, decisive, definitive, emphatic, express, firm, indisputable, real, unequivocal; affirmative; beneficial, constructive, efficacious, helpful, practical, progressive, useful; assured, confident, convinced, sure; absolute, complete, consummate, thorough, unmitigated; dogmatic, emphatic, forceful; insistent, obdurate, resolute, stubborn.

possess vb *lit:* be blessed with, enjoy, have, hold, keep, own, retain;

acquire, seize, take over, usurp; *fig:* bewitch, enchant, entrance, mesmerize, obsess, put under a spell; control, dominate.

possessed adj *lit:* berserk, bewitched, consumed, crazed, demented, enchanted, entranced, frenzied, haunted, hexed, obsessed.

possession n *lit:* asset(s), belonging(s), effect(s), estate, property; control, custody, hold, occupancy, ownership, proprietorship, tenure, title; colony, dominion, protectorate, territory.

possessive adj *lit:* acquisitive, covetous, grasping, greedy; retentive, tenacious; jealous, overprotective.

possible adj *lit:* conceivable, credible, feasible, imaginable, practicable, viable; hypothetical, potential, theoretical; on, realizable, within reach.

post n *lit:* column, pale, pillar, pole, stake, support, upright; mail, postal service; appointment, assignment, job, office, position, situation; beat, place, station; *spec:* (winning) line; pin (in a lock). **vb** *lit:* assign, establish, place, position, put, station; advertise, display, publicize, publish, put up; dispatch, mail, send; advise, brief, fill in on, notify, report to.

posture n *lit:* attitude, bearing, pose, position, set, stance; *fig:* disposition, frame of mind, outlook, point of view; circumstance, mode, phase, situation, state. **vb** *lit:* pose, put on airs, show off, strut, swagger.

pot n *lit:* bowl, container, dish, jar, pan, urn, vessel; hole, cave; lavatory, toilet; cup, trophy; *fig:* kitty, pool, stakes; shot, shy, throw; paunch, potbelly; *spec:* basket, trap (for catching lobsters); cone, stack (on a chimney); large sum (of money); cannabis, marijuana. **vb** *lit:* turn on the wheel; plant, replant; *fig:* bag, secure, shoot, win; hole, pocket.

potent adj *lit:* dynamic, effective, efficacious, forceful, mighty, powerful, strong, vigorous; cogent, compelling, impressive, persuasive; authoritative, commanding, dominant, influential.

potential n *lit:* capacity, power, resources; ability, aptitude, capability, makings. adj *lit:* budding, dormant, future, inherent, latent, possible, undeveloped.

pounce n *lit:* dart, jump, leap, spring, swoop; ambush. **vb** *lit:* fall (upon), jump (on), leap (on), swoop down (upon).

pout n *lit:* cross look, glower, grimace, lowering, moue. **vb** *lit:* glower, grimace, look petulant, look sullen, mope, pull a long face, sulk.

poverty n *lit:* beggary, destitution, insolvency, pennilessness, penury, privation; inadequacy, lack, paucity, scarcity, shortage; *fig:* aridity, barrenness, infertility, sterility.

power n *lit:* brawn, clout, force, might, muscle, strength; ability, capability, capacity, competence, faculty, potential; energy, vigor; authority, command, control, dominance, influence, supremacy, sway; authorization, licence, prerogative, right, warrant.

powerful adj *lit:* brawny, mighty, muscular, robust, stalwart, strapping, strong, sturdy; energetic, vigorous; authoritative, commanding, dominant, forceful, influential; compelling, convincing, effectual, impressive.

powerless adj *lit:* defenseless, helpless, impotent, incapable, ineffectual; disabled, incapacitated, paralyzed; debilitated, feeble, frail, vulnerable, weak; captive, chained, manacled, shackled.

practical adj *lit:* applied, functional, pragmatic, utilitarian; adept, ingenious, inventive, resourceful; businesslike, down-to-earth, factual, matter-of-fact, mundane, realistic, sensible; feasible, practicable, serviceable, sound, workable; accomplished, efficient, experienced, proficient, skilled, working.

practically adv *lit:* almost, in effect, just about, nearly, to all intents and purposes, virtually; factually, rationally, realistically, reasonably, sensibly; efficiently, ingeniously, inventively, resourcefully.

practice n *lit:* custom, habit, mode, routine, rule, tradition, usage, way; application, experience, operation, use; career, profession, vocation, work; drill, exercise, rehearsal, training, workout. **vb** *lit:* drill, exercise, prepare, rehearse, run through, train; apply, carry out, do, follow, live up to, observe; carry on, engage in, ply, pursue, work at.

practiced adj **(pa.pt)** *lit:* able, accomplished, adept, efficient, experienced, proficient, skilled, trained, well-rehearsed.

praise n *lit:* acclaim, accolades, applause, commendation, compliments, congratulation, eulogy, panegyric, tribute; *fig:* adoration, adulation, homage, worship. **vb** *lit:* acclaim, applaud, commend, compliment, congratulate, eulogize, extol, honor, pay tribute to; adore, adulate, worship.

preach vb *lit:* deliver a sermon, give an address (on); orate, speak, talk; harangue, lecture; *fig:* moralize.

precaution n *lit:* preventative measure, safeguard, safety measure; contingency plan; anticipation, caution, foresight, forethought, wariness.

precede vb *lit:* come before, go before, herald, introduce, lead; antedate; rank before.

preceding adj *lit:* above, aforementioned, earlier, former, previous, prior.

precious adj *lit:* cherished, favorite, prized, treasured, valued; adored, beloved, dearest; costly, expensive, invaluable, priceless, valuable; *fig:* affected, artificial, camp, overnice.

precipice n *lit:* cliff, cliff face, height, rock face, sheer drop; canyon, chasm, chine, gorge, ravine.

precise adj *lit:* accurate, clear-cut, definitive, exact, express, specific; fastidious, finicky, meticulous, nice, particular, scrupulous; prim, puritanical, strict.

precision n *lit:* accuracy, correctness, exactness, fidelity, meticulousness, scrupulousness, strictness.

precursor n *lit:* ancestor, forebear, predecessor; forerunner, harbinger, herald, messenger, vanguard; originator, pioneer.

predator n *lit:* carnivore, hunter, raptor; *fig:* marauder, plunderer, vulture.

predatory adj *lit:* carnivorous, rapacious, voracious, vulturine; *fig:* despoiling, destructive, marauding, plundering, raiding, ravaging.

predecessor n *lit:* antecedent, forerunner, precursor; previous occupant; ancestor, forebear, forefather.

predicament n *lit:* corner, dilemma, jam, mess, pickle, plight, quandary, scrape, situation, spot.

predict vb *lit:* augur, forecast, foresee, foretell, prophesy.

predominant **adj** *lit:* chief, dominant, leading, main, paramount, preponderant, prime, principal, prominent, ruling, supreme.

prefer **vb** *lit:* choose, favor, go for, like better, opt for, pick, plump for, select, single out; advance, elevate, promote, upgrade.

preferable **adj** *lit:* better, eligible, favored, more desirable, superior.

preference **n** *lit:* choice, favorite, first choice, option, pick, selection; advantage, precedence, priority.

pregnant **adj** *lit:* expectant, expecting, gravid, in the family way, with child; *fig:* charged, expressive, meaningful, pointed, revealing, significant, telling, weighty; creative, imaginative, inventive, original; abundant, fecund, fruitful, productive, prolific, teeming.

prejudiced **adj (pa.pt)** *lit:* biased, discriminatory, influenced, jaundiced, narrow-minded, opinionated, partial, partisan, slanted, swayed, unfair.

preliminary **n** *lit:* beginning, first round, foundation, groundwork, initiation, introduction, opening, preface, preparation, start. **adj** *lit:* beginning, exploratory, first, initial, introductory, opening, pilot, precursory, preparatory, qualifying, trial.

premature **adj** *lit:* early, immature, incomplete, undeveloped, untimely; *fig:* hasty, ill-considered, ill-timed, impulsive, inopportune, precipitate.

premier **n** *lit:* chancellor, head of government, prime minister, secretary of state. **adj** *lit:* first, foremost, leading, main, principal, top; earliest, inaugural, initial.

premises **n** *lit:* building, grounds, property, site.

preoccupation **n** *lit:* absentmindedness, absorption, abstraction, inattentiveness, oblivion, reverie; fixation, hang-up, hobbyhorse, obsession.

preparation **n** *lit:* anticipation, foresight, precaution, provision, readiness; fundamentals, groundwork, research and development; homework, revision, schoolwork, study; compound, concoction, medicine, mixture, tincture.

prepare **vb** *lit:* make ready, prime, put in order; coach, equip, fit out, groom, outfit, supply, train, warm up; concoct, contrive, draw up, fix up, make, put together; brace oneself (for), fortify (oneself for), ready (oneself for), strengthen (oneself for).

prepared adj (pa.pt) *lit:* all set, arranged, in order, in readiness, ready, set; able (to), disposed (to), inclined (to), of a mind (to), willing (to).

preposterous adj *lit:* absurd, incredible, insane, laughable, ludicrous, monstrous, nonsensical, outrageous, ridiculous, unreasonable, unthinkable.

prescription n *lit:* direction, instruction, specification; formula, recipe.

presence n *lit:* attendance, immediacy; company; occupancy, residence; closeness, propinquity, proximity; *fig:* air, carriage, demeanor, personality, poise, self-assurance; apparition, ghost, manifestation, specter, spirit, wraith.

present n *lit:* now, this moment, time being; donation, endowment, gift, gratuity. vb *lit:* acquaint (with), introduce (to), make known (to); demonstrate, display, exhibit, put on, show; advance, expound, introduce, offer, produce, proffer, raise, relate, state, submit, suggest, tender; award, donate (to), endow (with), give. adj *lit:* contemporary, current, existing, immediate; accounted for, at hand, available, near, ready, to hand.

preserve n *lit:* area, domain, realm, sphere; game reserve, reservation, sanctuary; conserve(s), jam, jelly, marmalade. vb *lit:* care for, conserve, keep, pickle, protect, safeguard, save, secure, shelter, store; keep up, maintain, perpetuate, sustain, uphold.

press n *lit:* bunch, crowd, crush, mob, multitude, pack, throng; bustle, hassle, pressure, strain, stress, urgency; printing house, printing machine; bookcase, cupboard; journalism, news media, newspapers; columnists, correspondents, journalists, newsmen, photographers, reporters. vb *lit:* compress, condense, crush, jam, push, squeeze; cluster, crowd, flock, gather, mill, push, rush, seethe, swarm, throng; flatten, iron, smooth, steam; clasp, embrace, enfold, hold close, hug; compel, constrain, demand, enforce, force, insist on; beg, exhort, implore, petition, plead, pressurize, sue, supplicate, urge; afflict, assail, beset, besiege, harass, plague, trouble, vex, worry.

pressure n *lit:* compression, crushing, force, squeezing, weight; *fig:*

coercion, constraint, influence, obligation, sway; adversity, affliction, demands, distress, hassle, strain, stress.

prestige   n *lit:* cachet, celebrity, distinction, eminence, fame, importance, influence, kudos, renown, standing, stature, status, weight.

prestigious   adj *lit:* celebrated, eminent, esteemed, exalted, great, illustrious, impressive, influential, prominent, renowned.

presume   vb *lit:* assume, believe, conjecture, postulate, suppose, take for granted, think; dare (to), go so far as (to), have the audacity (to), make so bold as (to), venture (to); count (on), depend (on), rely (on).

presumption   n *lit:* audacity, boldness, cheek, effrontery, forwardness, gall, impudence, insolence, nerve, presumptuousness; assumption, hypothesis, presupposition, supposition, surmise; grounds, likelihood, probability.

presumptuous   adj *lit:* audacious, bold, cheeky, forward, impudent, insolent, pushy, too big for one's boots, uppish, uppity.

pretend   vb *lit:* affect, dissemble, fake, feign, make out, put on, sham; make believe; purport (to be); aspire (to), lay claim (to).

pretense   n *lit:* affectation, artifice, charade, cover, deceit, display, fabrication, facade, falsehood, guise, make-believe, pose, pretext, semblance, sham, show, trickery.

pretext   n *lit:* affectation, cloak, cover, device, excuse, mask, ploy, pretense.

pretty   adj *lit:* appealing, attractive, bonny, charming, comely, cute, good-looking, pleasing, personable; dainty, delicate, neat, nice, trim. **adv** *lit:* fairly, moderately, quite, rather, reasonably, somewhat.

prevent   vb *lit:* bar, block, debar, foil, frustrate, obstruct, obviate, preclude, stop, thwart; avert, avoid, head off, inhibit, nip in the bud, stave off, ward off.

preventive   n *lit:* barrier, block, impediment, obstacle, obstruction; precaution, prophylactic, protection, safeguard; condom, rubber. **adj** *lit:* blocking, counteractive, obstructive; deterrent, precautionary, protective.

previously   adv *lit:* before, beforehand, earlier, in anticipation; formerly, in the past, once; hitherto, until now.

price n *lit:* bill, charge, cost, damage, expense, fee, premium, value; expenditure, outlay; estimate, evaluation; compensation, recompense, reward; odds; *fig:* consequences, penalty, toll. **vb** *lit:* cost, estimate, evaluate, rate, value.

prick n *lit:* perforation, pinhole, puncture; *fig:* pang, prickle, smart, sting. **vb** *lit:* drill, jab, perforate, pierce, puncture, stab; bite, prickle, smart, sting, tingle; *fig:* distress, trouble, wound.

prickly adj *lit:* barbed, spiny, thorny; itchy, smarting, stinging, tingling; *fig:* bad-tempered, cantankerous, edgy, grumpy, irritable, peevish, pettish, snappish, touchy, waspish; complicated, difficult, intricate, involved, knotty, tricky, troublesome.

pride n *lit:* honor, self-esteem, self-respect; arrogance, conceit, egotism, haughtiness, loftiness, presumption, pretension, self-importance; boast, prize, treasure; best, choice, elite, flower, glory; delight, gratification, joy, satisfaction. **vb** *lit:* be proud of (oneself), congratulate (oneself), flatter (oneself).

primarily adv *lit:* above all, chiefly, for the most part, mainly, mostly, on the whole, principally; basically, essentially, fundamentally; initially, in the first place, originally.

primary adj *lit:* basic, elemental, essential, fundamental, ultimate; capital, cardinal, chief, leading, main, paramount, principal, top; first, initial, introductory; elementary, rudimentary, simple; aboriginal, earliest, primal, primeval; crude, primitive, raw.

prime n *lit:* best, greatest, height, heyday, peak, perfection; *fig:* beginning, opening; spring; *spec:* (musical) keynote, tonic; (musical) octave. **vb** *lit:* coach, get ready, groom, prepare, train; charge, fuel, fill, load; brief, fill in, inform, tell; size, undercoat, whitewash. **adj** *lit:* best, choice, excellent, first-rate, highest, perfect, superior, top-grade; basic, fundamental, original, primary, underlying; leading, main, predominant, principal; *spec:* indivisible (number).

primitive adj *lit:* early, prehistoric, primeval, primordial; earliest, first; crude, elementary, rudimentary, unrefined, unsophisticated; barbarian, savage, uncivilized; childlike, naive, simple, untrained.

principal n *lit:* chairperson, chief, director, head, president; dean, director, headmaster, headmistress, rector; guarantor, security; culprit, ringleader; duelist; assets, capital, money; girder, main beam, rafter; *spec:* first violin (in an orchestra); lead, star (of a show). **adj** *lit:* cardinal, chief, crucial, dominant, essential, foremost, key, leading, main, paramount, preeminent, primary, prime, vital.

principle   n *lit:* axiom, doctrine, dogma, golden rule, law, maxim, precept, rule; belief, code, creed, ethic, tenet; approach, attitude, thesis, way of thinking; conscience, duty, honor, integrity, morality, virtue; *fig:* active ingredient, flavor.

print   n *lit:* impression; font, fount, type, typeface; engraving; photograph, positive, reproduction; fingerprint. **vb** *lit:* imprint, press in, stamp; go to press, run off.

priority   n *lit:* precedence, preeminence, preference, seniority, superiority, supremacy; essential, prerequisite, requirement, sine qua non.

prison   n *lit:* jail, lockup, penal institution, penitentiary; clink, jug, stir.

private   adj *lit:* exclusive, individual, intimate, own, personal; confidential, in camera, secret; concealed, isolated, not overlooked, secluded, solitary; independent, nonincorporated, unaffiliated.

prize   n *lit:* award, reward, trophy; jackpot, purse, winnings; booty, haul, loot, pickings, plunder, swag; *fig:* aim, ambition, desire, goal. **vb** *lit:* appreciate, esteem, regard highly, treasure, value. **adj** *lit:* award-winning, champion, first-rate, outstanding.

probably   adv *lit:* almost certainly, doubtless, in all likelihood, most likely, presumably, surely.

problem   n *lit:* brainteaser, conundrum, enigma, puzzle, riddle; difficulty, predicament, quandary, snag, trouble; complication, dilemma, doubt. **adj** *lit:* delinquent, difficult, unmanageable, unruly, wayward.

procedure   n *lit:* conduct, course, method, modus operandi, plan of action, policy, practice, process, routine, scheme, strategy, way of working.

proceed   vb *lit:* carry on, continue, get on, go ahead, go on, press on; arise (from), come (from), derive (from), emanate (from), issue (from), originate (from), stem (from); ensue, follow, result.

process   n *lit:* course of action, means, measure, method, mode, operation, practice; action, case, suit, trial. **vb** *lit:* deal with, handle, take care of; alter, prepare, refine, transform, treat.

procession n *lit:* cavalcade, cortege, motorcade, parade; crocodile, file, line, queue, sequence, series, succession; course, cycle.

proclaim vb *lit:* advertise, announce, blaze (abroad), circulate, declare, enunciate, give out, make known, promulgate, pronounce, publish, trumpet.

prod n *lit:* elbow, jab, nudge, poke, push, shove; goad, spur, stick; *fig:* cue, prompt, reminder, signal. **vb** *lit:* dig, elbow, jab, nudge, poke, push, shove; drive, egg on, goad, incite, motivate, prick, prompt, spur, stir, urge.

produce n *lit:* crop, harvest, yield; groceries, products. **vb** *lit:* come up with, construct, create, devise, invent, make, manufacture, put together, turn out; bear, bring forth, deliver, generate; furnish, render, supply, yield; bring about, cause, effect, give rise to, set off, start; elongate, extend, protract; advance, bring to light, demonstrate, exhibit, offer, put forward, set out; direct, do, mount, perform, present, put on, stage.

production n *lit:* assembly, construction, manufacture, preparation; creation, generation, origination; marketing, presentation, supply; bringing to light, disclosure, revelation; direction, mounting, performance, staging.

productive adj *lit:* creative, inventive; fecund, fertile, fruitful, prolific, vigorous; *fig:* advantageous, constructive, effective, effectual, efficacious, helpful, profitable, rewarding, useful, worthwhile.

profession n *lit:* business, calling, line of work, métier, occupation, vocation; acknowledgment, affirmation, assertion, confession, declaration, statement, testimony; claim.

professional n *lit:* business executive, career man or woman, employee, nonamateur, wage earner; artist, expert, master, virtuoso; specialist. **adj** *lit:* career-minded, employed, full-time, managerial, nonamateur, salaried, wage-earning; vocational; competent, experienced, expert, polished, proficient, qualified, skilled, trained.

profile n *lit:* contour, outline, side view, silhouette; drawing, figure, portrait, sketch; biography, cameo, character sketch, vignette; *fig:* chart, diagram, graph, table; analysis, study, survey.

profit   n *lit:* earnings, gains, proceeds, return, revenue, takings, yield; advantage, benefit, good, help, use, value. **vb** *lit:* aid, benefit, gain, help, improve, serve, stand in good stead; make a killing, make money.

profitable   adj *lit:* commercial, cost-effective, lucrative, money-making, remunerative, rewarding; advantageous, beneficial, productive, useful, valuable, worthwhile.

profound   adj *lit:* deep, insightful, penetrating, philosophical, sagacious, subtle, thoughtful, wise; erudite, learned, recondite; abstruse, difficult, serious; abyssal, bottomless, cavernous, infernal, yawning; heartfelt, intense, keen, sincere; extensive, extreme, far-reaching, great, immense, vast, wide-ranging.

program   n *lit:* agenda, list, order, plan, procedure, schedule, scheme, sequence, syllabus, timetable; cast list, lineup; performance, presentation, production, show. **vb** *lit:* arrange, bill, book, line up, schedule, organize; itemize, list, plan; order, put in sequence.

progress   n *lit:* advance, journey, movement, passage, way; advancement, betterment, development, growth, headway, improvement, promotion. **vb** *lit:* advance, come on, get farther, get on, make headway, move forward, proceed, travel, work one's way up; develop, grow, improve; blossom, gain, increase.

progressive   adj *lit:* accelerating, advancing, developing, increasing, intensifying, worsening; continuous, ongoing; dynamic, enterprising; *fig:* advanced, avant-garde, go-ahead, radical, reformist, revolutionary; enlightened, liberal, open.

prohibited   adj (pa.pt) *lit:* banned, barred, embargoed, forbidden, illegal, interdicted, proscribed, outlawed; made impossible, precluded, prevented, stopped.

project   n *lit:* assignment, enterprise, job, plan, program, scheme, task, undertaking, venture; proposal, proposition. **vb** *lit:* beetle, extend forward, jut out, overhang, protrude, stick out; fling, hurl; launch, propel, throw; broadcast, radiate, transmit; estimate, forecast, foretell, predict; design, devise, draft, frame, outline, plan, scheme.

projection   n *lit:* bulge, extension, overhang, protrusion; jetty, pier; ledge, ridge, shelf, sill; launch, propulsion; radiation, transmission; cinematography, screening; estimate, forecast, prediction, prognosis;

blueprint, outline, plan; *spec:* externalization (astral), independence, transference; telekinesis (mental), telepathy.

prolong vb *lit:* extend, lengthen, make longer, produce, project, protract; carry on, continue; drag out, stretch.

promenade n *lit:* esplanade, parade; pier, seafront, terrace; amble, constitutional, saunter, stroll; *fig:* drive, ride; dance. **vb** *lit:* amble, perambulate, saunter, stroll, take a walk; flaunt, parade, show off; *spec:* stand (at a concert).

prominence n *lit:* crag, headland, height, projection, promontory, spur; bulge, hummock, lump, mound, protrusion, protuberance, rise, swelling; conspicuousness, distinctiveness, dominance, salience, visibility; distinction, precedence; celebrity, eminence, fame, importance, prestige, reputation, standing.

prominent adj *lit:* jutting, protruding, protuberant; conspicuous, eye-catching, noticeable, obvious, pronounced, striking, unmistakable; celebrated, distinguished, eminent, famous, important, leading, main, outstanding, preeminent, renowned, top, well-known.

promise n *lit:* assurance, bond, commitment, oath, pledge, undertaking, vow, word of honor; *fig:* ability, aptitude, capability, flair, potential, talent. **vb** *lit:* assure, contract, engage, give an undertaking, give one's word, pledge, plight, take an oath, undertake, vouch; *fig:* augur, be likely (to), betoken, hint at, look like, seem to mean, suggest.

promising adj *lit:* auspicious, bright, encouraging, hopeful, optimistic, propitious, reassuring, rosy; *fig:* gifted, talented; likely, rising, up-and-coming.

promotion n *lit:* advancement, elevation, rise, upgrading; advocacy, backing, boosting, furtherance, support; advocacy, recommendation, sponsorship; advertising, marketing, media hype, plugging, publicity, sales pitch.

prompt n *lit:* cue, hint, prod, reminder, spur. **vb** *lit:* cue, jog the memory, prod, remind; cause, elicit, evoke, occasion, provoke; induce, inspire, instigate, move, spur. **adj** *lit:* immediate, instant, instantaneous, punctual, quick, speedy, swift, timely; *fig:* alert; willing.

pronounce **vb** *lit:* articulate, enunciate, say; accent, emphasize, stress; announce, assert, declare, decree, proclaim.

proof **n** *lit:* authentication, confirmation, corroboration, substantiation, verification; evidence, testimony; *spec:* galley, pull, slip (in publishing). **adj** *lit:* resistant (against), sealed (against), treated (against).

prop **n** *lit:* brace, buttress, stanchion, stay, support. **vb** *lit:* bolster, brace, buttress, hold up, shore up, support, sustain; *fig:* lean (against), put up (against), rest (against), set (against).

propaganda **n** *lit:* advertisement, hype, marketing, promotion, publicity, slogan; disinformation.

proper **adj** *lit:* decent, decorous, genteel, mannerly, polite, punctilious, refined; becoming, fitting, legitimate, right; appropriate, apt, suitable; accepted, conventional, established, formal; accurate, correct, exact, precise; characteristic, individual, own, particular, personal, specific.

property **n** *lit:* assets, belongings, capital, effects, estate, goods, holdings, possessions, resources, wealth; building, grounds, land, premises, territory; *fig:* attribute, characteristic, feature, idiosyncrasy, peculiarity, quality, trait; *spec:* article, bit of scenery (on stage).

prophet **n** *lit:* augur, oracle, seer, sibyl, soothsayer; astrologer, clairvoyant, crystal gazer, magus; forecaster, tipster; mouthpiece, spokesperson.

prophetic **adj** *lit:* oracular, prescient, sibylline, visionary; clairvoyant; apocalyptic, revelatory.

proportion **n** *lit:* cut, division, fraction, part, percentage, quota, ration, share; dimension(s), measurement(s); distribution, ratio, relationship; (in) agreement, (in) balance, (in) correspondence.

proposal **n** *lit:* motion, proposition, suggestion; plan, presentation, program, project, scheme; offer, tender; conditions, terms; *spec:* request for one's hand in marriage.

propose **vb** *lit:* advance, present, proffer, propound, put forward, submit, suggest, tender; aim, intend, mean, plan; introduce, invite, name, nominate, put up for membership, recommend; *spec:* request one's hand in marriage, pop the question.

prosecute vb *lit:* bring an action against, bring to trial, indict, litigate against, prefer charges against, sue, summons, take to court; carry on, discharge, engage in, perform, practice, work at; carry through, continue, persevere in, persist with, pursue, see through.

prospect n *lit:* panorama, scene, sight, view, vista; anticipation, expectation, outlook; chance, likelihood, possibility. vb *lit:* explore, look (for), pan (for), search, sift (for), survey.

prosperity n *lit:* affluence, plenty, riches, success, wealth, well-being.

prostitute n *lit:* call girl, harlot, hooker, hustler, streetwalker, tart, trollop, whore. vb *lit:* cheapen, debase, degrade, demean, profane; pimp for, sell.

protect vb *lit:* defend, give sanctuary to, keep safe, safeguard, shelter, shield; care for, harbor, look after, support, take under one's wing, watch over; conceal, hide, keep secret; cover up for.

protection n *lit:* armor, defenses, guard; barrier, cover, screen, shield; refuge, shelter; preservation, safety, security; care, charge, custody, guardianship, sake keeping.

protest n *lit:* complaint, demur, dissent, objection, outcry, remonstration, resistance. vb *lit:* complain, demur, disagree, dissent, expostulate, object, remonstrate; argue, assert, contend, declare, insist on, maintain, profess, testify to.

proud adj *lit:* honored; basking in the glory (of); gratified, pleased; glorious, gratifying, memorable, pleasing, satisfying; august, distinguished, eminent, grand, noble, splendid; arrogant, boastful, conceited, haughty, presumptuous, self-important, snobbish, snooty, supercilious, vain; *fig:* projecting, swelling.

prove vb *lit:* confirm, corroborate, demonstrate, establish, show, substantiate, verify; be found (to be), turn out; *fig:* analyze, assay, examine, experiment, put to the test, try.

provide vb *lit:* accommodate (with), contribute, equip (with), furnish, outfit (with), stock up (with), supply (with); afford, give, impart, lend, render, yield; determine, lay down, require, specify, stipulate; arrange (for), plan (for), prepare (for); care (for).

provided cnj *lit:* as long as, given (that), in the event (that), on condition (that), on the understanding (that).

providence n *lit:* destiny, divine intervention, fate, predestination; caution, foresight, forethought, prudence.

province n *lit:* colony, dependency, dominion, region, territory, zone; *fig:* area, business, duty, employment, field, function, line, responsibility, role, sphere.

provincial adj *lit:* backwoods, parochial, remote, small-town, upcountry; uninformed, unsophisticated; insular, inward-looking, limited, narrow-minded.

provision n *lit:* catering, equipping, furnishing, supplying, victualing; arrangement, plan, preparation; *fig:* agreement, clause, condition, specification, stipulation. **vb** *lit:* stock, supply, victual; accouter, equip.

provisional adj *lit:* conditional, contingent, interim, stopgap, temporary, tentative, transitional.

provocative adj *lit:* arousing, erotic, exciting, seductive, sensual, sexy, suggestive, tantalizing, titillating; aggravating, annoying, disturbing, galling, infuriating, offensive.

provoke vb *lit:* bring about, cause, elicit, evoke, excite, generate, give rise to, incite, induce, inflame, instigate, lead to, occasion, precipitate, promote, prompt, rouse, stir up; annoy, enrage, exasperate, gall, get on one's nerves, incense, infuriate, irk, irritate, madden, offend, pique, rile.

prowess n *lit:* ability, accomplishment, command, excellence, expertise, facility, mastery, skill; audacity, boldness, bravery, courage, daring, dauntlessness, intrepidity, valor.

prowl vb *lit:* cruise, lurk, patrol, ply, range, roam (around), skulk, sneak.

prudence n *lit:* care, caution, circumspection, common sense, discretion, forethought, judgment, judiciousness, precaution, sagacity, vigilance, wariness, wisdom; economy, frugality, husbandry, thrift.

prune n *lit:* dried plum. **vb** *lit:* clip, coppice, cut back, lop, pare down, pollard, reduce, shape, trim.

prying   adj (pr.pt) *lit:* inquisitive, nosy, snooping, spying; interfering, intrusive, meddlesome.

psychic   n *lit:* medium; clairvoyant, dowser. **adj** *lit:* clairvoyant, ESP, extrasensory, sensitive, supernatural, telekinetic, telepathic; mental, psychological; *fig:* astral.

public   n *lit:* citizens, community, electorate, nation, people, populace, population, society, voters; audience, buyers, clientele, market, patrons, supporters, trade. **adj** *lit:* civic, civil, national, popular, state, universal, widespread; communal, community, open to the public; accessible, unrestricted; exposed, known, open, overt, patent, plain, recognized; celebrated, important, prominent, well-known.

publication   n *lit:* appearance, broadcasting, declaration, disclosure, issue, printing, proclamation, promulgation; launch, marketing; book, brochure, leaflet, pamphlet, periodical.

publish   vb *lit:* print, produce, put out; bring out, issue, launch, market, sell; advertise, announce, broadcast, communicate, disclose, divulge, impart, leak, promulgate, publicize, spread.

pull   n *lit:* haul, heave, tow, tug; jerk, twitch, yank; strain, stretching; hit, stroke; row, scull; resistance; drag, inhalation, draft, swallow, swig; *fig:* ascent, climb; attraction, influence, magnetism, power; clout, influence, leverage, weight; *spec:* proof (in publishing). **vb** *lit:* draw, haul, heave, tow, tug; jerk, twitch, yank; strain, stretch; cull, pick, pluck, strip; extract, take out; hit, knock, strike; row, scull; move, steer; drag, inhale, suck; *fig:* attract, entice, lure; arrest, catch; *spec:* hold back (a horse, a punch).

pulp   n *lit:* flesh, marrow, pith; mash, mush, pap. **vb** *lit:* crush, grind, mash, mill, powder, squash. **adj** *lit:* cheap, trashy; lurid, sensational.

pulse   n *lit:* heartbeat; beat, beating, rhythm, throbbing, vibration. **vb** *lit:* beat, throb, vibrate.

pump   n *lit:* compressor, energizer, inflater, pressurizer, siphon, syringe; shoe. **vb** *lit:* drive, force, siphon, syringe; empty (out), inject (in); blow (up), inflate; energize, excite; *fig:* cross-examine, grill, interrogate, question, quiz; *spec:* contract (muscles).

punch   n *lit:* bash, blow, buffet, clout, hit, jab, knock, thump, wallop, whack; *fig:* bite, dynamism, energy, force, impact; *spec:* die, stamp. **vb** *lit:* bash, box, buffet, clout, hit, jab, knock, slam, smash, strike, thump, wallop, whack; imprint, indent, stamp; bore (through), drill (through); key, type; *spec:* drive (cattle).

punctual   **adj** *lit:* on the dot, on time, prompt, timely.

puncture   **n** *lit:* flat tire; break, hole, rupture, slit; escape, leak. **vb** *lit:* penetrate, perforate, pierce, prick, rupture; go down, go flat; *fig:* deflate, disillusion, humble, take down a peg.

pungent   **adj** *lit:* acrid, aromatic, bitter, peppery, piquant, sharp, spicy, strong, tart; *fig:* biting, caustic, cutting, incisive, keen, penetrating, piercing, poignant, pointed, sarcastic, scathing, stinging, trenchant.

punish   **vb** *lit:* castigate, chasten, chastise, correct, discipline, make one sorry, penalize; beat, cane, flog, spank, tan one's hide, whip; batter, hurt, injure, knock about, rough up.

punishment   **n** *lit:* castigation, chastening, chastisement, correction, discipline, penalty, penance; beating, caning, flogging, spanking, tanning, whipping; battering, injury, knocking about, rough treatment.

puny   **adj** *lit:* feeble, frail, pint-sized, runty, sickly, stunted, undersized, weakly; *fig:* inconsequential, insignificant, paltry, petty, trifling, trivial.

pup   **n** *lit:* cub, whelp, young dog; *fig:* jackanapes, popinjay, whippersnapper.

pupil   **n** *lit:* disciple, learner, schoolboy, schoolgirl, student; neophyte, novice, postulant; eye part.

purchase   **n** *lit:* buy; acquisition, gain, property; foothold, footing, grasp, grip, toehold; *fig:* edge, hold, influence, leverage. **vb** *lit:* buy; acquire, come by, invest in, obtain, pick up, procure, secure, shop for.

pure   **adj** *lit:* flawless, perfect, unalloyed; straight, unmixed; authentic, genuine, natural, real, simple, true; immaculate, pristine, spotless, virgin; clean, sanitary, sterile, uncontaminated, unpolluted, untainted, wholesome; *fig:* blameless, chaste, innocent, uncorrupted, virginal, virtuous; absolute, complete, mere, sheer, total, unqualified, utter; academic, hypothetical, speculative, theoretical.

purge   **n** *lit:* aperient, cathartic, emetic, laxative; *fig:* cleanup, sorting out, weeding out; pogrom, witch hunt. **vb** *lit:* absolve, cleanse, expiate, forgive, pardon, purify, wash clean; evacuate, use a laxative; *fig:* clean up, clear out, sort out, weed out.

purity n *lit:* flawlessness, perfection, spotlessness; clarity, cleanness, clearness, opacity; faultlessness, fineness, genuineness; simplicity; *fig:* blamelessness, chastity, innocence, virginity, virtue; piety; sincerity.

purpose n *lit:* aim, design, idea, intention, object, point, reason; end, goal, objective, target; aspiration, desire, wish; determination, firmness, persistence, resolve, single-mindedness, steadfastness, tenacity, will; avail, benefit, effect, gain, outcome, profit, result, return, use. **vb** *lit:* aim, aspire, commit oneself, determine, intend, mean, plan, propose, resolve.

purse n *lit:* money bag, pouch; funds, money, resources, treasury; award, prize, reward; gift, present. **vb** *lit:* draw tight, pucker, tighten.

pursue **vb** *lit:* chase, follow, go after, hound, hunt, tail, track; *fig:* chase after, court, pay court to, woo; aim for, aspire to, seek, strive for, work toward; apply oneself to, carry on, engage in, perform, ply, practice, work at; adhere to, continue, hold to, keep on, persist in.

push n *lit:* heave, ram, shove, thrust; assault, attack, charge, offensive, onslaught; *fig:* ambition, determination, drive, dynamism, energy, enterprise, vigor; effort, go, try. **vb** *lit:* drive, press, propel, ram, shove, thrust; elbow, jostle, shoulder, squeeze; browbeat, coerce, egg on, encourage, hurry, impel, incite, influence, oblige, persuade, urge; advertise, boost, plug, promote, publicize; hawk, peddle, market; *spec:* approach (in age).

put **vb** *lit:* bring, deposit, lay, place, position, rest, set, settle, situate; push (away), thrust (away); heave, hurl, lob, pitch, throw, toss; *fig:* arrange, fix; commit, condemn, consign, doom; assign (to), constrain (to), employ (to), make (to), oblige (to), require (to); express, phrase, pose, state, word; assess (at), estimate (at); advance, bring forward, posit, present, propose, submit.

puzzle n *lit:* brainteaser, conundrum, dilemma, enigma, problem, quandary, question, riddle; maze, mystery, paradox; difficulty, perplexity, uncertainty. **vb** *lit:* baffle, beat, bewilder, mystify, nonplus, perplex, stump; brood (over), mull (over), muse (over), ponder (over), thinking long and hard (over); figure (out), sort (out), work (out).

Q

quaint adj *lit:* antiquated, archaic, baroque, old-fashioned, old-world, rococo; picturesque, scenic; curious, eccentric, odd, peculiar, singular, unusual; bizarre, fantastic, grotesque, strange, whimsical.

quake n *lit:* convulsion, quiver, shaking, shiver, shudder, spasm, tremor, vibration; earthquake, seismic shock. **vb** *lit:* convulse, go into spasm, quail, quiver, shake, shiver, shudder, tremble, vibrate; flutter, palpitate, throb.

qualification n *lit:* authority, capability, eligibility, power; achievements, attainments, background, certificate, experience, history, past, record; attribute, capacity, skill; distinguishing feature, distinction; caveat, exception, limitation, modification, reservation, restriction; condition, proviso.

qualify vb *lit:* be accepted, be authorized, be certified, become eligible, be empowered, be entitled, be trained; equip, fit, prepare, ready, school; limit, moderate, modify, restrict, soften, temper; abate, diminish, lessen, mitigate, reduce; characterize, describe, distinguish; have an effect upon.

quality n *lit:* character, class, demeanor, description, essence, kind, make, manner, nature, sort, stamp, type; attribute, characteristic, feature, property, trait; timbre, tone; caliber, distinction, merit, standing, value, worth; position, rank, status, superiority; aristocracy, landed gentry, nobility, upper classes.

quantity n *lit:* amount, number, sum, total; aggregate, bulk, capacity, extent, magnitude, mass, measure, size, volume; dose, helping, part, portion, ration, share; *spec:* duration, length (of a musical note, of a syllable).

quarrel n *lit:* altercation, argument, clash, controversy, difference of opinion, disagreement, discord, dispute, dissension, feud, row, squabble, tiff, vendetta, wrangle; *spec:* arrow, bolt, dart (for a crossbow). **vb** *lit:* argue, bandy words, bicker, clash, differ, disagree, dispute, dissent, fall out, feud, have words, row, squabble, wrangle; carp, cavil, decry, demur, find fault, take exception.

quarry   n *lit:* excavation, open-cast mine, pit; game, hunted, kill, prey, victim; *fig:* reservoir, source, well; aim, end, goal, objective. **vb** *lit:* dig out (from), excavate; *fig:* extract.

quarter   n *lit:* fourth; 15 minutes; 3 months; area, district, locality, neighborhood, place, region, side, territory, zone; compass point, direction; clemency, leniency, mercy; *fig:* authority, source; *spec:* phase (of the moon); staff, upright, vertical (in construction). **vb** *lit:* chop up, divide into fourths; accommodate, billet, house, lodge, post, station; abide, be accommodated, board, put up, stay; range, roam; beat, search thoroughly; *fig:* compartment; impose.

queer   adj *lit:* abnormal, anomalous, extraordinary, odd, outlandish, peculiar, singular, strange, uncommon, unnatural, unusual, weird; curious, droll, funny, quaint; unconventional, unorthodox; dubious, fishy, questionable, suspicious; eerie, mysterious, uncanny; dizzy, faint, ill, light-headed, sick, queasy; crazy, touched; counterfeit, fake, sham.

quell   vb *lit:* crush, extinguish, overthrow, put down, quash, suppress; check, curb, repress, stifle, subdue; conquer, defeat, overcome; *fig:* allay, calm, mollify, pacify, quiet, soothe.

quench   vb *lit:* douse, drown, extinguish, put out, smother, snuff out, stifle; dip, plunge; allay, appease, cool, satiate, satisfy, slake; end, finish, stop; die down, fade out, subside.

query   n *lit:* inquiry, question; contention, controversy, debate, doubt, reservation, uncertainty; objection, problem; interrogation mark, question mark. **vb** *lit:* ask, challenge, debate, dispute, enquire, interrogate, question; doubt, wonder.

question   n *lit:* inquiry, query; contention, controversy, debate; demur, doubt, objection, problem, reservation, uncertainty; examination, interrogation; issue, motion, proposition, subject, topic. **vb** *lit:* ask, cross-examine, enquire, grill, interrogate, pump, query, quiz; challenge, debate, disbelieve, dispute, doubt, wonder about.

quick   n *lit:* living; flesh, sensitive part; *fig:* heart. **adj** *lit:* express, fast, fleet, meteoric, rapid, snappy, speedy, swift; abrupt, immediate, prompt, sudden; brief, brisk, cursory, hasty, hurried, perfunctory; active, adroit, alert, animated, energetic, keen, lively, nimble, ready, sharp, spry, vivacious; adept, clever, deft, dexterous, skillful, versatile; acute,

intelligent, perceptive, shrewd; excitable, irascible, touchy, volatile. **adv**
lit: fast, rapidly, speedily, swiftly; at once, immediately.

quicken vb *lit:* accelerate, expedite, hasten, hurry up, hustle, speed up;
activate, animate, arouse, awaken, excite, fire, kindle, reactivate,
reanimate, rekindle, resurrect, revitalize, revive, rouse, stimulate, stir up.

quickly adv *lit:* on the double, briskly, fast, flat out, rapidly, snappily,
speedily, swiftly, with alacrity; abruptly, immediately, instantly,
promptly, soon, suddenly; briefly, cursorily, hastily, hurriedly,
perfunctorily.

quiet n *lit:* peace, silence, stillness, tranquility; serenity; calm, repose,
rest. **vb** *lit:* hush, silence; calm down, pacify, soothe, still. **adj** *lit:*
noiseless, silent, soundless; hushed, low, peaceful, soft; at rest, calm,
motionless, placid, restful, serene, still, tranquil; dumb, mute,
unresponsive; private, secluded, secret, undisturbed, unfrequented;
modest, plain, restrained, sedate, sober, subdued, unobtrusive,
unpretentious; gentle, inoffensive, meek, mild, reserved, retiring, shy.

quietly adv *lit:* noiselessly, silently, soundlessly; gently, peacefully,
softly; complacently, contentedly, placidly, serenely, tranquilly;
confidentially, furtively, privately, secretively, secretly; inoffensively,
modestly, plainly, sedately, soberly, unobtrusively, unpretentiously;
demurely, meekly, shyly.

quit vb *lit:* depart, exit, go, leave, pull out; depart from, exit from, go
from, pull out from; abandon, desert, forsake, renounce; resign, retire;
cease, discontinue, drop, end, halt, stop, suspend; give up, surrender, yield;
pay off, repay, settle; absolve, discharge, free, remit. **adj** *lit:* clear (of), free
(of), rid (of); absolved, discharged.

quiver n *lit:* palpitation, shake, shiver, shudder, spasm, tic, tremor,
tremulousness, vibration; *spec:* arrow case, arrow holder. **vb** *lit:* quail,
quake, quaver, shake, shiver, shudder, tremble; flutter, oscillate, vibrate.

quiz n *lit:* examination, interrogation, test. **vb** *lit:* ask questions, grill,
interrogate, question; examine, test.

quota n *lit:* allocation, allowance, cut, helping, part, portion, proportion,
ration, share, slice, whack.

quotation n *lit:* allusion, excerpt, extract, passage, reference; citing, recital, repetition; *fig:* cost, estimate, price, quote, rate, tender; *spec:* company registration, share price (on the stock exchange).

quote n *lit:* allusion, quotation, reference, repetition; inverted comma, quotation mark; *fig:* cost, estimate, price, rate. **vb** *lit:* adduce, allude to, cite, declaim, instance, recite, refer to, repeat the words of; put in inverted commas; *fig:* give an estimate (for), put a price (on), tender (for); *spec:* state the market price (of shares or bonds).

R

rabble n *lit:* crowd, mob, throng; populace; commoners, hoi polloi, masses, proletariat, riffraff.

race n *lit:* chase, dash, sprint; competition, contest; blood, breed, clan, ethnic group, nation, people, stock. **vb** *lit:* career, dart, dash, fly, gallop, hurtle, speed, tear, zip, zoom; compete (against), contest (against), run (against).

racket n *lit:* ballyhoo, commotion, din, disturbance, fuss, hubbub, hullabaloo, noise, pandemonium, row, tumult, uproar; fraud, ramp, swindle; business, game, line.

radiant adj *lit:* beaming, brilliant, effulgent, gleaming, glittering, incandescent, luminous, resplendent, shining, sparkling; blissful, delighted, ecstatic, glowing, joyful, rapturous.

radical n *lit:* extremist, fanatic, militant, revolutionary. **adj** *lit:* constitutional, innate, natural, organic; basic, fundamental, profound, thoroughgoing; complete, entire, excessive, extreme, severe, sweeping, thorough; extremist, militant, revolutionary.

rag n *lit:* cloth, remnant, scrap, shred, tatter; jape, lark, practical joke, prank; ragtime music; *fig:* (lose one's) temper. **vb** *lit:* abrade, become frayed, become tattered, fray; *fig:* make fun of, play jokes on, tease; scold.

rage n *lit:* anger, fury, heat, ire, passion, wrath; craze, obsession; fad, latest, mode, vogue. **vb** *lit:* be beside oneself, blow one's top, fume, rave, seethe; blow, rampage, storm, surge.

raid n *lit:* attack, incursion, invasion, onset, onslaught, sally; foray, sortie; break-in; ambush. **vb** *lit:* assault, attack, despoil, invade, maraud, pillage, plunder, rifle, sack; break into, get into.

rail n *lit:* bar, barrier, fence; balustrade, banister; line, railway track. **vb** *lit:* enclose, fence round, hem in; rant (at), shout (at), yell (at).

rain n *lit:* cloudburst, downpour, drizzle, shower; deluge, flood, torrent; cascade, fountain, spray. **vb** *lit:* bucket down, drizzle, pour, sheet down, shower, teem; cascade, drop, fall, fountain, spray, sprinkle; *fig:* bestow, lavish.

raise vb *lit:* build, construct, erect, put up, set up; heave, hoist, lift; bring up, foster, rear; breed, cultivate, develop, grow, nurture, produce, propagate; augment, boost, enlarge, escalate, heighten, increase, intensify, strengthen; elevate, exalt, promote, upgrade; activate, arouse, excite, foment, incite, instigate, motivate, provoke, stir up, whip up; bring about, cause, create, give rise to, occasion, originate, start; advance, broach, introduce, put forward, suggest; assemble, form, gather, levy, mass, muster, obtain, rally, recruit; *spec:* abandon, give up, relieve, remove (a siege).

rally n *lit:* assembly, congregation, convention, gathering, mass meeting, muster; reformation, regrouping, reorganization, stand; improvement, recovery, renewal, resurgence, revival; road race. vb *lit:* assemble, convene, gather, get together, mobilize, muster, organize, round up, summon, unite; reassemble, reform, regroup, reorganize; come round, get better, improve, perk up, recover, revive.

ram n *lit:* male sheep; piston, plunger; pump; battering ram. vb *lit:* butt, collide with, crash into, drive (home), run into; cram, drum, force, hammer, jam, pack, pound, stamp, thrust.

ramble n *lit:* excursion, hike, perambulation, promenade, saunter, stroll, walk. vb *lit:* amble, perambulate, roam, rove, saunter, stray, stroll, walk, wander; meander, wind; babble, chatter, digress, maunder, rattle on.

rampage vb *lit:* be beside oneself, go berserk, rage, rant, rave, run amok, run riot, storm, tear.

rampant adj *lit:* dominant, raging, riotous, uncontrollable, unrestrained, wild; epidemic, exuberant, profuse, rife, unchecked, widespread; erect, rearing, upright.

range n *lit:* area, bounds, compass, confines, domain, extent, limits, orbit, province, radius, reach, scope, sphere, sweep; chain, file, line, rank, row, series, string; assortment, gamut, kind, lot, selection, sort, variety. vb *lit:* align, array, dispose, draw up, order; arrange, bracket, catalog, classify, file, grade, group, rank; aim, direct, level, point, train; cruise, explore, ramble, roam, straggle, stray, stroll, wander; extend, fluctuate, go, reach, stretch, vary (between).

rank n *lit:* caste, classification, division, grade, level, order, position, quality, standing, station, status, type; column, formation, group, line, row, series. **vb** *lit:* align, arrange, array, classify, grade, line up, marshal, order, position, range, sort. **adj** *lit:* abundant, dense, lush, productive, profuse, vigorous; bad, fetid, foul, fusty, noxious, off, offensive, pungent, rancid, stale, stinking; absolute, blatant, downright, excessive, flagrant, gross, rampant, sheer, total, unmitigated, utter; abusive, atrocious, coarse, filthy, gross, indecent, obscene, outrageous, scurrilous, vulgar.

rap n *lit:* blow, knock, tap; *fig:* blame, punishment, rebuke, reproof; conviction, prison sentence; atom, jot, whit. **vb** *lit:* knock, tap, strike; censure, condemn, criticize, rebuke, reprove.

rape n *lit:* ravishment, sexual assault, violation; defilement, defloration; abuse, maltreatment; *fig:* depredation, despoliation, looting pillage, plundering, ransacking, stripping. **vb** *lit:* outrage, ravish, sexually assault, violate; *fig:* despoil, loot, pillage, plunder, ransack, strip.

rare adj *lit:* exceptional, infrequent, scarce, singular, sparse, sporadic, uncommon, unusual; admirable, excellent, exquisite, extreme, fine, incomparable, superb, superlative; invaluable, precious, priceless.

rash n *lit:* eruption, inflammation; outbreak; *fig:* epidemic, flood, plague, series, spate, succession. **adj** *lit:* adventurous, audacious, brash, foolhardy, harebrained, hasty, headstrong, heedless, hot-headed, ill-advised, impetuous, impulsive, indiscreet, injudicious, madcap, premature, reckless, thoughtless, unthinking.

rate n *lit:* degree, percentage, proportion, ratio, scale; charge, cost, duty, fee, price, tariff, tax, toll; gait, pace, speed, time, velocity. **vb** *lit:* adjudge, appraise, assess, classify, count, evaluate, grade, rank, reckon, value, weigh; be worthy of, deserve, merit; admire, respect, think highly of.

ration n *lit:* allotment, allowance, dole, helping, portion, quota, share; provision(s), store(s), victual(s). **vb** *lit:* allocate, apportion, deal, distribute, dole, give, mete; budget, control, limit, restrict.

rational adj *lit:* intelligent, judicious, logical, lucid, realistic, reasonable, sensible, sound; cognitive, reasoning, thinking; all there, balanced, conscious, lucid, sane.

rationalize vb *lit:* account for, excuse, extenuate, justify, make allowance for, vindicate; elucidate, reason out, resolve, think through; cut back on, make cost-effective, make cuts in, streamline, trim.

rattle n *lit:* knock, knocking, pinking, rasp; castanet, maraca; clatter, racket, uproar; chatter, gossip, prattle. **vb** *lit:* bang, clatter, jangle; bounce, jiggle, jolt, shake, vibrate; chatter, gab, prattle, run on; disconcert, discountenance, disturb, perturb, scare, shake, upset; reel (off), recite, run (through).

ravage n *lit:* damage, desolation, destruction, devastation, havoc, pillage, plunder, ruin(s), waste. **vb** *lit:* demolish, desolate, destroy, lay waste, loot, pillage, plunder, ransack, raze, ruin, sack, shatter, wreck.

rave n *lit:* acclaim, applause, praise; celebration, do, party, thrash; craze, fashion, vogue. **vb** *lit:* babble, fume, rage, rant, roar, seethe, splutter, thunder; be mad (about), be wild (about), enthuse (about), rhapsodize (over). **adj** *lit:* commendatory, ecstatic, enthusiastic, excellent, laudatory.

ravishing adj (pr.pt) *lit:* bewitching, charming, dazzling, delightful, enchanting, gorgeous, radiant, stunning.

raw adj *lit:* bloody, fresh, uncooked, unprepared; basic, coarse, crude, natural, organic, rough, unrefined, untreated; abraded, grazed, open, scratched, sore, tender; callow, green, ignorant, immature, inexperienced, new, unskilled, untrained; blunt, brutal, candid, frank, naked, plain, realistic, unembellished; biting, bitter, bleak, chilly, cold, freezing, harsh, piercing.

reach n *lit:* capacity, compass, distance, extension, extent, grasp, influence, jurisdiction, power, range, scope, spread, stretch. **vb** *lit:* arrive at, attain, get to, make; extend to, get hold of, grasp, stretch to, touch; hand, hold (out), pass, stretch (out); amount to, come to; go down to, fall to; climb to, rise to; contact, find, get through to, make contact with.

read vb *lit:* look at, peruse, pore over, study; comprehend, construe, decipher, discover, interpret, perceive, see; deliver, recite; display, indicate, record, register, show.

reading n *lit:* examination, perusal, scrutiny, study; concept, grasp, interpretation, rendition, treatment, understanding, version; education, erudition, knowledge, learning, scholarship; homily, lecture, lesson, recital, sermon.

ready　vb *lit:* arrange, equip, fit out, organize, prepare, set up (for); nerve (oneself), steel (oneself). **adj** *lit:* arranged, fit, organized, prepared, set; mature, ripe; agreeable, eager, game, glad, inclined, keen, minded, prone, willing; acute, alert, apt, astute, bright, clever, deft, dexterous, perceptive, prompt, quick-witted, resourceful, sharp, skillful; about, close, near; to hand; liable (to), likely (to).

real　adj *lit:* absolute, actual, authentic, existent, factual, genuine, heartfelt, intrinsic, legitimate, positive, rightful, sincere, true, unfeigned, valid, veritable.

realistic　adj *lit:* businesslike, commonsense, down-to-earth, levelheaded, matter-of-fact, practical, rational, sensible, unsentimental; accurate, authentic, lifelike, naturalistic, true-to-life.

really　adv *lit:* absolutely, actually, assuredly, categorically, certainly, genuinely, indeed, in fact, positively, truly, undoubtedly.

rear　n *lit:* aft, back, back end, stern, tail; backside, behind, bottom, bum, posterior, seat. **vb** *lit:* breed, bring up, care for, cultivate, foster, grow, nurse, nurture, raise, train; build, construct, erect; stand upright; lift up; loom, rise, soar, tower. **adj** *lit:* aft, back, following, hindmost, last.

rearrange　vb *lit:* move, realign, redeploy, relocate, reorder, reposition; alter, change, turn round; decorate, refurnish, renovate; reorganize, reschedule, reset.

reason　n *lit:* apprehension, comprehension, intellect, logic, mentality, mind, rationality, reasoning, sanity, soundness, understanding; basis, cause, grounds, occasion, purpose; argument, defense, excuse, explanation, ground, justification, rationale, vindication; aim, end, goal, incentive, inducement, motive, object, target; moderation, propriety, sense, wisdom. **vb** *lit:* conclude, deduce, infer, make out, think, work out; argue (with), debate (with), dispute (with), expostulate (with).

reasonable　adj *lit:* advisable, believable, credible, intelligent, justifiable, logical, plausible, practical, rational, sensible, sound, tenable, well-advised, wise; acceptable, equitable, fair, fit, honest, inexpensive, just, moderate, modest, proper, right, within reason.

rebel　n *lit:* insurgent, mutineer, revolutionary, secessionist; dissenter, heretic, nonconformist, renegade, schismatic; anarchist; eccentric. **vb** *lit:*

mutiny, resist, revolt, rise up, take to the streets; come out against, defy, disobey, dissent; recoil, shy away.

rebellious adj *lit:* defiant, disloyal, insubordinate, insurgent, intractable, mutinous, revolutionary, seditious, subversive; disobedient, naughty; difficult, obstinate, recalcitrant, refractory, willful.

rebuff n *lit:* brush-off, cold shoulder, discouragement, refusal, rejection, repulse, slight, snub; setback. **vb** *lit:* brush off, cut, discourage, put off, reject, repulse, snub, spurn, turn down.

rebuke n *lit:* carpeting, reprimand, reproach, reproof, telling off, tongue-lashing. **vb** *lit:* castigate, censure, chide, lecture, reprimand, reproach, reprove, scold, take to task, tell off, tick off, upbraid.

recall n *lit:* summons; memory, recollection, remembrance, retrieval; repeal, retraction, withdrawal. **vb** *lit:* bring back, call back, summon; bring to mind, recollect, remember, reminisce about, revive one's memory of; renew, revive; be reminiscent of, hark back to; repeal, retract, withdraw.

receipt n *lit:* acknowledgment, counterfoil, proof of purchase; acceptance, reception; gain(s), proceed(s), profit(s), taking(s).

receive vb *lit:* accept, acquire, be given, get, obtain; take; have, own, possess; accommodate, admit, entertain, incorporate, meet, take in, welcome; *fig:* sustain, undergo.

recent adj *lit:* contemporary, current, late, new, present-day, up-to-date.

reception n *lit:* acceptance, acquisition, receipt; greeting, recognition, response, welcome; do, function, levee, party, soiree.

recess n *lit:* alcove, bay, cavity, depression, indentation, niche, nook; adjournment, break, holiday, intermission, interval, respite, rest. **vb** *lit:* set back; adjourn, take a break, take time off.

recipe n *lit:* constituents, formula, ingredients, instructions, method, prescription, procedure, technique.

reckless adj *lit:* careless, daredevil, foolhardy, heedless, imprudent, incautious, indiscreet, madcap, mindless, negligent, precipitate, rash, thoughtless.

recognize vb *lit:* identify, know, make out, place, recall, remember, spot; accept, acknowledge, admit, allow, be aware of, concede, grant, own, perceive, realize, see, understand; appreciate, approve, honor, salute.

recommend   vb *lit:* approve, commend, praise, speak well of, vouch for; advise, advocate, counsel, urge; advance, propose, suggest; be in one's favor, promote.

reconstruct   vb *lit:* reassemble, rebuild, re-create, renovate, reorganize, restore; build up, deduce, piece together.

record   n *lit:* account, annals, archives, chronicle, document, entry, file, log, memorandum, minute, register, report; documentation, evidence, remembrance, testimony, trace; background, curriculum vitae, performance; best performance, best time; album, disc, platter, release, single. vb *lit:* chronicle, document, enroll, enter, log, minute, note, put down, register, transcribe, write down; contain, indicate, read, say, show; cut, make a recording of, tape, video tape.

recover   vb *lit:* find, get back, recapture, reclaim, recoup, regain, restore, retrieve, win back; come round, get well, heal, improve, mend, pull through, rally, regain one's strength, revive; convalesce, recuperate.

recovery   n *lit:* recapture, reclamation, repossession, restoration, retrieval; convalescence, healing, mending, recuperation; improvement, rehabilitation, restoration, revival, upturn.

recreation   n *lit:* amusement, distraction, diversion, enjoyment, entertainment, leisure activity, pastime, pleasure, relaxation.

red   adj *lit:* carmine, coral, crimson, maroon, pink, ruby, scarlet, vermilion; bay, chestnut, flaming, titian; blushing, embarrassed, flushed, rubicund, shamefaced, suffused; blooming, glowing, healthy, rosy, ruddy; bloodshot, inflamed; bloodstained, gory, sanguine.

redeem   vb *lit:* buy back, reclaim, regain, repossess, retrieve, win back; cash in, exchange, trade in; abide by, acquit, adhere to, carry out, discharge, fulfill, keep, meet, satisfy; absolve, rehabilitate, reinstate; atone for, compensate for, make up for, offset, redress; deliver, emancipate, extricate, free, liberate, ransom, rescue, save, set free.

reduce   vb *lit:* abate, contract, curtail, cut down, decrease, dilute, diminish, impair, lessen, slow down, truncate, weaken; bankrupt, impoverish, ruin; bring, drive, force, subdue, vanquish; lose weight, shed weight, slim; cut, discount, lower, mark down, slash; bring low, degrade, demote, downgrade, humble.

redundant   adj *lit:* excess, inessential, inordinate, superfluous, surplus, unnecessary, useless; diffuse, repetitious, verbose.

refer   vb *lit:* allude (to); direct, guide, point, recommend; apply (to), turn (to); be directed (to), pertain (to), relate (to); attribute, credit, impute, put down (to); commit, consign, hand over, pass on, transfer.

referee   n *lit:* adjudicator, arbitrator, judge, umpire. **vb** *lit:* adjudicate, arbitrate, judge, umpire.

reference   n *lit:* allusion (to); applicability, connection, regard, relation; credential(s), endorsement, recommendation, testimonial.

refined   adj *lit:* civilized, cultured, genteel, gracious, polished, sophisticated, urbane, well-mannered; discerning, discriminating, exact, fastidious, nice, precise, punctilious, subtle; clarified, distilled, filtered, pure, purified.

refinement   n *lit:* clarification, cleansing, distillation, filtering, processing, purification; nicety, nuance, subtlety; civility, courtesy, cultivation, delicacy, discrimination, fastidiousness, finesse, gentility, good manners, graciousness, polish, sophistication, style, taste.

reflect   vb *lit:* echo, imitate, mirror; cogitate, contemplate, deliberate, meditate, mull over, ponder, ruminate, think; communicate, demonstrate, display, exhibit, express, indicate, manifest, reveal.

reform   n *lit:* amendment, correction, improvement, rectification, rehabilitation. **vb** *lit:* amend, better, correct, emend, mend, reconstruct, rectify, rehabilitate, renovate, reorganize, repair, restore; go straight.

refreshing   adj *lit:* bracing, cooling, fresh, invigorating, thirst-quenching; novel, original, stimulating.

refuse   n *lit:* debris, garbage, litter, rubbish, trash, waste; offal; detritus, parings; scrap. **vb** *lit:* decline, negate, reject, repudiate, spurn, turn down, veto, withhold.

regard   n *lit:* gaze, look, scrutiny, stare; attention, heed, notice; affection, attachment, concern, consideration, esteem, love, respect, sympathy, thought; aspect, detail, item, matter, particular, point; bearing, connection, reference, relation, relevance; best wish(es), compliment(s), greeting(s), respect(s). **vb** *lit:* behold, gaze at, observe, scrutinize, watch; consider, esteem, hold, look upon, rate, think, view; apply to, be relevant to, have to do with, pertain to, relate to; attend, heed, listen to, mind, note, pay attention to, take notice of.

region n *lit:* area, district, division, part, section, sector, territory, zone; locality, range, scope, vicinity; domain, field, sphere.

register n *lit:* annals, archives, chronicle, file, list, memorandum, record, roll, roster, schedule. **vb** *lit:* catalog, check in, chronicle, enlist, enroll, enter, list, note, record, sign on, take down; display, express, indicate, manifest, record, reflect, reveal, show; *fig:* dawn on, get through, have an effect, sink in.

regret n *lit:* bitterness, compunction, contrition, disappointment, grief, remorse, repentance, ruefulness, self-reproach. **vb** *lit:* bemoan, be upset, deplore, grieve, lament, mourn, repent, rue.

regular adj *lit:* commonplace, customary, everyday, habitual, normal, ordinary, routine, typical, usual; consistent, constant, even, fixed, ordered, periodic, rhythmic, set, steady; dependable, efficient, methodical, orderly, standardized, systematic; balanced, flat, level, smooth, straight, symmetrical; approved, correct, established, formal, official, orthodox, prevailing, proper, standard, traditional.

regulate vb *lit:* adjust, administer, arrange, control, direct, fit, handle, manage, moderate, monitor, organize, rule, run, supervise, systematize.

rehearse vb *lit:* act, drill, go over, practice, prepare, run through, train, try out.

rein n *lit:* bridle, control, curb; check, restraint, restriction. **vb** *lit:* control, curb, steer; hold (back), hold (in).

reinforce vb *lit:* augment, bolster, buttress, fortify, harden, prop, strengthen, supplement, support, toughen.

reject n *lit:* castoff, discard, second. **vb** *lit:* ban, bar, cast aside, discard, eliminate, exclude, rebuff, repulse, scrap, spurn, throw out, turn down, veto.

rejoicing n *lit:* celebration, cheer, elation, exultation, gladness, happiness, jubilation, triumph. **adj (pr.pt)** *lit:* celebrating, elated, exalted, exultant, glad, happy, joyful, joyous, jubilant, triumphant.

relate vb *lit:* chronicle, describe, detail, impart, narrate, present, recite, report, tell; ally, associate, coordinate, correlate, join, link; be allied (to), be cognate (to), be kin (to); appertain, apply, be relevant (to), pertain, refer.

relationship n *lit:* affair, association, bond, connection, exchange, kinship, liaison, parallel, rapport, similarity.

relative n *lit:* kinsman, kinswoman, relation. **adj** *lit:* allied, associated, comparative, contingent, corresponding, dependent, proportionate, reciprocal, related, respective; in proportion (to), proportional (to).

relax vb *lit:* abate, diminish, ease, loosen, lower, mitigate, reduce, relieve, slacken; flop, let oneself go, loosen up, rest, take it easy, unbend, unwind.

relaxation n *lit:* amusement, enjoyment, entertainment, leisure, recreation, refreshment; abatement, easing, letup, reduction, slackening, weakening.

release n *lit:* acquittal, deliverance, discharge, emancipation, liberation, liberty, relief; absolution, acquittal, dispensation, exemption, exoneration; announcement, issue, proclamation, publication. **vb** *lit:* discharge, disengage, drop, emancipate, extricate, let out, liberate, set free, turn loose, unchain, undo, unshackle, untie; absolve, acquit, dispense, excuse, exempt, exonerate, let off; break, circulate, distribute, issue, launch, make public, present, publish, put out.

relentless adj *lit:* fierce, grim, harsh, implacable, inexorable, inflexible, merciless, pitiless, ruthless, uncompromising, unrelenting, unyielding; incessant, persistent, punishing, sustained, unabated, unfaltering, unremitting, unstoppable.

relief n *lit:* abatement, alleviation, comfort, cure, deliverance, easement, mitigation, release, remedy, solace; aid, assistance, help, succor, support, sustenance; break, breather, relaxation, respite, rest; distraction, diversion.

relieve vb *lit:* abate, alleviate, appease, calm, comfort, console, diminish, dull, ease, mollify, palliate, salve, soften, soothe; aid, assist, help, succor, support, sustain; stand in for, substitute for, take over from;

deliver, discharge, exempt, release, unburden; break, interrupt, slacken, vary.

religious adj *lit:* devout, doctrinal, faithful, god-fearing, pious, reverent, sectarian, spiritual, theological; *fig:* conscientious, exact, fastidious, meticulous, punctilious, rigid, scrupulous, unswerving.

relish n *lit:* appetite, appreciation, enjoyment, fondness, gusto, liking, partiality, penchant, predilection, taste, zest; flavor, piquancy, savor, smack, tang, trace; appetizer, chutney, condiment, sauce. vb *lit:* appreciate, enjoy, fancy, like, revel in, savor.

remain vb *lit:* continue, go on, last, persist, prevail, stand, stay, survive, wait; dwell, live, stop; be left, be over.

remains n *lit:* crumbs, debris, fragments, leftovers, oddments, pieces, relics, remainder, residue, scraps, vestiges; bones, carcass, corpse, skeleton; hulk, ruins, shell, wreckage.

remark n *lit:* aside, assertion, comment, observation, statement, utterance, word; acknowledgment, attention, consideration, heed, mention, notice, recognition, regard, thought. vb *lit:* comment, mention, observe, say; espy, heed, make out, mark, notice, perceive, regard, see, take note of.

remarkable adj *lit:* conspicuous, distinguished, impressive, notable, noteworthy, outstanding, preeminent, prominent; extraordinary, singular, striking, uncommon, unusual.

remedy n *lit:* antidote, cure, medicament, medicine, panacea; corrective, countermeasure, redress, solution. vb *lit:* alleviate, cure, ease, heal, palliate, relieve, restore, soothe; correct, fix, rectify, redress, repair, solve.

remember vb *lit:* look back, recall, recollect, relive, reminisce, retain, think back.

reminder n *lit:* alarm; knot; memo, memorandum; keepsake, memento, souvenir.

remiss adj *lit:* careless, culpable, delinquent, derelict, dilatory, forgetful, inattentive, indifferent, lackadaisical, lax, neglectful, slack, slipshod, sloppy, tardy, thoughtless.

remit n *lit:* authorization, brief, guidelines, instructions, orders. **vb** *lit:* dispatch, forward, mail, post, transmit; cancel, halt, repeal, stop; abate, alleviate, decrease, diminish, dwindle, mitigate, reduce, relax, slacken, soften, wane; defer, delay, postpone, put off, suspend.

remorseful adj *lit:* apologetic, ashamed, conscience-stricken, contrite, guilt-ridden, penitent, regretful, repentant, rueful, self-reproachful, sorry.

remote adj *lit:* distant, faraway, godforsaken, isolated, lonely, secluded; alien, extraneous, extrinsic, immaterial, irrelevant, outside, removed, unrelated; doubtful, dubious, faint, implausible, meager, negligible, poor, slender, slight, slim, unlikely; aloof, cold, detached, indifferent, introverted, reserved, unapproachable, uninvolved, withdrawn.

remove vb *lit:* abstract, delete, eliminate, extract, get rid of, throw out; amputate, take off; doff; depart, move away, quit, relocate, transfer, transport, vacate; discharge, dismiss, expel, purge, relegate; depose, dethrone, dislodge, eject, oust, unseat; *fig:* assassinate, dispose of, do away with, execute, get rid of, liquidate, murder, wipe out.

render vb *lit:* contribute, furnish, give, make available, present, provide, submit, supply, tender, yield; display, exhibit, manifest, show; exchange, return, swap, trade; cause to become, leave; make; act, depict, do, interpret, perform, play, portray; construe, explain, reproduce, transcribe, translate; cede, give up, hand over, relinquish, surrender, turn over; give back, make restitution, pay back, restore.

rent n *lit:* fee, hire, lease, payment, rental, tariff; break, chink, crack, flaw, gash, hole, rip, slash, split, tear; *fig:* breach, dissension, disunity, division, rift, rupture, schism. **vb** *lit:* charter, hire, lease, let.

reorganize vb *lit:* adapt, adjust, move, realign, rearrange, redispose, relocate; remodel, restructure, rework; reschedule; reestablish, reset.

repair n *lit:* adjustment, mend, overhaul, patch, restoration; condition, fettle, form, shape, state. **vb** *lit:* fix, heal, mend, patch, put back together, rectify, renew, renovate, restore; retrieve; compensate for, make up for; go, move, retire; have recourse (to), resort (to), turn (to).

repay vb *lit:* pay back, refund, reimburse, remunerate, square; reciprocate, requite; avenge, get even with, settle the score with.

repeat   n *lit:* duplicate, echo, recapitulation, reiteration, repetition, replay, reshowing. **vb** *lit:* duplicate, echo, iterate, quote, recapitulate, recite, rehearse, reiterate, renew, rerun, reshow, restate.

repel   **vb** *lit:* drive off, fight off, hold off, parry, put to flight, rebuff, reject, repulse, resist, ward off; *fig:* disgust, nauseate, offend, put one off, revolt.

repetition   n *lit:* duplication, echo, iteration, recapitulation, recital, recurrence, reiteration, renewal, repeat, restatement, return, tautology.

replace   **vb** *lit:* restock, resupply, substitute, succeed, supersede, supplant, take over from.

reply   n *lit:* acknowledgment, answer, comeback, counter, rejoinder, response, retort, return, riposte. **vb** *lit:* acknowledge, answer, come back, counter, react (to), respond (to), retaliate, retort, riposte, write back.

report   n *lit:* account, article, broadcast, bulletin, communiqué, description, dispatch, message, piece, record, statement, story, summary; rumor; fame, reputation, repute; bang, blast, boom, crash, discharge, explosion, noise, sound. **vb** *lit:* announce, broadcast, communicate, describe, detail, document, inform of, notify of, pass on, publish, record, recount, relay, state, tell; appear, be present, clock in, show up, turn up.

represent   **vb** *lit:* be, correspond to, express, mean, serve as, stand for, symbolize; embody, epitomize, exemplify, personify, typify; denote, depict, describe, designate, illustrate, picture, portray, render, show, sketch.

representative   n *lit:* commercial traveler, rep, salesperson; archetype, embodiment, epitome, exemplar, personification, type; agent, counselor, delegate, member of congress, spokesperson. **adj** *lit:* archetypal, characteristic, evocative, exemplary, symbolic, typical; chosen, delegated, elected.

repress   **vb** *lit:* check, control, crush, curb, master, overcome, quash, quell, subdue, subjugate, suppress; bottle up, hold back, inhibit, muffle, restrain, smother, stifle, swallow.

reprieve   n *lit:* abeyance, amnesty, deferment, pardon, postponement, remission, stay of execution. **vb** *lit:* grant a stay of execution to, let off the hook, pardon.

reproach   n *lit:* censure, rebuke, reprimand, reproof; discredit (to), disgrace (to). **vb** *lit:* censure, chide, condemn, rebuke, reprimand, scold, take to task, upbraid; be a discredit to, condemn.

reproduce **vb** *lit:* copy, duplicate, emulate, imitate, mirror, parallel, print, re-create, replicate, represent; breed, generate, multiply, procreate, proliferate, propagate, spawn.

reproduction **n** *lit:* copy, duplicate, facsimile, imitation, print, replica; breeding, generation, multiplication, procreation, proliferation, propagation.

repulsive **adj** *lit:* disgusting, distasteful, foul, hideous, loathsome, nauseating, obnoxious, odious, offensive, revolting, sickening, vile; adverse, antagonistic, incompatible, opposed.

reputable **adj** *lit:* creditable, estimable, honest, honorable, law-abiding, reliable, respectable, trustworthy, upright.

reputation **n** *lit:* character, credit, distinction, fame, name, renown, repute, standing, stature.

request **n** *lit:* appeal, application, call, demand, entreaty, petition, requisition, solicitation, suit, supplication. **vb** *lit:* appeal for, apply for, ask for, entreat, petition, seek, solicit, sue for, supplicate.

require **vb** *lit:* call for, demand, necessitate, take; lack, miss, need, want, wish for; bid, call upon, command, compel, constrain, instruct, oblige.

rescue **n** *lit:* extrication, liberation, recovery, relief, salvage, saving. **vb** *lit:* deliver, extricate, free, get out, recover, release, salvage, save, set free; redeem.

resemble **vb** *lit:* be like, be similar to, echo, look like, mirror, remind one of, take after.

resent **vb** *lit:* be angry about, begrudge, be offended by, dislike, grudge, object to, take amiss, take exception to, take umbrage at.

resentment **n** *lit:* anger, animosity, bitterness, grudge, ill feeling, indignation, irritation, pique, rancor, umbrage, vexation; envy.

reserve **n** *lit:* capital, fund, reservoir, savings, stockpile, supply; asylum, park, reservation, sanctuary; aloofness, constraint, coolness, formality, reluctance, reservation, restraint, reticence, shyness, taciturnity. **vb** *lit:* conserve, hoard, hold, keep back, preserve, put by, save, set aside, store, withhold; book, engage, retain, secure; defer, delay, postpone, put off.

residence   **n** *lit:* abode, domicile, dwelling, habitation, household, lodging, home, quarters; hall, manor, mansion, palace, seat; occupancy, sojourn, stay, tenancy.

resident   **n** *lit:* citizen, denizen, inhabitant, local, lodger, occupant, tenant. **adj** *lit:* local, neighborhood, settled.

resign   **vb** *lit:* hand in one's notice; leave, quit, vacate; abandon, relinquish, surrender, yield; commit (oneself to).

resigned   **adj** *lit:* long-suffering, patient, stoical, subdued, submissive; committed (to); defeatist, fatalistic.

resist   **vb** *lit:* battle against, combat, contend with, counteract, curb, defy, fight back, hinder, hold out against, oppose, repel, stand up to, struggle against, thwart, weather, withstand; abstain from, avoid, forgo, leave alone, refrain from.

resistance   **n** *lit:* contention, counteraction, defiance, hindrance, impediment, intransigence, opposition.

resolute   **adj** *lit:* bold, dedicated, determined, dogged, fixed, inflexible, obstinate, persevering, purposeful, relentless, set, staunch, steadfast, stubborn, tenacious, undaunted, unflinching, unwavering.

resolution   **n** *lit:* boldness, dedication, determination, doggedness, firmness, fortitude, obstinacy, perseverance, purpose, relentlessness, stamina, steadfastness, stubbornness, tenacity, willpower; aim, intention; decision, declaration, finding, verdict; motion, proposition; settlement; answer, denouement, outcome, solution, unraveling, working out.

resolve   **n** *lit:* conclusion, decision, design, objective, purpose, resolution, undertaking; boldness, courage, determination, firmness, resoluteness, resolution, steadfastness, willpower. **vb** *lit:* agree, conclude, decide, design, determine, fix, intend, make up one's mind, settle, undertake; answer, clear up, crack, elucidate, fathom, work out; banish, dispel, explain, remove; analyze, break down, disentangle, disintegrate, dissolve, reduce, separate, solve, unravel; alter, convert, transform, transmute.

resources n *lit:* assets, capital, funds, holdings, means, money, property, reserves, wealth, wherewithal.

respect n *lit:* admiration, appreciation, deference, esteem, recognition, regard, reverence; aspect, characteristic, detail, facet, matter, particular, point, sense; bearing, connection, reference, relation; compliments, good wishes, greetings, regards. **vb** *lit:* admire, adore, appreciate, defer to, honor, look up to, revere, set store by, think highly of, value, venerate; abide by, adhere to, comply with, heed, obey, observe, pay attention to, show consideration for.

respectable adj *lit:* admirable, decent, decorous, estimable, honest, proper, reputable, respected, upright, worthy; ample, appreciable, considerable, fair, goodly, reasonable, sizable, substantial, tidy, tolerable.

response n *lit:* acknowledgment, answer, comeback, feedback, reaction, rejoinder, reply, retort, riposte.

responsible adj *lit:* in authority, in charge, in control; accountable, answerable, bound, liable, under obligation; authoritative, decision-making, executive; at fault, culpable, guilty, to blame; adult, conscientious, dependable, level-headed, mature, rational, reliable, sensible, sober, stable, trustworthy.

rest n *lit:* calm, doze, inactivity, leisure, nap, relaxation, relief, repose, siesta, slumber, snooze, standstill, tranquility; break, breathing space, cessation, halt, interlude, interval, lull, pause, stop, time off, vacation; haven, refuge, retreat, shelter; base, prop, stand, support, trestle; excess, leftovers, others, remainder, remains, residue, surplus. **vb** *lit:* be at ease, doze, have a snooze, idle, laze, lie down, nap, relax, sit down, sleep, slumber; lay, lean, lie, prop, recline, repose, stretch out; break off, cease, come to a standstill, discontinue, halt, knock off, stop, take a breather; be based, be founded, depend, hang, hinge, rely; be left, go on being, keep, remain, stay.

restless adj *lit:* active, bustling, footloose, inconstant, irresolute, nomadic, roving, transient, unsettled, unsteady, wandering; agitated, anxious, edgy, fidgeting, fretful, ill at ease, jumpy, nervous, on edge, restive, troubled, uneasy, worried.

restoration n *lit:* reconstruction, recovery, refurbishing, rejuvenation, renewal, renovation, repair, revival; reestablishment, reinstatement, restitution, return.

restraint   n *lit:* coercion, compulsion, confines, control, curtailment, grip, hindrance, hold, inhibition, moderation, restriction, self-discipline, suppression; bonds, captivity, confinement, detention, fetters, imprisonment, manacles, pinions, straitjacket; ban, check, curb, embargo, limitation, rein, taboo.

restrict   vb *lit:* bound, confine, contain, cramp, demarcate, hamper, handicap, hem in, impede, inhibit, limit, regulate, restrain.

restriction   n *lit:* check, condition, confinement, constraint, control, curb, demarcation, handicap, inhibition, limitation, regulation, restraint, rule, stipulation.

result   n *lit:* conclusion, consequence, decision, effect, end, event, issue, outcome, reaction, sequel, termination. vb *lit:* appear, arise, derive, develop, emanate, ensue, eventuate, follow, happen, issue, spring, turn out; culminate (in), end (in), terminate (in).

resume   vb *lit:* begin again, continue, go on, proceed, recommence, reinstitute, reopen, restart; assume again, reoccupy, take up again.

retain   vb *lit:* absorb, detain, grasp, grip, hang onto, hold fast, keep, maintain, preserve, reserve, save; bear in mind, keep in mind, memorize, recall, remember; commission, employ, engage, hire.

retard   vb *lit:* arrest, check, clog, decelerate, defer, delay, encumber, handicap, hinder, impede, obstruct, set back, slow down, stall.

retire   vb *lit:* be pensioned off, give up work; absent oneself, depart, exit, leave, remove, withdraw; go to bed, go to sleep, hit the sack, turn in; ebb, fall back, give ground, give way, pull out, recede, retreat.

retiring   adj *lit:* bashful, coy, demure, meek, modest, quiet, reclusive, reserved, reticent, self-effacing, shy, timorous, unassuming.

retreat   n *lit:* departure, ebb, evacuation, flight, withdrawal; den, haunt, hideaway, privacy, resort, sanctuary, seclusion. vb *lit:* back away, depart, draw back, ebb, give ground, leave, pull back, recede, retire, turn tail, withdraw.

retrieve vb *lit:* fetch back, get back, recapture, recoup, recover, regain, rescue, restore, salvage, win back.

return n *lit:* homecoming, reappearance, recurrence, retreat, reversion; reestablishment, reinstatement, restoration; advantage, benefit, gain, interest, proceeds, profit, revenue, takings, yield; compensation, reciprocation, recompense, reparation, repayment, retaliation, reward; account, report, statement, summary; answer, comeback, rejoinder, reply, retort, riposte. vb *lit:* come back, go back, reappear, recoil, recur, retreat, revert, turn back; convey, give back, reestablish, reinstate, remit, replace, restore, send back, transmit; pay back, reciprocate, recompense, refund, reimburse, repay, requite; bring in, earn, make, net, yield; answer, come back (with), rejoin, reply, retort; choose, pick, vote in; announce, arrive at, deliver, render, report, submit.

reveal vb *lit:* announce, betray, disclose, divulge, give away, impart, leak, let out, let slip, make public, proclaim, tell; bare, display, exhibit, lay bare, manifest, show, uncover, unearth, unveil.

revel n *lit:* bacchanal, carousal, celebration, debauch, festivity, merrymaking, saturnalia, spree. vb *lit:* bask (in), delight (in), gloat (in), indulge (in), rejoice (in), relish (in), take pleasure (in), wallow (in); carouse, go on a spree, live it up, rave, roister, whoop it up.

revenge n *lit:* reprisal, requital, retaliation, retribution, vengeance, vindictiveness. vb *lit:* avenge, repay, requite, retaliate, take revenge for, vindicate.

reverse n *lit:* antithesis, contradiction, contrary, converse, opposite; back, flip side, other side, rear, verso, wrong side; adversity, affliction, blow, check, defeat, disappointment, failure, misadventure, misfortune, mishap, repulse, setback, vicissitude. vb *lit:* invert, transpose, turn over, turn around, upend; alter, annul, cancel, change, invalidate, negate, overrule, overthrow, quash, repeal, retract, set aside, undo; back, backtrack, go backward, retreat. adj *lit:* back to front, backward, contrary, converse, inverted, opposite.

review n *lit:* analysis, examination, report, scrutiny, study, survey; commentary, criticism, evaluation, judgment, notice; journal, magazine, periodical; fresh look, reassessment, recapitulation, rethink, retrospect, revision; *spec:* inspection, march past, parade, procession. vb *lit:* go over again, reassess, recapitulate, reconsider, reevaluate, rethink, revise, think over; call to mind, recall, recollect, reflect on, summon up; assess, criticize, discuss, evaluate, judge, read through, scrutinize, study, weigh.

revive **vb** *lit:* animate, awaken, bring round, cheer, come round, comfort, invigorate, quicken, rally, recover, rekindle, restore, resuscitate, revitalize, rouse.

revolt **n** *lit:* defection, insurgency, insurrection, mutiny, rebellion, revolution, rising, sedition, uprising. **vb** *lit:* defect, mutiny, rebel, resist, rise, take up arms (against); disgust, nauseate, offend, repel, repulse, shock, sicken.

revolting **adj** *lit:* abhorrent, abominable, appalling, disgusting, distasteful, horrid, loathsome, nasty, nauseating, obnoxious, offensive, repellent, repugnant, repulsive, shocking, sickening.

revolution **n** *lit:* coup d'état, insurgency, mutiny, rebellion, revolt, uprising; drastic change, innovation, metamorphosis, reformation, shift, transformation, upheaval; circle, circuit, cycle, gyration, orbit, rotation, spin, turn, whirl.

revolutionary **n** *lit:* insurgent, insurrectionist, mutineer, rebel, revolutionist. **adj** *lit:* extremist, insurgent, mutinous, radical, rebel, seditious, subversive; avant-garde, different, drastic, experimental, fundamental, innovative, novel, progressive, radical, thoroughgoing.

reward **n** *lit:* benefit, bonus, compensation, gain, merit, payment, premium, profit, recompense, remuneration, requital, return, wages; just deserts, retribution. **vb** *lit:* compensate, honor, recompense, remunerate, repay, requite.

rich **n** *lit:* plutocracy; affluent, moneyed, opulent, wealthy, well off. **adj** *lit:* affluent, loaded, made of money, opulent, prosperous, wealthy, well-off, well-to-do; abounding, productive, well-provided, well-stocked, well-supplied; abundant, ample, copious, exuberant, fecund, fertile, fruitful, lush, plentiful, prolific; costly, elaborate, expensive, exquisite, lavish, precious, priceless, splendid, sumptuous, superb, valuable; creamy, fatty, full-bodied, heavy, juicy, luscious, savoury, succulent, sweet, tasty; bright, deep, intense, strong, vibrant, vivid; dulcet, full, mellifluous, mellow, resonant; amusing, funny, hilarious, humorous, ludicrous, ridiculous, side-splitting.

ridicule **n** *lit:* banter, chaff, derision, gibe, jeer, mockery, raillery, sarcasm, satire, scorn, sneer, taunting. **vb** *lit:* banter, caricature, deride, humiliate, jeer, lampoon, make fun of, mock, parody, poke fun at, pooh-pooh, satirize, scoff, sneer, taunt.

ridiculous   adj *lit:* absurd, contemptible, derisory, farcical, foolish, hilarious, laughable, ludicrous, outrageous, preposterous, silly, unbelievable.

right   n *lit:* authority, business, claim, due, interest, liberty, license, permission, power, prerogative, privilege; equity, good, honor, integrity, legality, morality, propriety, reason, rectitude, truth, uprightness, virtue. **vb** *lit:* compensate for, fix, rectify, repair, settle, sort out, vindicate. **adj** *lit:* equitable, ethical, fair, good, honorable, just, lawful, moral, proper, righteous, true, upright, virtuous; accurate, admissible, authentic, correct, exact, factual, genuine, precise, satisfactory, sound, valid; advantageous, appropriate, becoming, deserved, done, due, fitting, ideal, opportune, propitious, rightful, seemly, suitable; all there, balanced, fit, healthy, normal, rational, reasonable, sane, unimpaired, well; conservative, reactionary; absolute, complete, out-and-out, thorough, utter. **adv** *lit:* accurately, exactly, factually, genuinely, truly; appropriately, aptly, fittingly, properly, suitably; directly, immediately, instantly, promptly, quickly, straightaway; bang, precisely, squarely; absolutely, altogether, completely, entirely, quite, thoroughly, totally, utterly; fairly, honestly, justly, morally, virtuously; advantageously, beneficially, favorably, well.

rigorous   adj *lit:* austere, challenging, demanding, exacting, firm, hard, rigid, severe, tough; accurate, conscientious, meticulous, nice, precise, punctilious, scrupulous, thorough; bad, bleak, extreme, harsh, inhospitable.

ring   n *lit:* band, circle, circuit, halo, hoop, loop, round; arena, circus, rink; association, cabal, cartel, cell, clique, coterie, gang, group, mob, organization, syndicate; chime, knell, peal. **vb** *lit:* encircle, enclose, encompass, girdle, hem in, seal off, surround; chime, clang, peal, resound, reverberate, sound, toll.

riot   n *lit:* anarchy, commotion, confusion, disorder, disturbance, fray, lawlessness, quarrel, row, strife, tumult, turmoil, uproar; boisterousness, excess, frolic, high jinks, jollification, merrymaking, revelry, romp; display, extravaganza, show, splash. **vb** *lit:* go on the rampage, raise an uproar, run riot, take to the streets; carouse, cut loose, frolic, go on a binge, make merry, revel, roister, romp.

rip n *lit:* cut, gash, hole, rent, tear; current, rough water; cheat (off), con (off), loot (off), rifle (off). **vb** *lit:* cut, pull apart, rend, sunder, tear; strip, wrench, wrest; come asunder, open up, split; move fast, rush along.

ripe adj *lit:* fully developed, mature, mellow, ready, ripened; accomplished, complete, finished, in readiness, perfect, prepared; auspicious, favorable, ideal, opportune, right, suitable, timely.

rise n *lit:* advance, ascent, climb, improvement, increase, upsurge, upward turn; advancement, aggrandizement, progress, promotion; acclivity, elevation, hillock, incline, upward slope. **vb** *lit:* arise, get out of bed, get up, stand up, surface; ascend, climb, go up, grow, improve, increase, lift, mount, move up, swell, wax; advance, be promoted, get on, get somewhere, go places, progress, prosper, work one's way up; appear, become apparent, crop up, emanate, emerge, happen, issue, occur, turn up; mount the barricades, mutiny, rebel, resist, revolt, take up arms.

rival n *lit:* adversary, antagonist, challenger, contender, contestant, opponent; compeer, equal, equivalent, fellow, match, peer. **vb** *lit:* be a match for, come up to, compare with, compete, contend, emulate, equal, match, measure up to, oppose, vie with. **adj** *lit:* competing, competitive, conflicting, emulating, opposed, opposing.

road n *lit:* avenue, course, direction, highway, lane, pathway, route, street, thoroughfare, track.

roast vb *lit:* bake, cook; burn, calcine, desiccate, prepare by heating; *fig:* banter, chaff, make fun of, ridicule; criticize, reprove.

rob vb *lit:* burgle, cheat, con, defraud, deprive, dispossess, hold up, loot, pillage, plunder, raid, ransack, rifle, rip off, sack, swindle.

robbery n *lit:* burglary, depredation, embezzlement, filching, fraud, holdup, larceny, pillage, plunder, raid, rapine, rip-off, stealing, stickup, swindle, theft.

robust adj *lit:* athletic, brawny, fit, hale, hardy, hearty, husky, in fine fettle, muscular, rugged, sinewy, sound, staunch, stout, strapping, strong, sturdy, tough, vigorous, well; boisterous, coarse, earthy, raw, roisterous, rollicking, rough, rude, unsubtle; commonsensical, down-to-earth, hard-headed, practical, sensible, straightforward.

rock n *lit:* boulder, stone; anchor, bulwark, cornerstone, foundation, mainstay, protection, support. **vb** *lit:* lurch, reel, roll, sway, swing, toss, wobble; astonish, astound, daze, dumbfound, jar, shake, shock, stagger, surprise.

rogue n *lit:* blackguard, charlatan, cheat, con artist, crook, deceiver, fraud, mountebank, ne'er-do-well, rapscallion, rascal, reprobate, scamp, scoundrel, swindler, villain; mutant, sport, variant. **adj** *lit:* maverick, outcast, savage, wild; breakaway, disruptive, mischievous; defective, mutant, variant.

roll n *lit:* cycle, gyration, reel, revolution, rotation, run, spin, turn, twirl, wheel, whirl; ball, bobbin, cylinder, scroll, spool; annals, catalog, census, chronicle, directory, index, inventory, list, record, register, schedule, table; billowing, lurching, rocking, rolling, tossing, undulation, wallowing; boom, drumming, grumble, resonance, reverberation, roar, rumble, thunder. **vb** *lit:* elapse, flow, go past, gyrate, pass, pivot, reel, revolve, rock, rotate, run, spin, swivel, turn, twirl, undulate, wheel, whirl; coil, curl, enfold, entwine, furl, twist, wind, wrap; even, flatten, level, smooth, spread; billow, lurch, sway, swing, toss, tumble, wallow; lumber, stagger, swagger, waddle.

romantic adj *lit:* amorous, mushy, passionate, sentimental, sloppy, tender; charming, exciting, fascinating, glamorous, mysterious, nostalgic, dreamy, high-flown, idealistic, starry-eyed, unrealistic, utopian, visionary, whimsical; chimerical, exaggerated, extravagant, fairy-tale, fanciful, fictitious, idyllic, imaginary, legendary, made-up, wild.

root n *lit:* radicle, radix, rhizome, tuber; base, cause, core, crux, derivation, essence, foundation, heart, mainspring, nub, nucleus, occasion, source, starting point; beginnings, origins. **vb** *lit:* anchor, become established, entrench, fasten, fix, ground, implant, moor, set, stick, take root.

rot n *lit:* blight, canker, corrosion, decay, decomposition, disintegration, mould, putrefaction; balderdash, bosh, bunkum, claptrap, drivel, hogwash, moonshine, nonsense, poppycock, rubbish, twaddle. **vb** *lit:* corrode, corrupt, crumble, decay, decompose, deteriorate, disintegrate, fester, go bad, moulder, perish, putrefy; decline, degenerate, languish, waste away, wither away.

rotten   **adj** *lit:* bad, corroded, crumbling, decaying, decomposed, disintegrating, festering, fetid, foul, moldering, putrescent, putrid, rank, sour, unsound; bent, corrupt, crooked, degenerate, dishonest, disloyal, immoral, mercenary, perfidious, treacherous, untrustworthy, venal; base, contemptible, despicable, dirty, disagreeable, filthy, mean, nasty, scurrilous, vile, vicious; deplorable, disappointing, regrettable, unfortunate, unlucky; crummy, inadequate, inferior, lousy, low-grade, poor, sorry, substandard, unacceptable, unsatisfactory; below par, ill, off-color, poorly, rough, sick, under the weather.

rough   **n** *lit:* draft, outline, preliminary sketch; bruiser, bully, ruffian, thug. **vb** *lit:* block out, draft out, outline, sketch out; bash up, beat up, thrash up. **adj** *lit:* broken, bumpy, craggy, jagged, rocky, rugged, stony, uneven; bristly, coarse, dishevelled, fuzzy, hairy, shaggy, tangled, tousled, uncut; agitated, boisterous, choppy, stormy, tempestuous, turbulent, wild; bluff, blunt, brusque, churlish, curt, discourteous, ill-mannered, impolite, indelicate, loutish, rude, unceremonious, uncouth, unmannerly, unpolished, unrefined; cruel, drastic, extreme, harsh, nasty, severe, sharp, tough, unjust, violent; below par, ill, off-color, poorly, rotten, unwell, upset; cacophonous, discordant, grating, gruff, husky, inharmonious, jarring, rasping, raucous; arduous, austere, hard, Spartan, uncomfortable; basic, crude, cursory, hasty, incomplete, quick, raw, rudimentary, sketchy, unfinished, untutored; uncut, unprocessed, unwrought; approximate, estimated, foggy, general, hazy, inexact, vague.

roughly   **adv** *lit:* irregularly, unevenly; boisterously, choppily, turbulently, wildly; bluntly, brusquely, coarsely, curtly, impolitely, rudely, unceremoniously, ungraciously; drastically, extremely, hardly, severely, sharply, unjustly, unpleasantly, violently; discordantly, gruffly, harshly, raucously; arduously, toughly, uncomfortably; basically, crudely, hastily, imperfectly, quickly, sketchily; approximately, generally, hazily, inexactly, vaguely.

round   **n** *lit:* circle, disc, globe, orb, ring, sphere; bout, cycle, sequence, series, session; division, lap, level, period, stage; beat, circuit, compass, course, routine, schedule, turn; bullet, cartridge, discharge, shot. **vb** *lit:* bypass, circle, encircle, flank, skirt, turn. **adj** *lit:* annular, bowed, bulbous, circular, curved, cylindrical, disc-shaped, globular, orbicular, rotund, spherical; complete, entire, solid, unbroken, whole; ample, bountiful, considerable, generous, large, substantial; fleshy, full, plump, roly-poly, rounded; mellifluous, resonant, rich, sonorous; blunt, candid, frank, outspoken, plain, straightforward.

rouse vb *lit:* awaken, get up, rise, wake up; agitate, animate, bestir, disturb, excite, exhilarate, get going, incite, instigate, move, provoke, startle, stimulate, stir, whip up.

rout n *lit:* beating, debacle, defeat, drubbing, hiding, licking, overthrow, shambles, thrashing, trouncing. **vb** *lit:* beat, chase, conquer, crush, defeat, destroy, dispel, drive off, drub, lick, overpower, overthrow, scatter, thrash, trounce.

routine n *lit:* custom, formula, grind, method, pattern, practice, procedure, usage, way, wont; act, bit, line, performance, piece. **adj** *lit:* conventional, customary, everyday, familiar, normal, ordinary, standard, typical, usual, wonted; boring, dull, hackneyed, humdrum, run-of-the-mill, tedious, tiresome, unimaginative, unoriginal.

row n *lit:* bank, column, file, line, range, sequence, series, string, tier; altercation, brawl, commotion, controversy, disturbance, fracas, fuss, quarrel, racket, rumpus, squabble, tiff, trouble, uproar; castigation, dressing-down, lecture, reprimand, rollicking, telling-off. **vb** *lit:* paddle, scull; argue, brawl, dispute, fight, squabble, wrangle.

rub n *lit:* caress, kneading, massage, polish, stroke, wipe; catch, difficulty, drawback, hindrance, hitch, impediment, obstacle, problem, snag. **vb** *lit:* abrade, caress, chafe, clean, grate, knead, massage, polish, scour, scrape, shine, smooth, stroke, wipe; apply, smear, spread.

rubbish n *lit:* debris, dross, garbage, junk, litter, refuse, scrap, trash, waste; balderdash, bunkum, claptrap, drivel, gibberish, moonshine, nonsense, piffle, poppycock, rot, twaddle.

rude adj *lit:* abrupt, abusive, blunt, brusque, churlish, curt, ill-mannered, impertinent, impudent, insolent, offhand, peremptory, unmannerly; boorish, brutish, coarse, gross, loutish, oafish, obscene, rough, scurrilous, uncouth, ungracious, vulgar; artless, crude, makeshift, primitive, roughly made, simple; harsh, sharp, startling, sudden, unpleasant.

ruin n *lit:* bankruptcy, breakdown, collapse, crash, damage, decay, destitution, devastation, disrepair, downfall, failure, havoc, insolvency, overthrow, ruination, the end, undoing, wreckage. **vb** *lit:* bankrupt, break, bring down, crush, defeat, demolish, devastate, impoverish, lay waste, overturn, raze, shatter, smash, wreck; botch, damage, injure, make a mess of, mangle, mar, spoil.

rule n *lit:* axiom, canon, criterion, decree, guideline, law, maxim, ordinance, precept, principle, regulation, ruling, standard, tenet; administration, authority, command, control, domination, government, leadership, power, regime, reign, supremacy, sway; condition, convention, custom, habit, practice, procedure, routine, wont; course, formula, method, policy, way. **vb** *lit:* administer, command, control, dominate, govern, lead, manage, regulate, reign; adjudicate, decide, decree, determine, establish, find, judge, pronounce, resolve, settle; be customary, hold sway, predominate, prevail.

rumor n *lit:* buzz, gossip, hearsay, report, talk, tidings, whisper, word. **vb** *lit:* circulate, gossip, pass around, publish, put about, report, say, tell, whisper.

run n *lit:* dash, gallop, jog, race, rush, sprint, spurt; drive, excursion, lift, outing, ride, round, trip; chain, course, cycle, passage, period, season, sequence, series, spell, stretch, string; category, class, kind, sort, type, variety; application, demand, pressure; rip, snag, tear; current, direction, drift, flow, motion, path, stream, tendency, tide, trend, sway; coop, enclosure, pen. **vb** *lit:* bolt, career, dart, dash, gallop, hasten, hotfoot, hurry, jog, race, rush, scamper, scurry, speed, sprint; abscond, beat it, clear out, depart, escape, flee, make off, take off, take to one's heels; course, glide, go, move, pass, roll, skim; bear, carry, drive, maneuver, transport; operate, ply; function, perform, tick, work; administer, control, direct, head, look after, manage, mastermind, oversee, regulate, supervise, take care of; continue, extend, last, lie, proceed, range, reach, stretch; cascade, discharge, flow, gush, issue, leak, pour, spill, stream; dissolve, fuse, liquefy, melt, turn to liquid; be diffused, mix, spread; come apart, tear, unravel; be current, circulate, climb, creep, go round, trail; display, feature, print, publish; be a candidate, challenge, contend, stand, take part; bootleg, deal in, smuggle, sneak, traffic in.

rush n *lit:* dash, hurry, race, scramble; assault, charge, onslaught, storm; reed. **vb** *lit:* career, dart, dash, fly, hurry, race, run, scramble, scurry, speed; attack, charge (at), storm. **adj** *lit:* emergency, urgent; hasty, hurried, quick, rapid.

S

sabotage n *lit:* damage, destruction, disruption, subversion, treachery. **vb** *lit:* cripple, damage, destroy, disable, disrupt, incapacitate, subvert, undermine, vandalize, wreck.

sack n *lit:* bag; bagful; loose-hanging coat, trail; wine; dismissal, termination of employment, the axe, the boot, the chop; *fig:* despoliation, destruction, devastation, looting, pillage, plunder, ravage, ruin. **vb** *lit:* axe, discharge, dismiss, fire, kick out; *fig:* demolish, despoil, destroy, devastate, lay waste, loot, maraud, pillage, plunder, raid, ravage, rifle, ruin, spoil.

sacred adj *lit:* blessed, consecrated, hallowed, holy, revered, sanctified, venerable; invulnerable, precious, protected, sacrosanct, secure; holy, solemn.

sacrifice n *lit:* burnt offering, hecatomb, immolation, oblation; loss, renunciation, surrender. **vb** *lit:* immolate, offer, forego, forfeit, give up, immolate, let go, lose, offer, surrender.

sad adj *lit:* blue, cheerless, depressed, disconsolate, dismal, doleful, down, downcast, down in the dumps, gloomy, glum, heavyhearted, low, lugubrious, melancholy, mournful, sick at heart, somber, tearful, wistful, woebegone; *fig:* calamitous, dark, depressing, disastrous, grievous, heartrending, moving, pathetic, pitiful, sorry, tearful, tragic, upsetting; bad, deplorable, distressing, lamentable, miserable, regrettable, serious, unfortunate, unhappy, unsatisfactory, wretched.

saddle vb *lit:* burden, charge, encumber, load, lumber, task, tax.

safe n *lit:* coffer, repository, safe-deposit box, strongbox. **adj** *lit:* impregnable, intact, protected, secure, unharmed, unscathed; harmless, innocuous, nontoxic, pure, unpolluted, wholesome; bearish, cautious, circumspect, conservative, dependable, discreet, prudent, realistic, reliable, sure, trustworthy, unadventurous; certain, risk-free, secure, sound.

sail vb *lit:* embark, get under way, put to sea, set sail; captain, cruise, navigate, pilot, skipper, steer, voyage; *fig:* drift, float, fly, glide, shoot, skim, soar, sweep, wing.

sailor n *lit:* jack-tar, lascar, mariner, matelot, navigator, salt, sea dog, seafarer, seaman, tar.

saintly adj *lit:* angelic, blessed, devout, god-fearing, godly, pious, righteous, sainted, virtuous, worthy.

salary n *lit:* earnings, emolument, income, pay, remuneration, stipend.

sally n *lit:* foray, incursion, offensive, raid, sortie, thrust; *fig:* crack, jest, joke, quip, retort, riposte, wisecrack, witticism; escapade, excursion, frolic, jaunt, trip. **vb** *lit:* erupt, go forth, issue, rush, set out, surge.

salty adj *lit:* brackish, saline, salt, salted; *fig:* colorful, humorous, lively, piquant, pungent, racy, snappy, spicy, tangy, witty, zestful.

salute n *lit:* address, greeting, obeisance, recognition, salutation, tribute. **vb** *lit:* acknowledge, address, greet, hail, kiss, welcome; *fig:* honor, pay tribute to, recognize.

salvage vb *lit:* glean, recover, redeem, rescue, retrieve, save.

salve n *lit:* ointment, unguent; *fig:* balm, flattery, praise. **vb** *lit:* anoint; smear; *fig:* make good, soothe; account for, dispose of, harmonize, vindicate; *spec:* save (cargo).

same adj *lit:* aforementioned, selfsame, very; alike, corresponding, duplicate, equivalent, identical, indistinguishable, interchangeable, synonymous; *fig:* consistent, constant, invariable, unaltered, unchanged, unfailing, unvarying.

sample n *lit:* cross section, example, illustration, indication, instance, model, pattern, representative, sign, specimen. **vb** *lit:* experience, inspect, partake of, taste, test, try. **adj** *lit:* illustrative, pilot, representative, specimen, test, trial.

sanction n *lit:* allowance, approbation, approval, authority, authorization, backing, confirmation, endorsement, ratification, seal of approval, support; *fig:* ban, boycott, embargo, penalty. **vb** *lit:* allow, approve, authorize, back, countenance, endorse, permit, support, vouch for; confirm, ratify, warrant.

sanctuary n *lit:* altar, church, sanctum, shrine, temple; *fig:* asylum, haven, protection, refuge, retreat, shelter; conservation area, nature reserve.

sane   adj   *lit:* lucid, normal, of sound mind, rational; *fig:* balanced, judicious, levelheaded, moderate, reasonable, sensible, sober, sound.

sanity   n   *lit:* mental health, normality, rationality, reason, right mind, stability; *fig:* common sense, good sense, judiciousness, levelheadedness, sense.

sap   n   *lit:* essence, lifeblood, vital fluid; *fig:* chump, fool, jerk, nincompoop, ninny, nitwit, noodle, simpleton, twit, weakling.   vb   *lit:* bleed, deplete, drain, enervate, erode, exhaust, undermine, weaken, wear down.

sarcastic   adj   *lit:* acerbic, acrimonious, backhanded, biting, caustic, contemptuous, cutting, cynical, derisive, disparaging, ironic, mocking, mordant, sardonic, satirical, sharp, sneering, taunting.

satanic   adj   *lit:* accursed, demoniac, demonic, devilish, diabolic, evil, fiendish, hellish, infernal, iniquitous, malevolent, malignant, wicked.

satisfactory   adj   *lit:* acceptable, adequate, average, competent, fair, passable, sufficient.

satisfy   vb   *lit:* appease, assuage, content, fill, gratify, indulge, mollify, pacify, please, quench, sate, satiate, slake, surfeit; answer, be sufficient, fulfill, meet, qualify, serve, suffice; assure, convince, dispel doubts, persuade, quiet, reassure; comply with, discharge, pay off, settle, square up; *fig:* atone, compensate, indemnify, make good, recompense, remunerate, requite.

sauce   n   *lit:* dressing, gravy, ketchup, relish, topping; *fig:* brass, cheekiness, disrespect, impertinence, impudence, insolence, lip, nerve, rudeness.

saucy   adj   *fig:* cheeky, disrespectful, flippant, forward, impertinent, impudent, insolent, pert, presumptuous, rude; dashing, jaunty, natty, perky, rakish, smart, sporty.

saunter   n   *lit:* amble, constitutional, promenade, ramble, stroll, turn, walk.   vb   *lit:* amble, dally, linger, loiter, mosey, ramble, roam, stroll, tarry, wander.

savage   n   *lit:* aboriginal, heathen, primitive; *fig:* barbarian, boor, roughneck; beast, brute, fiend, monster.   vb   *lit:* attack, lacerate, mangle, maul.   adj   *lit:* feral, rough, rugged, uncivilized, uncultivated, untamed, wild; *fig:* barbarous, beastly, bestial, bloodthirsty, brutal, brutish, cruel, devilish, diabolical, ferocious, fierce, inhuman, merciless, murderous, ravening, ruthless, sadistic, vicious; primitive, unspoiled.

save   **vb** *lit:* bail out, deliver, free, liberate, redeem, rescue, salvage, set free; be frugal, be thrifty, collect, economize, hide away, hoard, hold, husband, lay by, put by, reserve, set aside, store, treasure up; *fig:* conserve, guard, keep safe, look after, preserve, protect, safeguard, shield; hinder, obviate, prevent, rule out, spare.

say   **n** *lit:* crack, turn to speak, voice, vote; *fig:* authority, influence, power, sway, weight. **vb** *lit:* add, affirm, announce, assert, declare, maintain, mention, pronounce, put into words, remark, speak, state, utter, voice; answer, disclose, divulge, make known, reply, respond, reveal, tell; allege, claim, noise abroad, put about, rumor, suggest; *fig:* deliver, do, orate, perform, read, recite, rehearse, render, repeat; assume, conjecture, dare say, estimate, imagine, judge, presume, suppose, surmise; communicate, convey, express, imply.

saying   **n** *lit:* adage, aphorism, apothegm, axiom, byword, dictum, maxim, proverb, saw.

scale   **n** *lit:* flake, lamina, layer, plate; calibration, degrees, gamut, gradation, graduation, hierarchy, ladder, pecking order, ranking, register, sequence, series, spectrum, spread, steps; *fig:* proportion, ratio; degree, extent, range, reach, scope, way. **vb** *lit:* ascend, clamber, climb, escalate, surmount; *fig:* adjust, calibrate, proportion, regulate.

scamper   **vb** *lit:* dart, dash, fly, hasten, romp, run, scoot, scurry, scuttle, sprint.

scan   **vb** *lit:* browse, check, examine, glance over, investigate, scour, scrutinize, search, size up, survey, sweep.

scandalous   **adj** *lit:* atrocious, disgraceful, disreputable, infamous, monstrous, odious, opprobrious, outrageous, shameful, shocking, unseemly; *fig:* defamatory, libelous, scurrilous, slanderous, untrue.

scanty   **adj** *lit:* bare, deficient, exiguous, inadequate, insufficient, meager, narrow, poor, restricted, scant, skimpy, slender, sparing, sparse, thin.

scarcely adv *lit:* barely, hardly, only just; *fig:* by no means, hardly, not at all, on no account, under no circumstances.

scarcity n *lit:* dearth, deficiency, famine, insufficiency, lack, paucity, rareness, shortage, undersupply, want.

scare n *lit:* alarm, alert, fright, panic, shock, start, terror. **vb** *lit:* alarm, daunt, dismay, frighten, give someone a turn, intimidate, panic, put the wind up someone, shock, startle, terrify, terrorize.

scathing adj *lit:* painful, biting, brutal, caustic, critical, cutting, harsh, mordant, sarcastic, scornful, searing, trenchant, withering.

scatter vb *lit:* broadcast, diffuse, disseminate, fling, litter, sew, shower, spread, sprinkle, strew; *fig:* disband, dispel, disperse, dissipate, separate.

scene n *lit:* display, exhibition, pageant, representation, show, sight, spectacle, tableau; area, locality, place, position, site, situation, spot, whereabouts; backdrop, background, set, setting; act, division, episode, incident, part, stage; landscape, panorama, prospect, view, vista; *fig:* commotion, confrontation, fuss, row, tantrum, to-do; arena, business, environment, field of interest, milieu, world.

scent n *lit:* aroma, bouquet, fragrance, nose, odor, perfume, redolence, smell; *fig:* spoor, track, trail. **vb** *lit:* detect, discern, get wind of, nose out, recognize, sense, smell, sniff, sniff out.

schedule n *lit:* agenda, calendar, catalog, inventory, itinerary, plan, program, timetable. **vb** *lit:* appoint, arrange, be due, book, organize, plan, program, time.

scheme n *lit:* contrivance, course of action, design, device, plan, program, project, proposal, strategy, system, tactics, theory; arrangement, blueprint, chart, codification, diagram, disposition, draft, layout, outline, pattern, schedule, system; *fig:* conspiracy, dodge, game, intrigue, machinations, maneuver, plot, ploy, ruse, shift, stratagem, subterfuge. **vb** *lit:* contrive, design, devise, imagine, lay plans, project, work out; *fig:* collude, conspire, intrigue, machinate, maneuver, plot, wheel and deal.

school n *lit:* academy, alma mater, college, discipline, faculty, institute, institution, seminary; *fig:* adherents, circle, class, clique, denomination, devotees, disciples, faction, followers, following, group, pupils, sect, set;

creed, faith, outlook, persuasion, stamp, way of life. **vb** *lit:* coach, discipline, drill, educate, indoctrinate, instruct, prepare, prime, teach, train, tutor, verse.

scintillating   adj *lit:* animated, bright, brilliant, dazzling, ebullient, glittering, lively, sparkling, stimulating, witty.

scoff   vb *lit:* belittle, deride, despise, flout, gibe, jeer, knock, mock, poke fun at, pooh-pooh, revile, ridicule, scorn, sneer, taunt, twit.

scold   n *lit:* nag, shrew, termagant, Xanthippe. **vb** *lit:* berate, blame, castigate, censure, chide, find fault with, lecture, nag, rate, rebuke, remonstrate with, reprimand, reproach, tell off, tick off, upbraid, vituperate.

scope   n *lit:* area, capacity, compass, confines, extent, freedom, latitude, liberty, opportunity, orbit, outlook, purview, range, reach, room, space, span, sphere.

scorch   vb *lit:* blacken, blister, burn, char, parch, roast, sear, shrivel, singe, wither.

score   n *lit:* grade, mark, outcome, points, record, result, total; the facts, the setup, the situation, the truth; crowds, droves, hosts, hundreds, legions, lots, masses, millions, multitudes, myriads, swarms; *fig:* account, basis, ground, reason; a bone to pick, grievance, grudge, injury, injustice, wrong; amount due, bill, charge, debt, obligation, reckoning, tally, total; *spec:* musical composition. **vb** *lit:* achieve, amass, gain, make, notch up, win; count, keep count, record, register, tally; crosshatch, cut, deface, gouge, graze, indent, mar, mark, nick, notch, scrape, scratch, slash; cross out, put a line through, strike out; gain an advantage, go down well with (someone), impress, make an impact, make a point, put oneself across, triumph; *spec:* adapt, arrange, orchestrate, set.

scorn   n *lit:* contempt, derision, disdain, mockery, sarcasm, scornfulness, slight, sneer. **vb** *lit:* be above, consider beneath one, contemn, deride, disdain, flout, hold in contempt, look down on, make fun of, scoff at, slight, sneer at, spurn.

scotch   vb *lit:* crush, eradicate, stamp out; foil, frustrate, prevent, thwart.

scour vb *lit:* abrade, rub, scrape clean, scrub; hose, syringe; burnish, polish; *fig:* beat, comb, rake, search.

scowl n *lit:* frown, glower, grimace, pout. vb *lit:* frown, glower, pout, snarl.

scramble n *lit:* hassle, race, rush, struggle, tussle; affray, commotion, melee, scrimmage; jumble, mess, muddle; hard ascent, stiff climb; *spec:* emergency takeoff. vb *lit:* jump, leap, race, rush, struggle; elbow, jostle, push; clamber, climb, scrabble; confuse, jumble, mix up, shuffle; encode.

scrap n *lit:* bit, crumb, fragment, morsel, part, piece, shred, sliver; leaving, leftover; junk, waste; affray, battle, brawl, fight, quarrel, row, scrimmage, scuffle, set-to, skirmish, wrangle. vb *lit:* abandon, discard, ditch, drop, write off; chuck out, get rid of, throw away; bicker, brawl, fight, quarrel, scuffle, wrangle.

scrape n *lit:* abrasion, dent, graze, rub, scratch, scuff mark; depression, excavation, hollow, pit; *fig:* fix, hole, jam, mess, plight, predicament. vb *lit:* abrade, dent, graze, scratch, scuff; rub, scour, scrub; file, grind, rasp; grate, screech, squeak; shave; excavate, hollow out; *fig:* put together, save up.

scratch n *lit:* abrasion, graze, laceration, mark, rip, scrape, tear; standard. vb *lit:* claw, etch, incise, lacerate, rip, rend, score, scrape, tear; scrawl; *fig:* cancel, delete, eliminate, rub; strike off; withdraw. adj *lit:* casual, impromptu, improvised, rough.

scrawny adj *lit:* bony, emaciated, gaunt, lean, scraggy, skeletal, skinny, spindly, thin, underweight.

scream n *lit:* screech, shriek, wail, yell; *fig:* hoot, laugh, riot. vb *lit:* cry, holler, screech, shout, shriek, wail, yell; *fig:* be conspicuous, be loud; clash, conflict, jar.

screen n *lit:* divider, partition; cover, defense, hide, shield; awning, canopy, guard, shade, shelter; fence, panel, railing, windbreak; grill, mesh, sieve; grid; white surface. vb *lit:* keep apart, partition, separate; cover, defend, protect, shelter, shield; conceal, mask, shade; filter, sieve, sift, test; examine, scan, vet; broadcast, present, project, transmit.

screw n *lit:* dowel, thread; propeller; spin, twist, wind. vb *lit:* compress, tighten, turn, twist, wind; coerce, constrain, force, pressurize; *fig:* contort, crumple, pucker; steel, summon (up); cheat, con, defraud, swindle; foul (up), mess (up), muck (up).

scrub n *lit:* brush, heath, veldt; runt. **vb** *lit:* bathe, brush, clean, rub hard, scour, soap, wash; *fig:* abandon, call off, cancel, drop, eliminate.

scrutiny n *lit:* contemplation, examination, investigation, observation, perusal, study; supervision.

scuffle n *lit:* affray, brawl, fight, fray, row, rumpus, scrimmage, set-to, skirmish, tussle, wrangle; scrape, shuffle. **vb** *lit:* brawl, fight, struggle, tussle, wrangle, wrestle; drag one's feet, shuffle.

seal n *lit:* arms, colophon, insignia, logo, mark; attestation, authentication, stamp; bond, fastening, lock, weld; cap, cover, lid, top. **vb** *lit:* close (up), make airtight, plug, stop, waterproof; fasten; lock (in), weld (in); *fig:* authenticate, ratify, stamp, validate; conclude, consummate, finalize, settle.

search n *lit:* exploration, hunt, quest; analysis, examination, inspection, study. **vb** *lit:* look for; comb, examine, frisk, rifle through, scour; go over, inquire in, investigate, probe; seek out.

searching adj *lit:* discriminating, intent, keen, minute, penetrating, probing, shrewd, subtle, thorough.

season n *lit:* division, period, term, time of year; interval. **vb** *lit:* flavor, pep up, spice; harden, mature, toughen, train; *fig:* moderate, temper.

seasoned adj *lit:* hardened, mature, weathered; *fig:* battle-scarred, experienced, practiced; well-versed.

seat n *lit:* bench, chair, pew, settee, sofa, stool; saddle; pillion; base, center, cradle, headquarters, site; ancestral home, manor, residence; constituency, incumbency, membership. **vb** *lit:* install, place, set, settle; accommodate, contain, sit, take.

second n *lit:* next, other; instant, jiffy, moment, tick, trice, twinkling; assistant, backer, supporter. **vb** *lit:* aid, assist, back, encourage, endorse, help, support; detach, lend, temporarily transfer. **adj** *lit:* following, next, succeeding; additional, alternative, extra, further, other; *fig:* inferior, lesser, subordinate, supporting.

secondary adj *lit:* alternative, auxiliary, relief, reserve, supporting; inferior, lesser, minor, subordinate; contingent, derivative, indirect, serial.

secret n *lit:* confidence; enigma, mystery; formula, key; in camera. **adj** *lit:* private, secluded, unfrequented; closet, covert, undisclosed; camouflaged, concealed, disguised, hidden; classified, hush-hush, undercover; clandestine, furtive, stealthy; arcane, cryptic, mysterious, recondite.

sect n *lit:* church, denomination, religion; faction, school of thought; philosophy; class; group, party.

section n *lit:* division, part, piece, portion, segment; branch, department; district, sector, zone; detachment, group, squad, team; *spec:* cutting, incision, operation.

secure vb *lit:* acquire, gain, get, obtain, pick up, procure; bolt, chain, fasten, fix, lock up, padlock, rivet, tie up; defend, fortify, make safe; guarantee, insure. **adj** *lit:* defended, impregnable, invulnerable, protected, safe, unassailable; fastened, fixed, immovable, tight; confined, in custody; assured, certain, confident, sure; absolute, definite, reliable.

sedate vb *lit:* anesthetize, drug, knock out, numb, pacify, tranquilize. **adj** *lit:* dignified, noble, stately; composed, decorous, deliberate, grave, solemn; calm, serious.

sediment n *lit:* dregs, grounds, lees; loess, silt; deposit.

seduce vb *lit:* beguile, entice, lure, tempt; lead astray, lead on; deflower.

see n *lit:* bishopric, diocese; cathedral city. **vb** *lit:* discern, distinguish, espy, make out, perceive, spot; behold, observe, view, watch, witness; look up, refer to; call in on, encounter, interview, meet, receive, speak to, visit; associate with, date, go out with, go steady with; *fig:* anticipate, envisage, envision, picture, visualize; be associated with, bring; experience, undergo; apprehend, fathom, get, grasp, learn, understand; appreciate, be aware of, comprehend, know, realize, recognize; deem, judge; ascertain, discover, find out, investigate; ensure, make certain, mind; consider, deliberate over, make up one's mind, reflect on, think over.

seed n *lit:* grain, kernel, spore; drupe, pip, stone; cell; semen; *fig:* beginning, germ, source, start; descendants, heirs, issue, progeny, successors; nation, race; *spec:* top-rated player. **vb** *lit:* plant, sow; dust, powder, scatter, sprinkle.

seedy   adj *fig:* abraded, dilapidated, faded, old, worn; scruffy, shabby, sleazy, sordid, squalid; ill, off-color, poor, run-down, sickly, unwell, wan.

seek   vb *lit:* ask, entreat, implore, petition, request; aim for, hope for, look for; hunt, pursue, search for; attempt, endeavor, strive, try.

seethe   vb *lit:* boil, bubble, ferment, foam, froth; *fig:* swarm, teem; fume, rage, simmer.

seize   vb *lit:* clasp, clutch, grab, grasp, snatch, take; apprehend, arrest, capture; repossess, take by force; appropriate, confiscate, impound, requisition, sequester; abduct, hijack, kidnap; *fig:* clog, jam, stick fast; lash down, make fast, tie up.

select   vb *lit:* choose, elect, opt for, pick out, single out, sort out. **adj** *lit:* choice, elite, prime, superior, top-quality, top-rated; exclusive, limited; privileged.

self-assertion   n *lit:* determination, dominance, insistence, masterfulness, positiveness; pushiness.

self-assured   adj *lit:* confident, poised, self-confident, self-reliant.

self-centered   adj *lit:* egotistic, monomaniacal, narcissistic, self-absorbed, selfish.

self-conscious   adj *lit:* abashed, bashful, diffident, embarrassed, ill-at-ease, insecure, nervous, shy.

self-esteem   n *lit:* confidence, ego, pride, self-regard, self-respect.

selfish   adj *lit:* self-centered, self-seeking; avaricious, greedy, mean.

selfless   adj *lit:* altruistic, generous, heroic, magnanimous, noble, unselfish.

self-reliant   adj *lit:* able, capable, independent, practical, self-confident, self-sufficient.

self-respect   n *lit:* dignity, pride, self-esteem, self-regard.

self-satisfied   adj *lit:* gratified, self-congratulatory, triumphant; complacent, overconfident, smug.

self-seeking adj *lit:* calculating, mercenary, opportunistic; selfish.

sell vb *lit:* deal, hawk, peddle, retail, trade, vend; dispose of, put up for sale; *fig:* market, promote, put across; convert to, convince of, persuade.

send vb *lit:* consign, convey, dispatch, forward, mail, post; broadcast, transmit; fling, hurl, sling, throw; fire, launch, propel, shoot; give (off), radiate; turn away; call for; *fig:* excite, intoxicate, stir, thrill.

senior adj *lit:* chief, elder, first, older, superior, upper.

sensation n *lit:* feeling; emotion; awareness, perception; effect, impression, sense; thrill; *fig:* agitation, commotion, excitement, stir; craze, fad, novelty.

sensational adj *lit:* astounding, dramatic, earth-shattering, epoch-making, exciting, fantastic, galvanizing, spectacular, staggering, stupendous, thrilling; appalling, horrifying, outrageous, scandalous, shocking; excellent, exceptional, marvelous, superb, wonderful.

sense n *lit:* appreciation, awareness, faculty, feeling, impression; air, aura, atmosphere; intuition, premonition, presentiment; discernment, imagination, logic, nous, practicability, practicality, reason, understanding; gist, implication, import, meaning, point, purport, significance, substance, use. vb *lit:* appreciate, apprehend, be aware of, feel, get the impression, grasp, hear, perceive, realize, scent, see, taste.

senseless adj *lit:* absurd, crazy, fatuous, half-witted, idiotic, ludicrous, mindless, nonsensical, ridiculous, stupid, unreasonable; futile, meaningless, pointless; anesthetized, deadened, insensible, knocked out, numb, unconscious.

sensible adj *lit:* canny, down-to-earth, matter-of-fact, no-nonsense, practical, straightforward; judicious, politic, prudent, realistic; intelligent, reasonable, shrewd, sound, wise; aware, conscious, mindful.

sensitive adj *lit:* feeling, keen, perceptive, reactive, responsive; allergic; delicate, emotional, high-strung, impressionable, nervous, tender; thin-skinned, touchy; *fig:* controversial, hot; awkward, embarrassing; embarrassed, shamefaced.

sensual adj *lit:* bodily, carnal, fleshly, physical; erotic, lascivious, lecherous, lustful, randy, sexual, voluptuous.

sensuous adj *lit:* bodily, fleshly, physical; feeling, perceptive, reactive, responsive, sensory; gratifying, pleasurable.

sentimental adj *lit:* emotional, maudlin, nostalgic, pathetic, simpering, sloppy, softhearted, tearful, tender.

sentry n *lit:* guard, lookout, picket, watch.

separate vb *lit:* break off, come apart, detach, disconnect, divide, keep apart, sever, split; put on one side, segregate, sort out; *fig:* break up, diverge, divorce, estrange, part company, split up. adj *lit:* detached, disconnected, disjointed, divided, divorced, unattached; alone, autonomous, independent, particular, single.

separation n *lit:* break, detachment, disconnection, dissociation, division, gap, severance; *fig:* breakup, divorce, estrangement, parting, rift, split.

sequence n *lit:* course, cycle, order, progression, succession.

serene adj *lit:* calm, composed, imperturbable, placid, unruffled; clear, cloudless, halcyon, unclouded.

series n *lit:* arrangement, course, order, sequence, string, succession, train.

serious adj *lit:* grave, pensive, solemn, thoughtful; determined, earnest, genuine, resolute, sincere; *fig:* crucial, difficult, important, momentous, pressing, significant, weighty; acute, critical, dangerous, severe.

serve vb *lit:* assist, attend to, help, minister to, wait on, work for; act, discharge, do, fulfill, officiate, perform; answer, be adequate, suffice, suit; deliver, dish up, distribute, provide, supply.

service n *lit:* assistance, avail, help, supply, use, utility; maintenance, overhaul, servicing; duty, employment, office, work; *fig:* ceremony, observance, worship. vb *lit:* check, maintain, overhaul, repair.

serving n *lit:* allotment, helping, portion, ration, share.

set n *lit:* attitude, bearing, position, posture, turn; scene, scenery, stage setting; band, circle, company, crew, faction, gang, group, outfit; *fig:* assortment, batch, collection, compendium, kit, series. vb *lit:* aim, apply, direct, fix, install, lay, locate, place, position, put, rest, situate, stick; *fig:*

agree upon, allocate, appoint, assign, determine, establish, resolve, schedule, settle; arrange, make ready, prepare; adjust, coordinate, regulate, synchronize; condense, congeal, crystallize, solidify, thicken; allot, impose, lay down, specify; decline, disappear, sink, vanish. **adj** *lit:* agreed, arranged, customary, definite, established, fixed, prearranged, regular, settled; *fig:* conventional, formal, routine, stock, traditional; entrenched, firm, hardened, inflexible, rigid, strict; bent, determined, intent.

setting n *lit:* background, context, frame, scene, set, site, surroundings.

settle vb *lit:* adjust, straighten out, work out; clear up, complete, conclude, put an end to, resolve; agree, come to an agreement, confirm, fix; calm, pacify, quell, reassure, sedate, soothe; bed down, come to rest, descend, land, dwell, live, move to, reside; colonize, found, people, populate; acquit oneself of, clear, liquidate, pay; decline, sink, subside.

sever vb *lit:* break off, cut apart, part from, slice; disjoin, divide, separate.

several adj *lit:* assorted, different, diverse, many, some, sundry, various.

severe adj *lit:* austere, draconian, hard, harsh, inflexible, oppressive, rigid, strict, unbending; cold, disapproving, dour, forbidding, grim, stern, straitlaced, tight-lipped; acute, bitter, critical, dangerous, fierce, grinding; *fig:* ascetic, chaste, plain, restrained, simple, Spartan, unembellished; arduous, demanding, exacting, punishing, rigorous, stringent, tough; astringent, caustic, cutting, satirical, scathing, unsparing.

sexy adj *lit:* arousing, erotic, inviting, naughty, provocative, seductive, sensual, suggestive, titillating, voluptuous.

shade n *lit:* dimness, dusk, gloom, shadiness, shadow; blind, canopy, cover, curtain, screen; *fig:* color, hue, tint, tone; dash, degree, hint, nuance, semblance, suggestion, trace; apparition, ghost, manes, phantom, specter, spirit. vb *lit:* cover, darken, dim, overshadow, protect, screen, shield, veil.

shadow n *lit:* cover, dimness, dusk, gloom, protection, shelter; hint, suggestion, trace; *fig:* ghost, image, representation, specter, vestige; blight, gloom, sadness. vb *lit:* darken, overhang, screen, shade, shield; *fig:* dog, follow, stalk, tail.

shady   **adj** *lit:* cool, dim, leafy, shadowy, umbrageous; *fig:* crooked, dubious, shifty, slippery, suspicious, unscrupulous, untrustworthy.

shake   **n** *lit:* agitation, convulsion, jerk, jolt, pulsation, quaking, shiver, tremor, vibration; *fig:* instant, jiffy, second, trice. **vb** *lit:* bump, fluctuate, jar, joggle, jounce, oscillate, quake, rock, shudder, totter, tremble, wobble; brandish, wave; *fig:* agitate, churn, rouse, stir; distress, disturb, intimidate, rattle, shock, unnerve; impair, undermine, weaken.

shallow   **n** *lit:* flat, sand bank, shelf, shoal. **adj** *lit:* empty, flimsy, frivolous, meaningless, puerile, skin-deep, superficial, trivial, unintelligent.

sham   **n** *lit:* counterfeit, forgery, fraud, hoax, pretense; impostor, phony, pretender. **vb** *lit:* affect, assume, fake, feign, imitate, put on, simulate. **adj** *lit:* artificial, bogus, counterfeit, false, imitation, mock, phony, pseudo, spurious, synthetic.

shame   **n** *lit:* blot, contempt, derision, disgrace, disrepute, infamy, opprobrium, reproach, scandal, smear; abashment, chagrin, embarrassment, humiliation, ignominy, mortification. **vb** *lit:* abash, confound, disconcert, disgrace, humble, humiliate, mortify, reproach, ridicule; debase, defile, discredit, smear, stain.

shape   **n** *lit:* build, contours, figure, form, make, outline; frame, mold, pattern; *fig:* appearance, aspect, guise, likeness, semblance; condition, fettle, health, state. **vb** *lit:* fashion, form, make, model, mold; *fig:* adapt, define, devise, frame, modify, plan, prepare, regulate.

share   **n** *lit:* allotment, allowance, contribution, due, lot, portion, quota, ration, whack. **vb** *lit:* apportion, assign, distribute, divide, go halves, partake, participate, split.

sharp   **adj** *lit:* acute, cutting, knife-edged, pointed, razor-sharp, serrated, spiky; abrupt, distinct, marked, sudden; *fig:* alert, apt, astute, bright, perceptive, quick-witted, subtle; artful, crafty, cunning, shrewd, sly, unscrupulous, wily; distressing, excruciating, fierce, piercing, sore, stabbing, stinging; clear-cut, crisp, well-defined; chic, classy, dressy, natty, smart, snappy, stylish; acrimonious, biting, bitter, caustic, harsh, hurtful, sarcastic, sardonic, scathing, trenchant, vitriolic; acid, acrid, burning, piquant, pungent, sour. **adv** *lit:* exactly, on the dot, on time, promptly, punctually; *fig:* abruptly, unexpectedly, without warning.

sharply **adv** *lit:* acutely, cuttingly, pointedly; abruptly, suddenly; aptly, brightly, subtly; cunningly, shrewdly; fiercely, piercingly; smartly, stylishly; bitterly, harshly.

shatter **vb** *lit:* break, crack, demolish, pulverize, smash; blast, destroy, devastate, impair, ruin, wreck.

shed **n** *lit:* cover, hut, shelter; ridge, watershed. **vb** *lit:* cause to flow, drop, let fall, pour out, spill; cast, diffuse, emit, give forth, radiate, scatter, throw; cast off, discard, molt, slough.

sheer **vb** *lit:* swerve, turn aside. **adj** *lit:* abrupt, precipitous, steep; absolute, complete, out-and-out, total, unadulterated, utter; fine, pure, see-through, thin.

shell **n** *lit:* case, husk, pod; frame, hull, skeleton, structure. **vb** *lit:* husk, shuck; barrage, blitz, bombard, strike.

shelter **n** *lit:* cover, guard, haven, refuge, safety, sanctuary, screen. **vb** *lit:* cover, defend, guard, harbor, hide, protect, safeguard, shield.

shield **n** *lit:* buckler, escutcheon; bulwark, defense, protection, rampart, safeguard, shelter. **vb** *lit:* cover, defend, guard, protect, screen, ward off.

shift **n** *lit:* alteration, change, fluctuation, modification, rearrangement, shifting, switch, veering; *fig:* contrivance, craft, dodge, evasion, move, stratagem, trick, wile. **vb** *lit:* alter, budge, displace, fluctuate, move, rearrange, remove, swerve, switch, transfer, vary, veer.

shifty **adj** *lit:* contriving, devious, evasive, furtive, scheming, slippery, tricky, underhand, untrustworthy, wily.

shimmering **adj** *lit:* gleaming, glistening, scintillating, sparkling, twinkling.

shine **n** *lit:* brightness, glare, gleam, luminosity, shimmer, sparkle; *fig:* glaze, gloss, luster, polish, sheen. **vb** *lit:* beam, emit light, glare, glitter, radiate, scintillate, sparkle, twinkle; *fig:* excel, stand out.

shining **adj** *lit:* beaming, bright, effulgent, glittering, luminous, radiant, resplendent, sparkling; *fig:* brilliant, distinguished, eminent, illustrious, leading, outstanding.

shirk **vb** *lit:* avoid, dodge, duck, shun, slack.

shock n *lit:* blow, breakdown, collapse, consternation, stupor, trauma, turn; clash, collision, impact, jolt. **vb** *lit:* appall, astound, disquiet, jar, jolt, numb, offend, outrage, scandalize, shake up, stagger, stun, stupefy, traumatize.

shocking adj *lit:* abominable, atrocious, disgraceful, disgusting, dreadful, ghastly, hideous, loathsome, outrageous, repulsive, revolting, scandalous, sickening, unspeakable.

shoot n *lit:* branch, bud, offshoot, sprig, sprout, sucker; current, rapids; chute, slide; shooting expedition, party. **vb** *lit:* bud, burgeon, sprout; bolt, dart, dash, fly, hurtle, rush, speed, tear, whisk; bag, blast, bring down, open fire, zap; discharge, fire, fling, hurl, let fly.

shore n *lit:* beach, coast, sands, seashore. **adj** *lit:* littoral, waterside.

short adj *lit:* abridged, compressed, concise, curtailed, laconic, pithy, summary, terse; diminutive, dumpy, petite, small; brief, fleeting, momentary; deficient, insufficient, lacking, low, scarce, sparse, wanting; abrupt, brusque, curt, discourteous, gruff, sharp, surly, terse, uncivil; direct, straight; crumbly. **adv** *lit:* abruptly, by surprise, suddenly, unaware.

shortage n *lit:* dearth, deficiency, famine, lack, scarcity, shortfall, want.

shorten vb *lit:* abbreviate, curtail, cut down, diminish, lessen, reduce, trim.

shortly adv *lit:* before long, presently, soon; briefly, concisely; abruptly, curtly.

shot n *lit:* discharge, lob, potshot; bullet, lead, pellet, projectile; marksman, shooter; *fig:* attempt, conjecture, crack, go, guess, stab, try.

shout n *lit:* bellow, cry, roar, yell. **vb** *lit:* bawl, bellow, call, cry, holler, roar, scream, yell.

shove vb *lit:* barge, crowd, elbow, jostle, press, push, shoulder, thrust.

show n *lit:* demonstration, display, exhibition, exposition, fair, pageant, parade, spectacle; affectation, appearance, likeness, pretense, semblance; *spec:* entertainment, presentation, production. **vb** *lit:* appear, display, divulge, exhibit, indicate, make known, reveal; demonstrate, explain, instruct, point out, prove; accompany, escort, guide, lead; accord, bestow, confer, grant.

shower n *lit:* downfall, downpour; *fig:* barrage, deluge, fusillade, torrent, volley. **vb** *lit:* deluge, inundate, lavish, pour, spray, sprinkle.

shred n *lit:* bit, fragment, piece, scrap, sliver, snippet, tatter; *fig:* grain, iota, jot, particle, trace, whit. **vb** *lit:* cut, tear.

shrewd adj *lit:* artful, calculating, canny, crafty, cunning, sly, smart, wily; discerning, farsighted, intelligent, keen, perceptive.

shriek n *lit:* howl, scream, screech, wail, yell. **vb** *lit:* cry, scream, screech, squeal, wail, yell.

shrill adj *lit:* earsplitting, high-pitched, penetrating, screeching, sharp.

shrink vb *lit:* decrease, deflate, drop off, dwindle, lessen, shrivel, wither; cower, draw back, flinch, hang back, recoil, shy away, wince.

shudder n *lit:* quiver, spasm, trembling, tremor. **vb** *lit:* quake, quiver, shake, shiver, tremble.

shuffle vb *lit:* drag, scuffle, shamble; disarrange, jumble, mix, shift; dodge, evade, fidget, prevaricate, pussyfoot, quibble.

shut vb *lit:* bar, close, fasten, seal, secure, slam. **adj** *lit:* closed, confined, enclosed, excluded.

shy vb *lit:* balk, draw back, flinch, rear, recoil, shrink, start, swerve, take fright. **adj** *lit:* bashful, coy, hesitant, reserved, reticent, timid, wary.

sick adj *lit:* ill, nauseated, queasy; ailing, indisposed; *fig:* perverted; bored, fed up, tired, weary.

sickly adj *lit:* ailing, bilious, delicate, faint, indisposed, in poor health, lackluster, languid, pallid, unhealthy, weak; mawkish, nauseating, revolting, syrupy.

sickness n *lit:* nausea, queasiness; ailment, bug, complaint, disease, disorder, illness, indisposition.

side n *lit:* border, boundary, edge, limit, margin, periphery, rim, verge; aspect, facet, part, surface, view; *fig:* angle, opinion, point of view, position, slant, stand; camp, faction, party, team; airs, arrogance. **vb** *lit:* ally with, associate oneself with, favor, go along with, second, support, team up with. **adj** *lit:* flanking, lateral; *fig:* ancillary, incidental, lesser, marginal, roundabout, secondary, subsidiary.

sidestep   **vb** *lit:* avoid, bypass, dodge, duck, elude, evade, skip.

sidetrack   **n** *lit:* railroad track, siding; *fig:* distraction, diversion, interruption. **vb** *fig:* deflect, deviate, distract, divert.

sift   **vb** *lit:* bolt, filter, pan, separate, sieve; *fig:* analyze, examine, go through, screen, scrutinize.

sight   **n** *lit:* eyesight, vision; appearance, eyeshot, range of vision, view, visibility; display, scene, show, spectacle, vista; *fig:* blot on the landscape, eyesore, mess, monstrosity. **vb** *lit:* discern, make out, see, spot.

sign   **n** *lit:* evidence, gesture, hint, indication, proof, suggestion, trace; board, notice, placard; badge, device, emblem, ensign, logo, symbol; auspice, foreboding, omen, portent, warning. **vb** *lit:* autograph, endorse, inscribe; beckon, gesture, signal, wave.

signal   **n** *lit:* beacon, cue, indication, sign, token. **vb** *lit:* beckon, gesticulate, indicate, motion, sign, wave. **adj** *lit:* conspicuous, eminent, extraordinary, memorable, noteworthy, outstanding, significant.

significant   **adj** *lit:* denoting, expressive, indicative, meaningful, suggestive; critical, important, material, momentous, serious, vital, weighty.

signify   **vb** *lit:* announce, communicate, connote, convey, express, imply, indicate, intimate, mean, portend, represent, stand for, suggest, symbolize; *fig:* carry weight, count, matter.

silence   **n** *lit:* calm, hush, lull, quiescence, stillness; dumbness, reticence, speechlessness, taciturnity. **vb** *lit:* cut off, deaden, gag, muffle, stifle, subdue, suppress.

silent   **adj** *lit:* hushed, muted, quiet, soundless, still; dumb, mum, nonvocal, speechless, taciturn, tongue-tied, voiceless, wordless; implied, tacit, understood, unspoken.

similar   **adj** *lit:* alike, comparable, congruous, in agreement, resembling.

similarity   **n** *lit:* affinity, agreement, analogy, comparability, concordance, congruency, likeness, resemblance, sameness, similitude.

simple   **adj** *lit:* clear, elementary, intelligible, lucid, straightforward, uncomplicated; classic, clean, natural, plain, uncluttered; pure, unalloyed, unblended, unmixed; artless, childlike, green, guileless, naive, sincere, unpretentious, unsophisticated; basic, direct, frank, honest, naked, plain, undeniable; homely, modest, rustic; brainless, dumb, feebleminded, moronic, silly, slow, thick.

simplify   **vb** *lit:* abridge, disentangle, facilitate, streamline.

simultaneous   **adj** *lit:* coincident, concurrent, contemporaneous, synchronous.

sin   **n** *lit:* crime, error, evil, misdeed, offense, transgression, trespass, unrighteousness, wrongdoing. **vb** *lit:* err, fall, go astray, lapse, offend, transgress.

sing   **vb** *lit:* carol, chant, chirp, croon, trill, warble, yodel; buzz, hum, purr, whistle; *fig:* blow the whistle (on), inform (on), rat (on), spill the beans, squeal, turn in.

single   **vb** *lit:* choose, distinguish, fix on, pick, select, separate. **adj** *lit:* distinct, individual, one, only, particular, singular, sole, unique; free, unattached, unmarried; exclusive, separate, unblended, undivided, unshared.

singular   **adj** *lit:* conspicuous, exceptional, noteworthy, outstanding, prodigious, rare, remarkable, unique; curious, eccentric, extraordinary, out-of-the-way, peculiar, queer, strange; separate, single, sole.

sinister   **adj** *lit:* dire, injurious, malevolent, malignant, menacing, threatening.

sink   **n** *lit:* basin, tub; drain, sewer; marsh, pool. **vb** *lit:* decline, descend, drop, drown, ebb, fall, founder, go down, merge, plummet, sag, submerge, subside; abate, lapse, retrogress, slump; deteriorate, die, dwindle, fade, weaken, worsen; bore, dig, drill, excavate, lay; *fig:* defeat, destroy, finish, overwhelm, ruin; stoop, succumb.

situation   **n** *lit:* locality, place, position, setting, site, spot; circumstances, plight, state of affairs, status quo, the picture; rank, station, status; employment, job, office, post.

size   **n** *lit:* amount, bulk, dimensions, extent, hugeness, immensity, magnitude, mass, measurement, proportions, range, volume. **vb** *lit:* arrange, classify; make of a certain size; *spec:* glaze, stiffen.

sizzling　adj (pr.pt) *lit:* crackling, frizzling, spitting, sputtering.

skeleton　n *lit:* framework; *fig:* bare bones, draft, outline, structure.

sketch　n *lit:* delineation, draft, drawing, etching, outline, plan. **vb** *lit:* delineate, depict, draft, draw, etch, outline, plot, represent.

skew　adj *lit:* askew, awry, slanting, twisted; bent, crooked, not symmetrical.

skewer　n *lit:* spit; nail, pin, stake; tent peg. **vb** *lit:* impale, spit, transfix; nail, pin, stake; peg.

skill　n *lit:* ability, accomplishment, aptitude, competence, dexterity, expertise, finesse, knack, proficiency, skillfulness, talent.

skin　n *lit:* fell, hide, pelt; coating, crust, husk, outside, rind. **vb** *lit:* abrade, bark, flay, graze, peel.

skinny　adj *lit:* emaciated, scraggy, skeletal, skin-and-bone, thin, undernourished.

skip　n *lit:* jump, leap, spring, trip. **vb** *lit:* bounce, caper, gambol, hop, prance; eschew, leave out, miss, omit, pass over.

skirt　n *lit:* kilt; border, edge, fringe, margin, outskirts, periphery. **vb** *lit:* border, edge, lie alongside; avoid, bypass, detour, evade.

slack　n *lit:* leeway, looseness, room. **vb** *lit:* dodge, idle, neglect, shirk, slacken. **adj** *lit:* baggy, flexible, lax, loose, relaxed; easygoing, idle, inactive, lazy, negligent, permissive, tardy; dull, slow-moving, sluggish.

slacken　vb *lit:* abate, diminish, drop off, lessen, reduce, relax, slow down.

slang　n *lit:* argot, cant, colloquialism, jargon, rhyming slang. **vb** *lit:* abuse, berate, call names, insult, inveigh against, rail against, revile, slander, vituperate.

slant　n *lit:* camber, incline, pitch, ramp, tilt; angle, bias, emphasis, leaning, prejudice, viewpoint. **vb** *lit:* bend, incline, lean, list, slope, tilt; bias, twist, weight.

slap   **n** *lit:* bang, clout, smack, spank, wallop, whack; *fig:* blow, rebuff, snub. **vb** *lit:* blow, clap, clout, cuff, hit, spank, whack.

slash   **n** *lit:* cut, gash, laceration, rip, slit. **vb** *lit:* gash, hack, lacerate, rend, score, slit; cut, lower, reduce.

slaughter   **n** *lit:* bloodbath, bloodshed, carnage, killing, liquidation, massacre, slaying. **vb** *lit:* butcher, do to death, exterminate, kill, massacre, murder, put to the sword, slay.

slave   **n** *lit:* drudge, serf, servant, vassal, villein. **vb** *lit:* drudge, slog, toil.

slavery   **n** *lit:* bondage, captivity, serfdom, servitude, thralldom, vassalage.

slavish   **adj** *lit:* abject, cringing, groveling, low, menial, servile, sycophantic; conventional, imitative, unimaginative, uninspired.

slay   **vb** *lit:* annihilate, assassinate, destroy, eliminate, exterminate, massacre, murder, slaughter; amuse, be the death of.

sleek   **adj** *lit:* glossy, shiny, smooth, well-groomed.

sleep   **n** *lit:* doze, nap, rest, slumber, snooze. **vb** *lit:* catnap, doze, drop off, drowse, nod off, slumber, snooze, take a nap.

slender   **adj** *lit:* lean, narrow, slim, sylphlike, willowy; inadequate, insufficient, meager, scanty, small; feeble, flimsy, remote, slight, thin, weak.

slick   **vb** *lit:* plaster down, sleek, smooth. **adj** *lit:* glossy, smooth, soft; glib, plausible, polished, sophistical, specious; adroit, deft, sharp, skillful, sly, tricky.

slight   **n** *lit:* affront, discourtesy, disdain, insult, rebuff, snub, (the) cold shoulder. **vb** *lit:* affront, cold-shoulder, disparage, give offense to, scorn, snub. **adj** *lit:* feeble, insignificant, minor, negligible, paltry, small, superficial, trivial, unimportant; delicate, fragile, lightly built.

slim   **vb** *lit:* diet, lose weight, reduce. **adj** *lit:* lean, narrow, sylphlike, thin, trim; faint, poor, remote, slender, slight.

slimy   **adj** *lit:* clammy, mucous, muddy, oozy, viscous; creeping, groveling, oily, servile, smarmy, sycophantic, toadying, unctuous.

sling   n *lit:* strap, string; casting, hurling, throw; band, chain, loop. **vb** *lit:* cast, chuck, fling, heave, hurl, throw, toss; dangle, hang, swing.

slip   n *lit:* blooper, blunder, error, fault, indiscretion, mistake, oversight, slip of the tongue. **vb** *lit:* glide, slide, slither; fall, lose one's footing, skid, trip (over); conceal, hide, insinuate oneself, sneak; blunder, miscalculate, mistake; break free from, disappear, dodge, elude, evade, get away, outwit.

slippery   adj *lit:* slippy, smooth, unsafe, unstable, unsteady; crafty, cunning, devious, evasive, false, shifty, sneaky, tricky, two-faced, unreliable, untrustworthy.

slope   n *lit:* declination, descent, gradient, inclination, ramp, scarp, slant, tilt. **vb** *lit:* drop away, fall, incline, lean, pitch, rise, tilt; creep, make oneself scare, skulk, slip.

sloth   n *lit:* idleness, inactivity, indolence, inertia, slackness, sluggishness, torpor.

slow   vb *lit:* check, curb, delay, detain, hold up, lag, reduce speed, restrict. **adj** *lit:* creeping, dawdling, easy, laggard, lazy, leaden, leisurely, plodding, ponderous, slow-moving, sluggish, unhurried; behind, delayed, dilatory, late, tardy, unpunctual; gradual, lingering, long-drawn-out, prolonged, protracted; dull, inactive, quiet, sleepy, stagnant, tedious, uneventful, wearisome; dim, dull-witted, dumb, obtuse, stupid, thick.

slur   n *fig:* affront, blot, brand, discredit, disgrace, innuendo, insinuation, reproach, smear, stain, stigma; *spec:* legato, slide (in music or speech). **vb** *lit:* conceal, go through hurriedly, minimize, pass lightly over; pronounce indistinctly; *fig:* affront, disgrace, discredit, insinuate, insult, smear, stain.

sly   adj *lit:* artful, clever, conniving, crafty, cunning, devious, guileful, scheming, shifty, stealthy, underhand, wily; impish, mischievous, roguish.

smack   n *lit:* flavor, taste; dash, suggestion, tinge, touch, trace; blow, crack, slap; sailing ship. **vb** *lit:* box, clap, hit, pat, slap, sock, spank, tap. **adv** *lit:* directly, exactly, pointblank, right, squarely, straight.

small   adj *lit:* diminutive, little, miniature, minute, petite, pint-sized, puny, tiny, undersized; insignificant, lesser, minor, paltry, petty, trifling, trivial; inadequate, insufficient, limited, meager, scanty; humble, modest, small-scale; base, grudging, mean, narrow, selfish.

smart   n *lit:* burning, pang, smarting, sting. **vb** *lit:* burn, hurt, sting, throb, tingle. **adj** *lit:* hard, painful, piercing, sharp, stinging; adept, apt, astute, bright, canny, ingenious, keen, nimble, quick-witted, sharp, shrewd; chic, elegant, fashionable, modish, natty, neat, snappy, stylish, trim; impertinent, ready, saucy, witty; brisk, lively, quick, spanking, spirited.

smear   n *lit:* blot, blotch, daub, smudge, splotch; defamation, libel, mudslinging, slander, vilification. **vb** *lit:* bedaub, blur, cover, daub, dirty, plaster, rub on, smudge, spread over, stain; asperse, blacken, calumniate, malign, sully, tarnish, vilify.

smell   n *lit:* aroma, bouquet, fragrance, odor, redolence, scent, whiff; stench, stink. **vb** *lit:* get a whiff of, scent, sniff; be malodorous, reek, stink.

smooth   vb *lit:* flatten, iron, polish, press; allay, alleviate, calm, extenuate, facilitate, mitigate, mollify, palliate, soften. **adj** *lit:* even, flat, flush, level, unwrinkled; glossy, shiny, silky, soft, velvety; calm, equable, peaceful, serene, tranquil, unruffled; agreeable, mellow, mild, soothing; glib, ingratiating, persuasive, slick, smarmy, suave, unctuous; easy, effortless, flowing, fluent, regular, rhythmic, unbroken, uninterrupted, well-ordered.

smothered   adj (pa.pt) *lit:* choked, stifled, strangled, suffocated; concealed, muffled, suppressed; cocooned, inundated, overwhelmed, showered.

smug   adj *lit:* complacent, conceited, priggish, self-opinionated, self-righteous, self-satisfied.

snag   n *lit:* catch, complication, disadvantage, drawback, hitch, problem, stumbling block. **vb** *lit:* catch, rip, tear.

snap   n *lit:* crackle, fillip, flick, pop; energy, go, liveliness, vigor, zip. **vb** *lit:* break, crack, give way, separate; bite, catch, grip, nip, snatch; bark, flare out, flash, lash out at, retort, snarl; click, crackle, pop; *fig:* take a photograph. **adj** *lit:* abrupt, immediate, instant, on-the-spot, sudden.

snare n *lit:* catch, net, noose, pitfall, trap, wire. **vb** *lit:* catch, entrap, net, seize, spring, wire.

snatch n *lit:* bit, fragment, piece, smattering, snippet, spell. **vb** *lit:* clutch, grab, grasp, grip, make off with, pluck, pull, seize, stolen, wrench, wrest.

sneer n *lit:* derision, disdain, gibe, jeer, mockery, ridicule, scorn. **vb** *lit:* deride, disdain, gibe, jeer, laugh, mock, ridicule, scoff, sniff at, snicker, snigger, turn up one's nose.

snobbish adj *lit:* arrogant, condescending, hoity-toity, patronizing, pretentious, snooty, uppish.

snooze n *lit:* catnap, doze, nap, siesta. **vb** *lit:* catnap, doze, drop off, nap, nod off.

snub n *lit:* affront, brush-off, insult, put-down. **vb** *lit:* cold-shoulder, cut dead, humble, humiliate, mortify, rebuff, slight.

snug adj *lit:* comfortable, cozy, homely, sheltered, warm; compact, neat, trim.

so adv *lit:* as shown, in that way, in the same way; as stated; to that degree, to this degree; in such a way, to such a degree; very; very much; accordingly, for that reason, therefore; also, likewise. **cnj** *lit:* in order that, with the result that; with the intention that; if, on the condition that. **interj** *lit:* well; all right, let it be that way; is that true?

soak vb *lit:* damp, drench, immerse, moisten, penetrate, permeate, saturate, wet; absorb, assimilate, suck in, take in.

sober vb *lit:* bring back to earth, calm down, clear one's head, come to one's senses. **adj** *lit:* abstinent, moderate, temperate; calm, clearheaded, composed, cool, levelheaded, rational, reasonable, sedate, serious, sound, steady, unruffled; dark, quiet, somber, subdued.

sociable adj *lit:* affable, approachable, convivial, cordial, friendly, genial, gregarious, neighborly, warm.

society n *lit:* community, humanity, mankind, people, social order, the public; companionship, company, fellowship; association, circle, club, corporation, fraternity, group, guild, institute, league, organization, sorority, union; elite, gentry, high society, smart set, top drawer, upper crust.

soft   adj *lit:* creamy, doughy, pulpy, spongy, squashy, yielding; bendable, elastic, flexible, malleable, plastic, pliable, supple; downy, fleecy, furry, silky, smooth, velvety; delicate, diffuse, dimmed, faint, low, mellow, melodious, murmured, pale, pastel, shaded, soothing, subdued, temperate, understated, whispered; compassionate, gentle, sensitive, sympathetic, tender; easygoing, lax, lenient, overindulgent, permissive, weak; comfortable, easy, undemanding; effeminate, flabby, overindulged, pampered; daft, feebleminded, foolish, silly, soft in the head.

soften   vb *lit:* allay, alleviate, appease, calm, diminish, lessen, melt, mitigate, modify, muffle, palliate, quell, relax, soothe, subdue, tone down.

soil   n *lit:* clay, dust, earth, ground; country, land, region. **vb** *lit:* besmirch, defile, foul, pollute, spatter, stain, tarnish.

solemn   adj *lit:* earnest, glum, portentous, serious, sober, thoughtful; august, ceremonious, dignified, grand, grave, imposing, momentous, stately; devotional, reverential, ritual, sacred, venerable.

solid   n *lit:* lump, mass. **adj** *lit:* compact, dense, firm, stable, strong, sturdy, substantial; genuine, pure, real, sound; complete, unalloyed, unanimous, unbroken, united, unmixed; *fig:* decent, dependable, levelheaded, reliable, sensible, sober, trusty, upright, worthy.

solitude   n *lit:* isolation, loneliness, privacy, reclusiveness, seclusion; emptiness, waste, wilderness.

solution   n *lit:* answer, clarification, explanation, key, resolution, unraveling; blend, emulsion, mix, solvent, suspension; dissolution, melting.

solve   vb *lit:* clarify, clear up, crack, decipher, disentangle, elucidate, explain, expound, interpret, unfold, unravel, work out.

somber   adj *lit:* dark, dim, doleful, drab, dull, funereal, gloomy, grave, melancholy, mournful, sad, shadowy, shady.

somebody   n *lit:* bigwig, celebrity, heavyweight, household name, public figure, VIP. **prn** *lit:* anybody, anyone, one, someone.

353   **sound**

sometimes **adv** *lit:* at times, every now and then, from time to time, now and again, now and then, occasionally, off and on, once in a while.

song n *lit:* air, anthem, ballad, canticle, carol, chant, ditty, hymn, melody, pop song, psalm, shanty, tune.

soon **adv** *lit:* before long, in a minute, presently, shortly; promptly, quickly; leaf, readily, willingly.

sophistication n *lit:* finesse, poise, savoir faire, urbanity, worldly wisdom.

sordid **adj** *lit:* dirty, filthy, foul, seamy, seedy, sleazy, squalid; backstreet, base, debauched, disreputable, shabby, vile; avaricious, covetous, grasping, mercenary, selfish, venal.

sore n *lit:* abscess, boil, inflammation, ulcer. **adj** *lit:* burning, chafed, inflamed, irritated, raw, smarting, tender; annoying, distressing, grievous, sharp, troublesome; acute, critical, dire, extreme, pressing, urgent; afflicted, aggrieved, angry, hurt, irked, peeved, resentful, vexed.

sorrow n *lit:* affliction, anguish, distress, grief, heartache, mourning, sadness, woe; blow, hardship, misfortune, trial, tribulation, trouble, worry. **vb** *lit:* agonize, bemoan, grieve, moan, mourn.

sorry **adj** *lit:* apologetic, conscience-stricken, contrite, penitent, remorseful, repentant, self-reproachful; disconsolate, distressed, grieved, melancholy, sad, sorrowful; compassionate, moved, pitying, sympathetic; abject, base, deplorable, dismal, mean, miserable, paltry, pathetic, piteous, shabby, wretched.

sort n *lit:* brand, breed, category, character, class, description, genus, ilk, kind, make, nature, order, species, style, type, variety. **vb** *lit:* arrange, assort, categorize, choose, classify, distribute, divide, grade, put in order, rank, select, separate.

soul n *lit:* life, mind, psyche, reason, spirit, vital force; being, body, individual, mortal, person; embodiment, essence, personification, quintessence, type; ardor, courage, energy, feeling, fervor, inspiration, vitality.

sound n *lit:* din, noise, report, resonance, reverberation, tone; drift, idea, impression, look, tenor; earshot, hearing, range. **vb** *lit:* echo, resonate, resound, reverberate; appear, look, seem; announce, articulate,

enunciate, express, signal; fathom, probe; examine, investigate, test.
adj *lit:* complete, entire, fit, hale, healthy, intact, perfect, robust, sturdy,
substantial, unimpaired, vigorous, whole; fair, just, levelheaded, logical,
proper, prudent, reasonable, reliable, right, sensible, true, valid, well-
founded; established, proven, recognized, reputable, safe, secure, solvent,
stable; peaceful, unbroken, undisturbed.

sour   **vb** *lit:* alienate, disenchant, embitter, exacerbate, exasperate, turn
off. **adj** *lit:* acid, bitter, sharp, tart; bad, fermented, gone off, rancid,
turned; acrimonious, churlish, cynical, disagreeable, embittered,
grudging, ill-tempered, peevish, waspish.

souvenir   **n** *lit:* keepsake, memento, reminder, token.

sovereign   **n** *lit:* autocrat, monarch, ruler. **adj** *lit:* absolute, chief,
dominant, monarchal, paramount, predominant, principal, regal, ruling,
supreme; effectual, efficient, excellent.

sow   **n** *lit:* female hog; main trough. **vb** *lit:* disseminate, implant,
inseminate, plant, scatter, seed.

space   **n** *lit:* capacity, elbowroom, expanse, extent, leeway, margin,
room, scope, volume; blank, distance, gap, lacuna; duration, interval,
period, span, time; accommodation, berth, place.

span   **n** *lit:* distance, extent, reach, spread, stretch; duration, period,
spell. **vb** *lit:* arch across, bridge, extend across, link, traverse, vault.

spare   **n** *lit:* duplicate, extra, spare part, surplus; extra tire. **vb** *lit:*
afford, dispense with, do without, give, let (someone) have, manage
without, part with; deal leniently with, go easy on, have mercy on, let off,
pardon, refrain from, relieve from, save from. **adj** *lit:* additional,
emergency, extra, free, over, superfluous, surplus, unoccupied; gaunt,
lank, meager, slender, slim, wiry; economical, frugal, modest, scanty,
sparing.

spark   **n** *lit:* flare, flash, flicker, glint; atom, hint, jot, trace, vestige. **vb**
lit: excite, inspire, kindle, precipitate, set off, start, stir, trigger (off).

sparkle   **n** *lit:* brilliance, dazzle, flash, flicker, glint, spark, twinkle;
animation, flash, life, panache, spirit, vim, vivacity, zip. **vb** *lit:* beam,
flash, gleam, glint, glitter, scintillate, shine, twinkle, wink; bubble,
effervesce, fizz.

spasm   n *lit:* contraction, paroxysm, twitch; burst, eruption, fit, frenzy, outburst, seizure.

speak   vb *lit:* articulate, converse, discourse, express, make known, pronounce, say, state, tell, utter, voice; address, declaim, harangue, lecture, plead.

special   adj *lit:* distinguished, exceptional, extraordinary, festive, gala, important, memorable, momentous, red-letter, significant, unique; certain, characteristic, especial, individual, particular, peculiar, specific; chief, main, major, primary.

specialist   n *lit:* authority, connoisseur, consultant, expert, master.

specific   adj *lit:* clear-cut, definite, exact, explicit, express, particular, precise, unambiguous; characteristic, distinguishing, peculiar, special.

specifications   n *lit:* details, items, particulars, requirements, stipulations.

specify   vb *lit:* cite, define, detail, enumerate, indicate, itemize, mention, name, spell out, stipulate.

speck   n *lit:* blemish, blot, defect, fault, flaw, fleck, mark, speckle, spot, stain; atom, bit, dot, grain, iota, mite, modicum, particle, shred, whit.

speckled   adj *lit:* brindled, dappled, dotted, freckled, mottled, spotted, spotty, stippled.

spectacle   n *lit:* display, event, extravaganza, pageant, performance, show; curiosity, laughingstock, marvel, phenomenon, scene, sight.

spectacular   n *lit:* display, extravaganza, show, spectacle. **adj** *lit:* breathtaking, dazzling, dramatic, fantastic, impressive, magnificent, sensational, splendid, striking, stunning.

spectator   n *lit:* beholder, eyewitness, observer, onlooker, viewer, watcher.

speculate   vb *lit:* cogitate, conjecture, contemplate, deliberate, hypothesize, meditate, scheme, surmise, theorize; gamble, hazard, risk, venture.

speech   n *lit:* conversation, dialogue, discussion, talk; address, discourse, disquisition, harangue, lecture, oration; articulation, dialect, diction, idiom, jargon, language, parlance, tongue.

speed n *lit:* acceleration, celerity, expedition, fleetness, momentum, pace, precipitation, quickness, rapidity, swiftness, velocity. **vb** *lit:* belt (along), career, expedite, flash, get a move on, hurry, make haste, press on, race, rush, tear, zoom; advance, boost, facilitate, further, help, promote.

spell n *lit:* bout, interval, period, season, stint, stretch, term, time, turn; charm, conjuration, exorcism, incantation, sorcery; allure, enchantment, fascination, magic, trance. **vb** *lit:* amount to, herald, imply, indicate, point to, portend, promise, signify, suggest.

spend vb *lit:* disburse, expend, lay out, pay out, splash out; consume, dissipate, drain, empty, exhaust, fritter away, squander, waste; bestow, devote, lavish, put in; fill, occupy, pass, while away.

sphere n *lit:* circle, globe, globule, orb; capacity, domain, field, function, range, scope, stratum, territory, walk of life.

spicy adj *lit:* aromatic, flavored, fragrant, savory, tangy; *fig:* indelicate, keen, lively, piquant, pungent, salacious, showy, smart, spirited

spin n *lit:* gyration, revolution, roll, whirl; drive, joy ride, turn. **vb** *lit:* gyrate, pirouette, revolve, rotate, twirl, twist; concoct, invent, recount, relate, tell, unfold; be giddy, grow dizzy, reel, swim.

spine n *lit:* backbone, spinal column, vertebrae; barb, quill, ray, spike, spur.

spineless adj *lit:* fainthearted, feeble, gutless, ineffective, irresolute, lily-livered, pusillanimous, soft, squeamish, submissive, vacillating, weak, yellow.

spiral n *lit:* coil, corkscrew, helix, volute, whorl. **adj** *lit:* circular, coiled, helical, scrolled, voluted, whorled, winding.

spirit n *lit:* air, breath, life force, psyche, soul; attitude, disposition, essence, humor, outlook, temper, temperament; ardor, backbone, courage, dauntlessness, energy, enthusiasm, force, grit, guts, life, mettle, sparkle, vigor, zest; motivation, resolution, willpower; atmosphere, feeling, gist, tenor, tone; intent, meaning, purport, sense, substance; apparition, ghost, phantom, specter, spook, sprite, vision. **vb** *lit:* carry (away), convey (off), steal (away), whisk (off).

spirited   adj *lit:* animated, ardent, bold, energetic, high-spirited, mettlesome, plucky, sprightly, vivacious.

spit   n *lit:* dribble, drool, saliva, spittle. **vb** *lit:* eject, expectorate, spew, splutter, throw out.

spite   n *lit:* animosity, grudge, hostility, ill will, malevolence, malice, pique, rancor, spitefulness, spleen, venom. **vb** *lit:* annoy, gall, harm, hurt, needle, nettle, offend, pique, put out, vex.

splendid   adj *lit:* admirable, exceptional, glorious, illustrious, magnificent, outstanding, remarkable, renowned, sublime, superb; costly, gorgeous, impressive, lavish, luxurious, rich, sumptuous; excellent, fantastic, fine, great, marvelous, wonderful; beaming, brilliant, glittering, lustrous, radiant.

splendor   n *lit:* brightness, brilliance, dazzle, glory, grandeur, luster, magnificence, pomp, renown, resplendence, solemnity, spectacle, stateliness.

splinter   n *lit:* chip, flake, paring, shaving, sliver. **vb** *lit:* disintegrate, fracture, shiver, split.

split   n *lit:* breach, crack, division, fissure, gap, rent, rip, slash, slit, tear; breakup, discord, disruption, dissension, divergence, estrangement, partition, rift, schism. **vb** *lit:* branch, break, burst, come apart, come undone, crack, disband, diverge, fork, give way, go separate ways, part, rend, rip, separate, slit, snap, splinter; allocate, allot, distribute, dole out, halve, partition, share out; grass on, inform on, squeal on. **adj** *lit:* ambivalent, bisected, broken, cracked, divided, fractured, ruptured.

spoil   n *lit:* refuse, slag. **vb** *lit:* blemish, damage, harm, impair, mess up, ruin, upset, wreck; cosset, indulge, mollycoddle, overindulge, pamper; curdle, decay, go bad, go off, rot, turn.

spot   n *lit:* blemish, blot, daub, flaw, mark, pimple, smudge, speck, stain; location, place, point, position, site; bit, little, morsel; mess, plight, predicament, quandary, trouble. **vb** *lit:* descry, detect, identify, make out, pick out, recognize, see, sight; blot, dot, fleck, mottle, soil, spatter, splotch, stain, taint, tarnish.

spread   n *lit:* advancement, dispersion, escalation, expansion, increase, proliferation, spreading; extent, period, span, stretch, sweep; array, feast repast. **vb** *lit:* broaden, expand, fan out, sprawl, stretch, unfold, widen; escalate, multiply, mushroom, proliferate; advertise, circulate, cover, distribute, make known, promulgate, propagate, publicize, scatter, shed, transmit; arrange, array, lay, prepare.

spring **n** *lit:* hop, jump, leap, vault; bounce, buoyancy, elasticity, flexibility, give, resilience; cause, origin, root, source, well. **vb** *lit:* bound, hop, jump, leap, rebound, recoil, vault; derive, descend, emanate, emerge, grow, originate, start, stem; burgeon, mushroom, shoot up.

spry **adj** *lit:* agile, brisk, nimble, quick, sprightly, supple.

spur **n** *lit:* goad, prick; impetus, impulse, incentive, motive, stimulus. **vb** *lit:* drive, goad, impel, incite, press, prod, prompt, stimulate, urge.

spurt **n** *lit:* burst, rush, spate, surge. **vb** *lit:* burst, erupt, gush, jet, spew, squirt, surge.

spy **n** *lit:* agent, mole. **vb** *lit:* shadow, tail, trail, watch; glimpse, notice, spot.

squander **vb** *lit:* blow, dissipate, fritter away, lavish, misuse, run through, spend, waste.

square **n** *lit:* equilateral rectangle; number multiplied by itself; *fig:* antediluvian, diehard, fuddy-duddy. **vb** *lit:* agree, conform, fit, match, reconcile, tally; balance, clear up, liquidate, pay off, satisfy, settle; adapt, align, even up, level, regulate, suit, tailor; bribe, buy off, fix, rig. **adj** *lit:* decent, equitable, ethical, fair, genuine, honest, just, straight; behind the times, conventional, old-fashioned, straitlaced, stuffy.

squash **n** *lit:* gourd, vegetable. **vb** *lit:* compress, crush, mash, pound, press, pulp, smash, trample down; annihilate, humiliate, put down, quash, quell, silence.

squeal **n** *lit:* scream, screech, shriek, wail, yell. **vb** *lit:* scream, screech, shout, shriek, shrill, wail, yelp; betray, blab, inform on; complain, protest.

squeeze **n** *lit:* cuddle, embrace, hold, hug; congestion, crowd, crush, jam, jostle, press, squash, thrust. **vb** *lit:* clutch, compress, crush, grip, pinch, squash, wring; cram, crowd, force, jam, jostle, pack, ram, thrust, wedge; clasp, cuddle, embrace, hold tight, hug; bleed, extort, lean on, pressurize, wrest.

stab n *lit:* gash, incision, jab, thrust; pang, prick, twinge; *fig:* attempt, crack, endeavor, go, try. **vb** *lit:* cut, gore, jab, knife, pierce, puncture, run through, stick, thrust, transfix; *fig:* deceive, double-cross, let down, sell.

stable n *lit:* barn, shed, stall; string, stud. **adj** *lit:* constant, deep-rooted, enduring, established, firm, fixed, lasting, permanent, reliable, secure, sound, steady, sure, unwavering, well-founded.

stage n *lit:* arena, theater; dais, platform, scaffold; jetty, pier, quay; division, juncture, lap, leg, level, phase, point. **vb** *lit:* arrange, do, engineer, lay on, orchestrate, organize, perform, play, present, produce, put on.

stagger **vb** *lit:* falter, lurch, reel, sway, totter, vacillate, waver, wobble; amaze, astonish, astound, bowl over, dumbfound, flabbergast, overwhelm, shake, shock, stun, stupefy, surprise, take aback; alternate, overlap, zigzag.

stain n *lit:* blemish, blot, discoloration, dye, spot, tint; disgrace, dishonor, infamy, shame, slur, stigma. **vb** *lit:* blemish, blot, color, discolor, dye, mark, soil, tarnish, tinge; corrupt, defile, deprave, disgrace, sully, taint.

stale **adj** *lit:* dry, fetid, flat, fusty, musty, old, sour, stagnant; antiquated, banal, cliché-ridden, common, drab, flat, hackneyed, insipid, platitudinous, stereotyped, trite, worn-out.

stall n *lit:* compartment (in a stable); booth (in a market); stalling, standstill; delay, pretense, pretext, prevarication. **vb** *lit:* confine (in a stall); become stuck, stop; block, delay, hedge, obstruct, play for time, prevaricate.

stand n *lit:* rest, standstill, stay, stopover; attitude, opinion, position, stance, standpoint; base, booth, dais, grandstand, platform, rack, stage, stall, support. **vb** *lit:* be upright, mount, place, position, put, set; be valid, continue, exist, halt, pause, rest, stay, stop; bear, cope with, countenance, endure, handle, put up with, stomach, sustain, take, tolerate, withstand.

standard n *lit:* average, criterion, example, gauge, guide, measure, model, norm, pattern, rule, specification, type, yardstick; ethics, ideals, moral principles; banner, colors, ensign, flag, pennant. **adj** *lit:* accepted, basic, customary, normal, orthodox, popular, regular, set, staple, stock, typical, usual.

standing   n *lit:* credit, estimation, footing, rank, reputation, station, status; duration, existence, experience. **adj** *lit:* fixed, lasting, permanent, perpetual, repeated; erect, perpendicular, upright, vertical.

stare   vb *lit:* gape, gawk, gaze, goggle, rubberneck.

start   n *lit:* beginning, commencement, dawn, foundation, inauguration, initiation, kickoff, onset, opening; advantage, head start, lead; break, chance, introduction, opportunity; convulsion, jar, spasm, twitch. **vb** *lit:* begin, commence, get under way, go ahead, leave, set off, set out; initiate, instigate, kick off, originate, set in motion, create, found, institute, launch, pioneer, set up; flinch, jerk, jump, recoil, twitch.

state   n *lit:* circumstances, condition, pass, plight, position, predicament, situation; attitude, frame of mind, mood; glory, grandeur, pomp, splendor, style; bother, flap, panic, tizzy; country, federation, land, nation. **vb** *lit:* affirm, articulate, assert, declare, enumerate, explain, expound, express, present, put, specify, voice.

station   n *lit:* depot, headquarters, location, place, position, situation; appointment, calling, grade, position, post, rank, situation, standing, status. **vb** *lit:* assign, fix, garrison, install, post, set.

stay   n *lit:* sojourn, stopover, visit; delay, halt, pause, postponement, remission, reprieve, suspension. **vb** *lit:* continue, delay, halt, hang around, linger, pause, remain, settle, sojourn, stop, tarry; lodge, put up at, visit; adjourn, defer, put off, suspend.

steady   vb *lit:* balance, brace, secure, support; compose oneself, cool down. **adj** *lit:* firm, fixed, stable, uniform; balanced, calm, dependable, levelheaded, reliable, sensible, settled, sober, steadfast; ceaseless, consistent, constant, even, faithful, habitual, persistent, regular, rhythmic, unbroken, unfaltering, uninterrupted, unwavering.

steal   vb *lit:* appropriate, embezzle, lift, misappropriate, pilfer, pinch, pirate, plagiarize, poach, purloin, thieve, make off with; creep, slip, sneak, tiptoe.

steep   vb *lit:* damp, drench, immerse, moisten, soak, submerge; fill, infuse, permeate, pervade, saturate, suffuse. **adj** *lit:* abrupt, precipitous, sheer; excessive, extortionate, overpriced, stiff, unreasonable.

stem   n *lit:* axis, peduncle, stalk, stock, trunk. **vb** *lit:* arise, derive, emanate, issue, originate; check, contain, curb, dam, hold back, resist, restrain, stop, withstand.

step   n *lit:* footstep, gait, pace, stride, trace, track; action, deed, expedient, means, measure, move, procedure; advancement, phase, point, progression; degree, level, rank; doorstep, stair, tread. **vb** *lit:* move, pace, tread, walk.

stick   n *lit:* baton, cane, rod, staff, stake, twig, wand; *fig:* fuddy-duddy, old fogy, pain, prig; blame, criticism, flak, hostility. **vb** *lit:* adhere, affix, bind, cling, fasten, hold on, join, paste; insert, jab, pierce, prod, puncture, stab, transfix; bulge, jut, poke, protrude; fix, lay, place, position, put, set; clog, jam, snag, stop; linger, remain, stay; endure, get on with, stand, stomach, take, tolerate; last out, put up with; stand up for, support.

sticky   adj *lit:* adhesive, clinging, glutinous, gooey, gummy, tacky, tenacious, viscous; awkward, difficult, embarrassing, nasty, thorny, tricky; clammy, humid, muggy, oppressive, sweltering.

stiff   adj *lit:* firm, hardened, inflexible, rigid, solid, taut, tense, tight, unbending; austere, chilly, constrained, formal, labored, pompous, prim, punctilious, starchy, uneasy; awkward, clumsy, crude, graceless, jerky, ungainly; arduous, exacting, formidable, hard, tough, trying, uphill; cruel, drastic, extreme, harsh, oppressive, pitiless, rigorous, severe, strict, stringent; brisk, powerful, strong, vigorous.

still   n *lit:* frame, photograph, picture; peace, quiet, stillness, tranquility. **vb** *lit:* distill; allay, alleviate, calm, hush, lull, settle, silence, smooth, soothe, tranquilize. **adj** *lit:* calm, hushed, inert, motionless, peaceful, placid, quiet, restful, silent, smooth, tranquil, undisturbed, unruffled. **adv** *lit:* even, yet; nevertheless; at that time, at this time; even to that time, even to this time; quietly, without moving. **cnj** *lit:* but, for all that, however, notwithstanding.

stir   n *lit:* ado, agitation, commotion, disturbance, excitement, flurry, fuss, to-do, uproar. **vb** *lit:* agitate, disturb, move, quiver, rustle, shake; arouse, excite, instigate, provoke, raise, urge; affect, inspire, thrill, touch; budge, get a move on, look lively.

stock   n *lit:* array, assortment, cache, commodities, fund, hoard, inventory, merchandise, range, stockpile, store, supply, variety; cattle, horses, livestock, sheep; breed, descent, extraction, forebears, lineage, parentage, pedigree; capital, funds, investment, property. **vb** *lit:* deal in, handle, keep, sell, supply, trade in; accumulate, buy up, hoard, replenish, store up; equip, fit out, furnish, provide with, provision. **adj** *lit:* banal, basic, conventional, customary, hackneyed, overused, regular, routine, set, standard, staple, stereotyped, trite, usual, worn-out.

stomach **n** *lit:* abdomen, belly, paunch, tummy; appetite, inclination, mind, taste. **vb** *lit:* bear, endure, put up with, resign oneself to, suffer, take, tolerate.

stoop **n** *lit:* droop, sag, slouch, slump. **vb** *lit:* bend, crouch, duck, hunch, incline, lean, squat; condescend, deign, demean oneself, resort, sink.

stop **n** *lit:* cessation, conclusion, end, finish, halt, standstill; sojourn, stay, stopover, visit; bar, block, break, check, hindrance, impediment, stoppage; depot, destination, station, terminus. **vb** *lit:* be over, break off, cease, conclude, cut short, discontinue, end, finish, leave off, peter out, pull up, quit, refrain, stall, terminate; arrest, bar, block, check, forestall, frustrate, hinder, hold back, impede, intercept, prevent, restrain, silence, stem, suspend; break one's journey, lodge, sojourn, stay, tarry.

store **n** *lit:* accumulation, cache, hoard, mine, provision, reserve, stock, supply; emporium, outlet, shop, supermarket; depository, storeroom, warehouse. **vb** *lit:* accumulate, deposit, hoard, keep, lay by, put aside, reserve, salt away, save, stock.

storm **n** *lit:* blizzard, cyclone, gale, gust, hurricane, tempest, tornado, whirlwind; assault, attack, blitz, offensive, onslaught; *fig:* agitation, commotion, disturbance, outburst, outcry, row, rumpus, strife, turmoil. **vb** *lit:* assail, assault, beset, charge, take by storm; complain, fume, rage, rant, scold, thunder; flounce, rush, stalk.

story **n** *lit:* account, anecdote, chronicle, history, legend, narrative, novel, recital, romance, tale, yarn; fib, fiction, lie, untruth; article, feature, news item, report.

straight **adj** *lit:* direct, undeviating, unswerving; aligned, erect, horizontal, level, perpendicular, upright, vertical; blunt, forthright, frank, outright, point-blank, straightforward, unqualified; above board, accurate, equitable, fair, honest, law-abiding, reliable, trustworthy; arranged, neat, orderly, organized, shipshape, tidy; continuous, nonstop, solid, sustained, uninterrupted; conventional, orthodox, traditional; pure, unadulterated, undiluted. **adv** *lit:* as the crow flies; at once, directly, immediately, instantly; frankly, honestly, point-blank, pulling no punches.

strain   n *lit:* effort, exertion, force, injury, struggle, tension, wrench; anxiety, burden, pressure, stress; air, melody, theme, tune; ancestry, descent, extraction, lineage, pedigree, stock; suggestion, tendency, trace, trait; manner, style, temper, tone, vein. **vb** *lit:* draw tight, extend, stretch, tighten; exert, fatigue, injure, overwork, sprain, tax, tire, twist, wrench; endeavor, strive, struggle; filter, percolate, separate, sieve, sift.

strange   adj *lit:* abnormal, bizarre, curious, extraordinary, fantastic, odd, peculiar, perplexing, queer, rare, singular, uncanny, weird; alien, foreign, novel, unfamiliar, untried; new to, unaccustomed to, unused to; awkward, bewildered, ill at ease, lost, out of place.

strangle   vb *lit:* asphyxiate, choke, smother, strangulate, throttle; gag, inhibit, stifle, suppress.

stray   n *lit:* lost animal, wanderer. **vb** *lit:* deviate, diverge, get sidetracked, ramble; be abandoned, drift, err, go astray, meander, roam, rove, straggle, wander. **adj** *lit:* abandoned, lost, roaming; accidental, chance, freak, odd, random.

stream   n *lit:* beck, brook, current, river, rivulet, torrent, tributary. **vb** *lit:* cascade, course, flow, gush, run, shed, spout.

strength   n *lit:* backbone, brawn, firmness, might, robustness, stamina, sturdiness, toughness; efficacy, energy, force, potency, vehemence, vigor; asset, mainstay, strong point, succor.

stress   n *lit:* emphasis, importance, significance, weight; anxiety, hassle, pressure, strain, tension, trauma, worry; accent, accentuation, beat. **vb** *lit:* accentuate, dwell on, emphasize, harp on, repeat, rub in, underline.

stretch   n *lit:* distance, expanse, extent, spread, tract; period, run, space, spell, stint, time. **vb** *lit:* cover, extend, reach, spread; draw out, elongate, expand, pull, rack, tighten.

strict   adj *lit:* austere, firm, harsh, no-nonsense, rigorous, stern, stringent; accurate, exact, meticulous, particular, precise, scrupulous; absolute, complete, utter.

strike   n *lit:* bang, blow, clout, hit, knock, slap, smack, wallop; stoppage, walkout. **vb** *lit:* bang, beat, chastise, clobber, clout, hit, knock, pound, smack, smite, thump, wallop; clash, collide with, run into, smash into; drive, force, thrust; come to mind, dawn upon, occur to, register; chance upon, discover, find, stumble upon, unearth; assail, assault, attack, fall upon, set upon; achieve, arrive at, reach; walk out.

strip **n** *lit:* belt, bit, fillet, piece, shred, slip, swathe. **vb** *lit:* bare, deprive, dismantle, empty, loot, pillage, plunder, ransack, rob, spoil; disrobe, unclothe, undress.

stroke **n** *lit:* achievement, blow, feat, hit, knock, movement, pat, rap, thump; apoplexy, attack, fit, seizure, shock. **vb** *lit:* caress, fondle, pat, pet.

stroll **n** *lit:* breath of air, constitutional, excursion, promenade, ramble, walk. **vb** *lit:* amble, make one's way, mosey, promenade, ramble, saunter, stretch one's legs, toddle, wander.

strong **adj** *lit:* athletic, beefy, burly, hale, hardy, muscular, robust, sound, stalwart, strapping, sturdy, tough, virile; brave, courageous, determined, high-powered, plucky, resilient, resourceful, steadfast, tenacious, unyielding; acute, dedicated, deep-rooted, eager, fervent, firm, intense, keen, staunch, vehement, zealous; clear-cut, cogent, compelling, distinct, formidable, marked, persuasive, potent, telling, unmistakable, weighty, well-founded; drastic, extreme, forceful, severe; durable, hard-wearing, heavy-duty, reinforced, substantial, well-built, well-protected; bold, bright, dazzling, glaring, loud; biting, heady, highly flavored, hot, intoxicating, piquant, pure, spicy, undiluted.

structure **n** *lit:* arrangement, conformation, design, form, interrelation of parts, make-up, organization; building, construction, edifice. **vb** *lit:* arrange, assemble, build up, design, put together, shape.

struggle **n** *lit:* effort, exertion, grind, long haul, scramble, toil; battle, brush, clash, conflict, contest, encounter, skirmish, strife, tussle. **vb** *lit:* exert oneself, go all out, strain, strive, toil, work; battle, compete, contend, fight, grapple, scuffle.

stubborn **adj** *lit:* bullheaded, dogged, headstrong, intractable, obstinate, persistent, pigheaded, recalcitrant, stiff-necked, tenacious, unshakable, willful.

stuck **adj (pa.pt)** *lit:* cemented, fastened, fixed, glued, joined; *fig:* at a loss, baffled, nonplussed; hung up on, infatuated, keen, mad, obsessed with.

student n *lit:* apprentice, disciple, observer, pupil, scholar, undergraduate.

study n *lit:* academic work, research; analysis, attention, contemplation, inquiry, investigation, scrutiny, survey; drawing, sketch; den, library. **vb** *lit:* apply oneself to, contemplate, examine, go into, meditate, ponder, read; analyze, deliberate, investigate, look into, peruse, research, survey.

stuff n *lit:* belongings, effects, equipment, gear, paraphernalia, possessions, tackle, trappings; cloth, fabric, material, textile; essence, matter, quintessence, substance; balderdash, bunkum, claptrap, humbug, nonsense, poppycock, rot, rubbish, tripe, twaddle, verbiage. **vb** *lit:* compress, cram, fill, jam, load, pad, ram, shove, squeeze, wedge; gobble, guzzle, make a pig of oneself, overindulge.

stuffy adj *lit:* airless, fetid, heavy, oppressive, stifling, suffocating, unventilated; conventional, dreary, dull, musty, priggish, prim, stodgy, straitlaced.

stumble vb *lit:* fall, falter, flounder, lurch, reel, slip, stagger, trip; falter, stammer, stutter.

stunted adj (pa.pt) *lit:* diminutive, dwarfed, small, tiny, undersized.

stupid adj *lit:* asinine, brainless, dim, feebleminded, imbecile, naive, slow, thickheaded; absurd, folly, foolhardy, inept, irresponsible, senseless, silly.

sturdy adj *lit:* athletic, brawny, durable, firm, hardy, hearty, muscular, robust, secure, stalwart, staunch, steadfast, vigorous, well-built.

style n *lit:* cut, design, form, manner, technique; fashion, mode, rage, trend, vogue; approach, custom, manner, way; chic, dash, elegance, flair, panache, smartness, sophistication, stylishness, taste; affluence, comfort, grandeur, luxury; category, characteristic, genre, kind, sort, spirit, tenor, tone, type; diction, expression, phraseology, turn of phrase, vein, wording. **vb** *lit:* adapt, cut, design, dress, fashion, tailor; address, call, dub, entitle, label, name, term.

subdued adj *lit:* chastened, dejected, downcast, grave, restrained, sad, serious, solemn; hushed, low-key, muted, quiet, sober, soft, subtle, toned down.

subject n *lit:* affair, business, issue, matter, object, point, question, theme, topic; case, guinea pig, participant, patient; citizen, dependent, national, vassal. **vb** *lit:* expose, lay open, put through, submit, treat. **adj** *lit:* exposed, liable, open, prone, susceptible, vulnerable; conditional, contingent, dependent; answerable, bound by, inferior, obedient, satellite, subjugated, subordinate.

submit vb *lit:* acquiesce, agree, bend, capitulate, comply, defer, give in, knuckle under, put up with, resign oneself, succumb, surrender, toe the line, tolerate, yield; commit, hand in, proffer, put forward, refer, tender; advance, argue, assert, contend, move, propose, propound, put, state, suggest.

substance n *lit:* body, fabric, material, stuff, texture; burden, gist, import, meaning, pith, significance, subject, theme; actuality, entity, force, reality; affluence, assets, estate, means, resources.

substitute n *lit:* agent, deputy, expedient, locum tenens, proxy, relief, replacement, reserve, standby, surrogate. **vb** *lit:* change, exchange, replace, swap, switch; act for, cover for, deputize, fill in for, stand in for. **adj** *lit:* acting, additional, proxy, replacement, reserve, surrogate, temporary.

subtle adj *lit:* delicate, ingenious, nice, penetrating, profound, refined, sophisticated; faint, slight, understated; artful, crafty, cunning, devious, intriguing, Machiavellian, scheming, shrewd, sly, wily.

succeed vb *lit:* flourish, make good, prosper, thrive; ensue, follow.

successful adj *lit:* best-selling, booming, efficacious, flourishing, lucky, lucrative, profitable, prosperous, thriving, top.

suffer vb *lit:* ache, grieve, hurt; bear, endure, experience, go through, put up with, sustain, undergo; be impaired, deteriorate, fall off; allow, let, permit.

suggestion n *lit:* motion, proposal, proposition, recommendation; hint, indication, insinuation, intimation, suspicion, trace.

suggestive adj *lit:* evocative, indicative, reminiscent; bawdy, blue, provocative, ribald, risqué, rude, smutty, spicy, titillating.

suit n *lit:* appeal, attentions, courtship, entreaty, petition, request; costume, dress, habit, outfit; *spec:* action, case, lawsuit, proceeding, prosecution, trial. **vb** *lit:* agree, answer, become, befit, be seemly, conform to, do, go with, match, satisfy, tally; accommodate, adjust, fashion, fit, tailor.

suitable   adj *lit:* acceptable, applicable, appropriate, apt, becoming, befitting, convenient, fitting, in character, in keeping, pertinent, proper, relevant, right, satisfactory, seemly, suited.

sulky   adj *lit:* aloof, churlish, disgruntled, moody, morose, petulant, put out, querulous, sullen, vexed.

sullen   adj. *lit:* glum, ill-humored, moody, morose, sulky.

sultry   adj *lit:* hot, humid, oppressive, sticky, stifling, stuffy; passionate, provocative, seductive, sensual, sexy, voluptuous.

sum   n *lit:* aggregate, amount, quantity, reckoning, score, tally, total, whole.

summary   n *lit:* abridgment, abstract, compendium, digest, epitome, essence, extract, outline, résumé, review, rundown, sum-up, synopsis. **adj** *lit:* arbitrary, compact, compendious, concise, condensed, cursory, hasty, perfunctory, pithy.

summit   n *lit:* acme, apex, crowning point, culmination, height, peak, pinnacle, top, zenith.

summon   vb *lit:* assemble, bid, call together, convene, invite, rally, send for; call into action, draw on, gather, muster.

sunken   adj *lit:* at a lower level, buried, depressed, immersed, recessed, submerged; drawn, haggard, hollowed.

sunny   adj *lit:* bright, clear, luminous, radiant, sunlit, unclouded; beaming, buoyant, cheery, genial, joyful, lighthearted, optimistic, pleasant.

superb   adj *lit:* admirable, breathtaking, choice, exquisite, first-rate, gorgeous, magnificent, splendid, superior.

superior   n *lit:* boss, chief, director, manager, principal, senior, supervisor. **adj** *lit:* better, greater, higher, more advanced, predominant, preferred, prevailing, surpassing; admirable, choice, deluxe, distinguished, excellent, exclusive, first-class, first-rate, good quality, high caliber, high-class; airy, condescending, haughty, lofty, patronizing, pretentious, snobbish, supercilious.

supervision n *lit:* administration, auspices, care, charge, control, guidance, management, oversight, surveillance.

supplant vb *lit:* displace, oust, overthrow, replace, supersede, take over, undermine, unseat.

supple adj *lit:* elastic, flexible, limber, lithe, plastic, pliable.

supplementary adj *lit:* accompanying, additional, auxiliary, complementary, extra, secondary.

supply n *lit:* cache, fund, hoard, reserve, reservoir, source, stockpile, store; foodstuff, items, materials, necessities, provisions, rations, stores. vb *lit:* afford, cater, contribute, endow, furnish, give, grant, produce, provide, purvey, replenish, stock, store, victual.

support n *lit:* back, brace, foundation, pillar, post, prop, stanchion, stay, underpinning; aid, assistance, backing, blessing, encouragement, furtherance, help, moral support, patronage, protection, relief, sustenance; livelihood, maintenance, subsistence; backbone, backer, mainstay, supporter. vb *lit:* bear, bolster, brace, buttress, hold up, prop, reinforce, sustain, underpin, uphold; cherish, finance, foster, fund, keep, look after, maintain, provide for, strengthen, subsidize, succor, take care of, underwrite; advocate, aid, assist, back, champion, defend, forward, go along with, promote, second, side with, stand behind, stick up for, take (someone's) part; attest to, authenticate, bear out, confirm, corroborate, endorse, substantiate, verify; countenance, endure, put up with, stand (for), submit, suffer, tolerate, undergo.

suppose vb *lit:* assume, conjecture, dare say, expect, imagine, presume, surmise, take for granted, think; believe, conceive, conclude, consider, fancy, postulate, pretend.

suppress vb *lit:* check, conquer, crush, drive underground, extinguish, overthrow, quash, quench, stamp out, subdue, trample; censor, conceal, cover up, curb, hold back, keep secret, muffle, repress, restrain, silence, smother, withhold.

supreme adj *lit:* cardinal, chief, culminating, extreme, first, foremost, greatest, leading, paramount, predominant, preeminent, prime, principal, superlative, surpassing, top, ultimate, utmost.

sure adj *lit:* assured, clear, confident, decided, definite, positive, satisfied; accurate, dependable, foolproof, honest, indisputable, infallible, precise, reliable, trusty, undeniable, undoubted, unmistakable; bound, guaranteed, inescapable, inevitable, irrevocable; fast, firm, fixed, safe, secure, solid, stable, steady.

surface n *lit:* exterior, facade, facet, outside, skin, top, veneer. **vb** *lit:* appear, come to light, crop up, emerge, rise, transpire. **adj** *lit:* apparent, exterior, external, outward, superficial.

surge n *lit:* billow, efflux, flood, flow, gush, intensification, rush, swell, upsurge, wave. **vb** *lit:* billow, eddy, flow, gush, heave, rise, rush, swell, swirl, undulate.

surly   **adj** *lit:* brusque, churlish, crusty, gruff, ill-natured, morose, sullen, testy, uncivil.

surplus n *lit:* balance, excess, remainder, residue, superfluity, surfeit. **adj** *lit:* excessive, extra, odd, remaining, spare, superfluous.

surprise n *lit:* amazement, astonishment, bewilderment, incredulity; bombshell, eye-opener, revelation, shock. **vb** *lit:* amaze, astonish, astound, bewilder, disconcert, flabbergast, stun, take aback; catch off guard, catch red-handed, discover, startle.

surrender n *lit:* capitulation, delivery, relinquishment, renunciation, resignation, submission. **vb** *lit:* abandon, concede, forego, give up, part with, relinquish, renounce, resign, waive, yield; capitulate, give oneself up, give way, quit, submit, succumb.

surround   **vb** *lit:* close in on, encircle, enclose, encompass, fence in, hem in, ring; *spec:* besiege, lay siege on.

surroundings n *lit:* environment, location, milieu, neighborhood, setting.

survive   **vb** *lit:* endure, hold out, last, live, pull through, subsist.

suspect   **vb** *lit:* distrust, mistrust, smell a rat; believe, conjecture, consider, feel, speculate, suppose, surmise, think probable. **adj** *lit:* doubtful, dubious, fishy, questionable.

suspend   **vb** *lit:* attach, dangle, hang, swing; adjourn, cease, cut short, defer, delay, hold off, interrupt, lay aside, postpone, put off, shelve, stay, withhold.

suspense   n *lit:* anticipation, anxiety, apprehension, doubt, expectation, indecision, tension, uncertainty, wavering.

suspicion   n *lit:* distrust, doubt, misgiving, mistrust, qualm, skepticism, wariness; conjecture, guess, hunch, impression, notion, supposition, surmise; glimmer, hint, shadow, strain, suggestion, tinge, touch, trace.

swamp   n *lit:* bog, fen, marsh, mire, morass, quagmire, slough. **vb** *lit:* capsize, engulf, flood, inundate, sink, submerge, swallow up, upset, waterlog; besiege, deluge, overload, overwhelm.

swear   vb *lit:* affirm, assert, attest, declare, give one's word, pledge oneself, promise, take an oath, testify, vow, warrant; blaspheme, curse, imprecate.

sweep   n *lit:* arc, curve, gesture, movement, stroke, swing; compass, extend, range, scope, span, stretch, vista. **vb** *lit:* brush, clean, clear; career, fly, glide, hurtle, sail, skim, tear, zoom.

sweet   n *lit:* confection, dessert, pudding, sweetmeat, treat, trifle. **adj** *lit:* cloying, honeyed, saccharine, sugary, syrupy, toothsome; affectionate, agreeable, amiable, attractive, charming, delightful, engaging, gentle, kind, sweet-tempered, taking, tender, winsome; beloved, darling, dear, precious; aromatic, fragrant, fresh, perfumed, redolent, sweet-smelling; euphonic, harmonious, mellow, silvery, soft, tuneful; fond of, keen on.

sympathetic   adj *lit:* affectionate, caring, compassionate, concerned, kindly, understanding, warmhearted; favorably disposed (to), in sympathy with, pro; agreeable, appreciative, compatible, congenial, like-minded.

system   n *lit:* arrangement, classification, combination, coordination, organization, scheme, setup, structure; fixed order, practice, procedure, routine, technique, theory, usage; logical process, method, orderliness, regularity, systematization.

T

table n *lit:* bar, counter, stand, surface; board, fare, food; flats, mesa, plain, plateau; *fig:* chart, diagram, key, list, tabulation. **vb** *lit:* introduce, move, propose, put forward; catalog, chart, list, tabulate.

tack n *lit:* drawing pin, nail, pin; gear, harness, riding equipment, saddle; basting, darn, temporary stitch; adhesiveness, bond; bearing, course, heading; angle, dogleg, zigzag; *fig:* approach, method, procedure, way. **vb** *lit:* nail, pin; baste, darn loosely, stitch temporarily; bond, glue, gum, paste, stick; change direction, veer, zigzag; *fig:* annex, append, attach.

tackle n *lit:* accouterments, equipment, gear, outfit, rig, trappings; attack, block, bringing down. **vb** *lit:* apply oneself to, attack, get to grips with, grapple with, have a go at, set about, take on, undertake, wrestle with; block, bring down, fell, grab, halt, hold, pounce on, stop.

tact n *lit:* address, decorousness, delicacy, diplomacy, discretion, finesse, sensitivity; judgment, sense, wisdom.

tactic n *lit:* gambit, maneuver, move, ploy, stratagem, strategy; line, method, plan, policy, scheme, way.

tactless adj *lit:* boorish, clumsy, inconsiderate, indelicate, inept, insensitive, thoughtless, unkind; imprudent, incautious, indiscreet, undiplomatic; discourteous, impolite, rude, uncivil.

tail n *lit:* appendage, end, extremity; backside, behind, bottom, posterior, rear, rump, seat, stern; file, line, train; coda, conclusion, finale; shadower, stalker, tracker, watcher. **vb** *lit:* dog, follow, shadow, trace, track, trail; die (away), drop (off), fade (away), taper (off).

tainted adj (pa.pt) *lit:* blighted, contaminated, dirty, foul, infected, poisoned, polluted, soiled; blackened, blemished, branded, disgraced, dishonored, ruined, stigmatized, sullied, tarnished.

take vb *lit:* carry (away), collect, gain possession of, get, get hold of, grasp, grip, have, hold, receive, win; bear, bring, convey, ferry, fetch, haul, lug, transport; accompany, conduct, escort, guide, lead, usher; acquire, come into possession of, obtain, procure, secure; marry, wed; arrest, capture, entrap, seize; fell, hit, kill, tackle; abduct, hijack, kidnap, run off with; abstract, liberate, misappropriate, pinch, purloin, steal, swipe; deduct, remove, subtract; consume, drink, eat, ingest; accommodate, contain, have room for; *fig:* do, effect, execute, make, perform; indulge in; accept, adopt, assume, be guided by, comply with, obey; call for, demand, need, require; spend, use (up); book, engage, hire, lease, rent, reserve; buy, purchase; choose, pick, select; brook, endure, go through, put up with, stand, stomach, swallow, tolerate, withstand; bilk, cheat, con, dupe, swindle; catch, go by, travel in; believe, consider, interpret, perceive, presume, regard, see; be attractive, charm, enchant, please; learn, study; photograph, shoot, snap; *spec:* be effective, operate, work.

tale n *lit:* account, anecdote, fable, legend, saga, story, yarn; fib, fiction, rigmarole, spiel; rumor, scandal, secret.

talent n *lit:* ability, aptitude, faculty, flair, forte, gift, knack.

talk n *lit:* address, dissertation, lecture, oration, sermon, speech; chat, chitchat, conversation, gab, gossip; confabulation, conference, consultation, dialogue, discussion, parley; words. vb *lit:* speak; chat, chatter, converse, gossip, prattle; confabulate, confer, consult, discuss, parley; negotiate; blab, spill the beans, sing, squeal.

tall adj *lit:* big, high, lanky, lofty, towering; *fig:* daunting, demanding, formidable, hard; absurd, farfetched, implausible, incredible, ludicrous, preposterous, ridiculous.

tamper vb *lit:* fiddle (with), fool about (with), interfere (with), meddle (with), muck about (with), tinker (with).

tan n *lit:* sunburn; tannin. vb *lit:* burn, sunburn; *fig:* beat, flog, thrash, whip. adj *lit:* beige, buff, khaki, light brown.

tangle n *lit:* coil, knot, mass, mesh, snarl, twist; imbroglio, mix-up; labyrinth, maze. vb *lit:* coil, interlace, intertwine, knot, mat, mesh, snarl, twist; embroil (in), involve (in); *fig:* contend (with), cross swords (with), lock horns (with), mess (with).

tank n *lit:* cistern, container, reservoir, vessel; lake, pool; armored vehicle.

tap n *lit:* bug, listening device; knock, pat, rap, touch; faucet, spout, stopcock; (on) draft; *fig:* (on) hand. vb *lit:* bug, listen in on; knock, pat, rap, touch; broach, draw off, open, siphon off; exploit, make use of, milk, mine, use, utilize.

tape n *lit:* band, cassette, film, ribbon, strip; binding; finishing line. **vb** *lit:* bind, secure, tie (up); record, videotape.

target n *lit:* butt, inner; bull's-eye, goal, mark, objective, quarry; prey, victim; *fig:* aim, ambition, intention, objective.

task n *lit:* assignment, charge, chore, duty, job, mission, occupation, work.

taste n *lit:* flavor, relish, savor, tang; bite, morsel, mouthful, nip, sip, snatch, swallow; appetite, fancy, fondness, inclination, liking, palate, partiality, predilection, preference; culture, discrimination, grace, judgment, refinement. **vb** *lit:* have a flavor (of), savor (of); discern, distinguish, sense; nibble, sample, sip, take a bite of, try; *fig:* encounter, experience, feel, know.

taunt n *lit:* dig, gibe, insult, snide remark; provocation. **vb** *lit:* deride, insult, jeer at, mock, sneer at, tease; provoke.

taut adj *lit:* flexed, strained, stressed, stretched, tense, tight; neat, orderly, shipshape, tidy, trim.

tax n *lit:* customs, duty, excise, impost, levy, rate, tariff, toll; assessment, contribution; burden, drain, load, stress, weight. **vb** *lit:* exact a toll from, impose a levy on, levy a rate on; burden, exhaust, load down, sap, strain, try, weaken, weigh upon; charge (with), reprove (with).

teach vb *lit:* educate, enlighten, impart, inculcate, inform; give lessons, lecture, tutor; coach, discipline, drill, instruct, school, train; demonstrate, show.

teacher n *lit:* educator, guru, lecturer, master, mentor, mistress, pedagogue, professor, tutor; coach, instructor, trainer; demonstrator.

team n *lit:* band, brigade, company, crew, gang, set, side, squad, troop, troupe; pair, span, yoke. **vb** *lit:* cooperate (with), join (up with), link (up with), unite (with).

teasing n *lit:* aggravation, badgering, baiting, gibes, mockery, needling, provocation, ragging, ridicule, taunts; carding, combing out, shredding.

technique n *lit:* art, craft, execution, knack, know-how, proficiency, skill; manner, means, method, procedure, system, way.

teeth n *lit:* dentition, dentures, occlusion; canines, incisors, molars, premolars; fangs, tusks; cogs, projections, prongs, serrations, tines; *fig:* bite, force, power.

telephone n *lit:* handset, phone, receiver; line. **vb** *lit:* buzz, call, call up, dial, give one a call, give one a ring, phone, ring.

tell vb *lit:* acquaint of, apprise of, communicate to, divulge to, impart to, inform of, let know, make known to, mention to, notify of, say to; blab, squeal; announce, proclaim, publish; depict, describe, narrate, recount, relate; command (to), direct (to), instruct (to), order (to); differentiate, discern, distinguish, identify, make out, see, understand; count, have an effect, register, weigh heavily.

temper n *lit:* consistency, density, homogeneity; disposition, frame of mind, humor, mood, nature; (lose one's) composure, cool, equanimity, self-control; fury, heat, passion, rage, tantrum. **vb** *lit:* mix, mold, work; moderate, soften; harden; check, curb, restrain; adjust the pitch of, tune.

temperament n *lit:* character, disposition, frame of mind, humor, make-up, nature, outlook, personality, stamp; excitability, hotheadedness, impatience, moods, volatility; tuning, variation in pitch.

temperance n *lit:* moderation, restraint, self-control, self-discipline; abstinence, continence, sobriety, teetotalism.

temperate adj *lit:* agreeable, clement, fair, mild, moderate, pleasant; balmy, cool, soft; calm, composed, equable, even-tempered, self-controlled, self-restrained, stable; abstinent, continent, sober, teetotal.

tempest n *lit:* cyclone, gale, hurricane, storm, typhoon; *fig:* agitation, commotion, furor, riot, tumult, turbulence, uproar.

tempestuous adj *lit:* blustery, boisterous, gusty, raging, stormy, turbulent; emotional, excited, feverish, furious, impassioned, intense, uncontrolled, violent, wild.

temporary adj *lit:* bridging, fleeting, impermanent, interim; casual, passing, stand-in, substitute, transient, transitory.

temptation   n *lit:* allure, attraction, enticement, lure, pull, seduction; bait, carrot, decoy, draw, invitation, loss leader.

tend   vb *lit:* attend, care for, feed, keep, look after, maintain, nurse, see to, serve, wait upon; guard, protect, watch over; aim, go, lead, move, point, be biased, gravitate, incline.

tender   n *lit:* bid, offer, proposal; coinage, currency, money, payment; supply vehicle. **vb** *lit:* give, offer, present, proffer, submit, volunteer. **adj** *lit:* delicate, fragile, frail, weak; callow, green, immature, new, unripe, young; affectionate, amorous, fond, kind, loving, sentimental, softhearted, sympathetic; compassionate, gentle, merciful; emotional, moving, romantic, touching; aching, painful, raw, sensitive, sore.

tenderness   n *lit:* delicacy, fragility, frailty, weakness; greenness, immaturity, unripeness, youth; affection, fondness, kindness, love, sentiment, softheartedness, sympathy; compassion, gentleness, mercy; painfulness, rawness, sensitivity, soreness.

tense   vb *lit:* clench, contract, flex, stiffen, tighten. **adj** *lit:* strained, stretched, taut, tight; *fig:* apprehensive, edgy, jittery, jumpy, keyed up, nervous, restless, strung up, wound up; nerve-racking, stressful.

tension   n *lit:* rigidity, tautness, tightness, torque; apprehension, edginess, nervousness, pressure, strain, stress, suspense.

term   n *lit:* appellation, designation, expression, name, phrase, title, word; duration, period, spell, time, while; semester, session; denominator, numerator; predicate, subject; *spec:* completion, culmination, end (of a pregnancy, of a period of grace). **vb** *lit:* call, christen, designate, dub, entitle, label, name, nickname, style.

terminal   n *lit:* airport, airport building; station, stop, terminus. **adj** *lit:* concluding, final, last, ultimate; endmost, hindmost, rear; fatal, incurable, lethal, mortal.

terminate   vb *lit:* come to an end, complete, conclude, end, finish, stop; bring to an end, close, cut off, discontinue, wind up; expire, lapse, run out.

terrible   adj *lit:* bad, grave, serious, severe; appalling, awful, dreadful, frightful, horrifying; hopeless, poor, rotten, useless.

terrific   adj *lit:* enormous, extreme, great, intense, serious, severe, tremendous; excellent, fantastic, fine, magnificent, outstanding, superb, wonderful.

territory   n *lit:* area, country, district, domain, land, manor, realm, region, tract, zone.

terror   n *lit:* dread, fear, fright, panic; alarm, awe, consternation, shock; *fig:* devil, fiend, monster; scoundrel, villain; rascal, rogue, scamp.

test   n *lit:* examination; checkup; analysis, assessment, evaluation, investigation; measure, proof. **vb** *lit:* analyze, assess, check up on, examine, gauge, investigate, measure, try, try out, verify.

testimonial   n *lit:* character reference, commendation, reference; honorarium, memorial gift; charity match.

testimony   n *lit:* evidence, submission, witness; affidavit, confession, deposition, statement; demonstration, indication, manifestation, proof, verification.

tether   vb *lit:* lash, rope, secure, tie up; moor; attach, bind.

text   n *lit:* contents, matter, words; book, reference work, source; passage, verse; motif, subject, theme, topic.

texture   n *lit:* composition, consistency, quality, structure, surface; fabric, grain, weave.

then   adj *lit:* concurrent, contemporary. **adv** *lit:* at that time; afterward, later, presently, soon, thereafter; next, subsequently; also, besides; accordingly, consequently, in that case.

theory   n *lit:* assumption, conjecture, estimate, explanation, guess, hypothesis, speculation, supposition; classification, philosophy, system.

thick   n *lit:* center, midst. adj *lit:* broad, deep, fat, substantial, wide; compact, concentrated, condensed, dense, impenetrable, opaque; crowded, jammed, packed; bristling, covered, crawling, swarming, teeming; *fig:* guttural, hoarse, husky, throaty; distinct, marked, pronounced, strong; friendly, inseparable, intimate; dim, dull, idiotic, obtuse, slow, stupid.

thief   n *lit:* burglar, housebreaker, mugger, pickpocket, robber; embezzler, fraud, swindler; kleptomaniac, shoplifter; pirate, plagiarizer, rip-off merchant.

thin vb *lit:* adulterate, attenuate, dilute, water down, weaken; prune back, trim; rarefy, refine; constrict, fine down, narrow, taper. **adj** *lit:* attenuated, fine, narrow; bony, emaciated, lanky, scraggy, scrawny, skeletal, skinny, slender, slim, spindly; meager, scanty, scarce, sparse; diaphanous, filmy, flimsy, see-through, sheer, skimpy, transparent, wispy; adulterated, dilute, insipid, watered down, watery, weak; rarefied, refined; *fig:* feeble, inadequate, lame, poor, superficial, unconvincing.

thing n *lit:* article, fact, item, object; affair, matter, subject, theme, topic; idea, importance, point, significance, thought; attribute, property, quality; event, incident, occasion, occurrence, phenomenon, proceedings; act, action, deed, feat, turn; apparatus, device, implement, instrument, machine, tool; belonging(s), effect(s), possession(s); *fig:* animal, creature, person; hobby, pastime, preoccupation; fixation, hang-up, obsession.

think vb *lit:* brood, cogitate, contemplate, deliberate, meditate, mull, muse, ponder, reflect, ruminate; call to mind, consider, recall, recollect, remember; believe, conceive (of), hold, suppose; conclude, decide, deem, judge; assume, gather, guess, imagine, reckon, surmise; envisage, expect, presume, suspect; intend (to), plan (to).

thirsty adj *lit:* dehydrated, dry, parched; arid; *fig:* avid, eager, greedy , hungry, longing (for), yearning (for).

thorough adj *lit:* careful, conscientious, efficient, meticulous, painstaking, scrupulous; complete, comprehensive, exhaustive, full; intensive; arrant, out-and-out, sheer, total, unmitigated, utter.

though adv *lit:* for all that, however, nevertheless, nonetheless. **cnj** *lit:* although, despite the fact that, notwithstanding the fact that, while; albeit, yet; (as) if.

thoughtful adj *lit:* caring, considerate, helpful, kind, solicitous; contemplative, deliberative, introspective, introverted, meditative, pensive, reflective, ruminative, studious; careful, provident, prudent.

threat n *lit:* intimidation, menace, warning; blackmail; danger, peril, risk.

through adj *lit:* fast, nonstop; arterial, linking, major; completed, done, finished; breaking up, separating; bust, washed up; exhausted, spent, whacked. **adv** *lit:* in and straight on out; from beginning to end, from one side to the other; all the way, directly, nonstop; to the skin. **prp** *lit:* in and

through 378

straight on out of; from beginning to end of, from one side to the other of; during the whole of, throughout; around, in, on, via; because of, by reason of, owing to; as a result of, by means of, by way of, with; done with, finished with.

throw n *lit:* cast, fling, heave, hurl, lob, put, shy, sling, toss; fall; attempt, bash, go, try, turn, venture; *fig:* article, item, unit. **vb** *lit:* cast, chuck, fling, heave, hurl, lob, put, shy, sling, toss; launch, propel; fell, floor, overturn, unseat; *fig:* catch unawares, confound, disconcert, put off altogether, screw.

thunder n *lit:* crash, detonation, peal, rumbling; din, resonance, reverberation, roar. **vb** *lit:* blast, boom, crack, crash, explode, peal, rumble; resound, reverberate, roar; *fig:* bellow, shout, trumpet, yell.

thunderous adj *lit:* deafening, earsplitting, reverberating, resounding, roaring; booming, crashing, pealing, rumbling; *fig:* dark, glowering, lowering, menacing, threatening.

thus adv *lit:* as follows, in this way; so; accordingly, consequently, hence, therefore, understandably.

tight adj *lit:* fast, firm, fixed, secure; close-fitting, hermetic, sealed; constricted, cramped, jammed, stuck; clenched, rigid, stiff, stretched, taut, tense; impervious, proof; *fig:* neat, trim; close, even, well-matched; austere, rigorous, severe, strict, stringent; difficult, hazardous, precarious, sticky, thorny, ticklish, tricky; hard to come by, scarce; grasping, mean, miserly, parsimonious, stingy; drunk, inebriated, intoxicated, pickled, plastered, smashed, stoned.

timber n *lit:* forest, trees, woods; lumber, wood; beams, boards, joists, planks.

time n *lit:* duration, interval, period, space, span, spell, term, while; age, date, epoch, era; day, generation, heyday, hour, season; life, lifetime, lifespan; juncture, moment, point, stage; beat, meter, rhythm, tempo; pace, rate, speed; *fig:* chance, opportunity. **vb** *lit:* clock, pace, rate; schedule.

tip n *lit:* apex, crest, crown, peak, point, top; cap, end, ferrule; bonus, extra, gratuity; cut, glance; hint, information, suggestion, warning, wrinkle. **vb** *lit:* cant, incline, lean, list, slant, tilt; chuck, dump, empty out, pour, unload; leave a gratuity for, reward; cut, glance; glue (in), paste (in).

tired adj (pa.pt) *lit:* all in, dead on one's feet, done in, drained, drooping, exhausted, fatigued, shattered, spent, worn out; sick (of), weary (of); *fig:* clichéd, corny, hackneyed, stale, trite.

tireless adj *lit:* diligent, energetic, indefatigable, industrious, persevering, unflagging, untiring; constant, continual, persistent.

tissue n *lit:* cells, structure, texture; mesh, network, system, web; fabric, gauze, nylon, weave; paper handkerchief; toilet paper; wrapping paper.

toast vb *lit:* brown, grill, heat, roast; drink the health of, drink to, salute.

together adv *lit:* as a body, as one, collectively, in unison, jointly, mutually; at once, en masse, in unison, simultaneously; continuously, nonstop.

toilet n *lit:* bathroom, closet, convenience, gents, ladies' room, latrine, lavatory, men's room, powder room, privy, rest room, washroom; ablutions, grooming, titivation, toilette.

tolerable adj *lit:* acceptable, adequate, fair, good enough, middling, not bad, passable; bearable, endurable, supportable.

tolerance n *lit:* forbearance, indulgence, patience, sufferance; fortitude, resilience, resistance, stamina, staying power; leeway, play, swing, variation.

tolerant adj *lit:* broad-minded, complaisant, easygoing, forbearing, indulgent, liberal, lenient, long-suffering, patient, permissive.

tolerate vb *lit:* bear, endure, put up with, stand, stomach, suffer, swallow, take; accept, allow, condone, let go, let pass, permit.

toll n *lit:* charge, duty, fee, payment, tariff, tax; cost, levy, loss; chime, clang, ding, ring. **vb** *lit:* chime, knell, peal, ring, sound.

tomb n *lit:* burial chamber, crypt, grave, sepulcher, vault; barrow, burial mound, catacomb, cave, chamber, pyramid; sarcophagus; shrine.

tone n *lit:* air, aspect, character, effect, feel, mood, spirit, temper, tenor; emphasis, inflection, intonation, stress; modulation, pitch, timbre; note; health, strength, vigor; color, hue, shade, tint. **vb** *lit:* blend (in), fit (in) well; play (down), soften (down), temper (down); brighten (up), strengthen (up).

torch n *lit:* firebrand, sconce; arc lamp, flame, welder; *fig:* beacon, illumination, light. **vb** *lit:* burn, ignite, set ablaze, set on fire.

torture n *lit:* agony, anguish, pain, suffering, torment; cruelty, sadism. **vb** *lit:* hurt, put on the rack, torment; *fig:* give hell, persecute.

total n *lit:* aggregate, amount, bottom line, sum, whole. **vb** *lit:* add up, reckon up, tot up; amount to, come to, work out at. **adj** *lit:* complete, comprehensive, entire, full, out-and-out, perfect, thorough, unconditional, undivided, utter, whole.

touch n *lit:* feel, feeling, physical sensation; brush, palpation, pat, stroke, tap; pressure; *fig:* effect, hand, influence; handiwork, method, style, technique; artistry, command, facility, knack, skill; acquaintance, contact, rapport; dash, hint, pinch, smattering, spot, suggestion, tinge, trace. **vb** *lit:* brush, caress, feel, finger, fondle, handle, palpate, pat, press, stroke, tap; lay hands upon; adjoin, be contiguous with, border, converge, meet, merge with, overlap; arrive at, come up to; stop over (at); *fig:* disturb, impress, move, stir, strike; affect, be pertinent to, concern, have to do with; be party to, get involved in, use; come near, compare with, equal, hold a candle to, match, rival; attain, reach; allude to, have a word (on), say something (on), speak (on); ask (for) a loan of; set (off), spark (off), trigger (off).

tough adj *lit:* all-weather, dense, durable, hard, resilient, resistant, rugged, solid, stiff, strong, sturdy, thick; brawny, hardy, iron, seasoned, stout, strapping; hard-nosed, inflexible, obdurate, obstinate, resolute, stern, stubborn, unyielding; demanding, exacting, unforgiving; aggressive, refractory, rough, violent; arduous, difficult, exhausting, knotty, laborious, strenuous, thorny, uphill; baffling, confounding, perplexing, puzzling; *fig:* bad luck, hard luck, too bad, unlucky.

tour n *lit:* excursion, jaunt, outing, trip; round-trip, sightseeing trip; circuit, course. **vb** *lit:* do, go round, journey in, see, sightsee, travel round, visit; go on the road, play.

tower n *lit:* barbican, bastion, citadel, fortress, turret, watchtower; belfry, dome, minaret, spire, steeple; condominium, high rise, skyscraper. **vb** *lit:* loom, rear, rise, soar.

track n *lit:* footprints, footsteps, mark, path, scent, spoor, trace, trail; wake; course, flight path, line, orbit, trajectory; bridle path, footpath, lane, road; lines, rails, railroad; (keep) sight (of), (lose) sight (of). vb *lit:* dog, follow, pursue, shadow, stalk, tail, trace, trail; hunt (down).

tradition n *lit:* convention, custom, folklore, institution, practice, usage.

traffic n *lit:* vehicles; transport, transportation; freight, passengers; business, commerce, dealing, exchange, trade; hawking, peddling, selling. vb *lit:* deal (in), trade (in).

train n *lit:* locomotive, rail, railway service; caravan, column, convoy, crocodile, file; cortege, entourage, followers, retinue, suite; chain, order, progression, sequence, series, succession. vb *lit:* coach, condition, drill, groom, instruct, teach, tutor, school; exercise; domesticate, tame.

trample vb *lit:* crush, flatten, squash, stamp (on), tread (on).

transit n *lit:* carriage, passage, portage, shipment, transportation; eclipse, occultation; change, conversion, transition. vb *lit:* cross, traverse; go, move, travel.

transition n *lit:* changeover, turnaround; alteration, change, conversion, evolution, metamorphosis, progression, transmutation.

transmit vb *lit:* carry, communicate, convey, forward, impart, pass on, send, transport; broadcast, radio, relay, send out, telecast, televise.

transparent adj *lit:* clear, limpid, pellucid, see-through, sheer, translucent; *fig:* apparent, manifest, obvious, patent, plain unambiguous, visible; candid, frank, open, straightforward.

transport n *lit:* conveyance, vehicle; carriage, postage, shipment, transportation; *fig:* ecstasy, euphoria, rapture. vb *lit:* bring, carry, convey, ferry, fetch, haul, move, ship, take, transfer; banish, exile; *fig:* captivate, enchant, enrapture, entrance.

trap n *lit:* pitfall, snare; ambush; ruse, subterfuge, trick. vb *lit:* catch, corner, ensnare, entrap, snare; ambush; dupe, trick.

tread n *lit:* footfall, footstep, step, stride, walk; sole; *spec:* depth, gauge, pattern (on a tire). vb *lit:* plod, stamp, step, stride, tramp, trudge, walk; crush, flatten, trample.

treat n *lit:* gift, present, reward; delight, pleasure, surprise, thrill. vb *lit:* behave toward, deal with, handle; apply medication to, care for, medicate, minister to, nurse, tend; denature, process, purify, recycle, refine; be concerned with, discuss, examine; bargain, negotiate, parley; lay on for, pay for, stand (to).

treatment **n** *lit:* care, medication, medicine, remedy, surgery, therapy; handling (of), management (of), reception (of), usage (of).

tremble **vb** *lit:* quake, quiver, shake, shudder; oscillate, vibrate, wobble.

trial **n** *lit:* court, hearing, tribunal; experiment, proof, test; attempt, effort, go, shot, stab, try; adversity, affliction, hardship, misery, tribulation; bane, bother, nuisance, pest. **adj** *lit:* experimental, pilot, provisional.

trouble **n** *lit:* anxiety, disquiet, distress, pain, suffering, tribulation, vexation, worry; bother, commotion, disorder, disturbance, row, unrest; ailment, complaint, disability, upset; care, effort, labor, pains; difficulty, hot water, pickle, predicament, scrape. **vb** *lit:* afflict, annoy, bother, disconcert, disquiet, distress, disturb, fret, incommode, inconvenience, pain, plague, upset; exert (oneself).

true **adj** *lit:* factual, valid, veritable; authentic, genuine, natural, pure, real; accurate, correct, exact, precise, unerring; confirmed, dedicated, faithful, firm, loyal, sincere, staunch, trustworthy, upright; reliable, sure; lawful, rightful.

tunnel **n** *lit:* cave, corridor, gallery, hole, passage, shaft, subway, tube. **vb** *lit:* burrow, dig, drive a shaft, excavate, mine.

turn **n** *lit:* angle, bend, corner, curve, deviation; coil, gyration, loop, revolution, rotation, spin, twist, whirl; change, deflection, shift; drive, excursion, outing, ride; constitutional, jaunt, saunter, stroll, walk; *fig:* go, round, spell, stint, time, try; aptitude, flair, gift, knack, propensity, talent; action, deed, gesture, service; act, performance; fright, shock, start; attack, bout, dizzy spell; cast, form, mold, shape. **vb** *lit:* arc, bend, corner, curve, deviate, go round, swerve, veer; tack, zigzag; coil, gyrate, loop, revolve, rotate, spin, twist, wheel, whirl; recoil, reverse; change direction, deflect, shift; aim, direct, point; construct, execute, fashion, form, make, mold, shape; employ, make use of, utilize; *fig:* become, get; alter (into), change (into), convert (into), render, transform (into), translate (into); go bad, go off, sour; sicken, upset; distract, unsettle; persuade, prevail upon, subvert.

U

ugly adj *lit:* frumpish, ill-favored, plain, unattractive, unprepossessing, unsightly; frightful, hideous, horrible, offensive, repugnant, repulsive, revolting, stomach-churning; dark, evil, malevolent, malign, nasty, surly; dangerous, menacing, ominous, sinister, threatening.

ultimate adj *lit:* conclusive, final, last, terminal; finite, limiting; extreme, greatest, highest, superlative, supreme; most important, most significant; basic, fundamental, primary.

umpire n *lit:* adjudicator, arbiter, arbitrator, judge, linesman, referee, scorer. vb *lit:* adjudicate, arbitrate, judge, referee; chair, moderate, preside over.

unable adj *lit:* helpless (to), powerless (to); unqualified (to); incapable, not up to it.

unacceptable adj *lit:* impermissible, inadequate, inadmissible, insupportable, intolerable, unsatisfactory.

unaccountable adj *lit:* incomprehensible, inexplicable, puzzling; extraordinary, odd, unheard-of; not answerable (to).

unaccustomed adj *lit:* unused (to); uncommon, unusual, unwonted.

unanswerable adj *lit:* insoluble, unsolvable; conclusive, incontestable, incontrovertible, indisputable, unassailable, undeniable; unaccountable (to).

unasked adj *lit:* uninvited, unsought, unwanted; gratuitous, spontaneous, unexpected. adv *lit:* of one's own accord, voluntarily; gratuitously, spontaneously, unexpectedly.

unaware adj *lit:* ignorant (of), unconscious (of), uninformed (of), unmindful (of); uncomprehending, untaught.

unbearable adj *lit:* intolerable, unendurable; insupportable, unacceptable; insufferable, unspeakable.

unbending adj *lit:* aloof, distant, formal, haughty, remote, rigid, stiff;

inflexible, intractable, severe, strict, uncompromising, unrelenting, unyielding.

unbroken adj *lit:* homogeneous, intact, solid, undivided, uniform, unimpaired, whole; deep, fast, profound, sound; constant, continual, continuous, incessant, undisturbed, uninterrupted; monotonous, relentless, unremitting; unbowed, undomesticated, untamed, wild.

uncertain adj *lit:* doubtful, indefinite, indeterminate, speculative, undetermined, unpredictable; dubious, irresolute, unclear, undecided, unresolved, unsure, vague as to; erratic, fitful, precarious, unreliable, vacillating, variable; inconstant, interrupted, varying; hazy, indefinite, indistinct, vague.

unclear adj *lit:* clouded, opaque; indistinct, obscure, uncertain, vague.

uncomfortable adj *lit:* crammed, cramped, hard, ill-fitting, lumpy, painful, rough; discomfited, distressed, disturbed, pained; *fig:* diffident, ill at ease, restless, self-conscious, uneasy.

uncommon adj *lit:* infrequent, novel, rare, scarce, unusual; curious, odd, peculiar, strange, untoward; amazing, exceptional, extraordinary, outstanding, remarkable, singular, special, surprising.

uncommunicative adj *lit:* close, dumb, guarded, mute, quiet, reserved, reticent, secretive, silent, taciturn, tight-lipped, unforthcoming, withdrawn.

unconditional adj *lit:* abject, complete, full, total, unlimited, unqualified, unrestricted.

unconscious adj *lit:* comatose, fainting, insensible, knocked out, out, out cold, stunned; anesthetized; accidental, automatic, inadvertent, instinctive, involuntary, reflex, unintentional, unpremeditated, unwitting; latent, repressed, subliminal, suppressed; ignorant (of), unaware (of), unmindful (of).

unconventional adj *lit:* eccentric, individual, irregular, nonconformist, odd, offbeat, original, unorthodox, unusual, way-out.

undecided adj *lit:* inconclusive, indefinite, in the balance, unresolved, unsettled; ambivalent, dithering, in two minds, irresolute, shilly-shallying, uncertain, tentative, vacillating, wavering; debatable, moot, open.

undeniably   adv *lit:* beyond doubt, certainly, evidently, incontestably, incontrovertibly, indisputably, indubitably, manifestly, obviously, patently, undoubtedly, unquestionably.

under   adj *lit:* inferior, junior, lesser, lower, minor, subordinate; minus, short. **adv** *lit:* below, beneath, beneath the surface; down, lower; below par. **prp** *lit:* below, beneath; inferior to, junior to, lesser than, lower than, subject to, subordinate to; as, beneath the heading, within; less than, short of.

undergo   vb *lit:* bear, endure, experience, go through, pass through, stand, suffer.

underhand   adj *lit:* crafty, crooked, deceptive, devious, dishonest, furtive, sly, sneaky.

underneath   adj *lit:* lower, under; below, beneath. **adv** *lit:* below, beneath, down below; next to the skin, under the skin. **prp** *lit:* below, beneath; inferior to, junior to, lesser than, lower than, subject to, subordinate to.

underrated   adj (pa.pt) *lit:* discounted, misjudged, sold short, underestimated, undervalued.

understanding   n *lit:* appreciation, comprehension, grasp, knowledge; apprising, insight, perception; belief, conclusion, view; assumption, supposition; sympathies; accord, agreement, entente, pact. **adj** *lit:* compassionate, considerate, insightful, kindly, perceptive, sensitive, sympathetic; charitable, forbearing, forgiving, magnanimous, tolerant.

undertake   vb *lit:* agree (to), commit oneself (to), engage (to), promise (to); attempt, embark on, endeavor (to), set about, tackle, take on, try.

undesirable   adj *lit:* deleterious, disagreeable, potentially harmful, unacceptable, unpleasant, unwanted, unwelcome; antisocial, obnoxious, shabby, squalid, unattractive, unsavory, unsuitable.

undignified   adj *lit:* indecorous, inelegant, unbecoming, unseemly; embarrassing, humiliating, ludicrous, ridiculous, risible, mortifying.

undisciplined   adj *lit:* boisterous, disobedient, naughty, obstreperous, uncontrollable, unmanageable, unruly, unschooled, untrained, wayward, wild, willful.

undisguised   adj *lit:* evident, frank, genuine, manifest, obvious, open, plain, transparent, unconcealed, unfeigned, unmistakable.

undisturbed   adj *lit:* placid, serene, tranquil; unruffled; uninterrupted; untouched.

undo   vb *lit:* loose, loosen, open, unfasten, untie; annul, cancel, invalidate, overturn, quash, reverse; defeat, destroy, ruin, wreck.

undone   adj (pa.pt) *lit:* loosened, opened, unfastened, untied; annulled, canceled, invalidated, overturned, quashed, reversed; defeated, destroyed, ruined, wrecked; incomplete, neglected, omitted, outstanding, unfinished.

undoubtedly   adv *lit:* certainly, definitely, naturally, of course, surely, unmistakably, unquestionably.

undress   n *lit:* dishabille, disarray, dishevelment, disorder; seminudity; nakedness, nudity; casual clothes, informal wear. vb *lit:* disrobe, strip, strip off.

unemployed   adj *lit:* idle, jobless, laid off, on the dole, out of work, redundant; between jobs, resting.

unenthusiastic   adj *lit:* casual, halfhearted, lukewarm, take-it-or-leave-it, wishy-washy; indifferent.

unerringly   adv *lit:* accurately, exactly, infallibly, precisely, specifically.

uneven   adj *lit:* broken, bumpy, corrugated, lumpy, ridged, rough, undulating; fluctuating, irregular, patchy, variable, varying; asymmetrical, lopsided, top-heavy, unbalanced; one-sided, unequal, unfair.

unexpected   adj *lit:* abrupt, startling, sudden, surprising; surprise, unforeseen; unasked, uninvited, unsought.

unfair   adj *lit:* biased, discriminatory, inequitable, partial, prejudiced, unjust; dishonest, unethical, unprincipled, unsporting.

unfaithful   adj *lit:* adulterous, deceitful, disloyal, promiscuous, two-timing; perfidious, traitorous, treacherous; *fig:* distorted, imperfect, inaccurate, unreliable; dissimilar (to).

unfamiliar   adj *lit:* alien, different, new, novel, strange, unknown; unacquainted (with), unconversant (with).

unfashionable   adj *lit:* antediluvian, antiquated, dated, démodé, dowdy, frumpish, fuddy-duddy, old-fashioned, old hat, outmoded, out of date, passé, unchic.

unfavorable   adj *lit:* adverse, bad, negative, poor; contrary, hostile, inclement, stormy; inauspicious, unlucky, unpromising, unpropitious; inopportune, untimely.

unfit   adj *lit:* inadequate (for), inappropriate (for), unsuitable (for), useless (for); ineligible (to), not cut out (to), physically unable (to), unprepared (to), unqualified (to); flabby, in poor condition, out of shape, unhealthy.

unfortunate   adj *lit:* hapless, luckless, unlucky; inauspicious, inopportune, unfavorable, unpropitious; deplorable, infelicitous, regrettable.

unfortunately   adv *lit:* unhappily, unluckily; inauspiciously, infelicitously; deplorably, regrettably.

unhappily   adv *lit:* unfortunately, unluckily; dejectedly, despondently, disconsolately, gloomily, miserably, mournfully, sadly, wretchedly; awkwardly, badly, infelicitously, injudiciously.

unhappy   adj *lit:* hapless, luckless, unfortunate, unlucky; dejected, depressed, despondent, disconsolate, gloomy, miserable, mournful, sad, wretched; awkward, inept, infelicitous, injudicious, tactless.

unharmed   adj *lit:* intact, safe and sound, scatheless, undamaged, unhurt, unimpaired, uninjured, unscathed, without a scratch.

unhealthy   adj *lit:* delicate, feeble, frail, puny, sickly, thin, weak; dirty, insanitary, unhygienic; corrupting, demoralizing, perverted, sick, warped.

unhesitating   adj *lit:* immediate, instant, prompt, ready; resolute, steadfast, unfaltering, unswerving, unwavering.

unidentified   adj *lit:* anonymous, nameless, unknown, unnamed; plain, unmarked.

unify   vb *lit:* bond, combine, fuse, join, weld; amalgamate, confederate, merge; marry, wed; unite.

unimaginative   adj *lit:* boring, dull, colorless, hackneyed, insipid, lifeless, pedestrian, tame, uninspired, unoriginal, vapid; derivative, plagiaristic.

unimpressed adj *lit:* apathetic, blasé, bored, impassive, indifferent, left cold, uninterested, unmoved, unperturbed, unruffled, unsurprised.

uninhabited adj *lit:* barren, desolate, empty, vacant, waste; deserted, unoccupied, unpopulated, untenanted.

uninhibited adj *lit:* free, liberated, natural, spontaneous, unselfconscious; open, unconstrained, unrepressed, unrestricted; unchecked, uncontrolled.

unintentional adj *lit:* accidental, inadvertent, unintended, unpremeditated, unthinking; involuntary, reflex; unwitting.

uninviting adj *lit:* disagreeable, off-putting, repellent, repugnant, unappealing, unappetizing, unattractive, unpleasant; depressing, dismal, dreary; daunting, formidable, ominous, sinister.

union n *lit:* bond, combination, coupling, fusion, joining, linkage, suture, synthesis, weld; affiliation, alliance, amalgamation, association, coalition, confederacy, confederation, league, merger; marriage, wedlock; brotherhood, fraternity, trade organization.

unique adj *lit:* isolated, single, sole; incomparable, unequaled, unmatched, unparalleled, unrivaled; unrepeatable; *fig:* ecstatic, magic, special; characteristic, idiosyncratic.

universal adj *lit:* blanket, catholic, common, comprehensive, general, unlimited, unrestricted, worldwide; ecumenical; adaptable, flexible, versatile.

universe n *lit:* cosmos, macrocosm; world.

unknown n *lit:* anonymity, nobody, nonentity; enigma, mystery, puzzle; dark, mysterious, unexplored. adj *lit:* anonymous, nameless, unidentified, unnamed; obscure, unfamiliar, unheard-of, unrecognized, unsung; alien, dark, mysterious, new, strange, unexplored.

unlike adj *lit:* different, dissimilar, distinct, diverse, incompatible, unequal, unrelated. prp *lit:* different from, dissimilar to, distinct from, incompatible with, unequal to, unrelated to.

unlikely adj *lit:* implausible, improbable, incredible, unbelievable; not expected (to), not likely (to); unconvincing; faint, remote, slight.

unnatural adj *lit:* anomalous, odd, strange, unusual; bizarre, extraordinary, freakish, outlandish, peculiar, weird; abnormal, perverse, perverted, warped; appalling, brutish, callous, cruel, heartless, inhuman, monstrous, shocking, unfeeling; artificial, assumed, contrived, false, forced, labored, self-conscious, stiff, stilted, strained.

unnecessary adj *lit:* unessential, needless, redundant, superfluous, surplus; pointless, useless, wasteful.

unpleasant adj *lit:* disagreeable, distasteful, irksome, objectionable, obnoxious, unattractive, unpalatable; disgusting, horrible, nasty, offensive, repellent, repugnant, repulsive, unlikable.

unpopular adj *lit:* avoided, disliked, friendless, ostracized, shunned, unwanted, unwelcome; difficult, inopportune, unfortunate, untimely.

unpredictable adj *lit:* chance, random, unforeseeable; changeable, erratic, inconstant, unreliable, variable; iffy, precarious, tricky.

unprepared adj *lit:* unready (for); caught on the hop, taken off guard; ill-considered, not thought through, unfinished, unpolished; ad lib, extemporaneous, improvised, spontaneous.

unprofitable adj *lit:* loss-making, uneconomic, unviable; bootless, fruitless, futile, unproductive, unremunerative, unrewarding, useless, valueless.

unqualified adj *lit:* incompetent (to), ineligible (to), not up (to), unfit (to); categorical, complete, outright, total, unconditional, unreserved, unrestricted.

unreal adj *lit:* immaterial, insubstantial, intangible, nebulous; dream, fictitious, illusory, imaginary, make-believe; artificial, false, insincere.

unrealistic adj *lit:* artificial, contrived, false, labored, stilted, unlifelike, unnatural; implausible, impracticable, impractical, improbable, unworkable; hopeful, idealistic, romantic, sentimental, wishful.

unreasonable adj *lit:* illogical, irrational, nonsensical, senseless, silly;

unfair, unjust, unwarranted; disproportionate, immoderate, uncalled-for, undue; capricious, erratic, inconstant, inconsistent.

unreliable adj *lit:* irresponsible, untrustworthy; disloyal, treacherous; deceptive, uncertain, unconvincing; erratic, fallible, unsound.

unrepentant adj *lit:* impenitent, incorrigible, shameless, supercilious, unruffled; callous, hard-bitten, indifferent, obdurate.

unrest n *lit:* agitation, demonstration, dissension, mutiny, rebellion, sedition, riotousness; affray, commotion, disturbance, hurly-burly, tumult, turmoil; disquiet, distress, uneasiness, worry.

unsafe adj *lit:* dangerous, hazardous, perilous, precarious, risky, treacherous, unsound, unstable; unclean, unhygienic; exposed, open, pregnable, vulnerable.

unselfish adj *lit:* altruistic, generous, kind, magnanimous, noble, philanthropic, selfless.

unsettled adj (pa.pt) *lit:* agitated, disordered, disturbed, flurried, restive, restless, tense, uneasy; insecure, loose, shaky, unstable, unsteady; changeable, inconstant, uncertain, variable; due, outstanding, payable, unpaid; debatable, moot, undecided, unresolved; deserted, empty, uninhabited, unoccupied, unpopulated, vacant.

unspoiled adj *lit:* genuine, intact, natural, preserved, real, unblemished, undamaged, unimpaired, untouched, wild; everyday, matter-of-fact, ordinary, unaffected, unassuming, unpretentious.

unsure adj *lit:* diffident, insecure, irresolute, uncertain, undecided; distrustful, skeptical, suspicious.

unthinking adj *lit:* careless, inconsiderate, insensitive, tactless, thoughtless, undiplomatic; inadvertent, mechanical, unconscious, vacant; impulsive, rash, reckless.

untried adj *lit:* alien, new, probationary, unfamiliar, untested; unexamined.

untrue adj *lit:* erroneous, inaccurate, incorrect, lying, wrong; deceptive, dishonest, false, misleading, spurious; disloyal, perfidious, unfaithful; treacherous, untrustworthy; bowed, distended, distorted, not straight, off, warped, wide.

unusual adj *lit:* abnormal, atypical, exceptional, rare, singular, uncommon, unconventional; bizarre, curious, extraordinary, queer, remarkable, surprising; fishy, odd, peculiar, strange, suspicious; characteristic, distinctive, special.

unwanted adj *lit:* extra, spare, superfluous, surplus; outcast, rejected; unasked, uninvited, unsolicited, unwelcome.

unwell adj *lit:* bedridden, ill, out of sorts, poorly, sick, under the weather; ailing, indisposed, sickly.

unwholesome adj *lit:* deleterious, noxious, unhealthy; corrupting, demoralizing, depraving, perverting; ailing, pale, pallid, sickly, wan.

unwise adj *lit:* foolish, ill-advised, ill-judged, inadvisable, irresponsible, silly, stupid; impolitic, imprudent, indiscreet, injudicious, rash, reckless.

unworldly adj *lit:* idealistic, inexperienced, naive, romantic, sentimental, unsophisticated; abstract, metaphysical; ethereal, extraterrestrial; religious, spiritual, transcendental.

unworthy adj *lit:* ineligible (to), undeserving (of), unfit (to); beneath the dignity (of), disappointing (of), uncharacteristic (of); contemptible, discreditable, dishonorable, ignoble, shameful.

uprising n *lit:* coup, coup d'état, insurrection, mutiny, putsch, rebellion, revolt, revolution.

uproar n *lit:* Babel, bedlam, clamor, commotion, din, furor, hullabaloo, outcry, pandemonium, racket, riot, ruckus, rumpus, turmoil.

upset n *lit:* defeat, reversal, reverse, setback; discomposure, distress, disturbance, shock; indisposition, queasiness, sickness. **vb** *lit:* capsize, knock over, overturn, spill, topple, turn over; confuse, disorder, disorganize, jumble, mix up, undo, untidy; agitate, annoy, bother, distress, disturb, fluster; best, defeat, overcome. **adj** *lit:* capsized, overturned, spilled, toppled, upside down; chaotic, confused, disordered, disorganized, jumbled, mixed up, untidy; agitated, annoyed, bothered, distressed, disturbed, flustered, hurt, put out, unhappy, worried; queasy, sick.

urban adj *lit:* city, civic, metropolitan, municipal, town.

urgent adj *lit:* compelling, compulsive, crucial, emergency, essential, exigent, imperative, necessary, pressing, vital; imploring, importunate, insistent.

use   **n** *lit:* application, employment, operation; custom, practice, treatment, usage, way; advantage, avail, benefit, good, help, object, point, profit, service, value. **vb** *lit:* apply, employ, exercise, ply, utilize, wield; exploit, take advantage of; behave toward, treat; consume, expend, spend, take (up).

used   **adj** *lit:* secondhand; cast-off, nearly new, shopworn, worn; not mint.

useful   **adj** *lit:* advantageous, beneficial, effective, good, helpful, profitable, serviceable, valuable, worthwhile; adaptable, general-purpose, practical, versatile.

usual   **adj** *lit:* common, customary, everyday, familiar, general, habitual, ordinary, regular, routine, standard, stock, typical.

W

wade vb *lit:* paddle (through), splash (through), walk (through); ford; *fig:* labor (through), plod (through), plow (through), toil (through).

wag n *lit:* shake, wave; comedian, humorist, jester, joker, wit. vb *lit:* shake, wave; flutter, oscillate, rock, vibrate, wiggle.

wage n *lit:* emolument, fee, pay, payment, remuneration, salary, stipend. vb *lit:* carry on, conduct, engage in, prosecute, pursue, undertake.

wail n *lit:* howl, ululation, yowl; cry, moan, sob; clamor, drone, scream, whine. vb *lit:* bemoan, cry, howl, moan, sob, ululate, weep, yowl; clamor, drone, scream, whine.

wait n *lit:* delay, halt, holdup, pause, rest, stop; hiatus, intermission, interval, space; ambush. vb *lit:* bide one's time, halt, hold back, hold on, pause, rest, stop, tarry; be delayed, remain, stay; attend (on), serve (at).

wake n *lit:* vigil, watch; funeral party; backwash, track, trail, wash. vb *lit:* awaken, be roused, come to, get up, stir; activate, arouse, reanimate, revive; *fig:* enliven, excite, galvanize, kindle, stimulate; evoke, fire, provoke.

walk n *lit:* constitutional, hike, perambulation, promenade, ramble, tramp; amble, saunter, stroll, traipse, trek, trudge; gait, pace, step, stride; aisle, alley, avenue, lane, path; pathway, trail; enclosure, pen, run; *fig:* activity, area, field, sphere. vb *lit:* amble, hike, perambulate, promenade, ramble, saunter, stroll, traipse, tramp, trek, trudge; foot it, hoof it, march, step out, stride out; inspect, pace out; advance, go, move, travel; go away, move off, withdraw; accompany, escort, take; exercise, lead.

wall n *lit:* brickwork; divider, panel, partition, screen; barricade, bulwark, fortification, palisade, rampart; barrier, fence; cliff, precipice; *fig:* obstacle, obstruction; defense; *spec:* membrane (surrounding or lining a body organ or a cell). vb *lit:* partition (off), screen (off), separate; enclose, surround; fortify; immure.

wander n *lit:* meander, perambulation, peregrination, promenade, ramble, roam. vb *lit:* drift, meander, perambulate, peregrinate, promenade, ramble, range, roam, rove, travel; deviate, digress, diverge, go astray, straggle, stray, veer off; *fig:* be led astray, err, lapse.

wandering adj (pr.pt) *lit:* aimless, circuitous, convoluted, meandering, rambling, ranging, roaming, sinuous, tortuous, winding; drifting, itinerant, nomadic, peripatetic, traveling, vagrant, wayfaring.

wane n *lit:* atrophy, decline, decay, dwindling, ebb, fading, falling off, shrinking, sinking, subsiding, withering; decrease, diminution, fall, lessening, lowering, tapering off, winding down. **vb** *lit:* abate, atrophy, decline, decay, dwindle, ebb, fade, fall off, get smaller, shrink, sink, subside, wither; decrease, diminish, fall, lessen, lower; die away, draw to a close, taper off, wear off, wind down.

want n *lit:* absence, default, demand, lack, need, requirement; craving, desire, longing, wish, yearning, yen; appetite, hunger, thirst; dearth, deficiency, insufficiency, paucity, poverty, privation, scarcity, shortage. **vb** *lit:* desire, need, require, wish; crave, hanker for, hunger for, long for, pine for, thirst for, yearn for; be deficient in, be short of, lack, miss; seek.

war n *lit:* battle, conflict, fighting, hostilities, strife, struggle; *fig:* contention, enmity, hostility; competition, rivalry; campaign. **vb** *lit:* battle, combat, fight, struggle; *fig:* campaign (against).

ward n *lit:* dependent, protégé; charge; care, custody, guardianship, keeping, protection; district, division, hundred, precinct, zone; *spec:* clinic, (hospital) dormitory, room, sanatorium; notch, slot (of a keyhole); parry (in fencing); section (in a prison). **vb** *lit:* guard, have custody of, keep, protect; deflect (away), fend (off), parry (off).

warden n *lit:* curator, executive officer, keeper, ranger, superintendent; caretaker, janitor, watchman; administrator, custodian, guardian.

warder n *lit:* guard, sentinel, sentry, watchman; jailer, keeper, prison officer.

warm vb *lit:* heat (up); melt, thaw; microwave, reheat; *fig:* limber (up); become more friendly (to), become more sympathetic (to); excite, interest, stimulate, stir (up). **adj** *lit:* pleasantly hot; unpleasantly hot; radiating; *fig:* affable, affectionate, cordial, friendly, hearty, kind, kindly, loving, tender; lively, severe, strenuous, vigorous; ardent, earnest, enthusiastic, fervent, keen, passionate; excited, stimulated; emotional, intense; fresh, strong, vivid.

warmth   n *lit:* heat, temperature; radiance, radiation, sunshine; blaze, fire, flame; *fig:* ardor, emotion, enthusiasm, feeling, fervor, intensity, passion; animation, excitement, spirit, vigor, zeal; affection, kindliness, love, tenderness; cordiality, heartiness; asperity, curtness, ferocity, sharpness.

warning   n *lit:* alarm, alert, caution, notice, tip, tip-off; threat; advice, notification, word; augury, omen, premonition, presage, sign; beacon, signal; beware. **adj (pr.pt)** *lit:* cautionary; threatening; ominous, premonitory; *spec:* aposematic (of the coloration of organisms).

warp   n *lit:* bend, distortion, twist; loop; *fig:* bias; defect, kink; perversion. **vb** *lit:* bend, be twisted, curve, distort, twist; haul, heave, hoist, winch; *fig:* misinterpret, misrepresent; pervert.

wash   n *lit:* ablution, bath, rinse, scrub, shampoo, shower; cleansing, laundering; surf, surge, swell, undertow; attrition, erosion, wear; coating, film, stain; coat, layer, suffusion; lotion, medication. **vb** *lit:* bath, bathe, launder, rinse, scrub, shampoo, shower; moisten, steep, wet; baptize, clean, cleanse; erode (away), sweep (away); *fig:* be convincing, be plausible, hold up, hold water, stick, work.

waste   n *lit:* debris, dross, garbage, leavings, litter, offal, refuse, rubbish, scrap, sweepings, trash; dissipation, extravagance, loss, misuse, prodigality, profligacy, squandering; desert, outback, veldt, wilds, wilderness; destruction, devastation, havoc, ravage, ruin; *spec:* silt (in rivers); excrement, excreta, feces, stools; urine. **vb** *lit:* be prodigal with, blow, dissipate, fritter away, misuse, squander, throw away; atrophy, corrode, crumble, decay, diminish, dwindle, eat (away), erode, fade (away), wear (away), wither; be spent, be used up; *fig:* assassinate, kill, murder. **adj** *lit:* extra, leftover, over, superfluous, unused; scrap, rejected, thrown away, unwanted; bare, barren, desolate, empty, uninhabited; wild; devastated, ravaged, ruined, unproductive.

watch   n *lit:* chronometer, timepiece; lookout, sentry; eye, observation, surveillance; guard, vigil; period. **vb** *lit:* eye, look at, mark, note, observe, pay attention to, stare at, survey, view; be on the alert, be vigilant, be wary of, look out (for), take heed of; guard, keep, look after, mind, protect, superintend, supervise; keep vigil.

water   n *lit:* lake, ocean, river, sea; tide; rain; *fig:* amniotic fluid, blood serum, saliva, tears; urine; class, grade, quality; *spec:* clarity, luster, transparency (of a diamond). **vb** *lit:* damp, dampen, douse, drench, flood, hose, irrigate, moisten, ret, soak, souse, spray, sprinkle, steep; adulterate, dilute, thin, weaken; give a drink; *fig:* cry, salivate.

wave n *lit:* flourish, flutter, gesticulation, gesture, shake, swing; billow, breaker, roller, undulation; oscillation, sine curve; *fig:* current, flood, movement, stream, surge, swell, upsurge; epidemic, outbreak, rash, trend. **vb** *lit:* brandish, flap, flourish, shake, stir, swing, undulate, wag; beckon, direct, gesticulate, gesture, indicate, make a sign, signal.

way n *lit:* avenue, channel, course, direction, lane, path, pathway, road, route, street, track; distance, journey, length; room, space; motion, movement, passage, progress; approach, course of action, means, method, mode, procedure, system, technique; custom, fashion, habit, idiosyncrasy, manner, practice, style, trait, usage, wont; aspect, feature, respect, sense; aim, desire, goal, will, wish; circumstance, condition, shape, state. **adv** *lit:* far; considerably, severely.

weak adj *lit:* debilitated, delicate, effete, feeble, flimsy, frail, puny; defenseless, exposed, helpless, impotent, unprotected, vulnerable; cowardly, ineffectual, irresolute, powerless, soft, spineless; inadequate, lacking, poor, substandard; distant, dull, faint, low, muffled, quiet, slight; *fig:* invalid, lame, pathetic, unconvincing; diluted, thin, watery, wishy-washy; *spec:* fluctuating (stock market prices); regular (verb inflection); unstressed (syllable).

weaken vb *lit:* fail, flag, give way, sap, soften up, temper, undermine, wane; abate, decrease, diminish, dwindle, fade, lessen, moderate; *fig:* adulterate, dilute, thin, water down; cut, debase.

wealth n *lit:* affluence, means, money, opulence, prosperity, riches, substance; fortune, lucre, pelf, property; resources; *fig:* abundance, copiousness, luxuriance, plenitude, plethora, profusion.

wear n *lit:* abrasion, attrition, depreciation, deterioration, erosion, friction damage; use; mileage, service, utility. **vb** *lit:* be dressed in, dress in, have on, sport; display, exhibit; abrade, depreciate, deteriorate, erode, fray, grind, rub; *fig:* bear up, endure, hold up, last; annoy, exasperate, fatigue, irk, tire (out), try, vex, weary; bring gradually (in); pass (on); accept, buy, credit, take on trust.

weary vb *lit:* drain, fatigue, jade, take it out of, tax, tire, wear out;

annoy, bore, burden, exasperate, harass, irk, pester, plague. **adj** *lit:* all in, dead beat, dog tired, done in, drained, exhausted, fatigued, jaded, spent, taxed, tired out, whacked, worn out; annoyed, bored, exasperated, irked, plagued.

weather n *lit:* atmospheric conditions, climate, elements; *fig:* normal, par; influence. **vb** *lit:* expose, season; harden, toughen; be discolored, be worn; *fig:* come through, get through, last, make it, ride, ride out, surmount, survive, withstand.

weave **vb** *lit:* braid, entwine, interlace, lace, plait; crisscross, intertwine, mesh; *fig:* create, make, spin, work; blend, combine; twist and turn, zigzag.

wedding n *lit:* marriage, matrimony, nuptials, solemnization of matrimony; *fig:* alliance, combination, joining, merger, union.

weep **vb** *lit:* blubber, cry, shed tears; greet; snivel, sob; grieve (for), mourn (for); *fig:* drip, leak, ooze; exude, suppurate.

weigh **vb** *lit:* have a weight of, tip the scales at; bear down, burden, load; apportion (out), dole (out), measure (out); balance, hold in the balance; *fig:* be influential, count, matter, tell; consider, contemplate, evaluate, mull over, ponder, think over; insert (in), interpolate (in); get stuck (in), lay (into); *spec:* hoist up (the anchor).

weight n *lit:* heaviness, ballast, burden, load, mass; poundage, tonnage; counterpoise; lead, sinker; pendulum; dumbbell; *fig:* millstone, pressure, strain; onus, preponderance; authority, clout, importance, influence, moment, power, substance; emphasis, impact, value; force, tension; impetus. **vb** *lit:* ballast, charge, load, make heavier; burden, handicap, weigh down; *fig:* add to, bias.

weighty **adj** *lit:* heavy, hefty, massive; burdensome, cumbersome, ponderous; *fig:* authoritative, consequential, important, influential, momentous, portentous, powerful, serious, significant, substantial; emphatic, forceful; demanding, exacting, exigent, onerous, taxing.

welcome n *lit:* greeting, reception, salutation; entertainment, hospitality. **vb** *lit:* give a reception to, go to meet, greet, offer hospitality to, receive, usher in; accept with pleasure, take gladly; please come in. **adj** *lit:* acceptable, agreeable, appreciated, desirable, gratifying, pleasing, pleasurable; *spec:* free of obligation.

welfare   n *lit:* health, well-being; benefit, good, prosperity; *fig:* benefits, social security, social services.

well   n *lit:* bore, hole, shaft; pool, spring; compartment, hollow, niche, pit; *fig:* fount, source; repository, store; mine. vb *lit:* arise, rise, spring; seep, spout, trickle; flow, gush, pour, run, spurt, stream; billow, surge. adj *lit:* fine, fit, hale, healthy, robust, sound; all right, okay; fortunate, lucky; advisable, prudent; useful. adv *lit:* ably, accurately, adeptly, correctly, efficiently, expertly, proficiently, properly, rightly, skillfully, suitably; carefully, closely; comfortably, more than satisfactorily; abundantly, amply, considerably, deeply, fully, greatly, heartily, highly, profoundly, substantially, thoroughly; easily, readily; approvingly, favorably, glowingly, kindly, warmly.

wet   n *lit:* dampness, moisture, water; drizzle, rain, storm; clamminess, condensation, damp, humidity. vb *lit:* damp, dampen, douse, drench, flood, moisten, ret, rinse, soak, souse, spray, sprinkle, steep; baptize, dip; urinate. adj *lit:* damp, dank, drenched, dripping, moist, saturated, soaked, soaking, sodden, soggy, sopping, waterlogged, watery, wringing; fluid, liquid; clammy, humid; rainy, showery.

wheel   n *lit:* hub, tire; helm, steering column; circle, disc; change of direction, rotation, turn; *fig:* cog, gear. vb *lit:* gyrate, pivot, rotate, spin, swing, swivel, turn; circle, loop, spin round, whirl round; drive, push along, take, transport.

whim   n *lit:* caprice, conceit, fancy, humor, impulse, notion, vagary; eccentricity, quirk; *spec:* horse-drawn capstan or winch.

whine   n *lit:* moan, wail; drone, noise, tone; nasal timbre. vb *lit:* moan, wail; complain, grouse, grumble; beef, bellyache, gripe, grizzle, yowl.

whip   n *lit:* cat-o'-nine-tails, crop, knout, lash, rawhide, scourge, switch, thong; *fig:* party manager; coachman, driver; *spec:* armature (in an electrical circuit); block and tackle, pulley. vb *lit:* beat, flagellate, flog, lash, scourge, strap, switch, thrash; birch, cane, leather, tan; hammer, lick; conquer, defeat, drub, overcome, overpower, rout, trounce; compel, drive, goad, incite, prick, prod, provoke, spur; force, jerk, pull, seize, snatch; dart, dash, dive, flash, fly, tear; mix, stir, whisk.

whirl   n *lit:* gyration, pirouette, revolution, rotation, spin, swirl, twirl; dizziness, giddiness; daze, dither; agitation, bustle, commotion, flurry, hurly-burly, stir; round, series, succession. **vb** *lit:* circle, gyrate, pirouette, revolve, rotate, spin, swirl, turn, twirl; reel; wheel.

whirlwind   **n** *lit:* dust devil, eddy, vortex; cyclone, tornado. **adj** *lit:* immediate, instant, lightning; hasty, rapid, speedy, swift; headlong, impetuous, impulsive.

whisk   **n** *lit:* beater, mixer; swat; brush, flick, sweep, whip. **vb** *lit:* beat, fluff up, mix, stiffen, whip; swat; brush, flick, sweep, wipe; hurry, race, rush, speed.

whisper   **n** *lit:* low voice, murmur, undertone; rustle, sighing, susurration, swish; white sound; *fig:* breath, hint, shadow, suggestion, trace, whiff; buzz, rumor, word. **vb** *lit:* breathe, murmur, say softly; rustle, sigh, swish; *fig:* gossip, hint, insinuate, spread a rumor.

whole   **n** *lit:* lot, sum, total; entirety, totality; aggregate, complete system, ensemble, total combination, unity. **adj** *lit:* complete, entire, full, integral, total; intact, perfect, sound, unbroken, undamaged, unscathed; unabridged, uncut; better, cured, healed, healthy; all at once, in one piece.

wholesome   **adj** *lit:* healthful, nourishing, nutritious; beneficial, hygienic; *fig:* clean, decent, edifying, good, moral, nice, respectable, uplifting, virtuous.

whore   **n** *lit:* harlot, strumpet, trollop; call girl, courtesan, lady of the night; hooker, hustler, prostitute, slut, streetwalker, tart, tramp. **vb** *lit:* be promiscuous, fornicate, sleep around; be a prostitute, solicit, walk the streets.

wicked   **adj** *lit:* bad, evil, impious, iniquitous, irreligious, sinful, ungodly, wrong; amoral, black-hearted, cruel, devilish, fiendish, inhuman, malevolent, malicious, malign, satanic, spiteful, vicious; abandoned, corrupt, debased, depraved, heinous, immoral, nefarious, villainous; *fig:* arch, impish, incorrigible, mischievous, naughty, roguish, sly.

wide   **adj** *lit:* ample, broad, expansive, extensive, great, large, thick, vast; dilated, distended, outspread, outstretched; capacious, commodious, full, loose, roomy, spacious; comprehensive, encyclopedic, sweeping; badly aimed, inaccurate, off-target. **adv** *lit:* as much as possible, fully; distantly, far, expansively, extensively, remotely; aside, astray, inaccurately, off, off-target.

width   n *lit:* breadth, bulk, compass, diameter, girth, span, thickness; extent, reach; depth, latitude, range, scope, sweep.

wield   vb *lit:* apply, control, employ, exercise, handle, have at one's disposal, maintain, make use of, ply, put to use, use, utilize; brandish, flourish, hold, retain.

wild   n *lit:* natural habitat; state of nature; backwoods, desert, outback, vastness, veldt, wasteland. **adj** *lit:* desert, desolate, empty, natural, uncivilized, uncultivated, uninhabited, unpopulated, virgin, waste; feral, unbroken, undomesticated, untamed; barbarous, brutish, primitive, rude; boisterous, disorderly, lawless, noisy, passionate, riotous, rowdy, turbulent, unbridled, uncontrolled, undisciplined, ungovernable, unmanageable, unruly, violent, wayward; berserk, crazed, demented, distracted, frenzied, hysterical, incoherent, irrational, mad, maniacal, possessed, rabid, raving; extravagant, fantastic, impracticable, irresponsible, madcap, preposterous, rash, reckless, unreasoned; disheveled, scruffy, tousled, unkempt, windblown, windswept; blustery, choppy, ferocious, fierce, howling, intense, raging, rough, tempestuous; avid, batty, crazy, eager, enthusiastic, excited, fanatical, nuts; *spec:* arbitrary, unassigned, unlimited (playing card). **adv** *lit:* freely, unchecked, unrestrainedly.

wilderness   n *lit:* jungle, wasteland, wilds; desert, desolation, waste; *fig:* bewildering mass, confusion, jumble, maze, tangle.

will   n *lit:* volition; choice, decision, discretion; desire, inclination, preference, wish; intention, mind, purpose, resolve; attitude, disposition, feeling; *spec:* last wishes, testament. **vb** *lit:* aim to, be going to, intend to, mean to; be determined to, be resolved to; choose, elect, opt, prefer, want, wish; command, desire, determine, direct, ordain; bequeath, endow, hand on, leave, pass on.

willful   adj *lit:* conscious, deliberate, intentional, volitional, voluntary; determined, headstrong, intransigent, mulish, obdurate, obstinate, pigheaded, single-minded, stubborn, uncompromising; intractable, perverse, refractory, unmanageable.

wilt   vb *lit:* become limp, droop, sag; dry up, shrivel, wither; *fig:* dwindle, fade, flag, wane; falter, waver, weaken.

win   n *lit:* success, triumph, victory. **vb** *lit:* be victorious, come first, prevail, succeed, triumph; attain, earn, gain, make, net, reach, secure; achieve, get, obtain, receive; charm, convert, induce, persuade.

wind n *lit:* air, blow, breeze, draught, gale, gust; breath, puff; respiration; flatulence, flatus, gas; scent, smell; *fig:* blather, bluster, empty talk, hot air; clue, hint, inkling, intimation, rumor, suggestion, whisper; near future, offing, pipeline; *spec:* brass and woodwind (in an orchestra). **vb** *lit:* have the breath knocked out of, puff out; scent, smell, sniff; blow, sound.

wind n *lit:* angle, bend, corner, curve, meander, spiral, turn, twist, wiggle. **vb** *lit:* bend, curve, meander, snake, spiral, turn, twist, wiggle, worm, writhe; coil, curl, encircle, loop, spiral, twine (around), twist, wreathe (around); fold (around), wrap (around); key, set; roll into a ball; reel (in), winch; *fig:* excite, make tense.

winding adj (pr.pt) *lit:* circuitous, convoluted, crooked, curling, helical, looping, meandering, roundabout, serpentine, sinuous, spiral, tortuous, twisting.

winning adj (pr.pt) *lit:* conquering, successful, triumphant, unbeaten, victorious; *fig:* alluring, attractive, captivating, charming, disarming, enchanting, engaging, fascinating, fetching, pleasing, sweet, taking; influential, persuasive.

wintry adj *lit:* arctic, bleak, chilly, cold, dark, freezing, frosty, icy, piercing, raw, snowy; *fig:* distant, frozen, unfriendly.

wipe n *lit:* brush, rub, swab; lick. **vb** *lit:* brush, mop, rub, sponge, swab; clean (off), erase, expunge; dry; *fig:* snuff (out), stamp (out).

wise adj *lit:* discerning, discriminating, enlightened, erudite, knowledgeable, learned, penetrating, percipient, sagacious, sage, understanding; judicious, politic, prudent, sensible, shrewd; aware, conscious, informed; clever, intelligent.

wish n *lit:* aspiration, hankering, hope, inclination; desire, longing, want, yearning; whim, will; bidding, entreaty, request. **vb** *lit:* hanker, hope; crave (for), desire, long, want, yearn; bid, express a hope (for, to); will; *fig:* foist (on), pass (on).

wit n *lit:* acumen, comprehension, discernment, intelligence, judgment, perception, penetration, percipience, understanding, wisdom; ingenuity, practicality, sense; humor, quip, repartee, sense of humor, wordplay; comedian, humorist, punster, wag.

witchcraft n *lit:* black arts, magic, sorcery, spells; enchantment, supernatural power.

withdraw vb *lit:* depart, fall back, go away, leave, retire, retreat; resign, scratch; disengage, draw back, pull out; debit, draw out, extract, remove, take out; recall, retract, take back, unsay.

withdrawal n *lit:* departure, exodus, going, leaving, resignation, retirement, retreat; disengagement, separation; extraction, pulling out, removal; recall, retraction, revocation; *spec:* deprivation (of drugs).

withering adj (pr.pt) *lit:* blasting, blighting, crushing, devastating, scorching, searing, trenchant; deadly, lethal, murderous; *fig:* humiliating, mortifying, scornful, shaming.

withhold vb *lit:* detain, hold back, keep back, reserve, restrain, retain, sit on; deduct, keep; deny, repress, suppress; forbear (from), refrain (from).

witness n *lit:* beholder, bystander, onlooker; spectator, viewer, watcher; deponent, testifier; corroboration, evidence, testimony, verification. vb *lit:* behold, look on at, observe, see, view, watch; attest to, corroborate, depone, give evidence, testify, verify; authenticate, countersign, endorse.

wits n *lit:* acumen, brains, intelligence, percipience; ingenuity, practicality, sense; consciousness, faculties, senses.

witty adj *lit:* ingenious, lively, original, pointed, topical, waggish; clever; amusing, droll, funny.

woe n *lit:* anguish, dejection, depression, distress, gloom, grief, heartbreak, melancholy, misery, sorrow, suffering, tribulation, unhappiness, wretchedness; adversity, burden, hardship, misfortune, trial.

woman n *lit:* female, girl, lady, lass, maiden, miss; bride, mistress, wife; dame, doll, gal, girlfriend; person; individual; domestic, female servant, housekeeper, maid, maidservant.

wonder n *lit:* curiosity, marvel, miracle, phenomenon, prodigy, rarity, spectacle; admiration, awe, fascination. vb *lit:* be curious, be inquisitive, inquire, query, question; conjecture, speculate, theorize, think; meditate, ponder, puzzle; be amazed, be awed, be fascinated, be flabbergasted, boggle, marvel.

wonderful *adj lit:* awesome, incredible, magnificent, marvelous, miraculous, outstanding, phenomenal, remarkable, staggering, superb; brilliant, excellent, fabulous, fantastic, great, magnificent, sensational, stupendous, super, terrific, tremendous.

wood *n lit:* xylem; forest, trees; coppice, copse, grove; planking, timber; branches, logs; *fig:* barrel, cask, keg.

wooden *adj lit:* ligneous, log, planking, slatted, timber; *fig:* awkward, clumsy, gawky, inelegant, rigid, stiff, ungainly; inflexible, obstinate, unbending, unyielding; blank, deadpan, emotionless, expressionless, unemotional, unresponsive; dull, muffled.

woolly *adj lit:* fleecy, flocculent, woolen; hairy, shaggy; *fig:* blurred, cloudy, confused, fuzzy, hazy, imprecise, indistinct, obscure, vague; rough, uncivilized.

word *n lit:* expression, term, vocable; speech, utterance; comment, declaration, remark, statement; chat, colloquy, consultation, conversation, discussion, talk; account, information, intelligence, news; command, go-ahead, green light, order, signal; countersign; decree, edict; assurance, guarantee, oath, pledge, promise, vow. **vb** *lit:* couch, express, phrase, put, say.

work *n lit:* employment, job, occupation, profession; business, craft, line, livelihood, métier, trade; assignment, chore, commission, duty, task, undertaking; achievement, composition, creation, opus, performance, piece, product, production; drudgery, effort, exertion, industry, labor, slog, toil, travail; fortification; *fig:* fuss, trouble. **vb** *lit:* drudge, labor, slave, slog, sweat, toil, travail; be employed, be in a profession, earn a living, have a job; do enough to be worth, earn; control, direct, drive, handle, manage, move, operate, ply, use, wield; cultivate, farm, till; fashion, form, knead, manipulate, mold, process, shape; accomplish, achieve, carry out, effect, execute, implement, perform; force (in), infiltrate, insinuate, inveigle, worm, wriggle; arrange, contrive, fix, pull off, swing; function, go, run, tick.

works *n lit:* factory, mill, plant; acts, deeds, doings; compositions, creations, output, pieces, productions, writings; action, guts, insides, machinery, mechanism, moving parts.

worldly   **adj** *lit:* lay, profane, secular, temporal; carnal, earthly, earthy, fleshly, mundane, physical; experienced, knowing, politic, sophisticated, urbane; cosmopolitan; *fig:* avaricious, grasping, greedy, materialistic, selfish.

worn   **adj (pa.pt)** *lit:* frayed, ragged, tattered, threadbare; *fig:* drawn, haggard, lined; fatigued, spent, tired, wearied; hackneyed, trite.

worry   **n** *lit:* anxiety, apprehension, care, concern, misgiving, perturbation, unease; pest, plague, problem, trial, trouble. **vb** *lit:* agonize, be anxious, be apprehensive, be concerned, be nervous, be perturbed, be uneasy, brood; be afraid, be fearful, be fretful, be frightened, fear, fret; annoy, badger, bother, distress, disturb, harass, harry, hassle, hector, importune, perturb, pester, plague, tease, unsettle, upset; attack, bite, savage.

worse   **adj** *lit:* less well, more ill; less good, more evil; more harmful, more painful, more unfavorable, more unpleasant; more incorrect; more ill-advised, more unsuitable; inferior, of lower quality, worth less; less fortunate. **adv** *lit:* more severely; more evilly; more harmfully, more painfully, more unfavorably, more unpleasantly; more incorrectly; more ill-advisedly, more unsuitably.

worship   **n** *lit:* devotion, glorification, homage, honor, praise, prayers; adoration, adulation, love; reverence. **vb** *lit:* glorify, honor, laud, praise, pray to, venerate; abase oneself to, make oblation to, prostrate oneself before, sacrifice to; participate in a service, praise God, praise the Lord, say devotions; adore, adulate, love; deify, idolize, put on a pedestal.

worst   **n** *lit:* least well, most ill; least good, most evil; most harmful, most painful, most unfavorable, most unpleasant; most incorrect, most ill-advised, most unsuitable; most inferior. **vb** *lit:* beat, best, conquer, defeat, gain an advantage over, get the better of, master, overcome, overpower, vanquish. **adj** *lit:* least well, most ill; least good, most evil; most harmful, most painful, most unfavorable, most unpleasant; most incorrect, most ill-advised, most unsuitable; most inferior, of the lowest quality; least fortunate. **adv** *lit:* most severely; most evilly; most harmfully, most painfully, most unfavorably, most unpleasantly; most incorrectly; most ill-advisedly, most unsuitably.

worth n *lit:* benefit, usefulness, utility, value; importance, quality; excellence, goodness, merit, virtue; cost, price, valuation. **adj** *lit:* deserving of, meriting, meritorious of; of a value of; at a cost of, at a price of, valued at.

worthless adj *lit:* futile, ineffectual, of no use, pointless, unavailing; insignificant, paltry, trifling, trivial, unimportant, valueless; unusable, useless; contemptible, despicable, ignoble.

wound n *lit:* abrasion, cut, gash, graze, incision, injury, laceration, lesion, scrape, slash; *fig:* hurt, offense, shock, slight, sting, trauma. **vb** *lit:* cut, gash, graze, injure, lacerate, pierce, scrape, slash, wing; damage, harm, hurt; *fig:* cut to the quick, grieve, mortify, offend, pain, shock. **adj (pa.pt)** *lit:* coiled, curled, looped, spiraled, turned (around), twined, twisted; folded (around), wrapped (around); keyed up, set up; *fig:* excited, nervous, tense.

wrangle n *lit:* altercation, argument, disagreement, dispute, quarrel, row, squabble, tiff; affray, brawl, clash, dustup, set-to, shoving match. **vb** *lit:* argue, bicker, disagree, dispute, fall out, have words, quarrel, row, squabble; brawl, clash, fight, scrap; *spec:* herd, tend (horses or cattle).

wreck n *lit:* hulk, sunken vessel; derelict, empty shell, husk, skeleton; destruction, ruin; *fig:* confounding, devastation, disruption, spoiling, undoing. **vb** *lit:* lure on to the rocks, run aground, strand; break up, demolish, destroy, ravage, ruin, shatter, smash, spoil.

wring vb *lit:* screw, squeeze, twist, wrench; dry, put through the mangle; extract (from), force (from), wrest (from); *fig:* coerce (from), extort (from); pain, pierce, rack, rend, tear at, wound; *spec:* clasp (hands) firmly, shake (hands) warmly.

wrinkle n *lit:* corrugation, crease, crinkle, crow's foot, fold, furrow, line, pucker, ridge; *fig:* device, dodge, easy method, gimmick, ploy, short cut, technique, trick; hint, tip; difficulty, problem. **vb** *lit:* corrugate, crease, crinkle, crumple, fold, furrow, line, rumple.

write vb *lit:* inscribe, pen, put down, scribble, set down; author, compose, publish; draft, draw up, jot down, record, take down, transcribe; letter, print, spell; correspond, send a note; endorse, sign; *fig:* display, exhibit, show.

writer n *lit:* author, pencil pusher, scribbler, wordsmith; columnist, hack, journalist, scribe; essayist, novelist, playwright, poet; litterateur, man or woman of letters.

wrong **n** *lit:* injury, misdeed, offense; evil, sin, sinfulness, transgression, wickedness; grievance, injustice, trespass. **vb** *lit:* aggrieve, harm, ill-treat, ill-use, injure, offend, oppress; be evil to, sin against; deflower, seduce; cheat, defraud, do out of a right; calumniate, malign; misrepresent. **adj** *lit:* erroneous, fallacious, false, inaccurate, incorrect, mistaken, untrue; bad, dishonorable, evil, immoral, improper, iniquitous, reprehensible, sinful, unethical, unjust, wicked; criminal, crooked, dishonest, felonious, illegal, illicit, unlawful; inappropriate, inapt, infelicitous, unsuitable; amiss, askew, astray, awry, not right; defective, faulty, out of order; *spec:* inner, reverse, under (side, surface). **adv** *lit:* amiss, astray, awry, badly, inaccurately; erroneously, incorrectly, mistakenly.

X

xenophobic   adj *lit:* racialist, racist; chauvinist; insular, isolationist.

xeric   adj *lit:* arid, dehydrated, dry, sear; desertlike, rainless, waterless.

xylograph   n *lit:* wood-block print, woodcut, wood engraving.

xylophone   n *lit:* gamelan, glockenspiel, marimba, vibraharp, vibraphone.

Y

yacht n *lit:* ketch, sailboat, skiff, smack; clipper, schooner, yawl; motor launch, pleasure boat.

yearly adj *lit:* annual, once-a-year; annual, 365-day, yearlong; annual, for one year, per annum, year's. **adv** *lit:* annually, once a year; annually, for one year at a time.

yearning n *lit:* aching, craving, desire, hunger, longing, lust, thirst, wish.

yellow adj *lit:* buttercup, canary, gold, golden, honey-colored, lemon, ocher, primrose, saffron, sandy, sulfur; jaundiced, sallow; *fig:* chicken, cowardly, craven, frightened, gutless, scared, timid.

yes adv *lit:* affirmative, all right, okay, roger; certainly, definitely, positively, surely; indeed so, quite so, really, that's true; affirmatively; furthermore, moreover.

yet adv *lit:* by now, hitherto, so far, thus far, till now, to date, until now, up to now; already, now, so soon; even, still; additionally, besides, further, to boot. **cnj** *lit:* all the same, but, however, nevertheless, nonetheless.

yield n *lit:* crop, harvest, produce; output, product; dividend, earnings, gain, income, profit, return, revenue, takings. **vb** *lit:* afford, bear, bring in, deliver, furnish, give, grant, produce, provide, render, supply; earn, generate, net, pay, return; accede, acquiesce, back down, bow, capitulate, cede, comply, give in, give up, relinquish, resign, submit, surrender; admit, concede, give way; bend, be pliant, flex, loosen, slacken.

young n *lit:* babes, children, girls and boys, juveniles, kids, toddlers, youth; babies, brood, cubs, infants, issue, litter, offspring, pups, progeny, sons and daughters. **adj** *lit:* adolescent, growing, immature, infant, junior, preschool, pubescent; coltish, juvenile, youthful; *fig:* fledgling, new, recently established; green, inexperienced, raw.

youth n *lit:* adolescence, boyhood, girlhood, immaturity, school days, teens; heyday, prime; boy, lad, stripling, teenager, youngster; teenagers, young, young generation, young people; juvenility, youthfulness.

Z

zeal n *lit:* ardor, fanaticism, fervor, militancy, passion, readiness, spirit, verve; commitment, dedication, devotion, earnestness, enthusiasm, keenness.

zealous adj *lit:* ardent, burning, fanatical, fervent, impassioned, militant, passionate, rabid, spirited; avid, committed, dedicated, devoted, earnest, enthusiastic, keen, unreserved, unstinting; card-carrying.

zero n *lit:* cipher, nil, nothing, naught; lowest point, minimum, nadir, rock bottom; least permissible. **vb** *lit:* calibrate; home (in on), target (in on).

zone n *lit:* area, district, region; band, belt, section, sector; field, sphere. **vb** *lit:* divide into areas, parcel out, partition, segment, section; encircle.